Happy Mother's Day
Mom!

Love,
T

SAVING AMERICAN ELECTIONS

SAVING AMERICAN ELECTIONS

A Diagnosis
and Prescription
for a
Healthier Democracy

Anthony Gierzynski

Politics, Institutions, and Public Policy in America series
Series editors: Scott A. Frisch and Sean Q. Kelly

CAMBRIA
PRESS

Amherst, New York

Requests for permission should be directed to:
permissions@cambriapress.com, or mailed to:
Cambria Press
20 Northpointe Parkway, Suite 188
Amherst, NY 14228

Library of Congress Cataloging-in-Publication Data

Gierzynski, Anthony, 1961–
Saving American elections : a diagnosis and prescription for a healthier
democracy/Anthony Gierzynski.
p. cm.
Includes bibliographical references and index.
ISBN 978-1-60497-752-3 (alk. paper)
1. Elections—United States. I. Title.

JK1976.G485 2011
324.60973—dc22

2011001588

For Kate

TABLE OF CONTENTS

LIST OF FIGURES

LIST OF TABLES

ACKNOWLEDGMENTS

I received a great deal of help and support in pulling together this book. I would like to thank my colleagues Paul Herrnson, Raymond La Raja, Alex Zakaras, Alec Ewald, David Mindich, Garrison Nelson, and the other anonymous reviewers who all read through the manuscript and gave me valuable feedback. I would also like to thank the students at the University of Vermont with whom I have had many great conversations about elections and democracy in the United States, discussions that helped me clarify and flesh out the ideas that went into this book. In particular I would like to single out the students of my class "The 2008 Election" who were forced to read and respond to an earlier version of this manuscript, including Bill Backhaus, Emelie Bailey, Leah Davis, Jason Depatie, Marietou Diouf, Benjamin Guttridge, Michael Lamb, Matthew McKeon, August Melita, Ally Perleoni, Janell Schafer, Brooke Sharpe, Jesse Simmons, and Margaret Walsh. I have had several teaching assistants who have helped me in various direct and indirect ways with this book, including Kensington Moore, Colin MacDonald, Yekaterina Kleyman, Kelsey Aroian, Ally Perleoni, and Claire Chevrier.

Taking an author's manuscript and getting it into print in a polished and professional manner is an arduous task. The entire staff at Cambria Press did a wonderful job refining the final manuscript I gave them. I am very grateful for all of their fine work. I would also like to express my appreciation to the Cambria Press series editors Scott Frisch and Sean Kelly for their work on this project.

In the course of writing this book, I lost two people to whom I am ever indebted: my father, Joe Gierzynski, whose unbounded support of and interest in my work were always encouraging (the same goes for you, Mom); and one of my intellectual "parents," Malcolm Jewell, whose wonderfully rich insights into politics and government helped shape the way I see elections, political parties and representative democracy.

I would also like to thank my in-laws, Martha and Jim Eddy, who, at various critical "crunch" times on this project watched our little boy, Chay ... and a thank you to Chay for his patience with his Daddy because he always seemed to have to be "working on his book." And, finally, there is my wife, Kate Eddy, to whom this volume is dedicated. Thank you for the happiness you have brought me, for all of your love and support, and for your feedback and help on this book.

SAVING AMERICAN ELECTIONS

INTRODUCTION

It is October 2010 and another election is in its final weeks. By all indications, the 2010 election is yet another one of many that seems to be screaming out that elections and the democracy these elections support are in a sorry state of health in the United States.

The Tea Party Movement, propelled by a nebulous anger and egged on by Fox News celebrity Glenn Beck and former vice presidential candidate Sarah Palin (and funded by large contributions from wealthy individuals and corporations[1]), has seized an outsized role in the political discourse, though not for its political ideals (which have not been clearly articulated because of the decentralized nature of the movement). Thanks to its unexpressed ideology and the media's penchant for focusing in on outrageous characters, the Tea Party's time in the spotlight during the run-up to the 2010 election has not involved a consideration of the movement's ideas, but attention has instead been focused on its members' indiscriminate anger and a parade of its seemingly wackiest members. These included a Delaware Senate candidate who grabbed national attention for, among other things, her public statements about dabbling in witchcraft and her opposition to masturbation, as well as a belligerent New York gubernatorial candidate who threatened to "take out" a reporter. Although benefiting from the Tea Party Movement, Republicans are not entirely sure what to do with this insurgency that has unseated a fair number of the party's incumbent officeholders in primary elections.

Liberals and Democrats, in contrast, appear to be lacking in enthusiasm and unlikely to vote despite a decent record of major policy successes that their party has accomplished in the first year and a half of the Obama administration—the massive stimulus bill that pumped money into a multitude of Democratic-supported programs in addition to saving millions of jobs,[2] actual health-care reform after more than a half-century of struggle, a budget full of liberal spending priorities, and legislation increasing the regulation of the financial industry, to name just a few.

As in all midterm elections, most of the electorate will not bother to vote in 2010. The consequence of this is that the minority of citizens that shows up at the polls will be able to reverse or stymie the effects of the prior presidential election. Indeed, such conflicting messages between presidential elections and the subsequent midterm elections appear to be the norm regardless of who is president.

In addition to focusing on the oddball personalities of and controversies involving those running, the media are in full final-quarter-of-the-game coverage, obsessed with polls, fundraising, and endless speculation about how the election will ultimately turn out, as well as with the political moves of the opposing sides. Will Obama be able to reignite any passion and save the day for the Democrats? Will the Republican's "Pledge" erase the perception of the Republicans as the "Party of 'no'" and help them repeat the electoral success of the "Contract for America"? Meanwhile discussions of the central meaning of the election—the policy implications—are so rare as to be invisible, as are serious analyses of the effectiveness of the policies enacted by Obama and the congressional majority Democrats.

Thanks to the 2010 U.S. Supreme Court ruling in *Citizens United v. Federal Election Commission*, the floodgates for direct corporate and labor union spending have been opened, contributing to a surge in interest group money, a fivefold increase over 2006, with Republican causes outspending Democratic causes more than two to one.[3] This money has fueled an explosion of misleading and flat-out false claims by both Democrats and Republicans on everything from social security and the healthcare and stimulus bills to the candidates' personal lives and records.[4]

Fittingly, in the midst of all of this, satirist Jon Stewart will have a "Rally to Restore Sanity" in Washington, DC, with a message for people to "take it down a notch" (while his Comedy Central partner, Stephen Colbert, plans a "March to Keep Fear Alive" and "notch it up a skosh").

With the absurdities of the media coverage, the lopsided funding, the barrage of false and misleading ads, and the expected low voter turnout, the potential for the 2010 election to be a genuine referendum on the policies of Obama and the Democrats is being lost. When all the votes are counted, politicians will claim that the public has spoken; however, less than half of the public would have voted and, given the absurd and distorted nature of the campaign, how can what "the public" said possibly be known? Such is the sad state of elections in the United States today.

The 2010 election is not unique in this failure to function as a means for citizens to make their preferences clear and to control their government. Elections in the United States have been unhealthy and in need of some serious "medical" attention for some time. Large segments of the population do not vote; public cynicism about politics, government, and the news media is high; the system of financing elections is lopsided in favor of some candidates and interests over others; most congressional and legislative campaigns are uncompetitive; the public appears ignorant of how their political system operates and of much of what goes on in it; political discourse is silly, mean, and distorted; and the media fail to provide the substantive coverage the electorate needs and fail to help the public sort through the claims and counterclaims of candidates, political parties, advocacy groups, viral emails, and even other media outlets.

Admittedly, elections in the United States have never been the picture of health—there have always been problems. Citizens were excluded from elections by law, discriminatory practices, or intimidation for well over a century because of their race or gender. Supporters were often rewarded with the material spoils of office, such as government contracts, jobs, and favorable legislation. Electoral discourse has always included issues of character, nasty personal attacks, and other trivia that could distract the electorate from the central meaning of the choice. Party machines also often exercised enough control over the process to guarantee the outcomes they desired, regardless of the preferences of the electorate. But now, in the twenty-first century, with the worst and most obvious of these abuses largely addressed, with technological advances in our ability to communicate, and a populace more highly educated than ever before, one would expect elections to be healthy and to function as democracy's vital instrument for popular control of government. But they are not and do not. Instead, they are still seriously ill with the same symptoms and ailments. And while there are signs of health that appear every now and then (such as the increased participation in the 2004 and 2008 presidential elections), we should not be fooled into believing that their health is improving, for even the most seriously ill patients can have a good day every now and then. Moreover, U.S. elections are sick with health problems which, as the diagnosis offered later in this book makes evident, will not simply heal and go away on their own. The past afflictions of discrimination and corruption did not just go away on their own, after all; they required legal and even constitutional changes that were driven by popular movements. The modern afflictions affecting U.S. elections are no different.

The unhealthy state of elections in the United States is evident to many. And just as it is when a person is sick and there is no shortage of "doctors" with remedies they believe can help, there is no shortage of election "doctors" out there with remedies they believe will restore elections to health (a group in which I include myself). Similar to the plethora of recommended remedies a person receives when they are ill, there are many cures suggested for ailing electoral campaigns. Some of these would include public funding for campaigns, the direct popular vote for the president, the elimination of the Electoral College, term limits, nonpartisan elections, more political parties, and improved civics education, among others (for a lengthier sampling of some of the more common remedies see the list in box 1).

Like the remedies people offer for the flu, some of these prescribed remedies for elections may be helpful, others not so helpful and maybe

---

**Box 1. A Sampling of Other Prescriptions
Offered by Reformers**

- free television time for candidates and political parties
- national primaries for presidential nominations
- nonpartisan, independent commissions for congressional and state legislative redistricting
- national voter initiatives and referenda
- regulating 527 and 501(c) committee activity
- improved civics education
- media awareness education for the public
- a reduction in the number and frequency of elections
- better, simpler ballot designs
- same-day voter registration
- "Rock the Vote"–style campaigns to increase youth turnout
- full disclosure of campaign contributions
- instant runoff voting (also called preferential voting)
- Internet voting
- postal voting
- easier absentee balloting
- a ban on candidate advertisements
- holding elections on weekends or designating Election Day a holiday
- mandatory spending limits for political candidates
- proportional representation
- compulsory voting

even a bit harmful; some are based on science, others merely on personal predilections. Indeed, a close reading of the list of proposed electoral reforms reveals a number of problems for those trying to make elections in the United States healthier. First, the sheer number of disjointed proposals vying for support makes it unlikely that anything will get done. Second, some of the remedies proposed contradict each other—for example, making the ballots easier to read and reducing the number of elections simplify the choice for voters while instant runoff voting and holding national referenda increase the complexity of voting. Third, the efficacy of some remedies is not supported by, or even goes against, the extant scientific research on elections—for example, full disclosure of campaign contributions or making absentee balloting easy. In the worst-case scenarios, reforms proposed sans an assessment of their effects can actually make things worse. Fourth, most of the remedies address only one part of the problem, such as holding a national primary for selecting the parties' presidential nominees or free television time for candidates. Fifth, in addressing one part of the problem, some proposals (like the "Rock the Vote"–style campaigns) merely address the symptoms as opposed to the illness itself. And finally, in the discussion surrounding these remedies, there is usually little consideration of potential side effects that could worsen the state and condition of the American electoral system.

The hodgepodge of remedies that constitutes the current approach to electoral reform suggests that the state of electoral "medicine" has progressed to the point where the medical field was at the time of "Theodoric of York."[5] The practice of electoral reform at the start of the twenty-first century is too often carried out without a clear understanding of what actually ails the U.S. elections, with little knowledge or assessment of the impact of proposed remedies. In addition, the practice is rarely informed by science (in this case, the extant social science research on elections). In this book, I aim to address these shortcomings in the practice of electoral reform. To do so, I first develop a full diagnosis of what ails elections, a diagnosis that is based on the extensive social science research on elections. Then, using that diagnosis and relevant research,

I evaluate the various prescriptions for electoral reform. In the process, I borrow from modern medicine's holistic approach, weighing how each reform would interact with the other prescribed changes to elections and how together the best of the reforms would address what is really making American elections "sick." I also take into consideration as much as possible the trade-offs and political costs of the treatments.

The process starts with cataloging the symptoms of the electoral illness in chapter 1. This is followed by a diagnosis of the illness afflicting U.S. elections and the causes of that illness in chapters 2 and 3. Then the subsequent chapters sort through the various remedies (and offer a few new ones) organized around the major causes of the illness—the state of the news media, the institutional structure of elections, the behavior of political parties and candidates, the laws governing elections, and habits of the public itself. The concluding chapter draws together the remedies that survive the analysis into an overall prescription for restoring health and vigor to U.S. elections and the democracy that depends on them.

SECTION I

DIAGNOSIS

CHAPTER 1

SYMPTOMS

As a political scientist who has spent his career studying elections, I have often struggled with the practical implications of all the research election scholars have done—with the question of how best to improve elections in the United States, given what we know. This desire to use what we know to facilitate better elections has driven me to help defend some election reforms in the courts[6] and ultimately to write this book. In considering how exactly U.S. elections might be rehabilitated, I was amazed and a bit overwhelmed by the vast number of ideas that aim to do just that, as well as by how many of them seem, at first glance, to be good ideas. Therefore I began thinking about how one might sort through all of these ideas: how can one know, beyond assessing each individual proposal on its own, what will work, what elections in the United States truly need in order to make them "healthier"? Then the obvious struck me: before trying to figure out how to fix U.S. elections, it might help to first understand precisely what is wrong with them. In other words, what is needed is a full diagnosis of the problem before anyone tries to solve it. Just as no good medical doctor would prescribe remedies without fully diagnosing the patient's problems, no one should take up election reform without a full diagnosis of what is ailing elections.

A full diagnosis requires cataloging the symptoms, identifying the illness, and locating the causes of the illness. Academics, pundits, and reformers have pointed out a wide range of problems with elections in the United States—including low voter turnout, problematic campaign finance laws, failures of the mass media, questionable redistricting practices, and so on—but few have performed the complete diagnosis of the system that is critical to prescribing treatment. The first section of this book is dedicated to that purpose; in the second section I discuss the prescriptions. I begin diagnosing the problem in this chapter by identifying the symptoms of the "illness" manifest in U.S. elections. Then in chapter 2, I catalog the specific afflictions that are making elections ill. In chapter 3, I complete the diagnosis by documenting the factors that have caused or contributed to illness.

The symptoms of the sickness afflicting elections are probably the best known aspects of the problem, recognizable to even the most casual observers: voter turnout in U.S. elections is low, substantially lower than voter turnout in most other democratic nations;[7] significant portions of the public are poorly informed and vulnerable to manipulation, often unaware of many important issues as well as lacking a basic understanding of the operation of the American political system; and a good number of citizens are overly cynical about the nature of politics and government.

LOW VOTER PARTICIPATION

The 2008 presidential contest took place at the end of eight years of a very unpopular presidency and at a time of tremendous economic upheaval. The problems blamed (rightly or wrongly) on the Bush administration— the Iraq war, the government's response to Hurricane Katrina, the expansion of executive authority in the war on terror, and the collapse of the economy—and the Republicans' very conservative and uncompromising approach to politics had left the public discontented and demanding a change. In October 2008, in response to the Gallup poll's question "In general, are you satisfied or dissatisfied with the way things are going in the United States at this time?," 90 percent of respondents said they were dissatisfied.[8] Additionally, the contest for the Democratic nomination between two historic candidacies was unusually close, keeping the attention of the country (and, almost to an obsessive degree, of the media) well into the summer months. As the news media would not let viewers forget, the general election contest was also a historic contest, with the first African American major-party nominee and the first female vice presidential nominee to be put forward by Republicans (the race was indeed historic, but the media's constant repetition of the fact was unnecessary).[9] The campaign also featured charismatic candidates—Barack Obama and Sarah Palin—who kept the media attention at a fever pitch. The Obama campaign broke spending records and put together a well-organized and well-funded grassroots movement to get out the vote; the campaign even purchased a simultaneous half-hour block of time on a number of broadcast and cable networks. And despite the final outcome, the election was perceived as close until the numbers started to come in. What more could win over the public and get them to the polls? Indeed, many *were* won over: the 2008 election broke recent records with the highest percentage of voter turnout since 1960. This was perhaps nearly the best modern American voters could do, but how good was it? The voter turnout for these elections was 63 percent; that is, a little over six in ten eligible voters were moved enough by the "historic" circumstances to vote.[10] And although turnout in 2008 increased over previous elections, the gains were not universal, as Curtis Gans and Jon Hussey noted:

> The overall increase in the national turnout rate masks a complex dynamic among the states. States that lost their battleground status, along with some safe Republican states, experienced turnout declines. These declines were more than offset by increases in states entering the battleground, by safe Democratic states, and by safe Republican states with large African American populations.[11]

Figure 1.1 shows voter turnout levels for presidential elections since 1960. As the chart shows, participation in presidential elections fell after the 1960s, and (with a few exceptions) remained low, with just over half of all eligible voters voting in most presidential elections. If the southern states are excluded, the decline in voter participation is even more dramatic, dropping more than twenty percentage points between 1960 and 1996.[12] The electorate's mediocre performance since the 1960s happened *despite changes that should have led to increases*—not decreases—in participation, including the removal of many of the barriers to participation, the increased use of same-day registration and no-excuse absentee or early voting, communications revolutions that have brought politics into nearly every American's home via television and the Internet, and increasing levels of formal education.

Although some might argue that six in ten eligible voters' participating in the two most recent presidential contests is not insignificant, the national levels of voting participation in presidential contests seem to represent the highest levels among the U.S. public. In presidential elections, participation varies widely from state to state. The highest turnout in the 2008 election was in Minnesota, where 76.1 percent of the eligible electorate voted in 2008; the lowest turnout was in Hawaii (coincidentally, the state where Barack Obama was born), where 49.4 percent voted.[13] Additionally, elections with presidential contests represent the high-water mark for voter turnout in the United States. Consider the 2002 election, in which voters decided on 34 members of the U.S. Senate, 435 members of the U.S. House, governors and statewide constitutional officers in 36 states, some 6,214 state legislators, and over 200 ballot measures. Despite the importance of these decisions and the fact that the election took place a year after the September 11 attacks—that is, at a time of heightened patriotism—only 39.5 percent of the eligible public voted.[14] There was little improvement for the 2006 election. As figure 1.2 shows, having just four in ten eligible voters cast ballots in a midterm election is typical in the United States.[15] By way of comparison, in an international ranking of voter turnout for parliamentary and legislative elections between 1945 and 2001, the United States ranked 138 out of 169 countries.[16]

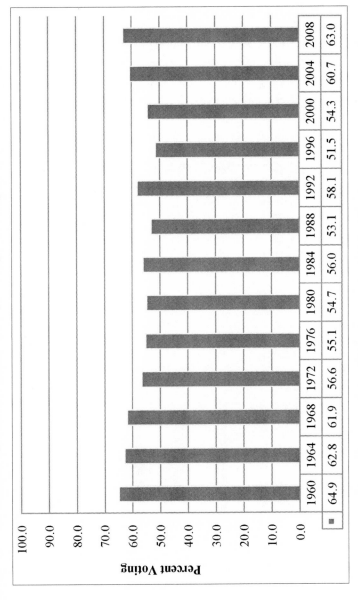

FIGURE 1.1. Voter turnout in presidential elections as a percentage of the eligible electorate, 1960–2004.

	1960	1964	1968	1972	1976	1980	1984	1988	1992	1996	2000	2004	2008
▓	64.9	62.8	61.9	56.6	55.1	54.7	56.0	53.1	58.1	51.5	54.3	60.7	63.0

Source. Committee for the Study of the American Electorate, "Turnout Exceeds Optimistic Predictions: More than 122 Million Vote," January 14, 2005, http://election04.ssrc.org/research/case_2004_final_report.pdf.

An examination of the levels of voter participation in primary elections
or state and local contests reveals an even bleaker picture. Participation
in presidential primaries and caucuses is very low and has dropped from
about 30 percent in the 1970s to 17 percent in 2000.[17] (There has been
a similar decline in congressional primaries, with an average turnout
in recent years of 15 percent.[18]) The presidential primary elections of
1996, 2000, and 2004 saw an overall voter turnout of under 20 percent

FIGURE 1.2. Voter turnout in midterm elections, 1982–2010.

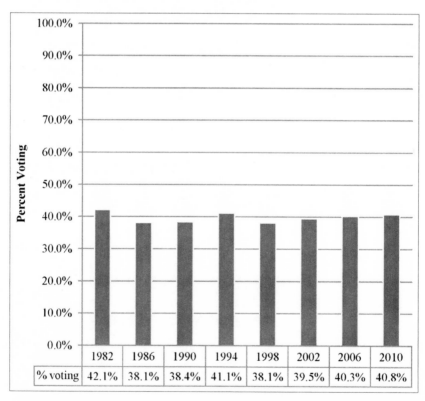

% voting	1982	1986	1990	1994	1998	2002	2006	2010
	42.1%	38.1%	38.4%	41.1%	38.1%	39.5%	40.3%	40.8%

Source. United States Election Project, George Mason University, http://elections.gmu.edu.

(see figure 1.3). For many states, turnout percentages for presidential primaries and caucuses is often in the single digits.

The 2008 contest for the Democratic presidential nomination witnessed a dramatic increase in participation, but it was an anomaly. The fact that neither party had an incumbent president or vice president running meant that both parties' contests would be more competitive than usual. Also, unlike all of the recent nomination contests, the battle

FIGURE 1.3. Overall turnout in presidential primaries, 1972–2008.

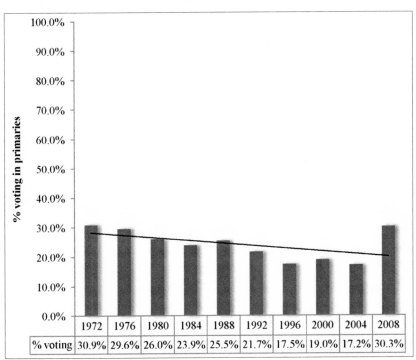

% voting	30.9%	29.6%	26.0%	23.9%	25.5%	21.7%	17.5%	19.0%	17.2%	30.3%
	1972	1976	1980	1984	1988	1992	1996	2000	2004	2008

Source. Curtis Gans, "The Primary Turnout Story: Presidential Races Miss Record High Senate and Governor Contests Hit Record Low," Report, Center for the Study of the American Electorate, American University, http://www1.media.american.edu/electionexperts/2008%20Primary%20Turnout_Final.pdf, accessed August 26, 2009.

between Barack Obama and Hillary Clinton did not end until all of the states had held their primaries and caucuses. Finally, the fact that the contest would conclude with either the first African American or first female to win a major party nomination—plus the charisma of Obama and the media's fascination with the Clintons—helped keep the media attention riveted on the race. In summary, these conditions plus the extreme discontent with the incumbent administration led to "perfect storm" conditions for stimulating participation. Ultimately,

> participation in the 2008 primaries and caucuses more than doubled over participation in the 2004 nominating contests .... reaching an eight-year high in 36 states. Among Democrats, presidential primary election participation doubled and participation in presidential nominating contests tripled over 2004 levels."[19]

Turnout for Republican contests increased, but not nearly as dramatically; this was not surprising because their contest was well over before all of the states were able to participate.

Despite the favorable conditions, the overall turnout in presidential primaries of both parties was 30.3 percent, shy of the record 30.9 percent turnout in 1972 (in which an incumbent ran for the Republican nomination and candidates far less compelling than Obama and Clinton ran in the Democratic contest).[20] See figure 1.3 for the trend since 1972, and note its downward movement until 2008. The overall primary turnout masks differences state by state. The highest turnout, as is typical given the amount of attention the state receives from candidates and the press, was in New Hampshire, where 51.9 percent of the eligible electorate turned out, beating the previous record in 2000 of 43.6 percent.[21] The lowest turnout was in Louisiana, where 16.4 percent of the eligible electorate voted; in eight states turnout did not exceed 25 percent.[22] The percentage of eligible citizens who participated in the presidential caucuses exceeded 10 percent only in Iowa, the first and most-watched caucus in the nation. See figure 1.4 for presidential caucus participation in other states.

Turning to state elections (the level of government most people tell pollsters they feel closest to), voter turnout levels are also well below

FIGURE **1.4.** Participation in presidential party caucuses, 2008, for states where both parties held caucuses simultaneously.

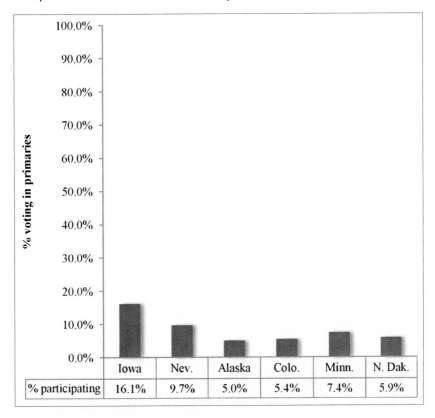

Source. Michael McDonald, The United States Election Project, "2008 Presidential Nomination Contest Turnout Rates," October 8, 2008, http://elections.gmu.edu/Turnout_2008P.html, accessed August 26, 2009.

those seen in presidential general elections. Overall, only about four in ten eligible voters vote in gubernatorial elections: the average voter turnout for gubernatorial elections from 1997 to 2002 was 43.5 percent; for gubernatorial elections held during nonpresidential election years, turnout averaged 41.2 percent.[23] Voter participation in gubernatorial elections held in nonpresidential election years is about 13 percentage points lower than those held with presidential elections. When it comes to electing their chief executive, some state residents are better at voting than others: about six in ten eligible voters in Minnesota, Montana, and South Dakota voted during this period, whereas only two out of ten eligible voters (19.4 percent) voted for governor in Kentucky's 1999 election.[24]

Turnout in statewide primary contests for governor and U.S. senator are also very low. Figure 1.5 charts turnout numbers for these contests during presidential election years, with separate figures for those gubernatorial or senate primary contests held on the same day as the presidential primary and those held on separate dates. As the chart shows, turnout for these contests, typically around the 20 to 25 percent mark, has declined—with a record low of 14 percent in the 2008 contests that were held on a day other than the state's presidential primary day.

As illustrated in figures 1.6 and 1.7, voter turnout in other—for offices such as lieutenant governor (when elected separately from the governor), secretary of state, attorney general, treasurer, auditor, agriculture commissioner, and education commissioner—is lower, even when these elections are held at the same time as the presidential or gubernatorial contests. It appears that people vote for candidates at the top of the ballot, and then—for lack of information, lack of a strong preference, or lack of choice (many of these races are uncontested)—they stop voting. This phenomenon is called *ballot falloff*, and the rate of falloff is most dramatic for races lower down on the ballot. It is a problem that has been exacerbated by the elimination of straight party voting in most states. Whereas Virginia, with only 3 statewide officers to elect, saw a drop of only one percentage point in voting for governor and lieutenant governor, Louisiana saw a drop of 3.4 percentage points between voting for governor and voting for the commissioner of agriculture and forestry; California, a drop of 6.7 percentage points between voting for governor and voting for superintendent of public education; and Vermont, an 8.4 percentage point drop between voting for president and voting for the Vermont secretary of state.

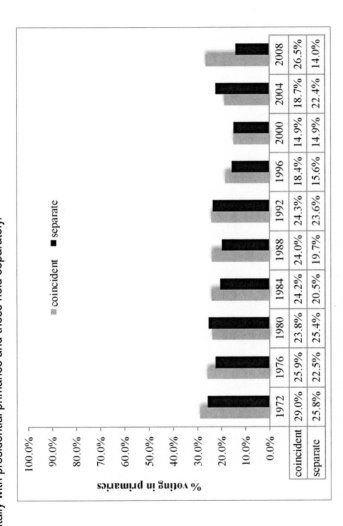

FIGURE 1.5. Voter turnout in statewide primaries for governor and U.S. Senate, 1972–2008, for primaries held coincidentally with presidential primaries and those held separately.

	1972	1976	1980	1984	1988	1992	1996	2000	2004	2008
coincident	29.0%	25.9%	23.8%	24.2%	24.0%	24.3%	18.4%	14.9%	18.7%	26.5%
separate	25.8%	22.5%	25.4%	20.5%	19.7%	23.6%	15.6%	14.9%	22.4%	14.0%

Source. Curtis Gans, "The Primary Turnout Story: Presidential Races Miss Record High Senate and Governor Contests Hit Record Low," Report, Center for the Study of the American Electorate, American University, http://www1.media.american.edu/electionexperts/2008%20 Primary%20Turnout_Final.pdf, accessed August 26, 2009.

FIGURE 1.6. Voter turnout for Virginia statewide officers, 2001, and for Louisiana statewide officers, first round, 2003.

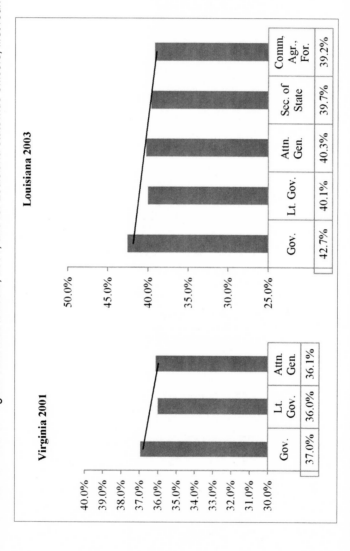

Sources. Vote data from Virginia State Board of Elections (http://www.sbe.state.va.us/web_docs/election/results/2001/nov2001/html/), voting eligible population extrapolated from United States Election project (http://elections.gmu.edu/). Vote data from Louisiana Secretary of State (http://www.sos.louisiana.gov:8090/cgibin/?rqstyp=elcms2&rqsdta=100403), voting eligible population extrapolated from United States Election project (http://elections.gmu.edu/).

FIGURE 1.7. Voter turnout for California statewide officers and propositions, 2002, and voter turnout for Vermont federal and statewide officers, 2004.

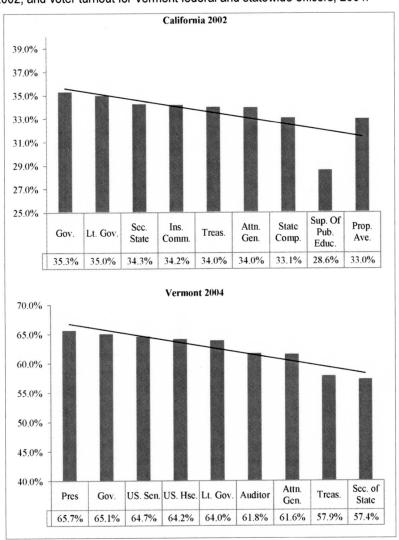

Source. Vote data from California Secretary of State (http://vote2002.ss.ca.gov/Returns/ voting eligible population from United States Election project (http://elections.gmu.edu/ Vermont Secretary of State (http://vermont-elections.org/elections1/2004_election_info. eligible population from United States Election project (http://elections.gmu.edu/).

Contests for the state legislature—law-making bodies that, thanks to the increasing power of state governments, have been making more and more of the important decisions that affect citizens' lives—engage even fewer voters than statewide contests. This can be observed both in states which hold separate elections for the state legislature and in states where legislators are selected simultaneously with statewide and federal officers (indicated by additional ballot falloff). In 2003, when New Jersey and Virginia (which hold legislative elections in odd-numbered years) selected their state legislators and no statewide officers, respectively 27.6 and 25 percent of the eligible public voted.[25]

Local electoral contests generally see the poorest level of participation—particularly if they are not held along with other elections, if they are nonpartisan, and if they have a weak mayor type of local government (a form of local government in which mayoral duties are split between a mayor and a city manager).[26] Figure 1.8 shows the voting levels for a number of cities. Average participation rates from 1974 to 1989 ranged from fewer than three in ten of voting-age citizens voting in Albuquerque, New Mexico, to under one in ten voting in Dallas, Texas. The numbers are similarly low when voter turnout is calculated as a percentage of registered voters. Between 1988 and 2001, only about one-third of registered voters voted in city elections in Boston, about one-fourth voted in Los Angeles city elections, and about one-fifth voted in local elections in Pensacola, Florida, and Austin, Texas.[27] Concerning participation in local *primary* elections, this satirical excerpt from *The Onion* is apropos:

> OLYMPIA, WA—A primary election of some sort is believed to have occurred in the past week or two in cities and counties across the nation, according to a report published by a citizens advocacy group. Although the report stopped short of affirming the claim, the Fair Election Advocacy Council believes that local political offices as diverse as mayor, city councilman, district attorney, and perhaps a judgeship or two may have been contested.[28]

As one might expect, turnout in these contests is miniscule.

FIGURE 1.8. Voter turnout as a percentage of voting age population for Albuquerque and other comparable cities, 1974–1989.

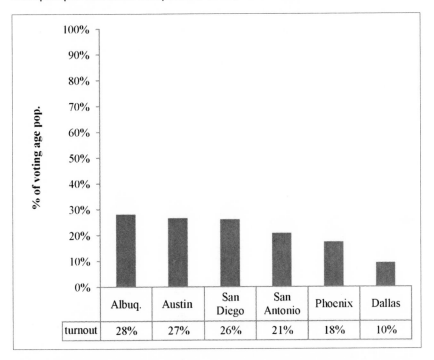

Source. Calculated from data presented by Amy Bridges in *Morning Glories: Municipal Reform in the Southwest* (Princeton, NJ: Princeton University Press, 1997).

And finally, in the quintessential town meetings that govern towns in New England (primarily Vermont at this point), participation is typically about 20 percent of the town's residents, with the rate of participation inversely related to the size of the town. (It should be noted that town meetings require a high level of commitment from citizens and are witness to a much deeper level of participation than voting.)[29]

Overall, the picture is quite clear: although Americans have many opportunities to vote, large proportions of the citizenry (majorities in most cases) often do not exercise their right to do so (figure 1.9 summarizes typical levels of participation for various types of elections in the United States). These low levels of voting represent the most visible symptom that something is wrong with U.S. elections. And if we expect elections to be the principal means for the governed to control their governments, such low levels of voter participation are harmful to democracy. The bulk of the evidence of political science research shows that low voter turnout is relevant: when fewer people vote, the voting public ceases to

FIGURE **1.9.** Typical voter turnout levels for various elections, highest office on ballot.

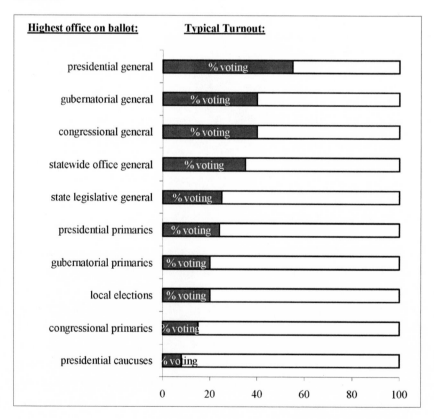

reflect the needs and desires of the public as a whole (in terms of social class, age, etc.), and the governments chosen by such voters become less representative of the majority—and consequently, less democratic.[30]

LACK OF KNOWLEDGE

Low voter participation is not the only symptom indicating that something is wrong with the health of U.S. elections. Not only do few participate in the political system by voting, but also very few—only about one in four—even claim to follow politics very closely.[31] And this lack of attention is accompanied by a lack of knowledge and understanding of politics, government, and policy. For example, three in ten respondents in 2007 could not name the vice president of the United States.[32] More than one person in four cannot name their states' governors, and four in ten do not know the party affiliation of their governors.[33] A little over half can name one of their two U.S. senators and less than one-third can name their U.S. representatives.[34]

One example of just how far off the public's understanding can be is a survey by *The Washington Post*, the Kaiser Family Foundation, and Harvard University; the poll found that about 60 percent of the public incorrectly believed that the U.S. government spends more on foreign aid than on Medicare (the U.S. government spends over one hundred times more on Medicare than on foreign aid).[35] In surveys during 2003 amid the Iraq conflict, about half of the public polled expressed the incorrect belief that the United States authorities had found clear evidence that Iraqi leader Saddam Hussein "was working closely with the al Qaeda terrorist organization" and that world opinion was supportive of the U.S.-led invasion. Twenty-two percent expressed the belief, also incorrectly, that the U.S. forces had found weapons of mass destruction (WMDs) in Iraq.[36] In all, six in ten people held at least one of these three misperceptions about the Iraq war—despite government statements and media reports to the contrary. By the eve of the 2004 election, after much public debate, notwithstanding the contents of a report by the September 11 Commission and the Duelfer Report, half of the public expressed the belief that Iraq had either weapons of mass destruction or WMD programs. And, whereas only 14 percent in 2004 said they believed that Iraq was directly involved in the September 11 attacks, 38 percent still believed that Iraq gave substantial support to al Qaeda;[37] by 2008, another poll found that the misunderstanding about the role of Iraq in September 11 had rebounded, with 46 percent of the public voicing the view that "Saddam Hussein had played a role in the attacks of September 11th."[38] On the issue of climate change, 43 percent of the public in a 2005 survey erroneously believed that President Bush favored U.S. participation in the Kyoto Treaty on global warming.[39] Even when it comes to money and taxes, the public seems poorly informed. Despite the massive tax cuts that were a major goal and accomplishment of George W. Bush's first term, only one in five of those surveyed knew that taxes had decreased under the Bush administration.[40] And the public greatly underestimates the magnitude of inequality in wealth in the United States. When researchers asked respondents to estimate the distribution of wealth in the United States in 2010, respondents estimated that the wealthiest 20 percent held 59 percent of the wealth, a far cry from the actual 84 percent of the wealth held by that group. When asked what proportion of wealth the top quintile should hold, the typical response was 32 percent.[41]

The situation is perhaps even more extreme than these studies indicate; research has suggested that when people get the facts wrong, they are often stubbornly resistant to correcting their misperceptions—perhaps preferring "truthiness" instead.[42] Research has also shown that although many people readily accept with little scrutiny information that confirms their existing beliefs, they tend to reject information incongruent with their beliefs even in the face of evidence. When they encounter evidence that contradicts their beliefs, many people tend to develop knee-jerk counterarguments—they frequently denigrate the source, the evidence, or the research—and then dismiss the information that does not support their viewpoints. The power of existing beliefs is such that studies indicate that people on opposite sides of an issue will disagree even more strongly after reading the same stream of information.[43]

Regarding some basics of U.S. government, one survey found that just 35 percent of the public could identify one of the First Amendment rights and that only 9 percent could identify three.[44] While about half of the public knew that the speaker of the house is third in the line of presidential succession,[45] only about one in ten knew who occupied that post in 2004.[46] Two-thirds of the public do not know who has the power to declare war.[47] A little over four out of ten citizens are unaware of the fact that the U.S. Supreme Court determines the constitutionality of a law or that the president appoints federal judges.[48] In 2007, fewer than four in ten knew that Chief Justice John Roberts was a conservative.[49] A 2002 preelection poll found that about two-thirds of the public did not know or incorrectly identified the majority party of the U.S. House of Representatives; and although this improved thanks to a significant amount of media attention paid to the Democratic victory in the 2006 election, by 2007 about one-fourth of the public was unaware of which party controlled the lower house.[50] On the whole, Americans today know about as much about public affairs as they did in the 1940s, "in spite of an unprecedented expansion in public education, a communications revolution that has shattered national and international boundaries, and the increasing relevance of national and international events and policies to the daily lives of Americans."[51] Even with the more recent aspects of this information revolution that have put a wealth of information literally at many people's fingertips—including the rise of the Internet, e-mail, and mobile devices and the spread of cable television—there has been no substantial improvement in public knowledge overall. Perhaps more disconcerting is that the gap between those who are informed about politics and those who are not informed and who do not care has increased substantially.[52]

The misunderstandings and fundamental lack of knowledge among large segments of the public matter; that is, they have political consequences, especially when elections are as closely divided as the recent presidential elections. Those who are less knowledgeable about politics tend to believe that the federal government makes every problem worse and are more likely to see the world in general as a cold and threatening place; these attitudes have consequences for support for governments and for the types of domestic and foreign policies governments pursue (resulting in more support for the use of the military and punitive policies and less support for foreign aid and diplomatic approaches).[53] Less knowledgeable citizens are also less likely to participate in politics or vote in elections than more knowledgeable citizens,[54] and therefore their opinions are less likely to be "heard and reflected in the political system."[55] Those who are misinformed may support policies or candidates that they would not support if they were properly informed.[56] For example, those who held just one misperception about the Iraq war—that Hussein was working closely with al Qaeda, or that world opinion supported the invasion, or that WMDs had been found—were twice as likely to support the Iraq war than those who had no misperceptions. Those persons who subscribed to all three misperceptions were four times as likely to support the war.[57] Additionally, holding any of these misperceptions was strongly associated with intent to vote for George W. Bush.[58] In this case, then, a better-informed public might have led to a different electoral outcome in 2004.

The lack of knowledge and its consequences can also be seen in studies of the American electorate. For the 2000 presidential election, Thomas Patterson's Vanishing Voter Project found that among respondents who were asked to identify twelve issue positions of Gore and Bush, "on the average issue, 38 percent correctly identified the candidate's position, 16 percent incorrectly identified it (an indicator that a third or more of the correct responses were also mere guesses), and 46 percent said they did not know it."[59] Though Patterson concludes that issue awareness in 2000 may have been the lowest in modern times, the fact is that substantial proportions of the electorate in every recent election are either unaware of or have incorrect ideas concerning what the candidates propose to do in office. Moreover, it is known from the research on voting behavior that a significant number of voters adopt the issue positions of their favorite candidates as opposed to opting for the candidate who fits their—the voters'—stands on the issues.[60]

The unusually closely followed and intensely fought 2004 election represented a significant improvement in public knowledge of the issues; nonetheless, large proportions of the public were either unaware of or misinformed about the candidates' positions. The 2004 National Annenberg Election Survey found that on average, 58 percent of registered voters[61] correctly identified the candidates' positions on fourteen issues, 31 percent incorrectly identified those positions, and 10 percent did not know. Figure 1.10 shows how aware voters were of the

FIGURE **1.10.** Knowledge of presidential candidates' issue positions, 2004.

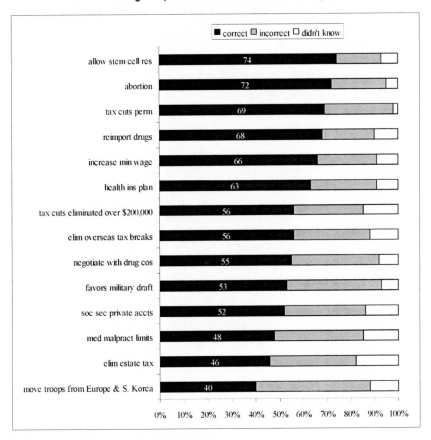

Source. National Annenberg Election Survey.

candidates' positions on each of those fourteen issues. On issues such as stem cell research, abortion, drug reimportation, and making Bush's tax cuts permanent, two-thirds to nearly three-fourths of the public knew where Bush and Kerry stood. This is not surprising given the simplified and emotionally charged nature of these issues, some of which garnered a great deal of media attention (especially stem cell research and drug reimportation). Knowledge levels drop off with more specific issues; barely a majority of registered voters knew that Kerry proposed to eliminate the Bush tax cuts only for the wealthiest taxpayers or that Bush planned to allow workers to invest social security contributions in private accounts. On one rather emotional issue, a sizeable proportion of registered voters—one in five—incorrectly believed that Bush was in favor of reinstating the military draft, and one survey found over half of eighteen- to twenty-nine-year-olds wrongly believed Bush wanted to reinstate the draft.[62]

As for the 2008 election, which dominated media coverage almost every week from late 2007 through Election Day and constituted a third of news coverage in 2008,[63] FactCheck.org's Kathleen Hall Jamieson and Brooks Jackson found that

> one in four (25.6 percent) of those who earned too little to have seen any tax increase under Obama's plan nevertheless believed that he intended to "increase your own federal income taxes," accepting McCain's repeated claims that "painful" tax hikes were being proposed on "families." Nearly two in five (39.8 percent) thought McCain had said he would keep troops in combat in Iraq for up to 100 years, though he'd actually spoken of a peacetime presence such as that in Japan or South Korea. Close to one in three (31 percent) believed widely disseminated claims that Obama would give Social Security or health care benefits to illegal immigrants, when in fact he would do neither.[64]

The implications of such lack of knowledge among significant portions of the electorate is an issue of contention among political scientists. Some argue that knowledge levels are high enough among some segments of the population and on certain issues for democracy to function properly, or that collectively, the dynamics of *mass* public opinion play out the way they should in a democracy regardless of the low levels of information among *individuals*.[65] Others argue that although people often do not remember specifics they may have heard or read, they do retain the broader beliefs or judgments derived from what they have heard.[66] Nevertheless, with election outcomes (especially outcomes of the close presidential contests typical in recent years) determined largely by that which sways the poorly informed segments of the public (the more sophisticated and knowledgeable voters know well in advance how they will vote), it is hard to believe that the low levels of public knowledge do not somehow allow for distortions of electoral outcomes. Furthermore, the demonstrated power of framing, priming, and spin, the emphasis placed on the personal qualities of the candidates, and the impact of events during campaigns all have the potential to influence voters—especially those least informed about politics—and deflect election results away from policy- or ideology-driven outcomes.[67] Under such circumstances, can elections truly be the vehicles of representation for public preferences?

In 2004, voters "preferred Kerry on most issues of domestic policy—education, health, and the economy," and there was growing discontent with President Bush over the Iraq war. Despite this, the combination of a continuing fear of terrorist attacks (primed by frequent announcements from the Department of Homeland Security about the level of threat in its color-coded warnings[68]), concern over terrorism in general, preferences for personal qualities associated in voters' minds with fighting terrorism (strong leadership, honesty, and trustworthiness), and Bush's emotional appeals rooted in religion and morality won the day.[69] Given such circumstances, what was the meaning of Bush's electoral mandate? What did the election results communicate about the public's wishes for the next four years?

Bush's answer to that question was to claim a mandate for creating personal investment accounts as part of social security, naming it his first priority. But one might question the legitimacy of that claim, considering that only about half of registered voters knew Bush's position on this issue before the election (see figure 1.10).[70] In a poll conducted shortly after the presidential election, only one-third of the public supported the newly reelected president's ideas on social security.[71] Just two months after the election, a majority of the public disapproved of Bush's handling of the economy and the war in Iraq, and the public was evenly split on his handling of the war on terror.[72] Less than one year later, in surveys taken in May and September 2005, some 61 percent of the public said they did not believe that George W. Bush had the same priorities for the country as they did.[73] The obvious discrepancy here raises the question of what the voters meant when the majority of them cast their vote for George W. Bush. The state of voter knowledge and the multitude of non-policy-related factors that affected voters' decisions make that question impossible to answer.

As they do in the case of voter turnout, presidential elections represent the high-water mark for voter knowledge. With less media attention devoted to local elections than to presidential campaigns, the public is often hard pressed to recognize the names of candidates for other offices (especially the candidates challenging incumbents)—and harder pressed to identify the candidates' issue positions. Name recognition, incumbency, service to constituents, and money all become more important the farther down the ballot (and away from presidential elections) a candidate appears. In primaries or nonpartisan local elections, where voters are not given the chance to infer candidate positions from party labels, issues play an even weaker or nonexistent role. All in all, American voters do not appear to be equipped with the knowledge necessary to make the enlightened decisions demanded of them by the U.S. political system as it is configured today.

LACK OF TRUST

The final symptom that indicates problems with the U.S. electoral system is the public's high level of cynicism about elections, politics, and government. Figure 1.11 shows the public's responses to a number of questions about how responsive and trustworthy they feel government

FIGURE **1.11.** Measures of public cynicism.

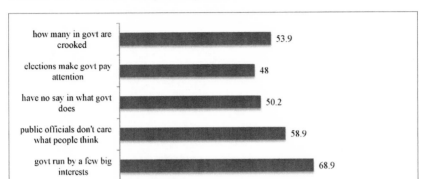

Source. American National Election Study, 2008.
Questions:
- Do you think that quite a few of the people running the government are crooked, not very many are, or do you think hardly any of them are crooked? Percent answering "quite a few."
- How much do you feel that having elections makes the government pay attention to what the people think—a good deal, some, or not much? Percent answering "a good deal."
- People like me don't have any say about what the government does. Percent agreeing.
- Would you say the government is pretty much run by a few big interests looking out for themselves or that it is run for the benefit of all the people? Percent answering "run by a few big interests."
- How much of the time do you think you can trust the federal government in Washington to make decisions in a fair way? Percent answering "always" or "most of the time."

and public officials are. Over half of the public believes that quite a few of the people running government are "crooked." Only about half of the public thinks that elections make government pay a good deal of attention to what people think. Almost six in ten think public officials do not care what people think. Almost seven in ten believe that government is run by a few big interests—as opposed to being run for the benefit of all people. And just 26 percent believes that citizens can trust the

FIGURE 1.12. Confidence in major institutions: Percent with a great deal or quite a lot of confidence.

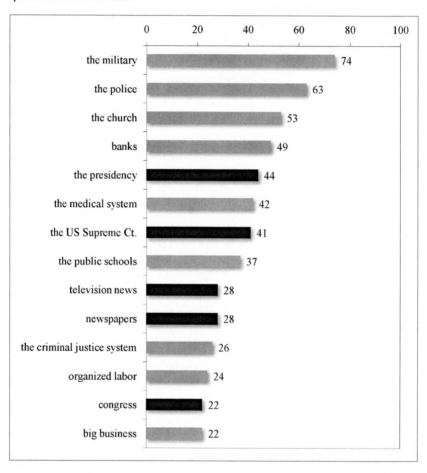

Source. Gallup Poll, May 23–26, 2005, accessed September 16, 2005, http://www.polling report.com/institut.htm.
Question: I am going to read you a list of institutions in American society. Please tell me how much confidence you, yourself, have in each one: a great deal, quite a lot, some, or very little.

government to make decisions in a fair way almost always or most of the time. As shown in figure 1.12, public cynicism extends to the major institutions in government and politics. Only 22 percent of the public has a great deal or quite a lot of confidence in the U.S. Congress; the numbers for the U.S. Supreme Court and the presidency are 41 percent and 44 percent, respectively. Additionally, the U.S. public has little confidence in its main window on the world of government and politics—the media—with only 28 percent voicing a great deal or quite a lot of confidence in television news or newspapers. In a separate poll, only 35 percent of the public said they believe that they can trust the media to report news fairly almost always or most of the time.[74]

Compared to the public several decades ago—and even considering the temporary drop in cynicism following the September 11 attacks—U.S. citizens are clearly more cynical today than they were in the past. For example, the percentage of the public who believe that government is run by a few big interests has doubled since 1964, and the percentage of the public who believe that they could trust the government in Washington almost always or most of the time dropped by almost half in the same time frame. These high levels of cynicism about government and politics, accompanied by the modern public's heightened cynicism for the institution once considered the primary source for objective information about government and politics—the mass media—make for a dangerously cynical public.

Box 1.1. On Bias

The lack of trust, the high levels of cynicism, and the weak understanding of politics and government that are prevalent in U.S. culture combine to make charges of bias the first and, unfortunately, often the only response to information and ideas that contradict one's own beliefs. Simply dismissing disagreeable points of view as biased appears to count as meaningful political discourse in the suspicious and intellectually lazy culture that has come to dominate political discussions in the United States. The use of the bias claim has perhaps been most aggressively cultivated by conservative media personnel and politicos who use the charge of bias (as in, "mainstream-media liberal bias") to inoculate their causes from unfavorable media coverage.[75] But use of the claim is not limited to any one ideological camp. There seems to be a widely held belief in the culture of the United States that there is no way to clearly discern reality independently from one's biases and a suspicion that everyone—journalists, politicians, governmental officials, scholars, interest group representatives, and ordinary citizens—is motivated by a political agenda and that such axe grinding is the only thing behind the evidence and arguments presented. Little credence seems to be given to professional norms that often motivate journalists, scientists, social scientists, historians, and economists, among others, to attain the most accurate picture of reality. (Certainly all professionals have their political perspectives, but those perspectives are generally not the primary considerations in their worldviews.) Furthermore, what counts as "unbiased" in this culture does not seem to be defined as objectivity or fairness in the United States. Instead, being unbiased seems to mean treating all perspectives as equally accurate when, as should be obvious, some assessments are usually closer to reality than the others. As a consequence of this widespread suspicion, competing political camps cannot agree on basic facts; and without any agreement on facts, it is impossible to have a productive, reasoned debate about politics.

I note this cultural phenomenon not just as part of the diagnosis (see chapter 8 for a discussion of this point under the prescription for skepticism), but because the very nature of the material in this book makes my arguments and evidence the likely targets of claims of bias. The truth is that sometimes one political party or ideological group is more inclined than another to act in ways that contribute to the poor health of elections. Sometimes the structure of elections and the laws that guide them favor one side over the other, and accordingly, no changes to the electoral system are going to be neutral. Sometimes, as Stephen Colbert has said, reality has a liberal "bias." At other times reality has a conservative "bias."

Therefore parts of the present discussion may reflect poorly on one party, candidate, or organization more than others. None of my discussion, however, has anything to do with the merit of the respective parties' governing philosophies. Judging the relative merits of the two parties' policies, programs, and ideology is not part of the purpose of this book; such judgments are, I argue, the realm of politics and elections—that is, the public should judge such issues. Parties should be supported or opposed on the basis of their governing philosophies, not according to the tactics that they use; and if more members of the public were aware of those differences in governing philosophies and made their electoral choices based on those differing philosophies, elections and the democracy they support would be healthier (and any misleading tactics rendered ineffective). My goal here is to show how the United States might clear the path for such elections and make them competitive on such policy-based partisanship—my aim is not to judge the parties on that basis myself. Although I do my utmost to navigate these areas as carefully and as objectively as possible (with help from expert colleagues who have reviewed this work), I cannot avoid describing the state of elections the way I have come to understand it through my own work and that of my fellow researchers. I certainly have my own political biases—it is impossible for anyone who follows politics closely to avoid this—but the professional norms that drive me to pursue accuracy are far more important to me, as is my bias toward a healthy, functioning democracy.

Although the problems discussed in this chapter—low turnout, lack of knowledge, and cynicism—are symptoms of a deeper illness afflicting elections, it is worth noting that the symptoms interact with each other, each elevating the magnitude of the others. Cynicism feeds on and contributes to both the lack of knowledge and lack of participation already discussed. Less knowledge of government and politics leads to more cynicism and a lower probability of any one individual's voting or participating. More cynicism makes people less likely to pay attention to politics and government—they are discouraged and frustrated by the idea that it is all simply a lie—thus leaving them less informed and reducing the likelihood that they will vote or otherwise participate in politics. This downward spiral, which involves far too many in the U.S. political system, leaves a segment of the population—mainly those at the lower end of the socioeconomic scale—outside of the electoral system and therefore makes it increasingly less likely that their interests will be represented.[76] Democracy, which values political equality, universal participation, and the responsiveness of public officials to the majority, cannot properly function under such conditions.

Something is clearly ailing U.S. elections. The root of the problem, however, runs deeper than the symptoms of low turnout, lack of knowledge, and high levels of cynicism—symptoms that, if ignored, could ruin the legitimacy of governments elected under the U.S. system. Fundamental to eliminating these symptoms is correctly diagnosing the "illness" that causes them, a task to which I turn in the next chapter. But first it is important to consider the nature of the U.S. political system in which elections operate.

NOTE ON THE NATURE OF THE SYSTEM: PLURALISM V. MAJORITARIANISM

Diagnosing a problem in any field requires an understanding of the system. As previously mentioned, no properly trained medical doctor would attempt to diagnose an illness or prescribe treatment without understanding how the body functions as a whole; the same is true of political bodies and elections. The fact that most political scientists consider the United States a pluralist system as opposed to a majoritarian system is critical to understanding U.S. elections and how they function within the country's democracy. A pluralist system is one in which the people exert influence mainly through organized interest groups, which utilize the fragmented nature of governmental power in the United States to effect change on behalf of those with common interests. A majoritarian system is one in which, simply put, the majority rules—that is, the government follows the preferences of those citizens who compose a majority on a particular issue.

Elections are generally critiqued from the perspective of majoritarianism, not pluralism. Indeed, elections are usually viewed as the key mechanisms of a majoritarian political system. In order for elections to function properly as mechanisms of majoritarianism, a number of conditions must be met, including (1) the presence of political parties that offer different visions of the role and purpose of government and (2) a knowledgeable and rational electorate that votes based on the sets of issues offered by the political parties (this is referred to as the *responsible parties model* of elections). Under such a system, the party (or coalition of parties, in the case of a multiparty parliamentary system) that wins the support of the majority implements its vision for government action (i.e., its platform), thus converting majority preferences into government policy.

The U.S. system does not operate in this way; indeed, judged by this standard, U.S. elections fail miserably. The electorate bears the bulk of the responsibility for this (though as is argued later, the citizens themselves are not entirely at fault). Though little appreciated, the political parties do actually act according to the responsible parties model: they offer different visions of the purpose of government, and when their members are in office, they implement policies in line with those visions.[77] But the electorate does not meet the requirement of citizens in a majoritarian democracy because, as mentioned earlier, barely half of those eligible actually vote in most elections. Moreover, many who *do* vote lack the necessary information to make a decision based on ideology and issues, and many choose their candidates for reasons other than

their policy positions, such as the personal characteristics of the candidates or a vague distaste for the other candidate. Such voting choices
may be considered legitimate by some, but even though these decisions
allow voters to determine who will govern, they impede majority control
over what governments *do*.

In addition to the failings of the electorate, the structure of the U.S.
system thwarts majority rule in that no single majority of voters chooses
the entire government, whether state or national. One set of voters (those
of each state[78]) determines the electors who select the president; other
groups of voters (those in each congressional district) select members of
the U.S. House; still another (those in each state) chooses U.S. senators.
The Supreme Court judges are appointed, not elected, and state and local
lawmakers are similarly elected by yet other, distinct sets of voters.[79]

Thus it is clear that the functioning of the U.S. system is not majoritarian in nature, but instead approximates what is known as a *pluralist
democracy*. The framers of the U.S. Constitution, using the principles
of separation of powers and checks and balances at the national level
as well as the division of power between the national and state governments, created a system that has multiple points of power and thus
multiple points of access to governmental decision makers. These points
of access are utilized by organized interests in attempts to influence government action through lobbying executives, lawmakers, and bureau-
crats, or by bringing cases before the courts. As long as all interests in a
society are represented fairly in this process, the result is a democratic
political system.

Elections in a pluralist democracy are one access point into the system: they represent one means to increase the number of government
officials who are ideologically predisposed to favor a group's interests;
elections are also a way to curry favor and gain access to those who will
hold power regardless of whether they are initially inclined to support
the group's interests. The former tactic—using elections to increase the
"friendly" lawmakers—is seen in interest group activities such as rat-
ing the voting records of officeholders (e.g., the National Rifle Association issues grades for candidates from president down to state legislator)

and providing money or volunteers to support one party's set of candidates (e.g., labor's nearly exclusive support for Democrats). The latter approach—trying to win access to lawmakers regardless of their views of the group's interest—is evident in the practice interest groups follow of giving money and support to incumbent candidates regardless of party or ideology and, in some cases, to candidates on opposing sides in a single contest.

Because elections are not the only means for changing what the government does in a pluralist democracy, elections can be judged differently in a pluralist system than those occurring in a majoritarian system. Elections in a pluralist system should be *open* and *fair*—that is, they should provide access and encourage participation from all of the various interests in society. Whether elections are open depends on the political freedom afforded groups in elections; whether elections are fair depends on the extent to which political equality exists in the process. In U.S. elections, all interests are, for the most part, free to participate in elections; whether they choose to do so or are capable of doing so—in terms of resources and organization—is another matter related to the fairness of elections. Whereas U.S. elections are certainly open, meeting the standard of fairness is where they fall short from a pluralist perspective. The structure and laws governing elections do not ensure fairness but instead exacerbate pluralism's tendency toward unequal political power.

As the present discussion of problematic elections proceeds, it is important to keep in mind these conceptions of the U.S. system, for the way the system is viewed—as majoritarian or pluralistic—affects the diagnosis of the problems with elections and ultimately the prescribed remedies for returning elections to a healthy state. That said, the fact that to most observers (myself included) the U.S. system closely approximates a pluralist democracy does not preclude suggestions for their improvement that would make the system more majoritarian. Indeed, one could argue that if elections functioned more properly along the lines of the majoritarian model, they could enhance the influence of electoral majorities, the size of which would necessitate the representation of interests otherwise left out of the flawed pluralist system.

CHAPTER 2

THE DISEASE

Why, then, is it the case that large segments of the American public don't vote, that much of the public has little knowledge about or interest in government and politics, and that most of the public is very cynical politics in general? These questions about conditions of the electorate have garnered a great deal of attention from the press and the political class, as well as from academics. Additionally, there have been many attempts to ameliorate these conditions, including the "Vote or Die" and "Rock the Vote" public campaigns; civics classes; websites such as FactCheck. org and that of Vote Smart; and government initiatives, such as same-day registration, postal voting, and no-excuse absentee voting. Though such activities may do some good, they are destined to make, at best, only marginal improvements.[80] Their impact is likely to be limited because all of these programs are aimed at *symptoms* of electoral problems in the United States and do not address the root causes of those problems.

If citizens are to vote, to inform themselves, and to be less cynical, they need more than encouragement or admonishment to participate, they need more than having the resources of a few Internet sites, and they need more than minor administrative adjustments that make it easier to vote. What members of the public really need are elections that matter, an understanding of *why* and *how* elections matter, and help in acquiring that understanding. These are the loci of the root causes of the United States of America's unhealthy elections. Identifying the actual causes requires first a diagnosis of the afflictions making U.S. elections ill and then a determination of the broader environmental and systemic conditions that contribute to and aggravate those conditions.

In brief, elections are diagnosed here as suffering from three ailments: political inequality, the failure of key supportive institutions, and an overburdened electorate. The major environmental and systemic factors that contribute to these ailments are (1) inadequate election laws and election administration, (2) an onerous electoral structure, (3) a mass media culture that is entertainment- and profit-driven, (4) the behavior of politicians, and (5) certain habits of the electorate. A map of the full diagnosis, with the ailments, causes, and symptoms, can be found in figure 2.1. The following sections of this chapter provide the details of the three ailments; the next chapter focuses on the five environmental and systemic causes.

THE ABSENCE OF POLITICAL EQUALITY

In order for elections to be "healthy," they must be open and fair or—to put it another way—free and equal. Elections must be open to anyone who wants to participate, whether that means voting, volunteering time, contributing money, or actually running for an office. U.S. elections meet the openness criterion for the most part: most barriers to voting were lifted in the twentieth century, there are no limits on volunteering, citizens can contribute money to campaigns (subject to certain, usually loose, restrictions), and anyone who meets the requirements for office and has a certain amount of appeal to the public can, with a little work, get on the ballot.[81] But whereas U.S. elections are relatively functional with respect to openness, the same is not true for fairness and equality.

FIGURE 2.1. Diagnosis of U.S. elections' illness.

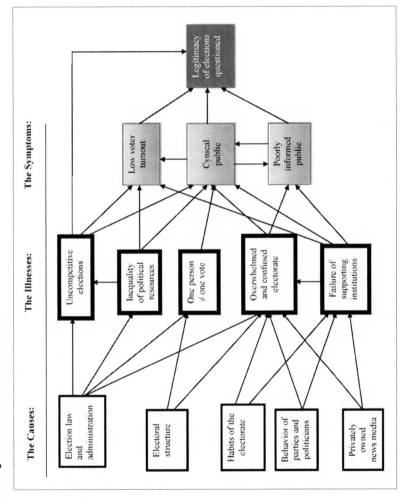

A certain level of political equality is required for elections to be considered fair and for them to function properly. First, each person's vote should be counted equally in order for elections to represent the will of the people. Second, there needs to be a rough balance in the electoral features that are extraneous to the vote choice in order for the races to be fair contests between opposing political viewpoints. For if the features of electoral contests are such that one side is favored over the other, then election winners owe victory not to any response of the voters to a candidate's philosophy of government or policy decisions, but to that politician's advantages in other areas unrelated to governing. Ultimately, when the answer to the question "Why did the candidates win?" is "Because they had more money" or "Because redistricting stacked the electorate in their favor," the legitimacy of both elections themselves and the governments they choose is questionable. Additionally, when contests are unequal or lopsided, supporters of the disadvantaged side are deprived of a chance to shape, through voting, the direction their governments take—contributing to cynicism about elections and the responsiveness of public officials. As one eminent political scientist put it years ago, "above everything, the people are powerless if the political enterprise is not competitive. It is the competition of political organizations that provides the people with the opportunity to make a choice. Without this opportunity, popular sovereignty amounts to nothing."[82]

One Person, One Vote
A basic principle of democracy is that each person's vote should be equal to that of every other person. This principle of *one person, one vote* was codified by the Supreme Court in its *Baker v. Carr* decision (369 U.S. 186, 1962), which ultimately forced state legislatures throughout the country to redraw congressional and state legislative districts so that they were equal in population.[83] Despite this stated principle, a great deal of inequality exists in U.S. elections. It exists in the unequal weight given each individual vote for president and for control of the U.S. Senate; it exists in the way the contests for the presidential nominations of the major parties are held; it exists in the way that electoral districts are

drawn; and it exists because of the uneven administration of elections and the machinery used for casting and counting ballots, which often fail to allow or count all legitimate votes.

The number of electoral votes each state casts for president is equal to the number of that state's U.S. representatives and senators. This arrangement guarantees every state at least three Electoral College votes and, as a consequence, gives more weight to voters in small states. Each of the three electors from the state of Vermont, for example, represents about 160,000 eligible voters, whereas each of the thirty-one electors in neighboring New York represents about 414,000 eligible voters. In other words, a Vermonter's vote for president is worth more than two and a half times a New Yorker's vote.[84] More importantly, because only a handful of states are truly competitive during any one presidential election, the citizens in the so-called battleground states receive the bulk of the attention from the candidates, parties, and media and ultimately exercise more influence over the outcome of the election, whereas the citizens in the remaining states are taken for granted and largely ignored. Writing about the 2000 election, which hinged on the outcome of the disputed Florida vote, Thomas Patterson wrote, "in what other democracy in the world would a margin of 537 votes in one state [Florida] be worth more than a nationwide margin of 537,179 votes?"[85]

The nomination contest for the presidency also grants disproportionate influence to residents of a small number of states that hold their contests early in the process, particularly Iowa, New Hampshire, and South Carolina. As is the case in the battleground states during the general election, the voters in states with early primaries or caucuses are courted heavily by the candidates and have tremendous influence on the eventual nominees for both political parties. In 2004 Howard Dean's third-place showing in the Iowa caucuses and his inability to recover in the New Hampshire primary sunk his once-popular campaign, whereas John Kerry's success in these states helped propel him to the Democratic nomination. In 2008 the Republican nomination was over in mid-February before many states had voted, thanks, in large part, to John McCain's surprise January victory in the New Hampshire primary. Even though the Democratic nomination contest in 2008 continued until the end of the voting in June, voters in the early states still had a disproportionate influence on the race—receiving the bulk of the attention from the candidates and media, as well as setting the parameters of the race.[86]

The voters of states that have primaries or caucuses later in the process are largely ignored, especially when those contests occur after one candidate has accumulated enough pledged delegates to ensure winning the vote of his or her party's convention. The importance of early nomination contests has led the legislatures in many states to schedule their contests earlier in the process, but such moves have not improved the situation for most voters because no matter how early other states set their contests, the Democratic National Convention guarantees Iowa and New Hampshire the right to go first. Thus in 2008, when Florida and Michigan ignored the Democratic Party rules and set the dates for their primaries earlier than allowed, the Democratic National Committee stripped both states of their convention delegates (who were later reinstated and granted half of a vote each).[87] Only a handful of the larger states that legally moved their contests up to the first allowable date become important in the crowded field, and voters in states that do not reschedule their contests find that they are even less likely to play any role in selecting the presidential nominees (the 2008 Democratic contest was a rare exception). In addition to making the votes of some more important than the votes of others, the front-loading of the nomination process also puts an even greater premium on money (giving advantages to those who give it and to those who can get lots of it) and on the media (granting journalists a powerful role in the process).[88]

Thus the influence of a select handful of states in the presidential nomination process and of the small number battleground states in the general election combine to the effect that from state to state, citizens' influence in selecting presidents is not at all equal. This geographically based inequality of the presidential electorate is reflected in the lower levels of interest, knowledge, and ultimately participation on the part of voters in states relegated to the sidelines by the configuration of the presidential election process.[89]

The constitutional guarantee of equal representation for each state in the U.S. Senate regardless of state population also results in a large degree of political inequality in the value of the vote, though this fact does not seem to be a distressing issue for the public at the moment. At the extremes, California's 36 million people have the same number of votes in the U.S. Senate as do the half a million people in Wyoming. In other words, when it comes to determining the makeup of the Senate, each voter in Wyoming has seventy-two times the voting power of each voter in California.[90] Because states with smaller populations tend to vote Republican, this imbalance in voting power for the Senate has partisan implications. In the three Senate elections between 2000 and 2004, "Democrats have actually received 2.4 million more votes than Republicans, yet the G.O.P. won 11 more seats. The Senate's 55 Republicans [in 2005] represent 131 million people; its 44 Democrats represent 161 million."[91] Thus the violation of the one person, one vote principle in electing U.S. senators results in a Senate composed of members who, as a whole, sometimes fail to represent the partisan preferences of the U.S. public as expressed in elections.[92] Thus the Senate deviates frequently from majority public preference when voting on policy, budgets (especially with regard to allocation of federal dollars among the states), and nominees to the U.S. Supreme Court, among other things.[93]

The uneven administration of elections and the varying error rates of the machinery and ballot design add other elements of inequality to U.S. elections. The Constitution allows the state governments to administer elections; the states have, for the most part, handed over responsibility to their county or other local governments. The result is widely varying practices at the local level with regard to ballot design and voting equipment, the assignment of polling places, the application of election law by poll workers, and the machinery that is used to tally the votes.[94] The unequal treatment of voters endemic to this system was brought to the public's attention most dramatically during the dispute over the Florida ballot count in the 2000 presidential election. For more than a month following Election Day, partisans, lawyers, and state and local officials battled in the glare of the media spotlight and in courtrooms over how and whether to count ballots that did not register a vote for president when run through vote-counting machines (not only the infamous hanging, dimpled, and pregnant chads of the punch card ballots but also electronic scan ballots with markings that did not register), absentee ballots that had arrived without postmarks or postmarked after Election Day, and ballots with such confusing designs (in some cases paired with poor instructions from poll workers) that tens of thousands of voters spoiled their ballots by unintentionally making a choice for more than one set of candidates for president and vice president. The fiasco of the Florida count shook voter confidence in how and whether their votes would count at all. The battle was settled when seven justices of the U.S. Supreme Court concluded that the uneven standards for counting ballots in the various Florida counties had led to unequal treatment of voters in violation the Fourteenth Amendment's equal protection clause and when five of those justices then ruled that time had run out for counting the ballots—handing the presidency to George W. Bush.[95]

Analyses of the ballots conducted the following year showed just how crucial the inequality in local elections practices can be. If the Florida ballots are examined according to various standards for counting the Florida votes (the ballots have been coded and computerized by the National Opinion Research Center at the University of Chicago and are available to the public), Al Gore is shown to win in as many cases as George Bush.[96] If the standard of deciding the outcome of the election is based on which candidate was preferred by the greatest number of those who attempted to legitimately cast a vote in Florida,[97] then Al Gore should have become the forty-third president of the United States.[98] Thus the unequal weight given to voters in Florida (because of the structure of the Electoral College) and the inequality in the actual count of Florida votes both led to an electoral outcome that was different from what would have happened had the one person, one vote principle of democratic elections been followed.

Additionally, analyses of ballots rejected in the 2000 Florida count show that the varying practices in administering elections, along with the structure of the ballots and the types of voting machines used, result in a class bias in vote counting and confusion for many voters. Studies have determined that votes are more likely to go uncounted in areas with greater nonwhite populations and lower socioeconomic status than in predominantly white, more educated, and wealthier areas of the country.[99] An analysis of the rate of ballot rejection in various counties in Florida in 2000 found that three times as many ballots were rejected in black precincts (where voters are more likely to vote for Democratic candidates) than in white precincts, even after taking into account the different education and income levels and the design of the ballots.[100] Other studies have found that the problem of higher rates of uncounted votes in areas with larger nonwhite, poor, and poorly educated populations is not limited to Florida or to the 2000 election.[101] Research has also demonstrated that the design and layout of some ballots and the types of voting machinery used can create voter confusion, leading some individuals to vote in unintended ways or overlook contests on the ballot.[102]

By 2002 the U.S. Congress had passed and the president had signed the Help America Vote Act (HAVA) in an attempt to address some of the problems associated with the uneven and often sloppy administration of elections, as well as the problems with the voting machinery. The HAVA provided federal funds for upgrading voting machinery and mandated a number of changes in state administration of elections, including the availability of ballots, standards for voting machines, and statewide computer voter databases. Whether the law is successful in establishing equality in vote counting will depend upon how much funding Congress ultimately appropriates to implement the act and how vigorously the national standards are applied.[103] The record to date seems mixed.[104] By 2004 many states had installed new voting machinery and made new regulations regarding provisional ballots. Still, many polling places continued using voting machines that had high rates of ballot rejection. Additionally, one of the newer types of machines—direct recording electronic (DRE) voting machines—raised questions about vote validation because the machines provide no paper record of the voters' choices and, as with any computer, are susceptible to programming problems and manipulation. In 2006 in Florida's Thirteenth Congressional District, for example, the DRE voting machines reported that more than eighteen thousand voters failed to cast a vote for Congress in a top-of-the-ballot contest that was won by a margin of only several hundred votes; there was no paper trail and thus no way to check for computer error. Recent research, however, has found that DRE voting, if designed correctly, can actually reduce voting errors. Studies have also found that the concerns about fraud are overshadowing the gains in accuracy and equality that such voting technology can offer.[105]

Evidence that these issues surrounding election administration, machinery, and ballot design affect the public's confidence in elections can be seen in public opinion polls. One 2004 postelection survey found that just 68 percent of voters were "very confident" that their vote was accurately counted, and only 48 percent were "very confident" that the "votes across the country were accurately counted."[106] As far as election administrators are concerned, a 2008 survey of local election officials found that only a minority thought that HAVA had made elections more fair and reliable, whereas a majority thought it made elections more expensive and more complicated to administer.[107]

Uncompetitive Elections
Beyond the simple issue of counting votes equally, U.S. elections are characterized by inequality in two other areas: in overall competitiveness and in the distribution of politically important resources. In too many electoral races, only one side has any chance of winning. This assertion may seem unfounded following two very close presidential elections and at a time when the electorate appears so divided along partisan lines, but far too many electoral contests in the U.S. are simply not competitive—or even contested. The national results of the presidential elections may have been close in 2004 and 2008, but competition was limited to between seventeen and nineteen battleground states. The other thirty-one to thirty-three states, plus the District of Columbia, were largely ignored by the presidential campaigns (neither the campaigns nor the national parties spent any money on television advertising in these states, for example[108]) because only one side had a real chance of winning their electoral votes.

In the battle for control of the narrowly divided U.S. Senate in 2008, only twelve of the thirty-five contests for U.S. Senate seats were competitive—that is, only about one-third of the races held the possibility that either party might win.[109] And only 64 of the 435 seats in the U.S. House of Representatives were determined in contests that were considered either battlegrounds or races in which one party would narrowly win in the 2008 election; that is, in less than 15 percent of U.S. House races did more than one candidate have a reasonable chance of winning.[110] In fact, there were almost half as many uncontested House races (30) as competitive ones. Despite these numbers, the election of 2008 was considered competitive by comparison to contests of other years.

The numbers for the election four years earlier are similar, when again only nine of the twenty-five contests for U.S. Senate seats were competitive—that is, only one-third of the races held the possibility that either party might win.[111] In the House, contests for 37 of the 435 seats were considered competitive in 2004: in less than 10 percent of U.S. House races that year did more than one candidate have a reasonable chance of winning.[112] There were more uncontested House races in 2004 (66) than competitive ones.[113] After the votes were counted, only 23 House races in 2004 were found to have been close contests (won by a margin of 10 percentage points, at most) compared to 68 in 1994.

The lack of competition in most electoral contests means not only that it is highly unlikely that voting will determine who is elected to the House or Senate in most districts and states but also that large partisan swings are required for elections to result in a change of partisan control of either chamber of Congress (or state legislatures).[114] It has been calculated that by 2004, a gain of 4.9 percent in the vote for the minority party nationally was needed to gain five seats in the U.S. House and 5.7 percent to gain ten seats (between 1946 and 1998 a 1.5 percent increase was required to gain five seats and 2.3 percent to gain ten).[115] The typical partisan vote swing nationally is below 5 percent. The 2004 election is an effective illustration of how difficult it usually is for the public to change party control of Congress through elections. Just how improbable was it that the election could have resulted in a change in party control of either chamber in 2004? Of the competitive Senate races, Democrats would have had to win the one contest that "leaned Democrat" and all of the "no-clear-favorite" contests in order to pick up the two seats needed to give them an effective majority in the U.S. Senate.[116] For the Republicans to lose control of the U.S. House, Democrats would have had to win all of the Democrat-leaning and all of the no-clear-favorite contests, *plus* twelve of the eighteen Republican-leaning contests.[117]

The thirty-seven competitive House seats in 2004 composed the smallest number of competitive seats in the last two decades and represent a continuation of a downward trend in competition. The 2006 and 2008 elections were something of an exception, given the overwhelming influence of the electorate's strong disapproval of the Bush administration and of the war in Iraq; nonetheless only a small fraction of those contests were competitive as well. Figure 2.2 shows the percentage of competitive seats for the U.S. House from 1982 to 2008 (the area shaded black represents the percentage of seats in which more than one candidate has a reasonable chance of winning; the area shaded in grey represents the percentage of seats in which only one candidate has a chance of winning).

Although the 2006 and 2010 elections did not represent a structural change in the number of competitive districts, they did result in a change in party control. Indeed, despite the low number of competitive seats and despite a swing in the national party vote of only 5.4 percent, the 2006 election witnessed a change in party control of the U.S. House, with the Democrats picking up thirty seats. There are good reasons to believe this election and the 2010 election are unique and not, in fact, an indication of an increase in competitiveness. According to one analysis, the 2006 election hinged upon a much wider swing in the partisan vote within Republican districts, a swing caused by the convergence of a number of unusual factors unique to that election—including an extremely unpopular president, the number of Iraq war deaths in each district, and a set of scandals that plagued a number of Republican candidates that year.[118] In 2008, the popularity of the Obama campaign (and continued unpopularity of President Bush) allowed the Democrats to retain many

FIGURE 2.2. Competitive and uncompetitive U.S. House races, 1982–2008.

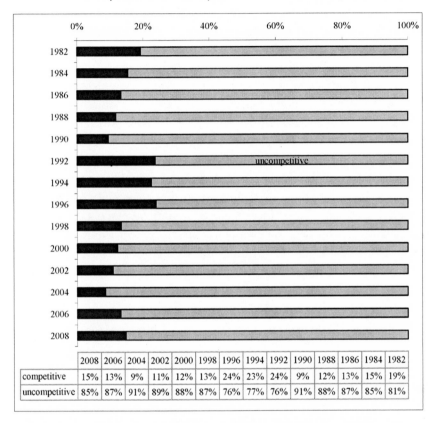

	2008	2006	2004	2002	2000	1998	1996	1994	1992	1990	1988	1986	1984	1982
competitive	15%	13%	9%	11%	12%	13%	24%	23%	24%	9%	12%	13%	15%	19%
uncompetitive	85%	87%	91%	89%	88%	87%	76%	77%	76%	91%	88%	87%	85%	81%

Source. Gray C. Jacobson, "The Congress: The Structural Basis of Republican Success," in *The Election of 2004*, ed. Michael Nelson (Washington, DC: CQ Press, 2005), 167.
Note. For 2006 and 2008 sum of the races considered battlegrounds (tossups) or narrow victories for either party (learning Democratic or leaning Republican) by *The New York Times*, accessed August 28, 2009, http://elections.nytimes.com/2008results/house/votes. html, and http://www.nytimes.com/ref/washington/2006ELECTIONGUIDE.html.

of those largely Republican districts won in 2006 and to make inroads into more typically Republican districts; in 2010 Democrats lost most of those districts resulting in a swing back to the partisan configuration of 2004 and a Republican majority in the U.S. House. In other words, the extraordinary conditions of the 2006 election led to a change in party control despite the low rate of district competitiveness, and the 2010 contest outcome was largely the result of the receding tide of that unusual election of 2006.

Finally, it should be noted that—Tea Party victories toppling some incumbent Republicans in 2010 notwithstanding—the lack of competition in House races is not balanced by intraparty competition in congressional primary elections. Between 1960 and 2000, only 11 percent of primaries for the U.S. House were competitive.[119]

Lack of competition in electoral contests is not a problem that afflicts only national congressional races. A study of competition in statewide contests (those for governor, lieutenant governor, secretary of state, etc.) found that serious competition occurred in only 59 percent of statewide races and 25 percent of statewide primaries between 1960 and 2000.[120] Only 55 percent of the forty contests for state governor were competitive in 2006 and fewer than half (five out of eleven) were competitive in 2008.[121] And both the number of competitive and contested races for statewide offices has been declining over time.[122]

With regard to contests for state legislatures, there was only one choice for voters in 35 percent of the 2004 races. Between 1996 and 2000, on average, 38 percent of state house seats were uncontested and only 28 percent of state house seats were deemed competitive. The percentage of uncontested seats ranged from 1 percent in Michigan to 70 percent in Massachusetts; the percentage of competitive seats ranged from a high of 56 percent in North Dakota to a low of 10 percent in Massachusetts. As in other elections, the overall number of contested and competitive races for state legislative seats has been decreasing.[123] Although partisan control of state legislatures does change (because many legislatures are closely divided or because of unique elections like the national congressional elections of 2006), such changes still depend on the outcomes of races in a handful of districts.

In sum, competition in U.S. elections is very low and has been declining in recent decades. That this lack of electoral competition comes at a time of intense partisan contention among the public suggests that elections are really ailing. Clearly, partisan conflict is *not* fully playing out in election contests where voters can have a role; most voters' choices come down to legitimizing (or not) the most probable winner. Instead, the political parties and incumbent officeholders battle for the advantage in other arenas—for instance, in obtaining electoral resources or drawing the electoral district maps—stacking the deck so that most electoral contests are foregone conclusions, leaving most voters out of the equation. Confronted with the choice of legitimizing the probable winner in most contests or staying home, it is little wonder that so many voters choose to stay home and that citizens are often cynical about elections and politics. The lack of competition is a key component of the sickness afflicting U.S. elections, for without real electoral competition (or any electoral competition, which is entirely lacking in too many contests) voting is, as E. E. Schattschneider wrote, meaningless.[124]

Unequal Distribution of Electoral Resources
In addition to unequal and often lopsided competition in many races, the current distribution of electoral resources, particularly money, contributes to the lack of political equality in U.S. elections. Although money is not the only factor that determines the outcome of elections, it plays an important role in successful campaigns. Indeed, money plays such a critical role that serious imbalances in the availability of funds can be decisive, determining whether candidates have any shot at winning in the first place and even tipping the balance in close electoral contests.[125] And serious imbalances in the availability of money certainly occur in U.S. elections: specifically, candidates running for reelection (that is, incumbent officeholders) and Republican Party organizations tend to hold significant financial advantages over their electoral opponents.

Most incumbent candidates running for reelection to legislative bodies (Congress, state legislatures, city councils) and many state and local executives (governors, secretaries of state, mayors, etc.) have tremendous advantages with respect to the amount of money they can spend campaigning. The typical candidate challenging a sitting senator in 2008 was able to raise and spend only a little over one-fourth (27.6 percent) of what the typical incumbent Senate candidate spent. Likewise, typical candidates challenging U.S. House incumbents were able to spend a little over one-third (38.4 percent) of what their incumbent opponents spent. Even in competitive races, incumbents had an overwhelming advantage: Senate challengers in close races raised just 45 percent of what incumbent senators in those races collected, and House challengers raised 65.9 percent of incumbent representatives' total revenues.[126]

As figure 2.3 shows, the financial disadvantage for candidates running against House incumbents has gotten worse since 1976; the last time challengers spent at least half of what incumbents spent (marked by the 50 percent line in the graph) was 1980. The jump in spending for candidates challenging sitting senators in 1994 and subsequent elections can be attributed to the fact that a number of Senate challengers spent large amounts of their own personal money in these years.[127] The downward trend in challenger financing, however, returned in 2004 despite continued self-financing,[128] with the average challenger spending only 36 percent of what incumbents did; in 2008 this dropped to 27 percent. Discontent regarding the Bush administration's handling of the war in Iraq and of Hurricane Katrina and scandals involving congressional Republicans helped fuel a slight increase in challenger spending in 2006 for Democrats. Nevertheless, even in competitive house races, as Paul Herrnson reported, "incumbents in jeopardy raised about 72 percent more in cash and party coordinated expenditures than hopeful challengers during the 2006 election."[129] In the six competitive Senate contests in 2006, average incumbent spending was $2 million more than the average challenger.[130]

This incumbent-challenger financial imbalance also holds true for state legislative seats. Figure 2.4 shows challenger spending as a percentage of incumbent spending for state house and senate candidates in 2004. In most of these cases, challengers had difficulty raising as little as half of what incumbents raised and often failed to raise even one-third of what the typical incumbent raised. Challengers do better in states where the amount of money involved in legislative contests is relatively small, as it is in Arkansas, Montana, and South Dakota; or where legislative

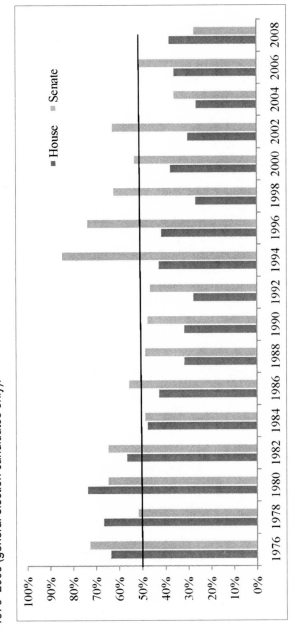

FIGURE 2.3. Challenger spending as a percentage of incumbent spending for U.S. House and Senate races from 1976–2008 (general election candidates only).

Source. Produced by author from data presented in Norman J. Ornstein, Thomas E. Mann, and Michael J. Malbin, *Vital Statistics on Congress, 1997–1998* (Washington, DC: Congressional Quarterly Press, 1998) and the Federal Election Commission, http://www.fec.gov/.

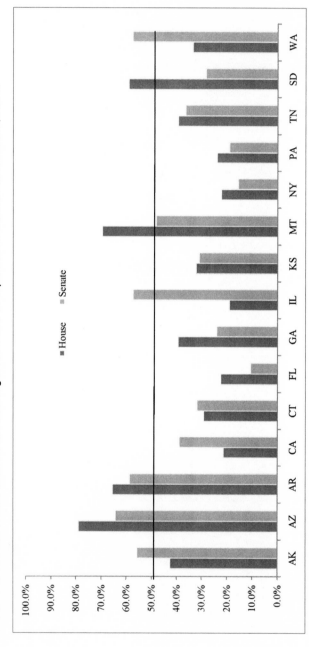

FIGURE **2.4.** State House and Senate challenger revenues as a percent of incumbent revenues, 2004.

Source. The Institute on Money in State Politics, http://www.followthemoney.org/index.phtml.

campaigns are publicly funded, as in Arizona. This pattern of an incumbent advantage in campaign money is evident in any year for almost any state, and there is plenty of evidence to show that this imbalance is worsening.[131]

Although gubernatorial races are not as visibly lopsided as legislative contests, incumbent governors are able to raise and spend more money than the typical challenger. Figure 2.5 shows the average spending by incumbent governors and their challengers for elections between 1997 and 2004. On average, challengers have been able to spend about

FIGURE 2.5. Average spending (in millions) in gubernatorial elections by incumbent governors and challengers, 1997–2004.

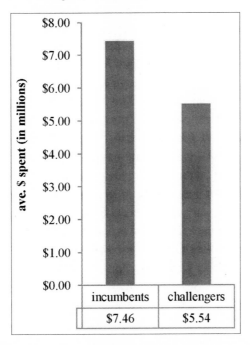

incumbents	challengers
$7.46	$5.54

Sources. Gubernatorial Campaign Expenditures Database, compiled by Thad Beyle and Jennifer Jensen, secretaries of state and state ethics committees, and the National Institute on Money in State Politics.

74 percent of what incumbents have spent. In an earlier analysis of guber-natorial elections between 1997 and 2000, I found that after controlling for a number of other factors that are related to fundraising levels,[132] incumbents raised, on average, $1.6 million more than challengers.[133]

As for presidential contests, no incumbent ran for reelection in 2008. During the 2004 election, both the incumbent Bush and his challenger, Kerry, accepted public funds for the general election contest, so their own campaign spending levels were legally limited and thus equal for the general election.[134] Neither candidate, however, used public funding for the nomination phase of the election. During the nomination phase of the election, George W. Bush, who faced no real competition, raised about $35 million more than John Kerry.[135] This difference, however, is less a reflection of the imbalance between incumbents and challeng-ers (in 1996 President Clinton, who also faced no serious opposition in the nomination phase, raised $2.4 million *less* than his Republican challenger, Bob Dole) than it is a reflection of the typical imbalance in election financing between the Republican and Democratic parties.

Republicans typically hold a large financial advantage over Demo-crats in fundraising for elections. This is especially true of the national political party organizations and of presidential and gubernatorial candi-dates.[136] The 2004 and 2008 elections, however, were unique in a num-ber of ways that require closer examination. In 2004, Bush's $35 million campaign finance advantage during the nomination phase of the election gave the president an upper hand in getting his message out and orga-nizing his campaign early.[137] Whereas Kerry had to spend nomination-phase money in the competition in order to win his party's nomination, the Bush campaign was able to leverage its superior resources on the general election. While Kerry was battling with fellow Democrats over the Democratic Party nomination, the Bush campaign spent its money on communicating with voters about the general election choice (including a $40 million, six-week television assault on Kerry immediately follow-ing Super Tuesday in March, when it had become clear that Kerry would win the nomination) and on organizing the Republican voter mobiliza-tion effort that garnered the party an additional 10.5 million votes over their total for 2000 (Democrats increased their vote by 6.8 million over 2000).[138] The Republican advantage in campaign funds was added to by the extra five weeks the Bush campaign had to spend nomination-phase money because of the later date of the Republican National Convention (public funding and the corresponding spending limits take effect shortly after candidates accept the party nominations at the conventions).[139] It was during this five-week period that Kerry—who was conserving his public funds to avoid an end-of-campaign shortfall like the one that plagued Gore in 2000—fell victim to the negative (and demonstrably false) attacks from the 527 committee Swift Boat Veterans for Truth.[140]

To get the full picture of the 2004 presidential contest, it is important to look beyond what the candidates themselves raised to what their party organizations and 527 committees raised. With bitterness lingering from the 2000 presidential election, a high level of ideological polarization, discontent about the war in Iraq, and the further development of the Internet's potential as a fundraising tool, more money than usual flowed into the accounts of the Democratic Party and Democratic Party candidates in 2004—reducing the traditional gap between the parties. In the 2003–2004 reporting cycle, the Democrat National Committee (DNC) actually raised $2 million more than the Republican National Committee (RNC). Between 2001 and 2002, however, the RNC raised $102.6 million more than the Democrats did. The RNC's advantage was used in an early start-up for the Bush reelection campaign, which spent millions of dollars beginning in 2001 devising and testing new ways to reach voters for the 2004 election.[141] Republicans were also able to raise $29 million more (51 percent more) than Democrats did for their party's 2004 nominating convention.[142]

In response to the Bipartisan Campaign Reform Act of 2002 (BCRA), which banned soft money (unregulated money used by the parties to run issue ads and voter-mobilization programs), a number of Democratic leaders channeled their efforts into 527 committees (named after the IRS tax-code section that regulates them). Contributions to and expenditures by 527 committees in 2004 were not limited by the Federal Election Commission (FEC) as long as the groups did not formally endorse a candidate or coordinate their efforts with the parties or candidates themselves. These committees could thus raise unlimited sums of money from wealthy individuals, corporations, and labor unions. Democrats had an advantage among major 527 committees trying to influence the presidential race in 2004, raising $181.8 million, compared to the major Republican 527 groups' $64.5 million—a $117.3 million advantage.[143]

Whether this money helped to eliminate the disadvantage the Democrats' presidential bid faced in candidate and party money is questionable, however. In order for that disadvantage to truly disappear, this 527 money would have to be considered de facto party or candidate money, which it is not. The parties and presidential candidates did not have control over the spending of this money; candidates and parties, by law, cannot coordinate with 527 committees. Therefore any advantage provided by having independent groups spend money to support or oppose candidates is reduced because of the lack of control and coordination with the campaign's own efforts, resulting in an unclear message and inefficient and overlapping administration. This was best illustrated by the fact that no 527 came to the aid of John Kerry when the Swift Boat Veterans attacked his war record immediately following the Democratic National Convention, and the attack carried serious consequences for the Kerry campaign.[144] The complicated nature of 527 spending was also highlighted by comments of those involved; Harold Ickes, for example, "who ran the Media Fund, a 527 organization that raised about $59 million in support of Kerry," told *Washington Post* reporters that "the federal election law prohibiting communication with the Kerry campaign created insurmountable obstacles in crafting effective, accurate responses to anti-Kerry ads."[145]

The complete financial picture of the 2004 presidential election is summarized in figure 2.6. The Republican candidate, Bush, had an advantage in fundraising during the nomination phase of the election—an advantage that was increased by the fact that Bush had no real opposition during that phase and by the additional five weeks that his campaign had to spend this money because of the timing of the two parties' national conventions. The Republicans had a monetary edge for their convention

FIGURE 2.6. Money raised for 2004 presidential campaign, in millions.

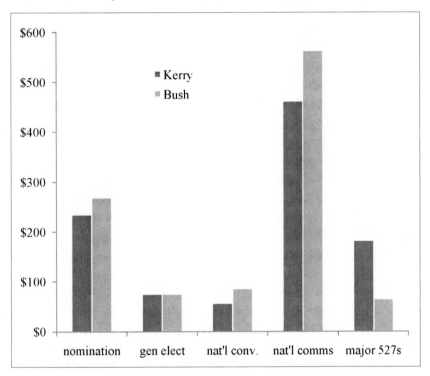

Sources. Federal Election Commission and the Center for Public Integrity, "527s in 2004 Shatter Previous Records for Political Fundraising," accessed September 27, 2005, http://www.publicintegrity.org/527/report.aspx?aid=435&sid=300.

as well—an event that showcases the party's nominee and is an important fundraising opportunity. The RNC had a $100 million advantage over the DNC during the period between 2001 and the 2004 election. And even though the Democrat's presidential bid had more 527 committee money, its use could not be coordinated with the party or the Kerry campaign. In all, the Republican bid to hold onto the presidency had a $47.2 million advantage over the Democrats if money raised by major 527 committees is counted, and a $117.3 million edge if 527 money is excluded. Either way, in a race as close as the 2004 presidential election, the inequality in campaign money between the Republicans and Democrats—characteristic of most U.S. elections—was an important factor in determining the outcome of that election.

In the 2008 presidential election, for the first time in recent history, the Democratic candidate, Barack Obama, had a clear financial advantage over his Republican opponent. Candidate Obama raised record amounts of money for the long nomination contest with Hillary Clinton as well as for the general election battle against John McCain. Whereas McCain opted for the $85 million in public funding for the general election, Obama, in a reversal of an earlier campaign promise, opted out of public funding and went on to raise over $336 million.[146] When combined with party money and 527 and 501(c) spending, the numbers show that Obama had about a $161 million advantage over McCain (see figure 2.7). The 2008 election was highly unusual in terms of Democratic fundraising. Eight years of the conservative and, from the Democrats' perspective, uncompromising Bush administration had made Democrats, liberals, and moderates incredibly unhappy and, as a consequence, willing to contribute vast amounts of money to end Republican control of the White House. The same conditions left Republican contributors dispirited and consequently less willing to open up their checkbooks to the extent that they normally do. Additionally, the Obama campaign refined the use of the Internet as a fundraising tool, and online drives yielded substantial amounts of money. Twenty-four percent of Obama's money ($181 million) came from contributors who gave $200 or less, mostly through the Internet.[147]

The financial advantage for Republicans is not limited to presidential contests. At the national level, Republican committees have long had a significant financial advantage over their Democratic counterparts. In 2008 the combined sum of Republican Party federal fundraising exceeded that of the Democratic Party by $29.6 million, and that was, by far, the narrowest fundraising gap between the two in recent decades. Between 2003 and 2004, the Republican Party committees raised $782.4 million federal dollars,[148] $103.6 million more than the Democratic Party committees' total of $678.8 million.[149]

In the same period, the Republican Governors' Association out-fund-raised the Democratic Governors' Association[150] by about $10 million ($34 million to $24 million).[151]

In terms of congressional campaign committees, the 2004 and 2008 elections were unique in that some of the congressional Democratic committees (the Democratic Senatorial Campaign Committee in 2004 and the Democratic Senatorial Campaign Committee and Democratic Congressional Campaign Committee in 2008) raised more money than their Republican counterparts. Those elections represented an extraordinary effort on the part of Democratic contributors motivated by serious discontent with Bush policies (the fact that in 2008 the Democrats held majorities in both

FIGURE 2.7. Money raised for 2008 presidential campaign, in millions.

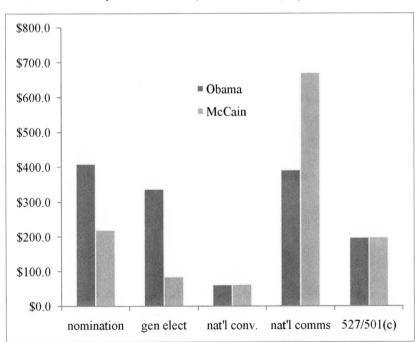

Source. Federal Election Commission and the Campaign Finance Institute.

chambers also helped). The success of some Democratic congressional committees in these years, like Obama's fundraising advantage, is likely to prove an exception to the general rule of Republican advantage. The Democratic committees' successes were driven by the unusual context of the preceding few years; as the normal pattern resumes, the Republican's historic advantage in fundraising will undoubtedly return because in general, Republican Party supporters—corporate interests and upper-income Americans—have more to contribute than Democratic Party supporters (see discussion of financial sources immediately following and in chapter 7). One can see a hint of the Republican advantage returning in the 2010 election, in which nonparty groups supporting Republican candidates outspent those favoring Democrats by more than a two to one margin, easily erasing the Democrats' advantage in party committee fundraising. Figure 2.8 shows the historical perspective on party fundraising, reporting the federal receipts for the two major parties' committees since 1978. The average election-cycle cash advantage of the Republican Party committees during this time frame was $137 million.

FIGURE 2.8. Money raised for federal campaigns by Democratic and Republican Party committees, 1977–2008.

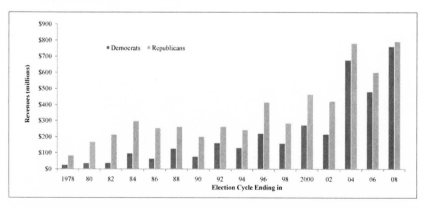

Source. Federal Election Commission, "Party Financial Activity Summarized For The 2006 Election Cycle," http://www.fec.gov/press/press2007/partyfinal2006/20070307party.shtml and Norman J. Ornstein, Thomas E. Mann, and Michael J. Malbin, *Vital Statistics on Congress. 1997-1998* (Washington, D.C.: Congressional Quarterly Press, 1998).

The problem with inequality in political resources is not limited to the imbalance between candidates and political parties but also extends to the question of who contributes money to candidates and parties. Though giving money to candidates or parties is not, as some claim, the equivalent of buying those politicians, those who give to election causes do have greater access to lawmakers (and access is critical in a pluralist system). Contributions have been found to affect the effort that lawmakers put into supporting or opposing legislation,[152] and contributions have been found to influence votes on legislation that is less visible to the public[153] or more closely tied to the interests of the contributors.[154] Moreover, analyses of contributions consistently find that most of the money given to candidates and political parties comes from the business or corporate sector and from wealthy Americans.[155] Figure 2.9 shows the sources of contributions to federal candidates and parties from 1990 to 2008 by the corporate sector, professionals, labor unions, ideological and single-interest groups, and others. The domination of the corporate sector is quite obvious: it provides more than $6 of every $10. This is true at the state level as well, as illustrated by the 2004 contributions to state party organizations in figure 2.10. Although 2004 and 2008 saw a jump in small contributions to campaigns, the bulk of money used by parties, candidates, and groups came in the form of large contributions and was provided by those on the upper end of the income scale. Figure 2.11 shows the makeup of 527 committees' 2004 money by the size of the contributions. Over half (56 percent) of the money raised by 527 committees came in contributions of $2 million or more. Surveys consistently find that most contributors to political campaigns are people who come from households with the highest income levels. Figure 2.12 shows contributors to candidates, parties, or groups by household income level in 2004. Those who made contributions were more likely to have higher household incomes, and 44.3 percent of those who contributed had household incomes of $80,000 or more.

All of these data make it abundantly clear that major inequities exist in the distribution of election money, a critical resource for campaigns.

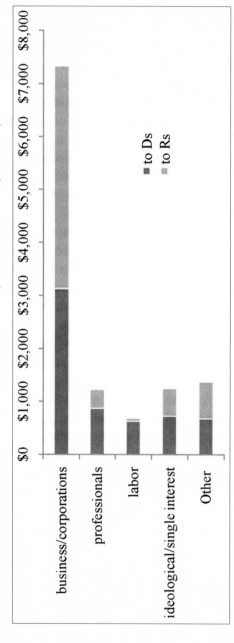

FIGURE 2.9. Source of contributions to federal candidates and parties, 1990–2008 (in millions).

Source. Calculated by author from data available from the Center for Responsive Politics, http://www.crp.org/bigpicture/sectors.asp?Cycle=All&Bkdn=DemRep&Sortby=Sector.

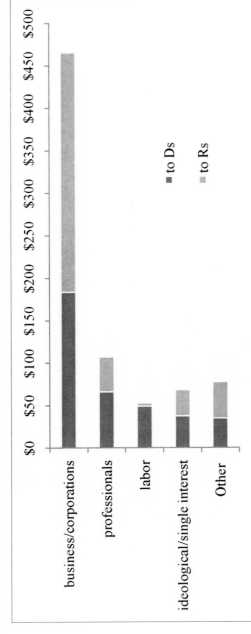

FIGURE 2.10. Sector contributions (in millions) to state party organizations, 2004.

Source. Calculated by author from data provided by the Center for Public Integrity, http://www.publicintegrity.org/partylines/.

FIGURE **2.11**. Distribution of contributions to 527 committees by size of contribution, 2004.

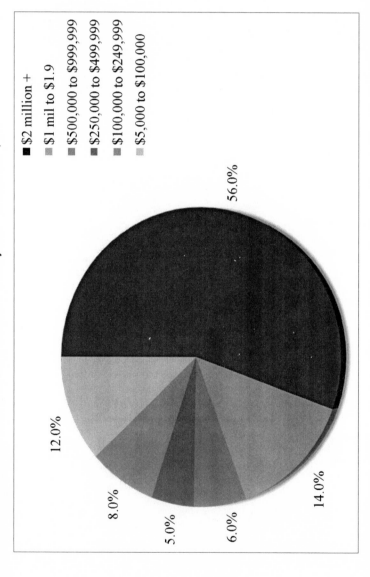

Legend:
- ■ $2 million +
- $1 mil to $1.9
- $500,000 to $999,999
- $250,000 to $499,999
- $100,000 to $249,999
- $5,000 to $100,000

56.0%

12.0%

8.0%

5.0%

6.0%

14.0%

Source. Steve Weissman and Ruth Hassan, "527 groups and BCRA," in *The Election after Reform: Money, Politics, and the Bipartisan Capaign Reform Act,* ed. Michael Malbin (Lanham, MD: Rowman & Littlefield Publishers, 2005).

FIGURE **2.12.** Contributors by household income, 2004.

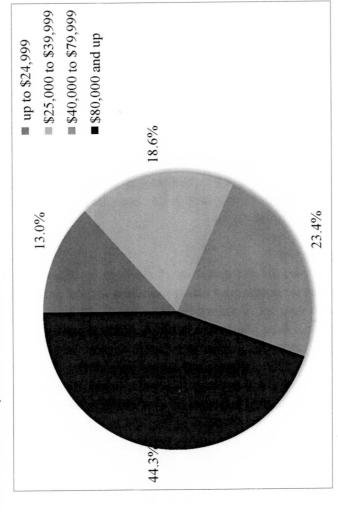

up to $24,999
$25,000 to $39,999
$40,000 to $79,999
$80,000 and up

18.6%

13.0%

23.4%

44.3%

Source. American National Election Studies, 2004.

As I document in chapter 7, these inequities are critically important; they play a crucial role in the "illness" of U.S. elections. Unequal resources contribute to uncompetitive campaigns, engender differences in political power, and help produce the symptoms of cynicism and low participation in elections.

THE FAILURE OF SUPPORTIVE INSTITUTIONS

Just as certain ailments in people involve the malfunctioning of organs that are critical for maintaining a healthy body, the sickness afflicting elections is characterized by the malfunctioning of a number of institutions that provide critical support for the electoral system. Three institutions necessary for a healthy electoral system—political parties that compete on ideological or programmatic grounds, an informative mass media, and an interest group system that is complementary, not dominating— are failing in harmful ways.

Political Parties
Political parties aid the operation of elections by offering alternative sets of plans for government action to address societal problems—plans rooted in a core set of values (in other words, an ideology)—and by implementing those plans once in office. Political parties in the United States function in this manner to a certain degree; the parties and their candidates do offer platforms and sets of policies that differ from those of the other party, and contrary to popular belief, those platforms and promises are very good indicators of what candidates will do if elected.[156] The parties do not run elections as they did in the nineteenth and early twentieth centuries, but they are by no means the marginal players they had become by the 1970s. Party organizations from national to state and local levels are very active in recruiting candidates, assisting candidates by providing services and financial help, and mobilizing voters.[157] Additionally, the Democrats and Republicans that have been elected to government positions are ideologically distinct from one another these

days as indicated by the sharp (and usually bitter) partisan divisions in national and state governments and in party-line voting in Congress and state legislatures.[158]

Where political parties are failing elections is in the way their candidates and spokespersons talk about politics. Instead of participating in debates about the merits of their respective approaches to governance in ways that could make the choice between the parties clearer to the public, the parties (and their candidates) use tactics that more often muddy the country's political discourse, ultimately obfuscating many of the genuine differences that exist between them. Even though such tactics have always been part of political discourse, it seems that they compose much more of it today in the modern media age, dominating the debate and distracting voters from the central meaning of their electoral choice.

Democrats and Republicans disagree over what government should be doing because they hold different sets of political values. Democrats believe governments should promote greater equality and greater personal freedoms. Republicans believe governments should be active in maintaining freedom in the marketplace and order in society, even at the cost of some personal freedom.[159] These differences offer an opportunity for the public to use elections as a means of determining what their governments will actually do. The debate between the two parties, however, is usually framed in ways that distract some voters and most nonvoters from the real differences between what each party believes should be done to address the problems facing the country. Instead of seeing the parties as offering alternatives in governance, the public sees the parties as bickering cliques engaged in personal conflict, name calling, battles over symbolic issues, and distortions that either mislead the public or caricature their opponents' policies and philosophies.

Instead of discussing their opponents' philosophies and policies, partisans too often attack their opponents on personal grounds. The 2008 election included, among other distractions, squabbles over Sarah Palin's daughter's out-of-wedlock child, whether Barack Obama supported

American troops, whether Obama was a Muslim, John McCain's age and lack of familiarity with the Internet, Hillary Clinton's erroneous account of a visit to Bosnia, comments made by the pastor of Obama's church, and John McCain's impulsiveness as reflected in his suspension of his campaign during the peak of the economic crisis. The 2004 presidential general election was sidetracked almost before it began by a misinformation campaign about John Kerry's record of military service in Vietnam and questions about George W. Bush's service in the National Guard. The main theme of the Bush campaign in 2004 was that John Kerry was a "flip-flopper" who would say anything to get elected. During the 2000 election George W. Bush was frequently portrayed as unintelligent, and Al Gore was condemned as a prevaricator. The revelation that Bush had been arrested for drunk driving twenty-five years earlier consumed more media attention in the year 2000 than all of the foreign policy issues combined.[160]

Republicans' personal attacks on members of the other party tend follow one of two approaches: Democrats are presented either as unprincipled and untrustworthy flip-floppers who will say whatever people want to hear or as liberals out of touch with the American public. In 2008 the liberal attack reached the point of calling Obama a socialist. The flip-flopper attack dominated the Republican's communications about Kerry in 2004, nicely symbolized in an ad which used footage of Kerry windsurfing to reinforce the portrayal of him constantly switching directions. Interestingly, they also tried to paint Kerry as one of the most liberal members of the Senate, an achievement that would have required a rather high level of consistency—and hence a claim at odds with the flip-flopper accusation. Republicans used the same flip-flopper attack against Al Gore in 2000 and Bill Clinton in 1992, and they used the liberal attack against Michael Dukakis in 1988 and Walter Mondale in 1984.

Democrats, when they get organized enough to keep up a focused attack (Republicans are usually more organized in their efforts and thus far better at presenting a common line of attack), also use the out-of-touch personal attack, suggesting that the Republicans are too right wing, too wealthy, or too much in the pocket of corporate interests. In 2008 Democrats tied McCain to the unpopular President Bush and portrayed him as too old and too rash in his judgments. One series of attacks in the Kerry campaign was that the Bush administration was too right wing and too friendly to corporate interests. In 2000, Bush's idiosyncratic use of the English language (including neologisms such as "misunderestimate") was used to question his competence, not with any consistency by the Gore campaign, but by the press.[161] Dole was painted as a cranky and out-of-touch ideologue by virtue of his association with Newt Gingrich and the conservatives in the U.S. Congress in 1996. George H. W. Bush was attacked by the Clinton campaign in 1992 as one whose family wealth made it impossible for him to relate to the economic suffering of Americans at the time.

Although these attacks (both the Republicans' and Democrats') have the potential to make points that are important in elections—whether leaders can be trusted, are out of touch with the public, or hold ideologically extreme positions—they stress the personal; that is, they are framed as personality-based, not value- or policy-based, accusations. As such, they caricature the candidates, make campaign discourse seem petty, distract voters from making reasoned judgments, and feed the cynicism of the public.

In addition to this overemphasis on the personal, much of what constitutes political debate is essentially name-calling—that is, the use of labels in lieu of argument. Disagreement with an administration's foreign or domestic security policy is labeled as *unpatriotic*. Domestic policies or their advocates are summarily dismissed as *right wing*, *liberal*, or *socialist*—negative labels whose meanings are rather obscure for most Americans. Indeed, for many Americans, these labels represent the people most commonly associated with them and not, in fact, actual policies or ideas—when people hear the word *liberal*, they see Ted Kennedy, Hillary Clinton, or Barack Obama; when they hear *conservative*, they think of Rush Limbaugh, George W. Bush, or Sarah Palin. Unpopular causes can also be enlisted in this tactic of smearing opponents as opposed to confronting their ideas. When the American Association of Retired Persons (AARP), for instance, publicly opposed President Bush's plan to allow workers to put some of their social security taxes into private investment accounts, a Republican group called USA Next responded by attacking the AARP for being antimilitary and pro–gay marriage. Attacking a political opponent for being associated with an unpopular cause or an unpopular personality as opposed to having a dispute over the facts, analysis, and reasons behind their political positions has unfortunately become the modus operandi of too many of those engaged in politics, turning political discourse in the United States into the equivalent of the name-calling and irrationality one may remember from the grade-school playground. Again, under such circumstances it is small wonder the public is so cynical about politics.

The political parties today also distract attention from their fundamental differences by focusing on symbolic issues, that is, issues that evoke emotional responses among the public but that are not related to change in governmental policy and that do not address important problems. Conflict over such issues keeps the more fundamental conflicts out of the public eye while making politics appear superficial. In a story that dominated the headlines in early 2005, Republicans went to great lengths to prevent the removal of feeding tubes from Terri Shiavo, a woman who was in a persistent vegetative state. The Republican-controlled Florida legislature, the state's Republican governor (Jeb Bush), the U.S. Congress, and President Bush passed legislation, subpoenaed Shiavo's husband, and took court action—all very publicly—to save a woman who had, as state and federal courts consistently ruled, made credible statements that she did not want to be kept alive in such a state.[162] President Bush even interrupted a vacation in order to fly to Washington and sign legislation (at one in the morning) that transferred the case to the federal courts. This enormous expenditure of energy by Republican government officials on behalf of one unfortunate woman in what the courts saw as a clear-cut case is the perfect example of symbolic politics. The Republicans' activity was not aimed at changing government policy (no broad changes took place); rather, the goal was to showcase their view on a sensitive and controversial issue in order to ensure continued support from a particular segment of the population (in this case, the country's conservative Christians). The episode may have clearly demonstrated to the public where the Republicans stood on this issue, which is a good thing, but it also made the Republicans appear superficial, willing to go to great lengths for political gain that had little effect on citizens' lives.

The Terri Shiavo case is probably the most extensive and concerted use of symbolic politics in recent years, but there are plenty of other examples from both parties (though the Republicans appear to use symbolic politics more frequently and perhaps more adeptly than Democrats). In 2010 the Democratic National Committee and President Obama mounted an unsubstantiated attack on the U.S. Chamber of Commerce, claiming that the chamber was trying to "steal our democracy" by using "secret foreign money" to influence elections.[163] This claim was promoted in part by a DNC ad showing a woman being robbed in a dark hallway by a shadowy male. Though it could be argued that this was a way to draw attention to the Democratic opposition to the *Citizens United* ruling, which allowed corporations to spend money to influence elections, this line of attack most likely simply fed public cynicism, not only because of its message and because the claims were unsubstantiated but also because it offered no plan of action to address the concerns it raised.

Also in 2010, the plan to build a mosque in Manhattan several blocks away from Ground Zero blew up into a political storm. Politicians jumped on the chance to show their patriotism and commitment to the war on terror by demanding that the project be halted, while denouncing anyone voicing tolerance of the project as being insensitive to the survivors of the attacks of September 11. Earlier in the year, poll results had shown that nearly one-fifth of the American public believed that President Obama is a Muslim, a perception that helped feed this storm. Outside of the effects on the project and those involved, however, nothing about this controversy moved beyond the symbolic; no broad policy was involved. Instead, one uproar inspired another—this time a media storm concerning the plan by a pastor of a small church in Florida to burn the Koran.

Other examples of symbolic politics from the 2008 campaign include much ado about Barack Obama's failure to wear a lapel pin and about Sarah Palin's wardrobe purchases. In the summer of 2006, Republicans in the House and Senate introduced proposed constitutional amendments to ban flag burning and same-sex marriage. Neither of these measures had much chance of winning the two-thirds vote needed in both chambers, but bringing these issues to the fore at that time had the potential to motivate the conservative base for the upcoming midterm elections. In order to boost the Gore-Lieberman image on moral issues in the 2000 presidential election, Joe Lieberman made a "series of high-profile attacks" on Hollywood and the entertainment industry for "corrupting American culture and its children."[164] "Such attacks are rarely part of a serious policy agenda, and both parties use the film industry as a whipping boy to impress that part of the electorate that responds to this sort of moral indignation."[165] This is the motivation that lies behind symbolic politics in general, and the more the parties and their candidates use such tactics, the more meaningless their true policy differences seem.

Finally, candidates from both parties engage in a significant amount of spin that distorts their records or those of their opponents and creates caricatures of the opposition politicians and their ideas. Ad messages in the run-up to the 2010 election were rife with distortions about the economic stimulus package and health-care reform passed by Democrats in 2009 and 2010, with claims that Republicans would destroy or privatize social security (scaring the elderly in this way seems to be one of the Democrats' favorite tactics), as well as with claims that Republicans believe that British Petroleum (BP) deserves an apology for harsh interrogation by members of Congress regarding the Deepwater Horizon oil spill. The 2008 election included false claims that McCain would keep combat troops in Iraq for one hundred years, that Obama would raise taxes for everyone, that McCain would cut social security, that Sarah

Palin opposed the "bridge to nowhere" earmark—and both sides distorted the facts relevant to energy policy.[166] FactCheck.org and Politifact.org provide abundant evidence of the level of distortion taking place in U.S. electoral politics.

Given the parties' tendency to fill rhetoric with distortions and to focus on the personal, the trivial, and the symbolic, and given modern media's ability to transmit such distortions to every segment of the electorate, it is a natural consequence that much of the public (1) knows little or nothing about what the two major parties and their candidates represent, (2) does not take party differences seriously, and (3) tends to be ambivalent about the importance of parties in general. Political parties and candidates are often perceived as unruly children on a playground, as a source of nastiness, lies, and partisan bickering— and the reason that very little is accomplished in Washington or Sacramento or Springfield. Parties are not usually thought of as broad coalitions that represent differing ideologies. In the "2000 Vanishing Voter survey, 75 percent of the respondents agreed with the statement 'political candidates are more concerned with fighting each other than with solving the nation's problems.'"[167] While 72 percent of the public said there was more mudslinging or negative campaigning in the 2004 election when compared to past elections, 42 percent said there was less discussion of issues.[168] As reported by the Pew Research/National Journal Congressional Connection Poll in 2010,

> one month before the midterm elections, Americans offer[ed] harsh judgments on Republicans and Democrats in Washington with roughly three-quarters saying partisans have been bickering more than usual.[169]

The petty, superficial, and distorted nature of partisan debate leaves voters without a sense of what the candidates and their parties represent. For this reason, many in the electorate fail to see the ideological differences between the political parties and thus cannot use the parties as tools to make a meaningful, policy-based choice during elections (the ability to make such distinctions is positively related to political participation).[170] A 2010 survey by the Pew Research Center found, for example, that among the 37 percent of those polled who reject the political parties, 53 percent said a major reason for rejecting both parties was that they did not trust either party, and 34 percent said a major reason was that they did not see much of a difference between the two parties.[171]

The news media are partially responsible for this perception of the political parties because of the media's penchant when covering politics for focusing on the politicians' personalities and on personal, emotionally charged conflicts and because of the media's relative inattention to policy differences between the parties.[172] Additionally, the game schema—according to which most people in the news business present elections—results in election coverage that portrays the main political parties as two opposing teams that will do whatever it takes to "win the game"—as opposed to a collection of individuals with shared values who wish government to reflect those values.[173] News coverage of party platforms is minimal and usually suggests that the platforms are meaningless (candidates have been known to dismiss party platforms as well, as Bob Dole did in 1996). The mass media thus add to the malfunctioning of the political parties by feeding the perception that political parties are largely irrelevant to healthy democracy.

News Media

The news media are, in their own right, a critical supportive institution for elections. Properly functioning news media provide additional and independent information for the electorate, helping members of the public understand their choices by evaluating the claims and records of partisans while presenting the bigger picture of what elections are all about. But the media fail to function in this manner in the United States. News coverage of elections—especially television news coverage, upon which most Americans rely for election news[174] is mostly devoid of the type of coverage that would help the public understand the fundamental meaning of their vote choice. Instead, news coverage is dominated by "horse-race" aspects of campaigns—polls, money, strategy—candidates' personal qualities, and a simplistic he said/she said coverage of political disputes, an approach that conveys candidates' arguments without any serious analysis of the veracity of those arguments.[175] According to one analysis, one out of two network news stories on the sharply divided ideological 2004 election was devoted to the horse race, although this was an improvement over the 2000 election, which saw about seven in ten stories focused on that aspect of the contest.[176] Local television news coverage of presidential elections—a primary source of news for many voters—spends even more of its time on horse-race coverage than does national news coverage.[177] And local coverage of the 2002 congressional and state elections, which was already minimal (fewer than half of the 10,000-plus local news shows randomly sampled between September 18 and November 4 had even one election story), devoted one-half of its election coverage to campaign strategy or to the horse race—and only one-quarter of its coverage to issues.[178]

Even when covering issues, the press usually fails to provide the type of analysis of candidates' positions that voters need in order to sort out claims and counterclaims or in order to contextualize these claims in terms of the values promoted by the contending sides.[179] Instead, the press simply reports what each side said, perhaps adding a superficial analysis of the accuracy of the statements. This was pointedly illustrated by Jon Stewart, comedian and host of *The Daily Show*, in the segment "CNN Leaves it There."[180] Additionally, when the media does attempt to fact-check partisans' claims, they usually do so by merely identifying flaws in both sides' arguments and making no attempt to assess which side is closer to the truth (the implicit message being, "They all lie"—fueling public cynicism instead of helping citizens parse the issue). And finally, the only context the media provide when covering issues is with regard to how candidates' issue positions might affect the candidates' chances of winning; again, the focus is on the game, the horse race. Regardless of the topic, television news—which three-fourths of the U.S. public cite as a main source for election news—by its very nature draws the audience's attention to the personal qualities of the candidates (those the audience can see) instead of to issues or ideology, which must be conceptualized from language rather than from an image.[181]

Interest Groups

Interest groups support the operation of elections by providing electoral resources—money and volunteers. They also help inform the public of electoral choices through newsletters to group members and public information campaigns, which often contain candidates' voting records and group endorsements. An interest group's natural alignment with the political party that best promotes the group's interests—labor and environmental groups with the Democrats, or the business sector with Republicans, for example—helps forge the broad-based coalitions that political parties represent.[182] The problem with interest groups today is not that they are not functioning well but rather that some of them are functioning so well that they have come to dominate elections and political parties. The political parties and candidates are very dependent on the resources—money and activists—provided by interest groups.[183] When political parties are extremely dependent on interest groups, the parties necessarily devote a great deal of energy to feeding the narrow interests of important groups. Thus even though the parties still offer different platforms rooted in their core values, the power of interest groups sometimes serves to distort party activity, focusing aspects of platforms and policy proposals on a narrow set of interests as opposed to broader societal concerns. This trend adds to the feeling among the public that the government is run for the benefit of a few big interests (in this case the interests lined up behind each of the major parties). Ultimately, there is some basis for that feeling, because interest group–driven politics of this sort exacerbates the inequalities among interests in the political arena.

OVERBURDENED CITIZENS

The last aspect of the sickness afflicting U.S. elections involves something most reformers seem to give little thought to: the demands placed on the voters. Many critics heap abuse on the uninformed, apathetic, nonvoting public (particularly the younger cohorts of the electorate) but give little consideration to the fact that the underlying issue may not be a simple matter of individual motivation or intelligence. Perhaps the poorly designed and malfunctioning system requires too much of the public. To return to the medical metaphor, when a person's physical environment demands too much of him or her and when the body's systems are under stress or are malfunctioning, energies become sapped, leaving the patient fatigued. The same is true of elections: the way the U.S. runs elections has left the body, the citizens, electorally fatigued—the public is worn out by the unreasonable demands placed on it by the electoral system. Elections require that voters pay attention, gather enough information to make an informed choice, register to vote, and vote. At first glance this perhaps seems simple, but one must consider the number of decisions voters are asked to make and with what frequency (and with very little help or guidance from the media). For example, the conscientious citizen of Burlington, Vermont, is asked to vote at least three times during each presidential election year: in the presidential primary and local elections in March, in the primaries for state officials in September, and in the general election in November. He or she is also asked to vote at least three times in midterm election years: in local elections in March, in the primary election for congressional, statewide, and legislative offices, and in the general election for those same offices. And he or she would be called to the polls at least once in odd-numbered years for local elections. In each of these election years, any number of addition issues (e.g., school budgets) might require a second or third vote.

Furthermore, each time voters go to the polls in the United States, they are asked to make what often seems like an overwhelming number of decisions. A typical ballot in a presidential election year will include multiple candidates for multiple offices and usually a complex set of ballot measure questions. The 2004 sample ballot for Kitsap County, Washington (figure 2.13), is a typical example of the task that U.S. voters are handed when they enter the polling place. The voters in Kitsap County in November 2004 were asked to vote on a large number of state and local issues. They were then asked to vote for president, U.S. senator, U.S. representative, governor, lieutenant governor, secretary of state, state treasurer, state auditor, attorney general, commissioner of public lands, superintendent of public instruction, insurance commissioner, state senator, two state representatives, county commissioner, three state supreme court justices, a public utility district commissioner, a charter amendment, and a limit on property tax increases. I have reproduced this list to make the following point: considering the time that would be required to gather enough information to make an informed choice among the alternatives for each of these contests and issues, as well as the time required to register and to actually vote, it is plain to see that the United States asks a great deal—too much—of its electorate. For this reason, large percentages of the public, especially those without college degrees, believe that politics is too complicated for them to understand or that they do not have a good understanding of important political issues (see figure 2.14).

Most other democracies (almost all of which have higher levels of voter turnout) require less of their citizens, asking them to go to the polls less often and demanding fewer decisions of them. Other democracies do not use primary elections to select party nominees (the fact that the United States does effectively doubles the number of elections that it holds). In parliamentary systems, voters simply determine control of the government by electing members of the parliament, often through simply voting for a political party (executives are usually not elected separately as they are in the United States). And most countries do not ask voters to decide on specific policies as initiatives and referenda do in the American states. By one count, the U.S. asked voters to go to the polls

FIGURE 2.13. Sample ballot, Kitsap County, WA, 2004.

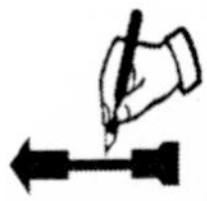

FIGURE 2.13. (Continued)

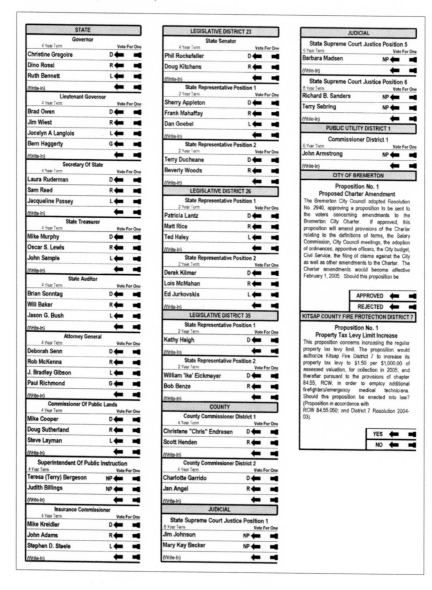

more frequently than every other democracy in the world but one; and according to empirical analyses, the frequency of elections has a strong negative impact on voter turnout.[184]

FIGURE **2.14.** Understanding of politics by education level.

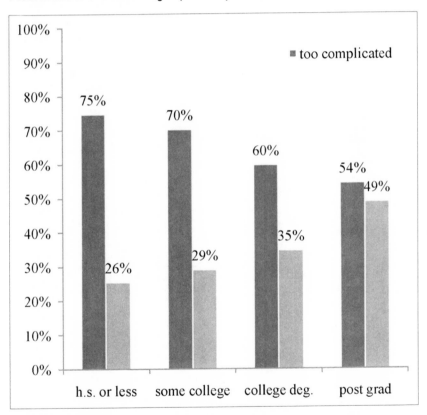

Source. ANES 2008.
Question 1: "Sometimes politics and government seem so complicated that a person like me can't really understand what's going on." Bars represent percent agreeing by education level.
Question 2: "How well do you understand the important political issues facing our country?" Bars represent percent responding extremely or very well by education level.

CONCLUSION

The diagnosis, then, is that U.S. elections are suffering from an illness characterized by an absence of competitive elections, by lack of political equality, by failing supportive institutions, and by a fatigued electorate. These are the ailments that produce the symptoms, more visible than their causes, of low voter turnout, political cynicism, and a poorly informed public. The next chapter examines the environmental and systemic conditions that have either caused or exacerbated these problems.

CHAPTER 3

THE CAUSES

People do not become ill simply because they "caught a cold"; the causes of illness are usually more complex. People fall ill because they contract a disease or a virus, certainly, but personal habits, genetics, and environment also play a critical role in wellness. If human beings do not maintain their bodies with proper nutrition, sleep, and exercise, they become much more susceptible to disease and require more time to recover from sickness. If a person's environment causes a great deal of stress, for example, or causes breathing difficulties, he or she becomes more likely to fall ill. The same is true of elections. The "disease" that is making U.S. elections ill must be considered separately from the unhealthy behaviors and the environment, factors that increase elections' susceptibility to dysfunction and make the system less likely to recover quickly. In this chapter, I identify several leading contributors to the poor health of U.S. elections: (1) the current legal environment surrounding elections, particularly campaign-finance law, redistricting, and election administration; (2) the structure of U.S. elections; (3) the nature of the mass media in the United States; and (4) the behavior and choices of the candidates and the public. (For a visual presentation of these aspects of the diagnosis, refer once again to figure 2.1.)

ELECTION LAW AND ADMINISTRATION

Healthy elections are open, fair, and competitive. Precisely how open, fair, and competitive elections are depends in large part on the laws governing election practices and administration. In terms of openness, the legal environment in the United States is probably currently at its best, though it is by no means perfect. Attempts to disenfranchise blacks—such as the poll tax, literacy tests, and the so-called white primary—have been abolished. Registration laws have been changed to facilitate voter registration: voters may register closer to Election Day and, in six states, on Election Day; and the motor-voter law allows citizens to register when they renew their driver's licenses or visit social service agencies. Absentee ballots and early voting have been made easier in many states; twenty-five states do not require an excuse for casting an absentee ballot, and twenty states allow early voting. Voting in primary elections may be limited to those who are registered or declare a party affiliation, but that is in the interest of allowing the parties to choose their candidates (a situation which leads to a more meaningful and differentiated choice in the general election, in which everyone can vote). Instances of unlawful and discriminatory limits on access to polling places still take place, as in 2000 with Florida's bungled purge of supposed ex-convicts that removed many legitimate (and mostly African American) voters from the roll. Nonetheless, although there continues to be room for improvement, the election laws that govern voting in the United States ensure a reasonable amount of openness in the electoral system.

Election laws concerning access to the ballot are a slightly different matter, but that is because governments must balance the interests of candidates, who want to get on the ballot, against the interests of voters, who would encounter the added complexity that would result from allowing anyone, regardless of initial support, to put his or her name on the ballot. States vary with regard to both the number of signatures an independent or minor-party candidate needs to get on the ballot and the deadlines by which those signatures must be submitted. The result is that elections in the United States are not as open as some would want them to be in terms of ballot access. But as the 2003 recall election in California demonstrated—there were 135 candidates for governor on the ballot—increasing access to the ballot would present already overburdened voters with ballots even more confusing than they currently are. Thus, U.S. election laws provide for open elections to a reasonable extent, given other considerations. These laws fail, however, to guarantee fair and competitive elections; instead, campaign finance laws, redistricting laws, and election administration laws allow for unhealthy practices that result in elections which lack equality and competition (for full discussion, see chapter 2).

Campaign Finance Law

Campaign finance laws contribute to the poor health of U.S. elections by allowing unequal distribution of a key electoral resource, a situation that ultimately contributes to the unequal competition in many electoral contests.[185] And the 2010 *Citizens United* Supreme Court ruling will likely exacerbate the situation.[186] The main justification for regulating the financing of campaigns is to prevent corruption. In one sense, the goal can be understood as preventing the unequal distribution of wealth in the economic sector from translating into inequalities of power in the political sector. Political equality—the notion that each person's vote (or influence) bears the same weight as anyone else's—is an important principle of democratic elections. Without it, a government cannot truly be representative of the electorate. Reporting requirements, public funding, and limits on contributions and expenditures are among the measures meant to ensure a certain amount of equality in the electoral process and prevent its corruption—but these laws have not, for the most part, been constructed or enforced so as to make them effective.[187] The Supreme Court has contributed to the problem by discarding certain campaign finance laws whose purpose is to enhance equity and competitiveness, giving preference to the freedom to spend and contribute over these other democratic values.

Campaign finance practices are regulated by a patchwork of federal, state, and local laws that have been limited in their scope by the U.S. Supreme Court ruling equating spending with speech in *Buckley v. Valeo* (424 U.S. 1, 1976).[188] Federal election law regulates the financing of federal campaigns, presidential and congressional. It bans direct corporate and labor union contributions, and it limits contributions from individuals and political action committees (PACs) to candidates and the political parties. Federal law also provides a system of public funding for the presidential nomination contest and for the general election contest. Candidates who accept public funding for their presidential campaigns must agree to spending limits. (In 2004 and 2008 the eventual nominees all decided to forgo public funding during the nomination phase, and only Barack Obama declined public funding for the general election.) State and local governments regulate state and local election finance, and those regulations vary widely. Some states have virtually no limits on campaign fundraising (Illinois and Alabama); others have bans on corporate contributions (Connecticut and Iowa), strict limits on the amounts that can be contributed (Missouri), or public-funding programs with matching spending limits (Minnesota, Arizona, and Maine). Local governments, including those in New York and Los Angeles, often have different sets of regulations for city elections.

The courts, following the precedent of the *Buckley* case, have struck down as unconstitutional federal, state, and local laws that limit out-of-state contributions, limit corporate campaign spending, regulate financing of ballot measure campaigns, mitigate the impact of independent spending, set contribution limits too low, or set limits on campaign spending.[189] Candidates and their consultants, political parties, and interest groups over the years have found ways to exploit the loopholes and weaknesses in the patchwork of laws, ensuring that the disparities in campaign finance discussed earlier persist. The soft money contributed to the 2004 party conventions and the use of 527 committees to skirt the changes made by the Bipartisan Campaign Reform Act of 2002 (BCRA, also called the McCain-Feingold Act) are good examples of how quickly campaign finance behavior adapts to exploit the holes in this ad hoc collection of laws.[190]

Redistricting

The drawing of electoral district boundaries has always been a source of unequal competition in U.S. elections; with the advent of modern technology it has become even more so.[191] District boundaries are redrawn every ten years (after each census) in order to make sure that district populations meet the one person, one vote criterion laid out by the Supreme Court in *Baker v. Carr* (369 U.S. 186, 1962).[192] In most states, the legislature and governor create the election districts for U.S. House elections as well as for their own state house, senate, and (in some states) judicial elections. In the process, partisans gerrymander districts, drawing boundaries in such a way as to ensure that as many districts as possible will include a majority of their partisans, or, under bipartisan redistricting agreements, they draw districts so as to make incumbent legislators' districts safer for the incumbents (gerrymandering has also been done in some places to dilute the influence of minorities). Those involved know that in order to improve their party's chances of controlling Congress or the state legislature, or in order to ensure their reelection and that of other incumbents, they merely need to analyze previous election results by precinct, fill as many electoral districts with a sufficient number of partisans to ensure victory, and pack voters of the opposing party into a smaller number of districts. Today computerized census maps and corresponding software provide partisans in the redistricting process with precision tools that remove any guesswork from this process. Drawing the electoral maps in this manner can create legislative districts with populations predisposed to vote for one party.

The extent to which such redistricting contributes to the lack of competitive elections in the United States is a matter of debate among political scientists and reformers, with recent research suggesting other more important reasons for the decline in competitive districts, including population movement, the effects of the Voting Rights Act of 1965 and its 1990 amendments, immigration, and ideological realignment.[193] Although such recent research findings demote redistricting as the main determinant of the decline in competitiveness, the authors of such work do not conclude that redistricting has had no effect on competition.

Furthermore, the fact that redistricting is not the only factor reducing competitiveness does not preclude the possibility that the process might be used in the future to increase the number of competitive districts.

In the redistricting that took place following the 2000 census, 19 of the 25 marginal Republican U.S. House seats and 16 of the 19 marginal Democratic seats were made safer for their parties' candidates by adding more Republican or Democratic voters. The result for the 2004 election was the lowest number of competitive seats—just 37 out of 435—in decades.[194] This paucity of competitive U.S. House seats reflects an overall trend that has taken place in competition in legislative contests. Between 1976 and 2004, the percentage of marginal districts in the U.S. House fell from 43 percent to 27 percent.[195] And that decrease in competition was mirrored at the state level, where the proportion of competitive and contested state legislative districts has also declined.[196] As noted earlier, this trend is not a result of redistricting alone; nonetheless, the way electoral districts are drawn is a contributing factor that can exacerbate the problem (or provide a potential fix). With fewer competitive seats because so many are stacked in favor of one party or the other, control of the U.S. House and of state legislatures is less sensitive to changes in the electorate's party preferences, weakening the effect of elections. Because such significant portions of the public have been placed in the role of legitimizing presumptive favorites in uncompetitive districts, much of the public sees no reason to go to the polls on Election Day.

Some reformers and other political observers argue that the effects of the redistricting process go beyond elections themselves; the way electoral maps are drawn may also contribute to ideological polarization in the U.S. House and in state legislative bodies. The argument is that because the median voter of districts populated with voters mostly from one party is likely to be ideologically further to the left or right than the median voter in more heterogeneous districts, these one-party districts tend to elect rigid ideologues to the U.S. House and to the state legislatures. These candidates have no interest in compromise and tend to add to the nastiness of political battles—thus feeding public cynicism about politics and government. Recent research, however, has shown that only a portion (20 percent) of the increase in polarization is attributable to redistricting; more important is the overall increase in the polarization of the voting public, polarization that makes it less likely that members of Congress will represent districts comprised of a majority of voters from the other party.[197] Nevertheless, though redistricting is not the only or even the most important cause of the phenomenon, past redistricting practices have contributed to the polarization evident in legislative bodies across the country.

Election Administration
The actual act of voting (along with voter registration) is administered by state and local governments. The ways these governments administer elections can affect the openness and fairness of elections as well the legitimacy of the outcomes. This point was demonstrated most dramatically in the 2000 election. Problems with voting machinery, ballot design, and registration rolls resulted in hundreds of thousands of uncounted votes and made an accurate count of the presidential vote in Florida impossible. But, as has become clear in subsequent elections and as a result of the work of scholars, such problems are not limited to Florida or the 2000 election. It appears that many voters make mistakes in casting their ballots (the rates of such errors vary based on ballot design and the nature of the voting machinery used), and these mistakes result in the failure to record the voter's preferences properly or even at all. The performance of voting machines is uneven and malfunctions can result in counting errors and long delays that discourage voters. The use of direct recording electronic (DRE) voting machines and the demonstrated ability of hackers to infiltrate the programming have raised questions about the security of such machinery and the accuracy of the vote totals it produces. In addition, the unequal allocation of polling places and election resources can also cause long lines that discourage voters, and a combination of poor training, poor pay, and understaffing increases the likelihood that election workers at the polling places may themselves make mistakes. In some places around the country, new

voters are required to show a government-issued ID; in other places voters are removed from the voter rolls because of slight inconsistencies between the names on their voter registration forms and the information in government databases.

What is magnitude of this problem with U.S. elections? As one scholar summarized, what we know from the research and data is that

> between one and a half and three million votes were lost solely because of problems with the registration process during the 2000 election, with several million more lost to other causes. According to the 2000 U.S. census, about one million registered voters said that they did not vote because polling lines were too long or polling hours were too short. In 2004, we were missing one-quarter of the two million poll workers needed to administer the election. In 2006, 43 percent of local officials surveyed about the prior presidential election reported that an electronic voting system malfunctioned, with 11 percent reporting a breakdown that could not be fixed. Twenty-one percent of those officials reported that poll workers did not understand their jobs, and 10 percent had problems with poll workers failing to show up for work. Twelve percent admitted that there were "excessively long lines" on Election Day.[198]

In short, the uneven administration of elections is a serious problem that can have major consequences for the legitimacy of elections, especially when the contests are close.

The voting problems that arise from the administration of elections do not result solely from local control (indeed, as political scientist Alec Ewald documented, there are advantages to the local dimension of the way we vote).[199] But, as argued by another political scientist, Heather Gerken, localism interacts with partisanship to make the administration of elections uneven, engendering inequality in the treatment of voters and presenting an ongoing potential for crises in the legitimacy of election outcomes.[200] Election administration, after all, is not only controlled at the state and local levels but is also controlled by state and local *partisan* officials. This opens the door to partisans who would use their authority in order to advantage their fellow partisans (it also makes election administration resistant to change). The combination of localism and partisanship in the administration of elections, according to Gerken, results in woefully inadequate resources for many election jurisdictions and results in poll workers who "lack the professional training and experience enjoyed by election administrators in other mature democracies."[201]

ELECTORAL STRUCTURE

Because of the federal nature of the U.S. system and because the United States has a political culture that has, over time, demanded more choices and more elections, the country is saddled with an electoral structure that is unnecessarily complex. This complexity is a leading cause of both political inequality and voter fatigue. The Electoral College, the rules governing presidential nomination contests, and the configuration of the U.S. Senate all create serious deviations from political equality, as argued in chapter 2. As also shown in that chapter, voters' time and energy are taxed by a multitude of decisions within multiple layers of elections. In a sense, the United States is suffering from too much democracy, because the voters are overburdened by this tendency to put everything and anything on the ballot. The national government limits choice to president and vice president, U.S. Senate, and U.S. House. The state governments, however, go well beyond having voters chose the chief executive and the legislature, presenting the electorate with everything from the selection of numerous state officers and judges to constitutional, policy, budget, and taxation decisions. Local government choices for voters run the gamut from mayor and councillor to county coroner, school board members, assistant judges, and justices of the peace, as well as charter changes, budget and taxing decisions, and policy questions. These elections are held at various times, requiring voters in many places to return to the polls several times each year.

Asking the voters to vote so often and to make so many choices exhausts the electorate; a tired electorate, in turn, affects the system as a whole. In order to reach weary voters, candidates constantly vie for attention from the electorate, oversimplify issues, and spend more and more money so as to cut through the cacophony of election communications and get voters to the polls. All of this activity eventually alienates most voters, who consequently distance themselves from the entire process. Additionally, the frequency of elections and the multitude of choices make it difficult for voters to see the connection between their votes and government action. Having so many elections and choices makes any one election less decisive, thus reducing the importance of voting and ultimately the incentive to do so. All of this is supported by research on the effects of electoral institutions; studies have shown that the manner in which elections are structured is strongly related to the level of political participation—more elections and more choices result in less participation in each election.[202]

ENTERTAINMENT-DRIVEN, PROFIT-DRIVEN MEDIA

The main reason the American news media fail as a useful linkage institution is that the media in the United States are, for the most part, businesses; the main exceptions are the semipublic National Public Radio (NPR) and the Public Broadcasting System (PBS). Consequently, coverage of government and politics is largely driven by business incentives, the dominant one of which is profit. Mass media programming, including news programs, makes its profit mainly from advertisers; the amount of money a media organization may charge advertisers depends on the size and nature of the media organization's audience. To garner a large, profit-generating audience, the news media must keep the public's attention and keep the costs of producing the news down. Holding the public's attention these days means entertaining them with personal conflict, controversy, scandal, violence, disaster, celebrities, and personal stories. Stories must be accompanied by abundant dramatic pictures or video and avoid the time-consuming complexities of context, background, or analysis. In other words, viewers are presented with simple stories about people they know fighting or doing something outrageous—accompanied by good sound and video. This is what captivates an audience and holds its attention, not coverage of government as it functions day to day affecting people's lives, not a presentation of the big-picture ideological and issue differences between the political parties and among the candidates, not a serious evaluation of the value of government programs or the record of the incumbents. Such aspects of government and politics, aspects that would present voters with critical information, can be found in certain newspapers and on some websites, but on the front pages of the most popular newspapers and on television—the source the U.S. public most relies upon for news—they are shoved aside or buried under the more audience-pleasing stories.[203]

The fact that the mass media industry is a business also means that its outlets are interested in keeping the costs of production down. For a media organization this means fewer journalists, which limits the capacity of media organizations. According to analysis by the Project for Excellence in Journalism, "nearly one out of every five journalists working for newspapers in 2001 was gone by 2008, and 2009 may be the worst year yet."[204] The number of journalists employed by television news has also dropped in past several decades, with local news cutting 7 percent of their staff in 2008.[205] These losses have not been balanced, moreover, by hiring in other media outlets. With fewer journalists covering the same amount of material, news coverage becomes more superficial, centered mostly around a few big stories, more reliant on information fed to the press and less likely to be based on intensive investigative reporting. The pressure to build and maintain an audience while keeping costs down has led two prominent journalists to call the period from the 1990s to the present the "era of profit maximization" for the press.[206] Journalists, most of whom take seriously their role of informing the public, express concern about these pressures. In a 2004 survey of journalists, for example, large majorities said they felt that the bottom-line business pressures were hurting coverage, reducing the quality of the news, and leading to a failure to cover complex issues.[207]

Thus, the coverage of government and politics in general leaves the public with little knowledge of what the government has been doing and how its decisions have been affecting their lives. Coverage of elections in particular is no different: it does little to inform the public in any amount of detail. Bottom-line business pressures lead the mass media to cover campaigns as they cover sports teams or horse races and to focus predominantly on the personalities of the presidential candidates almost to the exclusion of other contests. The news media present elections in this way because doing so makes the story more entertaining (most people enjoy a good race or game), avoids accusations of bias that would accompany a serious evaluation of candidates' positions or records, and is easy because it requires fewer journalists. The coverage also focuses on personalities because that, too, is more interesting than issues of governance and because it is the most salient aspect of any coverage in the dominant medium, television. Additionally, the bottom-line constraints that lead to this sort of coverage distract journalists from forcing political parties and their politicians to stay on subject, from focusing on the parties' overall agendas and the real differences between them.[208] In the end, this sort of election coverage leaves members of the audience *feeling* as though they are informed; people feel that they know the candidates personally (the politicians are in their living rooms every night) when, in fact, they know little.[209]

Thus, that the media today are basically in the entertainment business leads news shows and news publications to supply the public with a steady diet of political junk food that does little to provide any real sustenance.

POLITICS MADE PERSONAL:
BEHAVIOR OF CANDIDATES AND PARTIES

Of course, the media are not solely responsible for the poor state of political discourse in the United States; political parties and their candidates share some of the blame. While tactics of personalizing political conflict, name-calling, distortions, using symbolic issues and distorted caricatures of opponents play to the media's desire for entertaining politics, parties and politicians are certainly under no obligation to conduct their public debate in this manner. Contrary to the cynical perception among the public that politicians are in politics for their own personal gain, most of those who run for office are drawn by a call to public service—a desire to improve the lives of their fellow citizens and to change government policy on a set of issues. The problem is that when one side engages in the easy discourse of personal attack and symbolic politics, the other side can either answer in kind or suffer poor media coverage and weak performance at the polls. A mutual agreement among candidates to stick to the important issues of governance, however, could go a long way toward improving the political discourse and consequently the levels of knowledge and trust among the public. But that is unlikely to happen on the initiative of politicians alone.

HABITS OF THE ELECTORATE

JON STEWART: Your speech was really impressive at the convention.... When you said we should view the other party as our opponents not our enemy, was your mike on?

JOHN McCAIN: ... The message came through loud and clear [*laughter*].

STEWART: ... Have you ever seen anything like that? [*Referring to the blistering attack on John Kerry from the podium of the Republican National Convention the night before.*] ... So what happens now? Does everybody start hacking each other to pieces? Is there an inevitability there?

McCAIN: I think that ... there are operatives in both parties and those operatives sort of emerge every four years and they say, "Look, here's what works in the polls, here's what will appeal to people." They test it out and check it out, and sometimes, unfortunately, that's negative campaigning ... and the American people have got to demand that we change the debate [*applause*].

STEWART: But here's the thing ... we would [demand they change the debate], but *Who Wants to Marry My Dad* is on.[210]

As this exchange suggests, the American public is partially responsible for the problems that leave them politically ignorant, cynical, and on the political sidelines. Just as a person who has bad eating habits is more susceptible to diseases, the bad habits of the American public make the electoral system less immune to all of the problems already discussed. The two habits that weaken the system most are (1) the public's desire to be endlessly entertained and (2) certain ways of thinking about elections and political parties.

"Here We Are Now, Entertain Us"[211]

The demand for entertainment stems from the fact that Americans watch television (and Internet videos) and rely on it as their primary source of news about government and politics. Viewing television takes up about 40 percent of the average American's free time, or about 3 hours per day.[212] "During *every* period of the day at least one-quarter of all adults report some TV viewing. After work the fraction rises to more than half, peaking at 86 percent during the aptly named 'prime time' hours."[213] As illustrated in figure 3.1, America's appetite for entertainment leads to a preference for television over newspapers as a news source. In 2008, some 70 percent of the public said they got most of their news about national and international issues from television, and the Internet became the second-most cited source, passing newspapers for the first time. The same pattern holds true for the public's main source of news about presidential elections (see figure 3.2), for which nearly three-fourths of the public cite television as the main news source. And given the popularity of Internet sites like YouTube, the percentage of the public that relies on television's form of information delivery—video—is probably even higher.

The television shows that the public watches for news tend to be the ones that are the most amusing; the *NewsHour* on PBS, which is the most substantive television news program, is also the least-watched news program.[214] Evidence that the popular news shows are geared toward entertainment can be found in their very design, which includes dramatic music, audience-tested anchors and sets, and a flood of

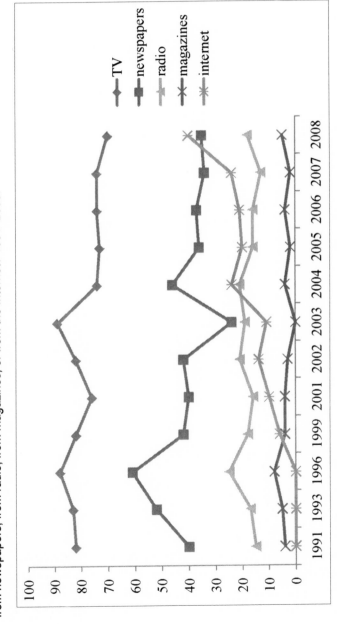

Figure 3.1. How have you been getting most of your news about national and international issues? From television, from newspapers, from radio, from magazines, or from the Internet? 1991–2008.

Source. The Pew Research Center for the People & the Press, accessed August 27, 2009, http://peoplepress.org/reports/ questionnaires/479.pdf.

FIGURE 3.2. Public's main source of news for presidential elections, 2000, 2004, and 2008.

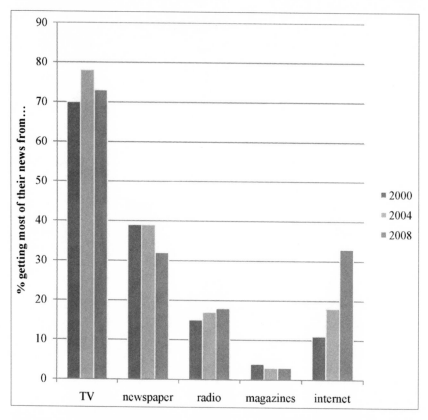

Source. The Pew Center for People and the Press, accessed August 27, 2009, http://peoplepress.org/reports/questionnaires/463.pdf.

Question: How did you get most of your news about the presidential election campaign? From television, from newspapers, from radio, from magazines, or from the Internet?

ever-changing video images meant to keep the audience from becoming bored.[215] Additionally, about the same percentage of eighteen- to twenty-nine-year olds as cited newspapers as a main source of news about the 2004 presidential election (one in five) cited comedy shows as a main source of news. This, however, is not much different than older age groups' habit of relying on television news, because "fake" news shows like *The Daily Show* appear to contain about as much actual news content as local, national, or cable television news.[216] Newspaper readership has declined over the past several decades, especially among the younger part of the population,[217] and when the public does choose newspapers, they opt for colorful and sensational newspapers over "serious" ones—as attested by the success of the widely circulating, colorful, and image-packed *USA Today*.

Not only does the American public's predilection for entertainment determine what people watch, but it also shapes what is produced and made available by the mass media. Audience demands largely determine what is available through the profit-driven media (audience demands also shape the programming of contributor-supported semipublic media in the United States—that is, PBS and NPR). By their very choices in media consumption, the public makes clear that they want to be amused, so media outlets strive to produce progressively more entertainment and less of the hard news citizens need to be an active part of their democracy. The Lewinsky scandal during Bill Clinton's second term in office offers an excellent example. Large majorities of the public told pollsters that the media were spending too much time on the Lewinsky story. Eighty percent of the public during the height of the uproar said that they thought "there ha[d] been too much discussion about [the Lewinsky scandal] by commentators and analysts on television and radio." Two-thirds of the public thought that "press coverage of the personal and ethical behavior of political leaders [was] excessive."[218] These opinions, however, were not reflected by the public consumption of the news on the subject: in fact, members of the public continued to display a voracious appetite for every new development and rumor that the media could feed them.[219] This drive for entertainment and reliance on television ultimately lead many Americans (especially the younger age-groups) to lose trust in the news media and tune politics out—with the end result that they know little about it, feel cynical about it, and ultimately decide not to participate.[220]

"Vote the Person, Not the Party" and Other Self-Defeating Approaches to Elections

The public has a number of bad habits with respect to thinking about parties and elections. Most people view politics in a way that deprives them of the simple means of controlling government actions through elections. These habits include (1) thinking that the individual candidate is more important than the party; (2) believing that there are no important differences between the two major parties; (3) failing to understand that voting is not simply individual self-expression but a form of mass action; and (4) failing to recognize their—the citizens'—own inconsistencies in what they demand from politics and government.

The one piece of information other than a candidate's name that appears on the ballot in most races in the United States is that candidate's party affiliation. This information, if used properly, could greatly simplify the decision-making process for voters; but instead of using it, a significant portion of the electorate eschews party affiliation, perhaps taking to heart the lesson of elementary school civics classes that one should vote for the person, not the party. But doing so requires learning enough information about each of the candidates in all of the races in order to make informed decisions. Consequently, the task of voting seems overwhelming, and if they are not up to it, voters cast their ballots on the basis of name recognition or some other factor unrelated to the policies that the candidates advocate. Party labels are, in fact, excellent clues as to the types of policies a candidate will pursue. This is especially true at the end of the twentieth and the beginning of the twenty-first century, when the elected officials of both parties are as ideologically polarized as the U.S. House (where there was "virtually no ideological common ground shared by the two parties" during the 106th Congress in 1999–2000).[221] Again, as documented in chapter 2, one of the reasons the public shuns party labels is that a sizeable segment of the population is unaware of the differences between the parties—and because television, upon which so many rely for their news, presents elections as popularity contests. Some citizens, moreover, are cynical about both parties and see them as part of the establishment; therefore they turn to independents or to other parties whose candidates more often than not feed this sort of cynicism and effectively disenfranchise voters.

There is a powerful current of individualism in the culture of the United States. That, along with the dominance of personality in the age of television, means that voters have a view of elections that is ultimately discouraging. Americans see voting as an individual act of political expression, something akin to the individual act of purchasing a good. Viewed in this way, voting makes little rational sense. The odds that any one person will affect the outcome of an election in which there are millions of other voters is extremely small. Additionally, it is highly unlikely that any of the major candidates will share all of your views on the issues, rendering the marking of a ballot wholly inadequate as a means of expressing the full range of one's political views.

The final bad habit of the American public is failing to see the contradictions in what they demand of elections and politicians. We want more choices of candidates and parties *and* we also want the winner to be supported by the majority. We value individualism *and* collective action. We want to be able to make more political decisions, but we are unwilling to invest the time or use the tools necessary to make informed decisions. We value political freedom and political equality, which clash when that freedom allows unequally distributed wealth to translate into political advantages.

Although these views and habits among members of the public are shaped in part by the mass media and the behavior of politicians and party organizations, they are also shaped by Americans' political socialization and are thus a result, in part, of the choices made by each successive generation of citizens.

CONCLUSION

The diagnosis is now complete (for a graphic summary refer to figure 2.1). Low voter turnout and a poorly informed and cynical public have been shown to be symptoms characteristic of an illness of political inequality, an overwhelmed electorate, and the failure of supporting institutions.

The causes of the illness reside in large part in (1) the laws that govern U.S. elections, (2) the structure of U.S. elections, (3) the behavior of politicians and the public, and (4) the profit-focused nature of the privately owned news media. Though many of these problems have been considered in discussions of election reform (e.g., redistricting and campaign finance laws), some (e.g., the notion of an overwhelmed electorate and the content of political discourse) have received scant attention. Beyond identifying individual problems, however, my purpose here has been to bring the real research-backed problems together into a coherent, evidence-based diagnosis that sheds light on the interconnectedness of all of the problems and provides a more thorough and complete view of the problems with U.S. elections—for the purpose of determining what type of "medical treatment" U.S. elections really need.

From the diagnosis it is easy to see that prescriptions meant to address the causes of the illness—such as those that deal with electoral law and administration, the structure of elections, the nature of the media, the behavior of politicians, or the habits of the electorate—are likely to be the most successful in making U.S. elections healthier. It is also clear from the diagnosis that prescriptions designed to deal merely with the symptoms—such as those that directly address low voter turnout or public cynicism—are bound to fail. And finally, the diagnosis makes it plain that prescriptions made without an awareness of the full nature of the illness—term limits, nonpartisan elections, national voter initiatives, and campaign-finance laws that require only public disclosure—are bound to, at best, do nothing, and at worst, exacerbate the conditions that have led to the poor health of U.S. elections in the first place.

With the diagnosis in hand, the next step is to examine proposed reforms for the U.S. electoral system—most made by others, some my own suggestions—in order to sort out the good medicine from the bad. Each subsequent chapter focuses on ways to deal with one of the causes of the elections' illness. The discussion within each chapter is, by necessity, limited to dealing with only part of the problem; however, the study's conclusion returns to the bigger picture.

SECTION II

THE PRESCRIPTIONS

CHAPTER 4

THE NEWS MEDIA

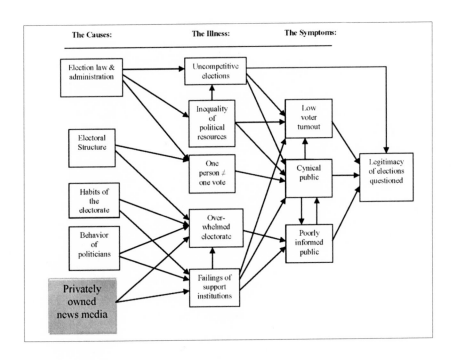

It is hard to conceive of elections in the United States without the mass media. Certainly, there remain small political jurisdictions where candidates can effectively run a race by directly contacting voters in a door-to-door campaign.[222] But even for those contests, voters need some way of assessing candidates' claims and performances as well as a means of connecting the contest and the candidates to the actions and performance of the government overall. For the most part, elections in the United States involve such large populations that most electoral contests would be impossible without channels of mass communication. The mass media are critical to elections because the media are the main institution through which the public can learn about the issues confronting their society and what their governments are or are not doing about those issues. The mass media, through the work of journalists, should also play the important roles of monitor, fact-checker, and referee during elections. This is especially true now, in the age of the Internet and of proliferating cable and satellite channels, when the public is confronted by a sea of competing, conflicting, and often misleading information. Good journalism in the media is necessary in order for people to understand the real meaning of the choices they confront in an election; without the media, the public would remain largely uninformed and open to manipulation.

U.S. citizens expect the media to fulfill these roles, to provide them with the information they need to make their choices during elections, and to hold elected officials accountable. But the media fail to meet these expectations. This failure has fueled the arguments of a number of books analyzing the state of the media in America, and it has prompted a fair amount of self-examination among journalists, a great deal of media bashing from politicos, and a low opinion of the press among much of the public. The media's failure even motivated one citizen, Jon Stewart—a well-known comedian who anchors *The Daily Show*, a "fake" news show—to plead with the hosts of the CNN program *Crossfire* in 2004 to change what they were doing.

JON STEWART: I made a special effort to come on the show today because I have privately, amongst my friends and also in occasional newspapers and television shows, mentioned this show as being bad.

PAUL BEGALA: We have noticed.

STEWART: And I wanted to—I felt that that wasn't fair and I should come here and tell you that I don't—it's not so much that it's bad, as it's hurting America. But I wanted to come here today and say ... stop, stop, stop, stop hurting America. And come work for us, because we, as the people ... we need your help. Right now, you're helping the politicians and the corporations.... What you do is not honest. What you do is partisan hackery. You have a responsibility to the public discourse, and you fail miserably.

BEGALA: And ... *Crossfire* reduces everything, as I said in the intro, to left, right, black, white.

STEWART: Yes.

BEGALA: Well, it's because, see, we're a debate show.

STEWART: No, no ... that would be great.... I would love to see a debate show.

BEGALA: We're thirty minutes in a twenty-four-hour day where we have each side on, as best we can get them, and have them fight it out.

STEWART: No, no ... that would be great. To do a debate would be great. But that's like saying pro wrestling is a show about athletic competition.... But the thing is ... this—you're doing theater, when you should be doing debate.[223]

Essentially, Stewart was pleading for meaningful discourse about the issues of governance so that the public could make some sense of their choices in the 2004 election. Voters were not being supplied with the information they needed, according to Stewart, from *Crossfire* or from the media coverage in general. Political discourse typically found on news shows today is a discourse that focuses on the trivial (e.g., George W. Bush's tendency to combine and mispronounce words); the personal (e.g., Kerry's war record); and the game ("What *are* the latest poll numbers Tucker?"), and often merely repeats the spin of the partisans without any real debate about how the election issues affect the lives of Americans. As Stewart put it, this sort of discourse is hurting America and it needs to stop.

CNN cancelled *Crossfire* shortly after Stewart's appearance.[224] But the immediate impact of his appeal stopped there; there were no more cancellations of television political talk shows and there was no change in the political discourse. Moreover, most politicos gave no indication in their reactions to the Begala-Stewart conversation that they understood or shared Stewart's concern. Stewart's own show, *The Daily Show*, and its spin-off, *The Colbert Report*, however, do attempt to make audiences aware that what is presented as news on television is not necessarily to be taken seriously. These comedies satirize television news itself—its format, its presentation, its pretense to be a serious source of information, its focus on the trivial and sensational. Satire is good medicine for democratic politics, but unfortunately its effects are limited in the "here we are now, entertain us" American culture if satire is just another reason to laugh, not a reason to take action or to think differently.[225] And in the meantime, most people are not getting from their news sources the information and tools they need in order to perform their duties as citizens of a democracy. Perhaps in this "era of profit maximization" it is unreasonable to expect that the news media fulfill this role.[226] It seems much more realistic to expect them to continue to do all they can to keep viewers amused so that the media organizations can deliver an audience to their advertisers, ultimately the source of the media business's profit. A review of the news fare available during the 2004 and 2008 elections makes clear the point that to the media, the audience comprises consumers, not citizens.

How the News Media Fail Voters

A potential voter looking for information to help him or her decide how to vote could turn on the national network news shows. These shows spend about twenty minutes per evening on the news, covering roughly seven to fifteen stories in an average time of about a minute and a half each. The text of the news shows—the actual words that are spoken—is equal to about the size of two full-length stories in the *New York Times*. Obviously, this time frame leaves very little room for substantive or in-depth coverage, especially because ABC, CBS and NBC have, since the 1980s, reduced the amount of "hard" news covered—government, policy issues, and international affairs—and increased their coverage of "soft" news—consumer interests, health, celebrity news, and the weather. Concerning elections, content analyses show that it is highly unlikely that a potential voter would hear about any contests other than the one for the presidency, and those stories would most likely be dominated by news of the horse race, not issues of governance. Content analyses of the coverage of the 2004 and 2008 presidential elections found that only 10 percent and 13 percent of television coverage, respectively, was devoted to explaining policy positions and differences.[227] Sixty-three percent of the television election coverage in 2008 was devoted to the horse race, and 69 percent of the 2004 election coverage focused on political internals—that is, tactics, campaigning, and "inside baseball" (coverage that focuses on background maneuverings and scheming) type of coverage. And if a voter expects to hear what the candidates have to say, he or she will have to settle for tiny snippets, or *sound bites*, of about eight seconds in length.

A voter could also turn to cable television news, which—despite its twenty-four-hour coverage—is home to an even more meager diet of information and is characterized by "continuous headlines, live cover-age of breaking stories and lots of chatter *about* the news, much of it mindless or tendentious."[228] Cable talk shows (of which CNN's *Crossfire* was one) provide little in the way of useful information because "com-mentary, chat, speculation, opinion, argument, controversy, and punditry cost far less than assembling a team of reporters, producers, fact check-ers, and editors" to gather and evaluate information for viewers.[229] As Leonard Downie, Jr., and Robert Kaiser put it, "while television talk shows give viewers the impression that they are engaging with the news, such shows seldom if ever produce new or reliable information.

More often, participants mislead viewers with the sound and fury of their noisy arguments."[230]

Alternatively, a potential voter could tune in to local news programs, but there, in any part of the country, potential news about the election (even news of local contests for Congress or state offices) will be crowded out by crime, weather, and sports.[231] One study found that local television news devotes only about 15 percent of its time to news of government and politics.[232] Another study that examined coverage on 122 randomly selected stations during the 2002 election found that fewer than half of the 10,000-plus local news shows that were analyzed between September 18 and November 4 had at least one election story, that only one-fourth of those stories dealt with issues, and that the average story was eighty-nine seconds long.[233] Aside from a few added stories on the presidential contest (about two minutes' worth during the typical half-hour, most of which focused on the horse race), coverage in 2004 was no different.[234] Local television coverage of local U.S. House and Senate races was so scant that the time devoted to advertisements for these contests was six times that of the news coverage.[235] Clearly, a voter cannot find much useful information about elections on local television news.

If television news is entirely inadequate to the task, what about talk radio? This medium comprises mostly one-sided arguments (designed to entertain) that are framed in a way that emphasizes the values and ideology of the show's hosts (arguments that, according to at least one study, are also very persuasive).[236] Additionally, as Kathleen Hall Jamieson and Joseph Cappella have shown, talk radio (along with Fox News and the editorial pages of the *Wall Street Journal*) leads to a balkanization of knowledge and the creation of insulated communities, each of which "differs in the kind of knowledge it holds and in its interpretation and distortion of political information."[237] Talk radio has also, according to the analysis of Jamieson and Cappella, helped pollute the political discourse by replacing argument with ridicule and ad hominem attacks, contributing to the sickness afflicting U.S. elections (see the discussion of the nature of political discourse in chapter 3).

On National Public Radio (NPR), shows like *All Things Considered* and *Morning Edition* provide more substance and policy analysis than any of the sources mentioned thus far. Nevertheless, these shows are not immune to audience pressures or to the general trends of journalism: covering the horse race, focusing almost exclusively on the presidency, and providing saturation coverage of breaking and blockbuster stories. In 2008 NPR was forced to cut about 7 percent of its workforce.[238] News stories that aired on *All Things Considered* in 2009 focused more on breaking news, entertainment, and celebrities and were about 170 words shorter than stories that aired in 1993.[239] The trend toward more superficial, less substantive coverage was illustrated when President Bush nominated Harriet Myers for Supreme Court justice. Following that announcement, *All Things Considered* suspended the normal news program for an hour of special coverage that (through several uninformative interviews with senators and court experts) made clear to listeners only three things: (1) Myers was President Bush's White House counsel, (2) she had worked with Bush for a long time, and (3) no one knew anything about her positions on any judicial issues. The same basic points were repeated for the entire length of the program. The content of public radio shows is, like that of commercial radio, driven by the need to amuse their audiences (as the increase in entertainment pieces and the addition of quirky stories to the headlines on *Morning Edition* in recent years illustrates), though for different reasons. Whereas commercial media relies on its programming to pull in profits, public radio relies on a satisfied audience for funding; during pledge drives, members of the audience are asked (begged, cajoled, etc.) to pay directly for the programming.

If a knowledge-hungry voter purchases the local paper (in almost any part of the United States), he or she will likely be reading a chain-owned newspaper with more fluff than substance, and the substance will come mostly in the way of wire stories (from, e.g., the Associated Press or Gannet News) that offer little more than horse-race coverage of (mainly) the presidential contest, without any analysis of what the voter's choice really means for how the country is governed.[240]

In the national newspapers, such as the *New York Times*, the *Washington Post*, and the *Wall Street Journal*, there is some very good journalism, including discussion and analysis of what candidates' propose to do as well what they have done in the past and often reprints of the entire text of candidates' speeches. Still, as these elite papers have not been immune to the business pressure to maintain high circulation numbers, the voter will have to dig a bit for the useful information (or search the online versions of the papers). According to one study of the critical weeks of the campaign in the first half of October 2004 (during which the presidential debates took place), only 16 percent of national newspaper front-page stories were framed around explaining the policy positions of the candidates; 43 percent were "inside baseball" type stories.[241] Changes to the *New York Times*, nicknamed "The Gray Lady" for its lack of color photos and dominant print, illustrate the point that it is becoming more and more difficult for voters to find the information they need. The *Times* now features numerous large color photographs, including one that takes up about one-third of the front page, above the fold; the paper has cut back on coverage, decreasing the width of the newspaper by an inch and a half (a full column); and it now uses more news briefs in lieu of full-length articles. However, whereas the substance in the print version of the *Times* has shrunk, the online version has the advantage of making the coverage available over a longer period of time so that one can indeed find substantial coverage on the *Times'* website over the course of an election. The same can be said of other major newspapers' websites—voters can find the information they need if they know how. This is not true of most news magazines, such as *Time* and *Newsweek*, in which a voter will find primarily soft news stories about celebrities, entertainment, health, and consumer news—accompanied by an abundance of glossy pictures.[242]

Similarly, a study of Internet news habits found that "the ... information users are searching for ... appears to be quite similar to the kinds of news people get from traditional news media."[243] Once a voter wanders beyond the major media outlets' pages, the question of what (or whom) to believe arises. Partisan sites are full of claims and counterclaims (often delivered in the form of compelling videos); voters are left to make sense of it all on their own. Moreover, the blogosphere exponentially expands what the Project of Excellence in Journalism calls *journalism of assertion* and

> brings to it an affirmative philosophy: publish anything, especially
> points of view, and the reporting and verification will occur after-
> ward in the response of fellow bloggers. The result is sometimes
> true and sometimes false. Blogs helped unmask errors at CBS,
> but also spread the unfounded conspiracy theory that the GOP
> stole the presidential election in Ohio. All this makes it easier for
> those who would manipulate public opinion—government, inter-
> est groups and corporations—to deliver unchecked messages,
> through independent outlets or their own faux-news Web sites,
> video and text news releases and paid commentators.[244]

The information that voters need in order to make their choices is indeed available, and excellent journalism is not entirely a thing of the past—but the public must diligently search for information or listen patiently for it because it is buried beneath entertainment and nonsubstantive news that is designed to entice people to watch or listen and buy. Most members of the public have neither the motivation nor patience for this; most, especially the younger generations, are content to be endlessly amused.[245] These circumstances leave the United States with a poorly informed, confused, cynical, and apathetic public and ultimately with unhealthy, less-than-democratic elections. This is, of course, a condition caused in part by the public's poor choices with respect to information sources. But it is also the result of the fact that the news media in the United States are, for the most part, privately owned businesses; as a result, business needs, not citizens' needs, determine the nature of the news provided.

The assertion that the news media in America are a business and that as such they are driven by a desire to make a profit is not meant as a denigration of the media. Rather, it is a recognition of the nature of the beast that, though obvious, carries implications that seem to escape many of those who complain about the media and most of those who look to them for information. We rely on and expect too much from news media businesses given that they are *businesses*. The cultural expectation in the United States that the news media exist in order to inform the public and provide citizens with what they need in order to make informed electoral choices is unrealistic given the nature of news media organizations today. At one time the owners of media organizations ran their news divisions with a directive to provide a public service (which was government mandated for the electronic media), informing the public even if the news divisions operated at a financial loss for the company. The government's failure to pressure media organizations for that public service, the public's growing taste for entertainment, and developments in the media industry—particularly the incredible concentration of media ownership—have left news organizations much more motivated by profit than by the task of informing citizens as a public service.[246] As discussed in the previous chapters, this circumstance—the reliance on business organizations to provide the important political function of maintaining an informed citizenry—is one of the leading causes of the illness afflicting U.S. elections. The remainder of this chapter discusses prescriptions designed to ameliorate this condition by addressing the harmful aspects of privately owned news media.

WHAT TO DO?

One fact medical doctors face while treating patients is that there are things they simply cannot do. It is not always possible to directly eradicate the causes of an illness; doctors cannot, for example, kill certain viruses that infect the body. But in most cases they are still able to help their patients through other, less direct means—counseling patients to reduce exposure to causes of the illness, helping patients build up immunities in case of additional exposure, and reducing the consequences of exposure and contraction of the illness. Dealing with the private news media as a cause of ailing elections in the United States is similar. In a free, market-oriented society, it is impossible to eliminate privately owned news media, nor is this a desirable approach because even though private media are consumed with profit margins, they continue to represent a potential check on government excess that other modes of media ownership might not provide. In the past, good journalism exposed the illegal activities of the Nixon presidency, the irrationality of McCarthy's communist witch hunt, the grossly unfair and humiliating treatment of African Americans, the costs of the Vietnam War, the illegalities of the Reagan administration's dealings with Iran and the Nicaraguan Contras, and the White House benefits (overnight stays) granted to large contributors to the Democratic Party during the Clinton administration. More recently, journalists pressured the Bush administration to explain why its rationale for the war in Iraq had proved false; exposed the CIA's secret prisons, the abuse of prisoners in Iraq, and the harsh and unfair treatment of those suspected of terrorism; identified problems with the No Child Left Behind Act; documented the unequal distribution of the recent tax cuts and their effect on the national deficit; and revealed President Bush's secret directive authorizing spying on U.S. citizens.[247] During the 2010 election season, *New York Times* investigative reporter Eric Lipton produced a series of pieces on ethics in Congress, exposing questionable practices of Democrats and Republicans in Congress.[248]

Since eliminating private news media is neither viable nor entirely desirable, what can be done to address the virus of hypercompetitive, profit-driven, entertainment-dominated media—are there less direct approaches that can help restore U.S. elections to health? In short, the answer is yes. There are a number of ways the detrimental effects of the media's drive for profit can be minimized. First, the United States could enhance alternatives to commercial news sources in order to allow some of the public to avoid the effects of private news media. In addition, the federal government could mandate that the private media live up to the requirement that they operate in the public service with respect to elections. And finally, steps could be taken to strengthen the one force within the news media that is driven by a professional desire to inform instead of by profit—namely, journalism.

R_x: PROVIDE BETTER ALTERNATIVES

Setting up alternatives to private news media is not a new idea; the United States already has the Public Broadcasting System (public television) and National Public Radio. In many other countries, electronic media are or were dominated by publicly held organizations, such as the BBC in Britain and the CBC in Canada. Many countries have a mix of privately, publicly, and government-owned media.[249] And in countries with authoritarian governments, such as China and Cuba, the government owns and runs all media outlets.

Government-run media is generally not a good idea in a democracy. Allowing the government to control information invites abuse, invites attempts to control the public by controlling the information available to them. One need only look to the behavior of politicians in the United States to see that such temptation would be nearly impossible to resist; politicians and their consultants have developed sophisticated ways to put their interpretations on the news as it is, and some have gone even further, as a number of Bush administration public-relations projects demonstrate. George W. Bush's administration paid one columnist $240,000 to write positive stories about its No Child Left Behind program and paid two other columnists to act as consultants in promoting the administration's marriage initiatives.[250] In 2004 the General Accountability Office (the investigative agency of the U.S. Congress) concluded that the Bush administration had broken U.S. laws against propaganda by distributing "video news releases" touting the benefits of the Bush administration's prescription drug program.[251] These videos were made available to local television news programs, which could not pass up the free material and aired the videos, often without identifying the government as the source. And someone in the White House granted regular daily passes to the press room to a bogus reporter who, operating under the assumed name Jeff Gannon and working for the GOP-linked Talon News website, would ask questions with a pro-administration slant during press conferences.[252] Obviously, some politicians go to great lengths to control information and the way it is presented under the current system. Therefore government-owned news media would not address the problems inherent in a privately owned system but indeed would likely exacerbate another problem—political manipulation of information—by granting even greater control to those in power.

For good reason then, the federal government does not own any of the media that broadcast within the United States.[253] Instead, the country has what are called *semipublic* media outlets (*semi* because they include both publicly and privately owned television and radio stations supported by a mix of public and private funds).[254] Public television (PBS) and National Public Radio (NPR) are governed by the Corporation for Public Broadcasting (CPB) and funded by the federal government, state and local governments, corporate sponsors, and viewers and listeners. The federal government's contribution to semipublic broadcasting is actually small (a total of about $455 million, comprising 19 percent of semipublic broadcasting revenues) and is third in the ranking of sources of funding for semipublic broadcasting. The first two sources are subscribers, who provide 26 percent of the revenues, and state and local government sources, which supply 25 percent of public broadcasting revenues.[255] Corporate contributions constitute 15 percent of semipublic broadcasting revenues.[256] The rest of the funding comes from foundations and other fundraising activities.

Semipublic broadcasting is supposed to provide a public service, offering alternative programming to that which airs on commercial media, and it is meant to be insulated from partisan political pressures. Semipublic broadcasting in the United States does provide some different and better-quality programming with respect to political news, but as recent developments show, it is far from insulated from political pressures.

The NewsHour with Jim Lehrer on PBS and *All Things Considered* and *Morning Edition* on NPR offer audiences solid news coverage and some excellent journalism. According to an annual study by the Project for Excellence in Journalism, an institute affiliated with Columbia University Graduate School of Journalism, *The NewsHour* "by some measures, exceeded [in 2004]... the three commercial nightly newscasts in its reporting.... It also stands out for its orientation to hard news."[257] *The NewsHour* offers more background that most programs to help viewers understand stories, and "interviews are often discussions with two or more analysts, rather than one guest or two opposing advocates in a debate format."[258] *The NewsHour* was also remarkable in this study because of the infrequency with which reporters injected their own opinions into stories.[259] Likewise, National Public Radio's major news programs—*All Things Considered* and *Morning Edition*—offer news programs between one and two hours long, a span of time which allows them to deal with the news in longer news segments than television network or cable news shows (although, as mentioned earlier, these NPR segments are shorter now than in the past) and in that extra time they can provide greater background and analysis. The programs often air long segments of candidates' speeches during election periods (compared to the eight-second-long average sound bites on network television) and provide more rigorous analysis of issues during campaigns.

The governing body of public broadcasting in the United States, the CPB, comprises political appointees who administer public broadcasting. In order to keep the programming free of political pressures, the CPB is not supposed to be directly involved in programming. Keeping public broadcasting insulated from political pressures, however, has not proved entirely workable. The CPB has used its control of the purse strings in order to influence programming, and under the chairmanship of Kenneth Tomlinson, the group actually became directly involved in programming.[260] Tomlinson, a conservative, campaigned against what he perceived as a left-wing bias in public broadcasting from his position as chairman of the CPB until he resigned under investigation for possible violations of federal law. According to a report by CBP Inspector General Konz, Tomlinson's attempts to exert partisan control over public broadcasting included direct involvement in attempting to put conservative talk show *The Journal Editorial Report* onto PBS's schedule; hiring Republican consultants and lobbyists (to conduct "analyses" of incidents of left-wing bias on several PBS shows and to lobby Congress) without the CPB board's knowledge; and using "'political tests' to recruit a former co-chairman of the Republican National Committee as PBS's president."[261] Tomlinson's activities represent the most egregious case of direct political interference with public broadcasting, but public broadcasting has historically been subject to partisan political pressure—especially through the budgeting process, in which conservative

Republicans in Congress, who claim that the programming has a liberal bias, have repeatedly targeted the corporation's budget so as to make cuts in, or entirely eliminate its funding.

Semipublic broadcasting in the United States as it is currently configured is clearly not without problems. On the one hand, it provides programming and quality news of the sort that is not available on commercial broadcasts; but on the other hand, its funding and management are regularly the target both of partisans, some of whom believe it to be promoting the wrong values, and of the privately owned media, whose owners don't appreciate publicly-financed competition. The assaults have taken their toll, limiting public broadcasting's part in the media world of the United States. Audiences are small: those tuned into *The NewsHour with Jim Lehrer* represent only 6.4 percent of the total audience for television news,[262] and though the number has seen considerable growth in the past decade, just 16 percent of the U.S. public regularly listens to NPR, and these listeners tend to be a "young, culturally elite group."[263]

In sum, government-owned media is not acceptable; semipublic broadcasting as it exists neither functions well nor reaches a large audience. What alternatives could attract a large proportion of the population and provide them with the information that they need in order to participate meaningfully in elections? Here I explore two possibilities: a partisan press and the BBC model. In some democracies, including many of those in Europe, the news media are partisan—that is, they are affiliated with partisan ideological positions, and they overtly cover politics and government from those perspectives.[264] This alternative to corporate media would probably not work well in the United States, however, because most of the public is more interested in getting news from objective, nonpartisan sources.[265] Besides, in this age of the Internet, political discourse teems with rumor and half-truths; additional journalism of assertion or affirmation, which characterizes partisan media, would not be helpful. Rather, U.S. citizens would benefit from more source-checking and verification of facts, characteristics of the traditional model of journalism.[266]

The model of the British Broadcasting Corporation (BBC) offers an interesting possible alternative to private media in America. The BBC has been very successful in providing high-quality information, and it is a respected and popular news source throughout the world. The BBC is more independent from the government and politics and less dependent on audience appeal than the semipublic system in the United States. In their book *Comparing Media Systems*, Hallin and Mancini wrote that the BBC exemplifies the professional model of media, with a high level of journalistic autonomy, professional norms, and a commitment to providing a public service.[267] These qualities are in part the result of the strong tradition in Britain of the BBC's political independence and of the fact that the corporation is funded largely by a tax (or license fee) on televisions, a tax which is dedicated solely to funding the BBC and thus is relatively insulated from politicians who might wish to exert influence through the budgetary process.[268] The BBC's revenue as a percent of GDP in 2001 was 0.30 percent, as compared to 0.02 percent for semipublic broadcasting in the United States (the BBC's audience share in Britain is 39 percent, as compared to 2 percent for semipublic broadcasting in the United States).[269]

Could America create a public broadcasting system that would be as successful an alternative to private media as the BBC? The answer depends on whether the conditions under which the BBC has thrived could be replicated. The BBC is more successful than U.S. semipublic broadcasting for the three reasons indicated in the previous paragraph: it has substantial funding, the type of funding protects the BBC from political pressures, and those appointed to run the BBC sustain the traditional political independence of British broadcasting.[270] Certainly the U.S. government could spend more money on public broadcasting; federal spending on semipublic broadcasting represents two one-hundredths of 1 percent of the federal government outlays in 2003 (a little over $450 million).[271] To put that in more personal terms, 0.02 percent of, say, one person's annual salary of $50,000 amounts to about $10, or sixty-three cents a month. The federal government spends as much on just two F-22 fighter planes (about $250 million each) annually as it does on providing the much-needed alternative to commercial media. At such low levels, funding for public broadcasting is by no means a zero-sum game; doubling or tripling the funding would have a negligible effect on overall government financing. Politically, though, it seems impossible to increase federal government spending on public broadcasting—as already mentioned, conservative Republicans and the corporate media are strongly opposed to public broadcasting, and at the moment they are far too powerful in Washington to make such an increase feasible. A review of the research analyses of the offerings of private news media and the corresponding lack of political awareness among the public, however, should make it clear to those of any ideological stripe that better-funded, public service–oriented news media outlets are critical for democracy in the United States. And as for conservatives' concern about liberal bias in American public broadcasting, such claims have not been substantiated by any published peer-reviewed empirical research.[272]

The BBC is insulated from politics because its funding is based on a dedicated source, whereas the level of federal CPB funding is determined by Congress each year. A source like the BBC's—an annual tax on televisions—would, to put it mildly, be a nonstarter in the United States (indeed, I have trouble thinking of anything that would be more likely to spark a massive uprising of Americans than a tax on their televisions). There are, however, more palatable alternatives for funding sources. A number of groups advocating reform of public broadcasting have proposed the creation of a trust fund that would provide a stream of funding immune from partisan interference. The organization Citizens for Independent Public Broadcasting (CIPB), for example, proposes that a onetime $20 billion trust fund be created to provide $1 billion a year for public broadcasting (over twice the amount that the federal government currently provides for public broadcasting). As for the sources of the $20 billion, the CIPB suggests a number of possibilities:

> a five percent tax on factory sales of digital television sets, a five percent tax on the sale or transfer of commercial broadcast licenses, a two percent tax on annual broadcast advertising, a two percent annual spectrum fee, or a modest tax on the auction of up to $100 billion in digital spectrum.[273]

Likewise, a proposal for a Digital Opportunity Investment Trust (DOIT) is advocated by two former PBS executives, by Representative Ed Markey (D-MA, the legislative sponsor), and by Digital Promise, a "coalition of technology executives, university officials like retired Sen. Bob Kerry and famous individuals like *Star Wars* creator George Lucas."[274] The DOIT would "direct [digital] spectrum-auction proceeds to a public trust that would back digital education and workforce-training projects of universities, cultural institutions, libraries and public broadcasters."[275] Although the opportunities for raising money in some of these ways are slipping by, these proposals demonstrate that there are creative ways to ensure greater and increased funding for public broadcasting, most of which do not involve increasing taxes on the U.S. public.

The final difference between U.S. public broadcasting and the BBC that helps account for the latter's greater success is the BBC's independence from politics.[276] The direct, politically motivated involvement in PBS programming by former CPB chairman Kenneth Tomlinson, as well as past behavior of the board of governors, shows that such a norm either does not exist or is largely ignored in the United States. Since it is unlikely that a norm of political independence will be adopted by political appointees of the CPB, the solution must lie in developing a new way to select members of the governing board. CIPB suggests that a new Public Broadcasting Trust replace the CPB; the new trust would comprise nine trustees, three of whom would be selected from the public broadcasting community, three from the educational community, and the final three from the President's Commission on the Arts and Humanities.[277] Appointing board members in such a way would not necessarily eliminate political interference in public broadcasting, but it would be a start. Any new configuration of the governing body of public broadcasting would also need to include a strong expectation that the board members and public broadcasting operate in the public interest and free of political considerations.

There are, then, ways to change public broadcasting in the United States that would allow it to operate more like its successful cousin, the BBC, and thus provide a better and perhaps more popular alternative to news delivered by businesses. The main obstacle is political. Conservatives simply object to publicly funded media. While they level charges of liberal bias against the mainstream media on a daily basis (charges that, as already mentioned, are unsubstantiated), most conservatives harbor an even greater animosity toward public broadcasting. This hostility appears to exist in the United Kingdom as well as in the United States. Part of conservatives' dislike of public broadcasting is undoubtedly tied to their governing philosophy, which prefers a minimal role for government in the market, including the media business sector. But perhaps conservatives' animosity toward public broadcasting also stems in part from their distaste for the adversarial role often played by the media. Many journalists see their professional role as one of neutral adversary with respect to those in power, or as that of a watchdog whose job it is to expose the wrongdoings of public officials. This role of challenging authority figures is directly opposed to conservatives' more deferential orientation to authority.[278] A comment made on Fox News by John McCain's 2008 campaign manager, Rick Davis, neatly illustrates this point: Davis stated that McCain's running mate, Sarah Palin, would not be subject to interviews by journalists until reporters treated her "with some level of respect and deference." Republicans want deference from those whose job is to challenge and question political figures.[279] Therefore conservatives will rarely be happy with the news media, where this professional journalistic norm of serving as a neutral adversary thrives. In the business-owned media in the United States, this professional role for journalists has been largely subverted by the bottom-line profit pressure. Publicly funded media operate without such pressures and thus allow the professional norms of journalists to play a larger role in shaping news coverage.[280]

Although conservative Republicans have often been the more skillful group in terms of manipulating the for-profit media's delivery of information, this may not always be the case.[281] And because Republicans may be outmaneuvered in the political spin contest at some point, it is as much in their interests as it is in the interests of liberals, Democrats, and centrists that the public have access to a widely consumed, independent, and professional source of information that is concerned more about an informed citizenship than about profit. Any supporter of democracy will realize that healthy elections require the support of a professional press to help the public sort through and evaluate the claims of the parties involved so that citizens can make an informed choice and render elections meaningful vehicles of representation. Because the profit motives of businesses lead the U.S. media to stress entertainment over information, a strong noncommercial alternative is needed. And it appears that the best way of providing that alternative is to make some substantial changes in the funding and operation of public broadcasting.

Thus, the first prescription for America's sick elections is to enhance the alternative to private, corporate media news. This should be done through creation of a trust fund that would provide public broadcasting with a politically insulated and greatly increased revenue stream for public broadcasting. The trust fund should be established by means other than the general revenue fund—that is, by the sale of the digital spectrum, charges for use of the public airwaves, or a tax on advertising revenue—and should provide public broadcasting with a stream of financing that is at least twice what it receives now. Enhancing public broadcasting would also require instituting a shift in the culture of public broadcasting governance— namely, changing the means of appointment of those who administer public broadcasting and stressing the expectation that those running public broadcasting will maintain its independence from politics.[282]

R$_x$: REQUIRE THAT TELEVISION FULFILL ITS PUBLIC SERVICE MANDATE

In exchange for allowing media businesses to broadcast over public airwaves, the federal government requires that those radio and television businesses "serve the public interest, convenience and necessity."[283] The Federal Communications Commission (FCC) has done little over the years to ensure that television and radio broadcasters serve the public interest; enforcing this requirement is the second way to indirectly deal with the problems caused by relying on private media as a source of information about elections. The FCC should use the public-service requirement to mandate programming that would give the public greater opportunities to learn about the meaning of electoral choices. Specifically, broadcasters could be mandated to (1) expand their coverage of the political parties' national conventions, (2) provide free television time to the political parties, and (3) host substantive political debates.

Covering Conventions
The quadrennial conventions of the two major political parties have become scripted and staged events that offer little in the way of news as defined by the major networks or journalists. But the party conventions do offer the public a chance to hear the leaders of the political parties address the problems facing the nation in blocks of time significantly longer than the average eight-second sound bite of television news coverage. Moreover, it is clear from public opinion research that the *people who watch the national party conventions become more interested in and more positive about the election and while at the same time learn about the parties' and candidates' positions on the issues.*[284] The University of Pennsylvania's National Annenberg Election Survey found that "despite minimal network television coverage, the Democratic National Convention increased the public's knowledge of the positions John Kerry and George W. Bush [held] on a range of issues," including Kerry's positions on reversing Bush's income tax cuts for those who earn over $200,000 annually, his opposition to tax breaks for U.S. corporations operating overseas, and his plan for concluding matters in Iraq.[285] The Vanishing Voter survey found similar increases in knowledge of candidate positions from the party conventions in 2000, with "awareness of Bush's and Gore's issue positions [rising] 17 percent during" the convention period.[286] Finally, because the audience patterns suggest that the more convention coverage the networks provide, the more the public watches, it is reasonable to expect even greater improvements in public knowledge, interest, and involvement if the networks expand their coverage.[287]

Allowing the public to view more of the conventions—scripted and staged though they may be—clearly provides a public service by increasing the available information about elections, thus enhancing interest and involvement. Nonetheless, the three major television networks provided a total of only four hours of coverage of each convention in 2008 and only three hours of coverage of each convention in 2004 (down from sixty hours of coverage in 1972 and twenty-five hours of coverage in 1984). In 2004 the broadcast networks even declined to cover the keynote speech at the DNC, given by Barak Obama (by most accounts, probably the best speech of that convention). Though viewers could—and millions did in 2004—turn to cable for extended coverage, they would have found that the proceedings and speeches of the convention were used mainly as video wallpaper for the cable stations' programs, limiting what viewers could actually hear from the parties (C-SPAN's unfiltered coverage is an exception).[288]

The major networks may not consider the conventions news events because nothing "new" or controversial happens at these meetings. This is a poor excuse on two fronts. First, as the Project for Excellence in Journalism points out, the networks cover other political rituals that are scripted and staged, such as presidential inaugurations and State of the Union addresses. Second, the networks should consider giving airtime to the political parties during their conventions *as a public service*. Given the research evidence indication that the public learns from the coverage and becomes more interested and less cynical about politics in the process, providing this coverage would clearly be a valuable public service. The real reason the networks have almost eliminated convention coverage is because they see no profit in it. Because profit will not motivate them to cover the conventions, then, the federal government needs to mandate convention coverage as part of the networks' public service obligation. As the fictional White House director of communications Toby Ziegler put it to television executives in an episode of *The West Wing*,

> There isn't going to be a horse race to cover [at either convention], but we gave you the airwaves for free seventy years ago and 357 days a year you can say who's up and who's down, who won

the West and who lost the South—but what's wrong with eight days, not every year but every four years, showing our leaders talking to us? Not a fraction of what they said but what they said. And then th-the balloons.[289]

Mandating expanded coverage of the conventions is logical given the sound-bite-dominated, horse-race-focused nature of news coverage of political campaigns. The positive effects of convention coverage for elections have been clearly demonstrated in the research literature. Allowing the public to hear the speeches of the party leaders, presidential and vice presidential nominees, and some of the convention proceedings without interruptions from commentators would certainly be good medicine for U.S. elections.

Free Television Time
The principle behind requiring the broadcast networks to provide free television time to candidates or political parties is similar to that behind mandating expanded convention coverage. Additionally, providing free television time could supplement campaign finance regulations aimed at reducing the inequalities between candidates with regard to their ability to reach voters over the airwaves. Free airtime could thus alleviate some of the pressure to raise enormous sums of money. And given that presidential candidates do not normally buy ad time nationally (they buy media time from local stations only in the limited number of states they wish to contest),[290] free national network airtime could spread electoral discourse more widely and keep the discourse focused on issues of concern to the entire nation.

Mandating that all television stations provide a block of time to the political parties or the candidates in the weeks prior to an election is justified by the fact (well supported by research) that news coverage of elections is insubstantial and lacking in the kind of information voters need. By granting the free television time to candidates or parties, station owners would be serving the public interest and the public's needs in ways that their news programs fail to do. If handled properly, free television time would allow the different sides to make their cases to the public in a more substantive manner than they are typically afforded on television news, imbuing the campaign discourse with more in-depth discussion of issues and policy. Proper handling means that the use of the airtime would be contingent upon the acceptance of certain stipulations designed to ensure that the free time segments would be used to talk about issues and governance. For instance, representatives of the political party or candidates could be required to talk directly to the camera, without visual aids or video clips, for the entire time granted. Such a stipulation would make it difficult for candidates to use the time to mount unsubstantiated attacks on their opponents or to manipulate audiences with emotional video images. The amount of airtime should be long enough that candidates and parties would be forced to address issues in a comprehensive manner. Finally, the candidate's or party's messages should be broadcast during prime time and across all broadcast channels so as to reach the broadest possible audience.

A number of reform groups, academic study groups, government commissions, politicians of both political parties, and even media owners themselves have made proposals for some form of free television time for candidates and political parties. In 1990 a group appointed by Senate leaders George Mitchell (D-ME) and Bob Dole (R-KS) recommended that television and radio broadcasters give eight hours of free time to national and state party committees.[291] In 1996 media mogul Rupert Murdoch offered to give a half-hour spot and ten one-minute spots to the presidential candidates in the last month of the campaign. In 1998, an advisory commission appointed by president Bill Clinton and headed by vice president Al Gore recommended, among other things, that "if Congress undertakes comprehensive campaign finance reform, broadcasters should commit firmly to do their part to reform the role of television in campaigns. This could include repeal of the 'lowest unit rate' requirement in exchange for free airtime, a broadcast bank to distribute money or vouchers for airtime, and shorter time periods of selling political airtime."[292] Additionally, the commission recommended that "the television broadcasting industry should voluntarily provide 5 minutes each night for candidate-centered discourse in the 30 days before an election" (the 5/30 standard). A number of stations did adopt the 5/30 standard in 2000, and a study of local coverage during that election found that, although stations that had committed to the 5/30 standard did not completely fulfill their time commitment, they did provide more and better coverage of elections—more issue coverage, longer sound bites, and less horse-race coverage.[293]

In 2004 former FCC chairman Newton Minow and former FCC general counsel Henry Geller requested that the FCC

> commence an expedited rulemaking proceeding to adopt a policy requiring broadcast licensees, during a short specified period (30 days) before a general election, to devote a reasonable amount of public service time (20 minutes) during the broadcast day to appearances of candidates in significant local races which otherwise would not receive coverage informing the electorate.[294]

Minow and Geller argued that such a requirement is necessary, "especially in view of recent research showing failed broadcast efforts to inform the public on such local campaign issues." Along similar lines, the Our Democracy, Our Airwaves Campaign has formed a coalition of the following organizations: the Brennan Center, Common Cause, the National Urban League, Democracy 21, the Sierra Club, AARP, AFSCME (American Federation of State, County and Municipal Employees), Moveon.org, the National Council of Churches, the National Education Association, and the Center for Voting and Democracy, led by Media Policy Program of the Campaign Legal Center. The group is advocating the "Our Democracy, Our Airwaves Act," a bill introduced in 2003 by senators John McCain (R-AZ), Russell Feingold (D-WI), and Richard Durbin (D-IL) that "amends the Communications Act of 1934 to establish minimum airtime requirements on television and radio stations for candidate-centered and issue-centered programming prior to primary and general elections." The bill's recommendations include

> a minimum of two hours per week of candidate-centered or issue-centered programming for a total of six weeks preceding a

primary or general federal election, at least four of which must be immediately preceding the general election. Half these segments must air between 5 p.m. and 11:35 p.m., and no segment that airs between midnight to 6 a.m. counts toward meeting this requirement. "Candidate-centered programming" refers to debates, interviews, candidate statements and other news or public affairs formats that provide for a discussion of issues by candidates; it does not include paid political advertisements. "Issue-centered programming" refers to debates, interviews and other formats that provide for a discussion of ballot measures on the ballot in the forthcoming election. It does not include paid political ads.[295]

Academic analyses of free television time have found evidence that it does have the potential to improve political discourse during elections. As mentioned previously, a Lear Center study of local coverage during the 2000 election found that stations that committed to providing free airtime provided more issue coverage, longer sound bites, and less horse-race coverage.[296] An Annenberg Center analysis of free television time in the 1996 presidential election found that the free television spots provided useful information with more policy substance than news broadcasts—and did so with less alarmism, fewer inflammatory attacks, and more accurate and fact-based comparisons between the two major-party candidates than appeared in the news.[297] A study of a sample of Chicagoans by the National Opinion Research Center for that same election year found that "those who viewed the [free television] segments learned relevant information about the candidates that they had not learned from other sources" and that "there is some evidence for increased voting behavior among viewers" of the free television segments.[298] The effects were the largest for those who were prompted to watch the segments through an outreach program, suggesting that free television time needs to be aggressively advertised to have the most beneficial effect. Paul Waldman's study of the free television time granted to New Jersey gubernatorial candidates in 1997 found that

> the free time presentations that the candidates gave supplied voters with messages that were less negative in form, more accurate,

and weighted heavily toward specific policy proposals. As such, free time was a superior format for the dissemination of information on the candidates.[299]

Finally, most other western democracies find it important to give free airtime to candidates or parties. Austria, Britain, Canada, Denmark, Finland, Germany, and Sweden, for example, provide free television time to the political parties while banning or strictly regulating paid advertising by parties and individual candidates.[300]

Clearly then, there is strong support for mandating that broadcasters give free airtime to candidates or political parties—research evidence supports it, the experience and practice of other democracies support it, and a wide range of groups and members of both political parties support it. Despite the voluntary efforts of some broadcasters to provide free television time, the main obstacle is the power of the broadcasting industry, led by the National Association of Broadcasters, the powerful interest group that represents broadcasters. Broadcasters do not want to lose valuable airtime to such a program and they do not want to lose the revenue that comes from candidate and party advertisements during an election. The broadcasting industry is powerful because it contributes large sums of money to campaigns (e.g., a total of about $5.8 million during the 2008 election cycle[301]), because it has a powerful and active lobby in Washington,[302] and because it owns the news programs that report on politicians.

Representatives of the broadcasting industry argue that they (the broadcasters) already provide hundreds of hours of election and political coverage.[303] Such claims, however, fail to consider the quality (or lack thereof) of coverage, which extensive research has shown to be deficient in the substance voters need.[304] In the end, media corporations take more from elections than they give. They use elections as fodder for their news and talk shows—the 2008 election, for example, kept them well stocked with material, filling one-third of the news slot from late 2007 until Election Day[305]—while failing to provide the substantive coverage needed in order to show voters the essential electoral choice. Media corporations also earn vast sums of money from political advertising during elections; in 2004 an estimated \$1.6 billion was spent for political advertising on local television stations only, and in 2008 the Obama and McCain campaigns alone spent well over \$60 million.[306] As many have already pointed out, the media corporations benefit from being given license to use the public airwaves (an expanding benefit as the digital spectrum is divided up). Demanding that, in return, broadcasters turn those public airwaves over for a brief period in order to air election messages every two years does not seem an unreasonable requirement. Broadcasters may even benefit from the free airtime, as party and candidate messages would give them additional material for their news and talk programs. The public image of corporate media could potentially improve if such a public service were provided.

Free airtime, combined with extended convention coverage, would go a long way to injecting greater substance into election-year discourse. As evident from the discussion here, there are a variety of proposals for free airtime. Which one should the United States adopt? I would recommend the Mitchell-Dole proposal of giving eight hours of free television time to the national and state political parties—two hours each to the RNC and DNC, and two hours to each state party committee in the broadcaster's area of dominant influence—during prime time throughout the four weeks leading up to the general election during both presidential and midterm elections. The parties could then use the time at their discretion, issuing party messages or showcasing their candidates (this would also strengthen the hand of the political parties, which carries added benefits, as discussed in chapter 6). The time would be used in half-hour blocks; each half hour would be divided up by the political parties as they saw fit. Granting longer blocks of time (as opposed to the five-minute blocks proposed by some) should increase the likelihood that at least a portion of the spots would be seen by the public. Again, the spots should feature candidates or representatives of the parties speaking directly to the camera—no video clips and no studio audiences. Additionally, broadcasters would be required to air public-service announcements throughout the day advertising the election messages and encouraging the public to tune in. And finally, all paid political advertisements would be banned for one hour before and one hour after the airing of each of the free broadcasts in order to prevent sandwiching the more substantive free time with discourse typical of campaign ads.

A note is in order here about banning candidate advertisements from television. As already mentioned, some political systems that give free airtime to the parties prohibit paid candidate advertisements altogether. Should the United States ban candidate ads on television or ban all tele-vised political ads if free airtime were made available to the political parties? Whereas doing so might give television viewers respite from the raucous cacophony of candidate, party, and group messages during an election, such a ban is not necessary for the health of U.S. elections (other reforms discussed in subsequent chapters will address the "noise level" of election campaigns). The purpose behind requiring broadcast-ers to provide free television time (and the reason for mandating con-vention coverage) is to inject a higher level of issue substance into the campaign discourse. Prohibiting candidate ads does nothing to further that goal and is thus unnecessary.

Finally, some might argue that the development of the Internet makes free television time unnecessary. It could be argued that the party mes-sages should simply be made available on an Internet site. The problem with this alternative to free television time is that these election messages would not have the widespread reach that a simultaneous broadcast and cable time block would have. In this high-choice media environment, the people who most need to be reached with the information (people who are poorly informed because they tend to choose entertainment programming over news programming) would be those least likely to seek out the election messages on the Internet.[307]

Debates

The national broadcast networks already provide coverage of the presi-dential and vice presidential debates. Providing airtime for the debates injects more issue consideration into elections (at least into presiden-tial elections). Research has consistently shown that members of the public learn from these debates.[308] Debates can also heighten public interest in an election and prompt people to talk about what they have seen.[309] Local broadcasters often air debates for state and local election contests, and there is evidence to suggest that such forums are also effective in informing the public.[310] In general, then, this is one area of elections that clearly functions well. There are, however, some concerns that need to be addressed so as to ensure that debates continue to contribute to the health of elections to the fullest extent possible.[311] First, there is a need to guarantee that there will be debates every election year and that the networks and local television stations will air them. Second, serious improvements should be made in the news media's postdebate coverage.

A number of reform proposals have suggested that presidential candidates who accept public funds should be required to participate in a minimum number of televised debates. This seems a reasonable requirement given that the public is providing the candidates with millions of dollars for their campaigns; the effectiveness of such a provision, however, depends on the maintenance of a public-funding system that entices the Democratic and Republican nominees to participate (a topic dealt with in chapter 7). A debate requirement could also be attached to a party's acceptance of free television time: in exchange for the free airtime, each party's candidates for major offices (U.S. Senate and House and state governor) must appear in, for instance, a minimum of two televised debates between Labor Day and Election Day. All debates should be limited to the two major political parties unless polling shows that a third-party or independent candidate has the support of at least 10 percent of the electorate.[312]

Broadcasters have found it in their interest to air presidential and vice presidential debates live in most recent elections. This seems unlikely to change, but some mechanism should be put in place to guarantee the broadcasting of the debates. The extent to which local broadcasting stations air debates by U.S. Senate, House, and gubernatorial candidates varies from one media market to the next. Again, as with free airtime provisions, local broadcasters could be required to air such debates as part of their mandate to serve the public's interest and necessity.

Postdebate coverage by journalists has fallen short of the ideal for the same reasons that overall campaign coverage falls short: the media's incentives to entertain overwhelm their desire to inform, and many journalists have a penchant for seeing elections as a game. Most coverage following the debates focuses on who won the debate in the eyes of the public, journalists, campaign representatives, and the ubiquitous pundits, all supplemented by instant polling numbers or panels of "undecided voters."[313] And winners are often determined based on style, mannerisms, the ability of a candidate to provide a memorable quote or moment, or whether a candidate committed a gaffe. Barack Obama was declared the winner of all three debates with John McCain in 2008 because he "kept his cool," seemed presidential, and did not allow McCain to rattle him. George W. Bush was deemed to have lost the first debate of the 2004 election because he seemed defensive and dismissive and because he fidgeted, slouched over the lectern, and reacted visibly as John Kerry talked.[314] Al Gore "lost" the first debate in 2000 because he made audible, exasperated sighs off-camera while George Bush spoke; the third debate that year prompted criticism of Gore for his physically aggressive manner.[315] Such is the nature of postdebate coverage: systematic studies of the content of media coverage of the presidential debates find little of value to voters who are trying to make their decisions. A study of debate coverage in 2004 found that

> nearly eight out of ten stories (79%) assessing the debates focused on political matters rather than where the candidates differed on issues, where they proposed to take the country or questions of character, record or veracity.... Only 4% of the debate stories explained policy differences between the two candidates.[316]

Most of the stories (91 percent) were framed around the aftermath of the debate events with respect to the politicians—that is, the debate's implications for each candidate's bid for the White House. "Only 8 percent of debate stories were written in ways that made clear how these events might impact Americans."[317] Researchers have found similar results in studies of the media coverage of other presidential election debates. Only 11 percent of the postdebate coverage in 2000 discussed the policy differences between the candidates; 70 percent was background machinations coverage, focusing on candidate performance, tactics, and strategy.[318] One study that tracked television postdebate coverage over time found that focus on issues dropped from 38.4 percent in 1976 to 5.7 percent in 1988.[319]

To their credit, media organizations have in recent years begun to run fact checks during the debates (though fact checking amounted to only 7 percent of the overall postdebate coverage in 2004).[320] The problem with these fact checks, however, is that the journalists or analysts they hire do not sort out the big, distorting errors from the small, technical ones. The fact-checking stories, in the interest of so-called balance, tend to conclude that both candidates made misstatements, a conclusion that undoubtedly reinforces the public's belief that no politician can be trusted. Ultimately, the postdebate coverage muddles the real differences that exist on the issues—differences that are usually made clear during the debates.

Clearly, media debate coverage is lacking. The minimal postdebate discussion of issue differences not only represents a failure on the part of journalists to augment the learning that comes from debates but also may actually reduce the debate's potential effect on voter learning by drawing attention away from real issue differences between the candidates by focusing instead on trivial matters that have no consequence for how the country will be governed. Instead of clarifying and reinforcing the lessons of the debate, postdebate coverage muddies the water and distracts voters from what is important. Therefore the health of U.S. elections would benefit from a different kind of journalism in the coverage of debates as well as in the overall coverage of elections. Elections call for journalism that conceives of campaigns not as games but as vehicles for choosing governments; elections need news organizations that conceive of their audiences as citizens, not consumers.

R$_{X:}$ Strengthening Journalism

Most of the reforms discussed up to this point are related to media organizations—the profit motive and public-service requirements for broadcasters. Although journalists are constrained by the nature of the media
organizations for which they work—problems that some of the reforms
already mentioned would address—there are changes that journalists
themselves could make that would improve the knowledge of citizens
and, ultimately, the health of elections. Moreover, governments could
take action in order to support good journalism.

Journalists as a group are quite aware of the current problems with
their profession. One survey of journalists conducted by the Pew Center for the People and the Press found that 57 percent of local journalists and 66 percent of national journalists believe that the increased
bottom-line pressure for profits is seriously hurting journalism. Chief
among the more specific concerns is the belief that too little attention is
being paid to complex issues; about 80 percent of journalists agreed that
this was a valid criticism of the media.[321] In response to such concerns
about the quality of journalism, journalists—along with editors, producers, publishers, owners, and academics—have organized to address the
problems they see. The Project for Excellence in Journalism (PEJ) "is
an initiative by journalists to clarify and raise the standards of American journalism."[322] The PEJ, affiliated with the Columbia University
Graduate School of Journalism until July 2006 and now part of the Pew
Research Center, does research to provide journalists with the tools they
need to do better work. Similarly, the Committee of Concerned Journalists (CCJ)—a group initially affiliated with the PEJ and comprising about
nine thousand journalists, editors, producers, owners, and educators—
has made its goal reform in journalism. The CCJ runs public forums
and newsroom training programs and offers various publications to contribute to the improvement of journalists' work.[323] From discussions and
forums with journalists and the public around the nation, the group has
compiled a set of principles that journalists agree on. The overarching

principle is "that the purpose of journalism is to provide people with the information they need to be free and self-governing."[324] With this primary goal in mind, the journalists interviewed for the study supported the following statements about the nature of the craft:

- Journalism's first obligation is to the truth.
- Its first loyalty is to citizens.
- Its essence is a discipline of verification.
- Its practitioners must maintain an independence from those they cover.
- It must serve as an independent monitor of power.
- It must provide a forum for public criticism and compromise.
- It must strive to make the significant interesting and relevant.
- It must keep the news comprehensive and proportional.
- Its practitioners must be allowed to exercise their personal conscience.[325]

Some of these principles are similar to those suggested by Kathleen Hall Jamieson and Paul Waldman in their book *The Press Effect*. Jamieson and Waldman suggest that journalists adopt a set of measures in producing their coverage of campaigns, measures designed to help the public sort through the claims and counterclaims and develop a better understanding of the meaning of elections. These measures are (1) using a *reasonable person standard* when judging what is meant by the terms used by politicians and when judging the accuracy of candidates' claims; (2) defining terms used in political discourse; (3) requiring those covered "to define their terms and apply the same definitions to claims about themselves and their opponents"; (4) "hold[ing] leaders accountable to consistently applied standards"; (5) using "widely accepted indicators to assess claims"; (6) examining the underlying assumptions politicians make when predicting the effects of policies, programs, or leadership; (7) asking whether examples offered by politicians accurately describe the effects of policies; (8) fitting the story to the facts, not the facts to the story—that is, not allowing the narrative that develops during coverage of events to determine which facts are covered and which facts ignored; (9) tying "the facts to a larger context to make sense of current debates"; and (10) being "skeptical of the frames offered by those with an interest in shaping the news."[326]

The principles outlined by the CCJ and the measures suggested by Jamieson and Waldman are exactly what democratic elections require of the press: (1) an independent and reliable way for citizens to make sense of the competing messages they receive, (2) assistance sorting truth from fiction, (3) an understanding of the issues and conflicts of the day put into context with history and background, and (4) a big-picture view of how the issues affect citizens' lives. Such principles and standards for coverage are beyond the capabilities of most *citizen journalists*[327] and therefore require professionals whose job is to take the time necessary to provide journalism that meets these standards.

Were professional journalists as a broad group to adopt such principles, the public's understanding of their choices in elections would be greatly enhanced, and elections would be made healthier. Research shows that many journalists do, in fact, understand their role in terms of upholding such principles. Additionally, organizations such as the CCJ and the PEJ are doing the necessary work to support these professional values. Two main obstacles prevent journalists from fully following such norms: the drive for profit within the organizations that employ journalists, and audiences' hunger for entertainment. American audiences' ever-increasing demand for entertainment and their corresponding poor appetite for substantive journalism must change in order to create a demand for good journalism (see full discussion of this issue in chapter 8) because in a media business driven by profit, media organizations will not reward good journalism until the public shows an interest in buying it. Expanding public sources of news and reinvigorating the public-service expectations for broadcasters, as discussed previously, are a few of the other ways to ease the constraints on journalists created by the business aspect of the media industry.

The government itself could encourage change, creating a new generation of journalists committed to public service through journalism internship and fellowship programs. Such programs, which would place graduate students from journalism and political science programs in media outlets throughout the United States, might address some of the problems journalists as professionals face, while training a new cohort of journalists who are dedicated to the principles of excellent journalism. The internship program, modeled on the medical field's practice of placing interns in hospitals at the final stage of their education, could draw participants from both graduate and undergraduate programs in journalism. That is, journalism students would serve as paid interns, working for a newspaper, television, radio, or Internet news organization for one year prior to entering the field as a full-fledged journalist. Likewise, political science graduate students could serve as fellows for a year in news media outlets, enhancing their understanding of U.S. politics, international relations, or the politics of a specific region or country, while contributing to the journalism on the matter with the more substantive and broad perspectives learned in their programs. The federal government, and perhaps even some state and local governments, could sponsor the internships and fellowships, providing a living stipend for those who participate.

Through a program like this, the government could provide public support for good journalism without having to pay for or run the media organizations themselves. The resulting infusion of well-trained journalists into newsrooms around the country would address the shortage of journalists and associated problems created by business cuts in their workforces. With more journalists, news organizations could return to gathering more news and doing more investigative reporting—and cease relying so heavily on government sources and newswire services. The Committee for Concerned Journalists could be in charge of nominating interns and fellows, creating a pool from which news media organizations could choose. Acceptance of media interns by news outlets would come with conditions, ensuring that the organizations would use the interns as journalists (that they would actually write and investigate stories as opposed to performing clerical or sales duties) and that the businesses would not use the interns to replace existing journalists on staff.

CONCLUSION

The prescriptions discussed in this chapter are summarized in the following section. Elections in the United States depend heavily on the mass media to inform the electorate of their choices on the ballot and to act as referees of the campaign discourse. By almost any account, the media have failed to provide that support, thus contributing to the poor health of U.S. elections. The key reason is that the mass media in the United States are owned by private businesses whose main motivation is profit. That basic fact is unlikely to change, thus prescriptions for improving the health of U.S. elections through changes in the mass media must, as those suggested here do, work around that circumstance. The proposals offered here would probably help the system if they were implemented apart from any other changes, but the impact they might have on the health of elections would be greatly enhanced if they were adopted in conjunction with the reforms discussed in the following chapters.

Anthony Gierzynski, Ph.D.
Department of Political Science
The University of Vermont

Patient: U.S. Elections   D.O.B.: September 17, 1789

R$_x$

Enhance public broadcasting through better (and dedicated) funding and greater insulation from political pressures.

Require that broadcasters fulfill public service mandate through requiring greater coverage of conventions, providing free airtime to the political parties, and continuing their coverage of candidate debates.

Support journalists' drive to spread professional principles so that they "provide people with the information they need to be free and self-governing." As part of this effort, establish a government-supported internship and fellowship program to increase the number of professionally trained journalists in news media organizations.

Signature of the Prescriber: *Dr. Anthony Gierzynski*

CHAPTER 5

ELECTORAL STRUCTURE AND INSTITUTIONAL CHANGES

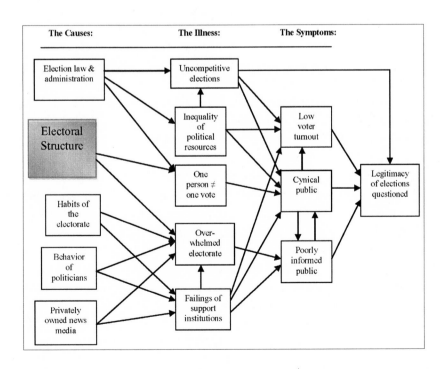

The basic setup of elections in terms of who is elected, when, and how—what I refer to as *electoral structure*—affects the functioning of elections in a number of different ways. To understand why this is so, imagine a political system in which the citizenry is asked to vote about once every four years in order to decide simply which party controls the government. Then imagine another system in which the citizenry is asked to vote two or three times *each year* and must decide which individuals are to hold multiple executive, legislative, and judicial offices, as well as what government policy ought to be on a number of different issues. More people would be likely to turn out for the elections in the first system because elections are less frequent, easier to understand, and more significant. This, then, is how the electoral structure affects the way choices are made in the system. Consider another paired example of systems: in one, each person's vote counts equally with all others and the voters directly choose the government; in the other, the weight of a person's vote depends on where a person lives and voters do not directly choose the most important public official. In this case, it seems only natural that some voters in the second system may be discouraged by their unequal treatment and by the fact that their votes do not directly elect the most important public official; here, too, the electoral structure is key. These comparisons do not represent extreme hypothetical cases contrived in order to make a point; they represent, in somewhat simple terms, real political systems—two of which (the second and fourth) reflect the structure of the U.S. electoral system.

In this chapter, I examine the effects the U.S. electoral structure has on the health of elections, and I discuss the impact of changes to that structure. Any serious consideration of the structure of U.S. elections (especially when compared with the electoral structure of other democracies) makes clear that the way the United States has set up its elections contributes to the poor health of those elections (1) by overburdening and confusing its citizens and (2) by creating political inequalities that can discourage voting. Therefore changes to the structure of choices for American citizens could have far-reaching effects on the condition of the country's electoral system in these areas.

THE BURDEN IMPOSED BY THE ELECTORAL STRUCTURE

Americans love to have choices. In general, they demand—and get—a seemingly endless variety of options, whether groceries, home-improvement supplies, shoes, clothes, electronics, or cars. To the American way of thinking, more is always better when it comes to choices. This obsession with choice extends to all aspects of U.S. culture, including elections. Following the more-choices-are-better mindset, the United States has, through the course of its history, haphazardly constructed a byzantine electoral structure (often in the name of reform) that affords U.S. citizens the opportunity to make more decisions about their governments than citizens in almost all other democracies. But having more choices actually renders the choices voters make less important.

Elections in the United States have not always featured so many choices. The framers of the U.S. Constitution did not create a system that would maximize direct popular control, nor did they intend to do so. Only one part of the government as originally established by the framers was popularly elected—the U.S. House of Representatives. Originally, the Senate was chosen by state legislatures until the early twentieth century, the president by the Electoral College, and the Supreme Court justices were (as they still are) appointed. The separation of powers and the division of governmental authority between the national and state governments were designed to moderate direct popular control of government for fear that factions, "whether amounting to a majority or minority of the whole," might promote their interests at the expense of others' or at the expense of what is good for the nation as a whole.[328]

In the time since the work of the framers was adopted, the desire for more popular control of government led to an extraordinary expansion of the avenues through which the public can have its say in government.[329] Shortly after the Constitution was adopted, states began to give voters the power to choose presidential electors. By 1828 the selection of the president had become a mass election, albeit through the mediation of the Electoral College. Likewise, states began to allow for the popular election of governors in the 1800s (legislatures chose the governors of nine of the first thirteen states), and a number of states adopted partisan elections as the means of choosing state judges. The Seventeenth Amendment (1913) established the direct popular election of U.S. Senators. The Progressive movement at the turn of the twentieth century then led to an explosion in the number of decisions to be made by American voters. Progressives successfully championed the adoption of (1) the direct primary as the means to nominate candidates for most state and Congressional offices, (2) the direct election of a number of state agency heads (such as attorney general, secretary of state, and treasurer), (3) elections on policy issues through voter referenda and initiatives, (4) nonpartisan election of state judges, and (4) recall elections.

The Progressive movement also promoted the use of nonpartisan elections, which were adopted by many city and town governments, ultimately depriving voters of the one piece of information on the ballot that could help them vote: candidates' party labels. The proliferation of special districts (or single-purpose governments)—for schools, parks, transportation, and so forth—added additional decisions to voters' responsibilities in areas where these districts are governed by elected officials. The later part of the twentieth century saw an explosion in the use of voter initiatives and referenda—fueled largely by interest group money—resulting in yet another sizeable increase in the number of decisions put before the voters. And finally, new national party rules for nominating presidential candidates were adopted after 1968, leading most state parties to replace party caucuses with presidential primary elections as their means of participating in the presidential nomination contest—not only adding another decision but sometimes also adding another election altogether because many states schedule presidential primaries separately from the primaries in which candidates for state and congressional offices are nominated.

The resulting electoral structure is unique among the world's democracies in its complexity and its demands on voters. U.S. citizens are expected to participate in at least twice as many elections as democratic citizens elsewhere because the U.S. is the only major democracy to use elections to nominate party candidates. America's relatively unique split executive-legislative system (wherein members of each branch are elected separately) and a preference for bicameralism (Congress and all state legislatures except Nebraska's have two legislative chambers) also multiplies the decisions voters must make in the United States. Finally, the U.S. federal system, with the concomitant need to make decisions about state and local governments (usually at times separate from national elections), piles on even more decisions. Adding it all up, there are about 490,000 elected local officials in the United States.[330]

The unique electoral structure that has evolved in America is dysfunctional because Americans have overreached, taking on more political decision making than they can meaningfully handle. Americans are asked to go to the polls too often, and when they do they are confronted with a myriad of decisions (see figure 2.13). The size of the task overwhelms many citizens, leaving them feeling that politics and government are too complicated to understand (see figure 2.14), so they do not bother to try (see voter turnout discussion in chapter 1). The media fail to help the public understand what the elections are about, and most of the public are either unable or unwilling to use political party affiliations as a way to simplify their decision making. These factors combine to make the cost of voting in the United States too high for too many of its citizens.[331] And whereas costs are high, the benefits of each effort at participation—each decision made on a ballot or each journey made to the polls—are low because the individual elected officials have only a fragment of the authority necessary to carry out the voters' wishes.[332] The relationship between the number of decisions voters are asked to make in elections and the costs and benefits of voting is illustrated in figure 5.1. If countries were placed on the graph in figure 5.1, the United States would be on the far right of the graph; America asks voters to go to the polls more often than all but one democracy, and according to empirical analyses the frequency of elections has a strong negative impact on voter turnout.[333] In addition to the high costs and low benefits, the complexity of the electoral structure allows voters to undermine the benefit of their participation by sending contradictory messages in the different choices that they make.

FIGURE 5.1. Relationship between the number of electoral decisions, costs and benefits of voting, and voter turnout.

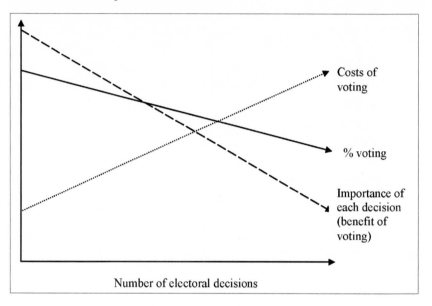

To gain a sense of the demands the electoral structure puts on American citizens, consider what is asked of residents of Milwaukee, Wisconsin, over a four-year period (see table 5.1). Counting only regularly scheduled elections from 2003 through 2006, the citizens of Milwaukee were asked to go to the polls twelve times in the four-year period and make 102 decisions (through primaries and general elections, both partisan and nonpartisan) about who should fill a number of positions from president to recorder of deeds and whether to adopt one state and three county referenda. In addition to that, depending on the district in which they live, citizens may have been asked to participate in one of five special elections (adding ten more decisions on filling government positions) and one recall election. When one considers the effort needed to gather the information necessary to make an informed choice in all of these contests as well as the time it takes to vote, it should be clear that this is

TABLE 5.1. Voting opportunities for Citizens of Milwaukee, WI.

Year	Date & Election	Decisions To Be Made
2003	February 18 Primary	Justice of the state supreme court Circuit court judges Alderperson School board
	April 1 General and special election primary	Justice of the state supreme court Court of appeals judge Circuit court judge Alderperson Nominees for state senator, district 7 Nominees for state assembly representative, district 18 School board member at-large School board district representative
	April 29 Special election	State senator, district 7 State assembly representative, district 18
	June 24 Special primary election	Nominees for state assembly representative, district 21 Alderman, district 13
	June 18 Special election	County board of supervisors, district 2
	July 22 Special election	State assembly representative, district 21 Alderman, district 13
	November 18 Recall election	State senator, district 6
2004	January 27 Special election	State assembly representative, district 17
	February 17 Spring primary and presidential primary	Presidential nominee Court of appeals judge Circuit court judge County executive County board of supervisors Mayor Alderperson
	February 17 Spring primary and presidential primary	Presidential nominee Court of appeals judge Circuit court judge County executive County board of supervisors Mayor Alderperson

(continued on next page)

TABLE 5.1. (*continued*)

Year	Date & Election	Decisions To Be Made
2004	September 14 Primary	U.S. senator U.S. representative State Senators (even-numbered districts) State assembly representatives District attorneys County clerk County treasurer Clerk of the circuit court Register
	November 2 General election	President of U.S. U.S. senator U.S. representative State senators (even-numbered districts) State assembly representatives District attorneys County clerk County treasurer Clerk of the circuit court Register of deeds
2005	February 15 Spring Primary	Superintendent of public instruction
	April 5 Spring election	Superintendent of public instruction Supreme court Court of appeals judge Circuit court judge Municipal judge School board State referendum Three county referenda
2006	February 21 Primary	Supreme court judge Court of appeals Judge Circuit court judge County executive County supervisors Municipal judges
	April 4 General election	Supreme court judge Court of appeals Judge Circuit court judges County executive County supervisors Municipal judges

(*continued on next page*)

TABLE **5.1.** (*continued*)

Year	Date & Election	Decisions To Be Made
2006	September 12 Primary	Governor Lieutenant governor Attorney general Secretary of state State treasurer U.S. senator U.S. representative State senators (odd-numbered districts) State assembly representatives District attorneys County clerk County treasurer County sheriff Clerk of the circuit court
	November 7	Governor Lieutenant governor Attorney general Secretary of state State treasurer U.S. senator U.S. representative State Senators (odd-numbered districts) State assembly representatives District attorneys County clerk County treasurer County sheriff Clerk of the circuit court

Source. City of Milwaukee Election Commission (accessed August 17, 2006, http://www.ci.mil.wi.us/display/router.asp?docid=1717).

too much to ask. Small wonder that voter turnout is so low for most of these elections.

Thus, the tendency to continually expand the ways voters have their say in government has led to considerably greater demands placed by the electoral structure on citizens in the twenty-first century than the electoral demands made of eighteenth-century Americans. While there is no question that the cause of popular democracy in the United States has been furthered by the increased role of citizens in electing certain public officials, it is also evident that at some point the electoral structure became too burdensome and too complex to be effective. Political science professor Steven Schier summed it up well, writing that

> the history of progressive and participatory reforms in [the twentieth] century has been a tragedy of inflated expectations. By demanding too much of America's citizens and electoral system, they [the progressives] have helped to create a system that does not produce clear results, has made it more difficult to hold officials accountable for their actions, and has perplexed and confused millions of well-meaning voters.[334]

Moreover, the belief that more choices and more decisions are tantamount to more democracy still dominates the American mindset today. The typical response when the political system is deemed unresponsive is to advocate reforms that offer even more choices, which would require even more of citizens: more citizen initiatives, more political parties, nonpartisan elections, ranking candidates instead of just choosing one, and so forth. As the preceding discussion makes clear, such changes are exactly what U.S. elections do *not* need.

Thus the more-choices-are-better approach to democracy has resulted in an overly democratic electoral structure that in fact discourages participation through the high cost and low benefits of voting. The situation is not unlike that faced by individuals who try to do too many things: attempting too much depletes people's energies and generates stress, making it difficult to do anything well and endangering one's ability to do anything at all. Such levels of activity also make people more susceptible to illnesses and may lead to a doctor's recommendation that the patient stop trying to do so much. The U.S. public has become involved in too many things, and few of its members are aware of the downside of this electoral overreaching or of the tradeoffs involved in taking on even more. To improve the health of elections, then, the United States should make some changes that simplify the task of voting and reduce the burden of the electoral system on the citizens.

What to Do?

U.S. elections are handicapped by an overly complex electoral structure that makes demands on voters so burdensome as to interfere with the healthy functioning of elections by overwhelming and sidelining citizens, ultimately weakening the citizens' ability to maintain some degree of popular control of their governments. What can be done about this? Providing voters with the means to navigate the system via information (see chapter 4 on the media and chapter 6 on the parties and politicians and convincing the public of the value and usefulness of an effective voting tool (the topic of chapters 6 and 8) undoubtedly would help. But can or should anything be done about the electoral structure itself? Can elections in the United States be organized in a way that would be somewhat less overwhelming to the public?

Given Americans' love of choices and given that the number of decisions voters are asked to make is in part a function of the federal nature of the U.S. governmental system with its layers of national, state, and local governments, such restructuring would seem a near-impossible task. Certainly, eliminating federalism or adopting a parliamentary system is out of the question in every sense but an imaginary one (even if such radical changes were possible, I am not convinced that they would be desirable). Short of those major changes, some things could be done to simplify elections a bit for voters in order to make elections more effective mechanisms of popular control. The first change is to stop the situation from getting any worse—that is, to end the behavior that has placed America in this mess in the first place. This means blocking any reforms to the system that ask more of the voters, whether the reforms entail choosing from among more options, making more policy decisions, or having to go to the polls more often. The second change is to remove some of the decisions that are put before the voters. This may sound radical and undemocratic, but the truth is that the multitude of decisions voters are asked to make weakens the overall electoral system. Counterintuitive as it may seem, eliminating some of these decisions would make elections more democratic by making them a more effective means of popular control of government. The third change that could improve the way elections are set up is to consolidate some elections in order to reduce their frequency, decreasing the number of times voters are asked to go to the polls.

Considering the real trade-offs and the effectiveness of some of the decisions that voters make, it makes sense to streamline the electoral structure. What, after all, is the value of asking voters to choose, for example, the state treasurer or circuit court judge? Does this value outweigh the added strain on the electoral system, the extra burden it places on the state's citizens? Do the state's citizens take advantage of the opportunity in a meaningful way that makes electing such officers better than other means of holding these public officials accountable? Simply asking these questions—simply considering on the one hand the costs for voters (and for elections as a whole) versus the benefit on the other hand of electing various officials—is a start, a start that could lead to consolidating responsibility in certain offices, ultimately reducing the total number of political officials chosen by the voters. Likewise, if elections were held less often, more voters would be more inclined to go to the polls, increasing the effectiveness of those elections.

R$_x$: Stop Taking On More Decisions

The first thing a doctor will tell a sick patient is to stop any behavior that is causing or exacerbating the illness; the same type of counseling is pertinent for U.S. elections. In this case the unhealthy practice is the tendency to believe that every problem with democratic governance in the United States can be solved by adding more choices, putting more decisions before the voters and letting the voters decide. This tendency needs to be checked. The solution to governance problems in America will not be found in asking voters to do more. Unfortunately, most reformers do not hold this view, and many proposed electoral reforms would only exacerbate this problem.

Instant runoff voting (IRV) is one such reform, advocated by various groups in the United States including FairVote, the Center for Voting and Democracy, the Green Party, and local IRV coalitions. IRV systems ask voters to rank each candidate in order of preference on the ballot instead of voting for only one. At first glance this seems appealing: the runoff aspect is supposed to eliminate the spoiler effect that can occur when voting for minor-party candidates or independents, and ranking candidates allows voters to express more with their voting than making a single choice does. But in the context of the already labyrinthine electoral system in America, it is clear that IRV would only make the problem worse. Rank-order voting systems like IRV multiply the number of decisions and the amount of information voters need—they need to know not only which choice is best for them but also which choice is second best, third best, and so on. Such systems also increase the complexity of the ballot, a factor that has been shown to pose problems for certain types of voters, particularly those with less education, the elderly, and those for whom English is a second language. Again, the history of ballot confusion in Florida during the 2000 presidential election demonstrates this problem: tens of thousands of ballots were spoiled because of confusion over complex ballots, ultimately costing Al Gore the election.[335] Recent experiments with IRV in Burlington, Vermont, and San Francisco, California, have confirmed that IRV may cause similar problems. The studies found that those with lower levels of education and those for whom English was a second language were more likely to have trouble with the IRV system.[336] Additionally, rank-order voting has the potential to result in outcomes that do not accurately reflect the preferences of the majority as claimed by IRV supporters. Rank order voting systems like IRV can also lead to what are known in the literature on voting systems as voting *paradoxes*. In only its second election using IRV in 2009, the mayoral candidate preferred by a majority of Burlington voters in one-on-one matchups with each and every one of the other candidates (as indicated by the way voters had ranked candidates on the ballot) lost the election.[337] The election also featured a *no-show paradox* (supporters of the Republican candidate would have served their own interests better by not voting) and *nonmonotonicity* (adding votes to the winning candidate's total would have led to his defeat.[338]

Other reforms that would increase the burden on voters and should thus be avoided include expanding voter initiatives to more states and the national government, making initiatives easier to place on the ballot in the states that already allow them, expanding recall elections, shifting to nonpartisan elections, and increasing the number of viable political parties to choose from.

Groups such as the Initiatives and Referendum Institute, the United States Public Interest Research Group, the National Initiative for Democracy, and various other interest groups including the Humane Society of the United States advocate the expansion of voter initiatives in states and the adoption of a national voter initiative.[339] Increasing the number of voter initiatives or creating a national initiative process means not only asking the voters to make more decisions but also asking them to do so on matters of policy that are often complex and require substantial knowledge and information, which we know voters are lacking. Additionally, experience has shown that the initiative and referendum (I&R) process has done more to empower interest groups than to enhance control of government by the people.[340] Interest groups are better able to use I&R because they have the money to do so; the process of gathering sufficient signatures to put an initiative or referendum on the ballot and then winning support from a majority of voters (or conversely, mobilizing enough voters to oppose it) requires huge sums of money, typically making the amount of money spent in the process the best predictor of the success or failure of an initiative or referendum.[341]

An expansion of the option for recall elections obviously means making more decisions more often. Perhaps the most notable example of a recall election was the California recall of Governor Gray Davis and his replacement by Arnold Schwarzenegger in 2003. The recall was set in motion when a wealthy Republican congressman (who himself wanted to be governor) provided the money necessary to collect signatures to place the recall on the ballot. After deciding whether to recall Davis, voters chose a replacement for Davis from a list of 135 names.

Under such circumstances, it is no surprise that the most recognizable name on the list was that of a popular movie actor, who won the contest. This case illustrates that recall elections not only increase the demands on voters but they also provide an avenue for moneyed interests to oust officials whose policies they dislike. Recall elections can also cause officials to shy away from taking unpopular but necessary actions. While the 2003 California recall is a well-known instance, most recall elections take place at the local level, where an interest group, business, or wealthy individual need not put up too much money to challenge a local official who threatens a particular group's or individual's interests.[342]

Nonpartisan elections deprive voters of a useful informational cue on the ballot—namely, the party label of the candidates—and have been found to reduce voter turnout.[343] As is discussed more fully in the following chapter, party affiliation can and should be used by voters as a means of assessing candidates' views on the issues; doing so is a logical way to simplify the task of voting. Increasing the number of major political parties vying for political office increases the level of knowledge required of voters and the complexity of the electoral choice. Voters need to sort out new parties' positions on issues as well as the implications of supporting each party—the need for a majority to control the government will require that parties build a governing coalition following the election (see full discussion in chapter 6).

Though each of these reforms may have some merit on its own, in the context of an already overwhelmingly complex and burdensome electoral structure, clearly any of them would do more harm than good. Changes to the electoral structure that increase the costs to voters and add to the complexity of the electoral structure would only compound the problem. Instead, the United States should be moving in the opposite direction, simplifying the way elections are set up and reducing the number of choices and decisions in order to make the connection between voting and governmental decisions clearer. Simplifying elections to strengthen the voting-policy connection reduces the burden on voters and increases the power of their choices. Therefore it would lead to more effective control of the government by *more people*, ultimately enhancing the democratic nature of U.S. elections.

R_x: Reduce the Number of Decisions

Out of context, the idea of taking decisions away from voters may seem undemocratic; when put in context of the U.S. elections, however, it becomes clear that reducing the number of voting decisions (and shifting the United States more to the left side of figure 5.1) would lead to an improvement in the overall health of U.S. elections. But which decisions should be taken out of voters' hands? This question can be answered by assessing the need for direct popular control of each elective office as well as the value of having voters decide directly on policy through initiatives and referenda. In order to make such assessments, three questions should be asked about each elected office: (1) To what extent is direct popular control of the office desirable? (2) How much direct popular control has actually been exercised over those elected to the office? (3) Could other means of holding the elected official responsible be as effective as or even more effective than the direct election of those officials? This set of questions can also be applied in a modified form to voter initiatives and referenda.

Elected Officials

When these questions are applied to all of the elected positions in the United States, it becomes clear that for a number of offices, the benefits of having the voters choose the occupants are negligible or even nonexistent; a greater benefit could accrue to the electoral system as a whole by removing those positions from the ballot. Whether it is desirable to fill governmental positions via elections depends in part on the powers and responsibilities of the office in question. In the U.S. system, primary responsibility for making, implementing, and interpreting the law is divided among the three branches of the national, state, and most local governments. Do all of these functions need to be controlled directly by the citizenry?

Given that the legislative branch has the primary responsibility for making law, it is important that the public choose those who will

e national, state, and local levels.
ives who determine the laws that
e basic mechanism for representa-
nment need two legislative bodies?
–usually a city council or commis-
forty-nine of the states, however,
ifferent bases of representation in
some justification for the existence
it creates political inequalities that
d in chapter 2). There is no paral-
the state level; state senators merely
than state representatives. Therefore
ne of their legislative chambers in
order to simplify their electoral structure for voters. Nebraska did so in
the 1930s without any apparent harm to their system of representation
(though I would not recommend Nebraska's nonpartisan selection process). The variation in the sizes of state senate and house chambers, however, produces different types of legislative bodies and different forms
of representation in the states; the states' citizens might not want to give
this up. Like the U.S. Senate, the smaller senate chambers tend to be less
centralized, with individual senators having a great deal of power, while
the larger house chambers tend to have a centralized, party-controlled
system in which party leaders and committee chairs hold most of the
power.[344] Additionally, if the state's senate districts coincide with areas
in the state whose interests may differ from the interests of the smaller
constituencies of house districts—if senate districts represented cities
or counties, for example, whereas house districts represented neighborhoods—that in itself might justify maintaining both chambers. Consequently, the bicameral legislature may or may not be the best locus for
streamlining the electoral structure.

The chief executive's modern role in legislating and the public's desire
to hold the executive responsible for administering the laws mean that
electing a chief executive makes sense.[345] But what about the administrative heads of various departments within the executive branch? At the

national level, voters in the United States choose only the chief executive (the president) and his or her second in command (the vice president); the president then appoints the top administrators for the rest of the governmental departments and agencies (with the consent of one or both of the legislative chambers, depending on the post). The president is accountable for the performance of those appointed administrators. The departure of secretary of defense Donald Rumsfeld, whom many blamed for the poor execution of the war in Iraq, a day after the 2006 election illustrates the working of such accountability.

In the states, however, voters are asked to choose not only the chief executive (governor) and his or her second in command (lieutenant governor)[346] but also the administrative heads of a number of different departments of state government, such as state attorney general, treasurer, auditor, and secretary of state. North Dakota's voters must choose twelve different executives; Georgia's, eleven; while voters in three other states elect ten. The average number of statewide executive officers chosen by voters is six.[347] This is neither effective nor necessary.[348] Does directly electing these administrators make them more responsible to public than they would be if appointed by the chief executive with consent of a legislative body, as is done at the national level? Given the low levels of voter information, this seems highly unlikely. Most voters would be challenged to describe what their state's auditor, secretary of state, or attorney general does—let alone judge the incumbent's performance in that office. Many voters do not even bother to vote for candidates for these offices, as the data on ballot falloff shows. Additionally, party labels are often irrelevant to the functioning of many of these positions, making this voter shortcut less useful in these contests (and in the process, adding to the misperception that party affiliation is meaningless).

It makes little difference whether the state's treasurer or auditor is a Democrat or a Republican, according to most who study elections and state government, apart from determining which individual has a better shot at winning future races for governor. In some cases, including that of the secretary of state (the official who administers elections), partisanship perhaps *should not* play a role. The Florida secretary of state's purge of voter registration rolls prior to the 2000 election—a purge that disproportionately disenfranchised minority voters who were likely to vote Democratic—and the actions of the Ohio secretary of state during the 2004 and 2006 elections that made it much more difficult for Democratic-leaning groups to register voters, provide two examples that highlight concerns over partisan control of the chief elections officer's position. These and other examples of partisan actions on the part of secretaries of state led the Commission on Federal Election Reform (cochaired by former president Jimmy Carter and former U.S. secretary of state James A. Baker, III) to suggest that "states should consider transferring the authority for conducting elections from the secretary of state to a chief elections officer, who would serve as a nonpartisan official…. subject to approval by a super-majority of two-thirds of one or both chambers of the state legislature."[349]

There appears to be little benefit for the democratic system in asking voters to choose the various state administrative positions, and in the case of the partisan administration of elections, there appears to be a potential cost in terms of the integrity of elections. Consequently, removing these offices from the ballot could reduce the complexity of the electoral structure, decrease the number of decisions asked of voters, and as a result ease the electoral burden placed on the public. The only purpose the election of state administration officials appears to serve is to help politicians by providing stepping stones to higher offices. Five states—Alaska, Hawaii, Maine, New Hampshire, and New Jersey—ask voters to choose only the governor or the governor–lieutenant governor team.[350] There is no reason the rest of the states cannot follow suit. Elections would be healthier if states adopted the national model, in which all administrative positions are appointed by the chief executive with the approval of the legislative body.

Finally, while the U.S. does not elect judges to its federal court system, about half of the states use elections (partisan, nonpartisan, and retention) to choose their judges.[351] Judges apply the law to individual cases, they decide whether the actions of governments violate the U.S.

or state constitutions, and they make common law. In applying the law, it is desirable to have impartial judges who can weigh the cases before them without prejudice or bias. Does the election of judges lead to impartial justice? The findings of a study of Pennsylvania criminal cases suggests that it does not: Gregory Huber and Sanford Gordon found that judges become more punitive as elections near, adding to the typical sentences handed down in nonelection years between 1,818 and 2,705 years of incarceration for the cases they examined.[352] Since judges also make law through the common-law process and through interpretation of legislative intent and constitutional provisions, should they be elected just as representatives are? If so, does the election of judges give the public more say in judicial decision making than the appointment of judges by elected executive and legislative branches? One could spend a great deal of time arguing over the merits of electing judges in theory, but the reality of judicial elections, especially in context of the electoral system as a whole, gives good cause to take judgeships off of the ballot.

Judicial elections in the thirty-nine states that hold them are plagued by low voter information, low voter turnout, or heavy ballot falloff. A study charting voter turnout for state supreme court races (the judicial races with the highest visibility) from 1980 to 1995 found that on average, more than a quarter of the voters who showed up at the polls failed to vote for a candidate in the supreme court races.[353] A survey conducted in the state of Washington found that two-thirds of voters said they did not have enough information to cast an informed vote in judicial elections.[354] The lack of knowledge and involvement in judicial elections is not surprising given the absence of media coverage of judicial elections—even newspapers basically ignore judicial elections, and when they do report on them, the papers follow the standard horse-race approach to coverage.[355] Most judicial elections are uncontested or lacking in serious competition.[356] Many judges are initially appointed by governors because judges often resign mid-term in order to give their party's governor a chance to appoint someone, who then becomes the incumbent with minimal opposition in the next scheduled election.[357] On the flip side, judicial contests that are heavily contested require increasingly high levels of campaign contributions. That money comes mainly from parties (in the legal sense of the word) that have cases before the court and from lawyers and big businesses whose interests are affected by the judges' decisions, a fact that raises concerns of political corruption.[358] It is a concern that was recognized by the U.S. Supreme Court in *Caperton v. Massey* (556 U.S. _____, 2009). The Court's decision invalidated a ruling by the West Virginia Supreme Court because Judge Brent Benjamin had not recused himself from the case despite the fact that one of the parties to the case had spent $3 million to help Benjamin get elected to the court three years earlier (the amount was 300 percent of Benjamin's own campaign spending).[359] Justice Kennedy, writing for the majority, stated:

> We conclude that there is a serious risk of actual bias—based on objective and reasonable perceptions—when a person with a personal stake in a particular case had a significant and disproportionate influence in placing the judge on the case by raising funds or directing the judge's election campaign when the case was pending or imminent.[360]

And the outcome of judicial contests *is* affected by campaign spending as well as by partisan trends stemming from races at the top of the ballot.[361] All told, little popular control of judges is exercised through elections, and there is no evidence to suggest that other forms of selecting judges—appointment or merit selection—produce judges that are any less accountable to the public.

It would seem, then, that the electoral system as a whole could benefit from the elimination of judicial elections (and of judicial retention elections[362]) while losing naught but the illusion of electoral control of state judiciaries. Removing judicial candidates would shorten the ballot and reduce the burden placed on voters in about half of the states. Only two other countries, Switzerland and Japan, hold judicial elections, and they do so in a much more limited fashion. All other countries eschew judicial elections because, as former justice Sandra Day O'Conner put it, "they realize you're not going to get fair and impartial judges that way."[363]

Finally, a great deal of paring down could take place at the local level, where voter participation is at its lowest. If local government charters narrowed the voters' role to choosing the legislators and chief executives (e.g., city councils and mayors, county commissions, school boards) and eliminated the plethora of special districts, the ballot could be greatly simplified. It is questionable whether many voters would protest if they no longer elected local sheriffs, assessors, coroners, justices of the peace, assistant judges, police chiefs, registers of deeds, county clerks, county treasurers, public utility commissioners, members of the board of directors for the airport authority, municipal judges, and clerks of the superior court.[364] Given the data about elections and the low level of voter turnout and knowledge about candidates in these positions, the value of voting for such officials is next to nothing.

All things considered, the ballots voters are handed on Election Day could be greatly simplified without losing much. Limiting the decisions voters are asked to make to choosing legislators and chief executives of each government and making those officials responsible for appointing all of the rest—as is the case for the national government—would greatly reduce the burden placed on voters and ultimately improve the health of elections.

Ballot Measures

One of the biggest contributors to the burden of voting in many states is the initiative and referendum (I&R) process, which asks voters to decide on policy matters and amendments to state constitutions and local government charters. These ballot measures have asked voters a myriad of questions in recent years, including whether to ban same-sex marriage, increase the minimum wage, allow for doctor-assisted suicide, provide state funding of stem-cell research, limit the terms of elected officials, establish a state lottery, set a three-strikes policy for crimes, limit state budgets, eliminate affirmative action, cap property taxes, ban the practice of baiting bears, establish the rights of property owners under eminent domain laws, allow for the medical use of marijuana, institute campaign finance reforms, and so on.[365] Twenty-four states allow citizens to put such policy questions on the ballot via the initiative process, and twenty-four states (many of which also allow initiatives) have provisions for popular referenda, which give voters an opportunity to repeal acts of the legislature. Most states are required by their constitutions to put constitutional changes on the ballot.[366] The number of initiatives placed on state ballots exploded in the 1990s: there were 458 initiatives between 1990 and 2000, more than three times as many as in the 1940s, 1950s, or 1960s, with the increase in the use of the initiative concentrated in six states.[367] As political scientist Richard Ellis put it, initiatives, once seen as a "gun behind the door" to keep state government honest, have become a gun that

> is madly brandished about and fired in almost every conceivable direction. Politicians scatter, running for cover, desperately trying to keep their heads down. Citizens appear bewildered, unsure of what to think. The gunmen cry "power to the people," but few of the people seem to feel more empowered by the blaze of gunfire.[368]

Initiatives and referenda were originally adopted about one hundred years ago, at a time that many state legislatures were corrupt and controlled by special interest groups. Initiatives and referenda were designed to provide an avenue for the public to address issues the interest group–captured legislatures refused to consider. Theoretically, I&R appears to be the model of popular democracy—citizens place issues on the ballot and those issues are then determined by a majority vote. But does the process live up to that ideal? Is it a tool of popular democracy? Do ballot measures still serve their original purpose today? Can their existence be justified? Overall, does asking voters to make these decisions enhance democracy enough to justify the added strain it puts on the electoral system? The three questions used in the previous section can be modified in order to examine whether initiatives and referenda ought to remain a part of U.S. elections: (1) To what extent is it desirable to have the public directly choose government policy? (2) How much direct popular control has actually been exercised in initiative and referenda elections?

(3) Are other means of setting government policies more representative than initiative and referenda elections?

The first and third questions can be addressed together. *Is it desirable to have the public directly choose government policy via I&R? Are other means of setting governmental policies more representative than initiative and referenda elections?* No and yes are the short answers to the two questions, respectively. First, the I&R process is inferior to the decision-making process of deliberative legislative bodies. Consider legislators versus citizens as decision makers. Legislators acquire more information than the public does in their decision-making process; legislatures have committees that develop specialized knowledge in policy—they study the issue, take testimony from the public, and have professional staff to provide research on the subject. Legislators can draw from the expertise of the committees and from the cumulative knowledge of the entire legislature. And legislators, unlike voters, are potentially held responsible for their decisions in the next election. The act of legislating on all governmental decisions forces legislators to see the connections among all of the decisions that they make, whereas voters make decisions in isolation from other decisions, which can lead to contradictory policy—for instance, limiting taxes while increasing services. Finally, legislators are forced to bargain and compromise, resulting in laws that may take more interests into consideration than the simple yes-or-no votes of ballot measures.[369]

This all seems reason enough to leave policy decisions in the hands of elected legislative bodies. The response from supporters of the I&R process would probably match the original justification for I&R—namely, legislatures are corrupt and cannot always be trusted to enact policies in the best interests of the public. But although plenty of examples of corruption pop up in the news, modern legislatures overall appear to be doing a fair job of representing state public interests.[370] Furthermore, there is no evidence to show that the public in initiative states is any better represented than the public in noninitiative states.[371] Additionally, the U.S. system would be better served by addressing the existing shortcomings of legislatures (some of which are related to elections and addressed throughout this book) than by abandoning them for direct democracy under I&R.

How much direct popular control has actually been exercised in initiative and referenda elections? Not much. Not only are I&R less desirable when compared to the legislative process, but research on I&R has cast serious doubt on the extent to which the processes afford the public popular control over governmental policy.[372] The process is expensive, requiring substantial amounts of money to obtain the number of signatures required to put questions on the ballot and then to educate the public about the effects of voting for or against the proposition (this is especially true in the states where the process is most used). As a consequence, successful ballot measures need to be supported by organizations and well-financed groups or individuals. In other words, it is a process that seems designed not for ordinary citizens, but for the wealthy and for interest groups with money.[373] As Richard Ellis showed, I&R is the realm of interest groups, politicians, initiative activists, and the very rich. While average citizens do endeavor to put questions on the ballot, "the best place to find amateur citizen initiatives is not on the ballot, but in the large number of initiatives that get filed but never make it to the ballot."[374] Research into the extent of voter knowledge when it comes to ballot measures suggests that at best, some voters are adequately informed of their choices.[375]

Voters clearly have less information than legislators, a circumstance that makes voters especially susceptible to manipulation through issue framing and priming effects, bringing into question the extent to which ballot measures really reflect popular will. Not surprisingly, then, research has shown that ballot measures appear to exert no positive impact on the overall responsiveness of state officials (though they have had an impact on three specific policy matters—abortion, the death penalty, and governance reform—which, as one set of researchers put it, may merely be the exceptions to the rule).[376] Additionally, I&R may be used to manipulate the outcome of other elections by using emotional issues to stimulate turnout among certain segments of the population and by priming issues that then affect the choices voters make among candidates for political offices. This was the case in 2004, when eleven states asked voters whether same-sex marriage should be banned. The ballot measures stimulated turnout among the Christian right and likely enhanced the importance of culture-war social issues in the decision-making processes of many voters.[377]

Overall, the I&R process has little to offer that might justify the costs it imposes on the democratic electoral system in the United States. While U.S. elections with their lengthy ballots are perhaps appealing to those who wish to feel in control, the initiative and referendum processes represent the worst of the system's controlling tendencies—the public does not trust their elected representatives to do what they have been elected to do, so the people must do it themselves. In a democracy, as with anything else, the desire to control everything ultimately leads to control of nothing. The U.S. system offers representative deliberative bodies whose process is superior to that of I&R; focusing the public's attention on those legislatures would do much more to ensure governments act in the public interest than even an improved I&R process. Thus, in the interest of simplifying the ballot, reducing the electoral costs to voters, and focusing voters' efforts to make them more effective, the I&R process should be eliminated.

R_x: Reduce the Frequency of Elections

In addition to shortening the ballot (or at the very least preventing it from getting any longer), the burden on voters could be eased by reducing the number of times they are asked to vote. The need to return to the polls for different elections exhausts voters and reduces the number of citizens who participate in state and local elections (voter turnout is highest in national elections, lowest in local elections; see chapter 1). The high frequency of elections in the United States is largely a function of the desire to insulate local and state elections from national partisan trends and of the systems used to nominate candidates.

State and Local Elections

While the scheduling of some state elections in odd-numbered years contributes to the frequency of elections, it is the irregular scheduling of local elections that accounts for the need for yearly trips to the polls in most places. Kentucky, Louisiana, Mississippi, New Jersey, and Virginia hold their gubernatorial and other statewide elections during odd-numbered years. Louisiana, Mississippi, New Jersey, and Virginia hold their state legislative contests in odd-numbered years; the rest of the states hold their statewide and legislative elections at the same time as presidential and congressional elections. Most U.S. cities' elections (about 60 percent) occur at times that are separate from presidential and gubernatorial contests.[378] In 2007, some 573 cities with populations of 30,000 or more held elections for mayor; of those, 373 cities held mayoral contests in 2005.[379] And even when held in even-numbered years, many local elections are not scheduled in November (the general election month for presidential and congressional elections).

The rationale for scheduling local elections at different times from national or state elections is to insulate local elections from national trends and to allow voters to prevent local issues from being crowded out by national or state issues.[380] This makes sense given the current unhealthy state of affairs, characterized by long ballots and the mad cacophonies of election messages generated by candidates, parties, and interest groups. Research has shown that national trends can affect contests down to the state legislative level, though this is perhaps less true now than in the past.[381] When the Republicans won control of the U.S. House and Senate in 1994, they also won control of twenty state legislative chambers, with a net gain of 472 state legislative seats. In 2006, the Democrats' victory at the national level was mirrored at the state level, where they won control of twenty-four chambers, with a net gain of 339 state house and senate seats nationwide.[382]

Separating local elections insulates them to some degree from national trends and potentially allows for focus on local issues, but it does so at the cost of involvement on the part of citizens. One study of turnout in fifty-seven U.S. cities found that voter turnout averaged twenty-nine percentage points lower when city elections were held separately.[383] Such low levels of voter turnout mean that local decisions hinge on the opinion of a small portion of the local electorate—between one-fifth to one-third of the local area's population. The need to schedule local elections at odd times to separate them from state and national electoral influences could be mitigated, however, if the changes suggested in this book are adopted. If elections were held once every two years and focused solely on electing chief executives and legislators at the national, state, and local levels, the noise level of elections (that stems from the plethora of competing campaign messages) might diminish, allowing for a focus on both state and local issues (or national and local issues) when their elections were held at the same time. Furthermore, scheduling elections only once every two years would also increase the proportion of the citizenry making local, state, and national decisions by reducing the overall demands on U.S. voters and thus encouraging greater participation.

Primaries

The frequency of elections could be cut in half if the U.S. eliminated the primary elections that are used to choose party nominees for general elections. Primary elections, after all, have been found to result in lower turnout in general elections in the American states.[384] Or, short of that change, the number of times voters are asked to go to the polls could be reduced by scheduling primaries for both presidential candidates and candidates for other offices at the same time.

Most other democracies and some localities in the United States allow the political parties to choose their nominees, with no apparent negative effects. Indeed, political parties have a strong incentive to put forward the best candidates possible in order to win the general election. Furthermore, the question arises whether the small numbers of voters who participate in primary elections do a better job than the political party would if they chose nominees in party caucuses or conventions. Only a fraction of the population bothers to vote in primaries. In 2002, for example, the average turnout in primaries for congressional and statewide officeholders was 9.1 percent for Democratic contests, and 7.7 percent for Republican contests.[385] Primaries for most public offices other than the presidency are rarely contested, meaning that the nomination is won by the candidate who goes to the trouble of acquiring the requisite number of signatures on his or her petition.[386] When primaries are contested, they are usually won by the candidate who spends the most money.[387] The importance of spending money is increased by the fact that primaries garner little in the way of media attention and by the fact that primary ballots lack the voting cue that assists voters in choosing among candidates in general elections—party labels.

As the U.S. experience with primaries seems to show, little harm would come to the system by eliminating the direct primary for most offices in the country. Nominees would not have to be selected in "smoke-filled back rooms" by party bosses, however, a practice that contributed to the adoption of the direct primary as part of the Progressive movement one hundred years ago. Instead, local party caucuses, open to all would-be primary voters (registered party members and independents, say), could select nominees for the state legislature, mayor, and city council, as well as delegates to state conventions—state conventions in turn could select parties' nominees for governor, members of Congress, and delegates to the parties' national conventions. Such a system would allow the parties to maintain a certain amount of ideological consistency; voters would know what they are getting when they vote for members of the party, reinforcing the value of the party label on the ballot. This would make it more difficult for individuals whose values differ dramatically from a party's to capture the nomination, as can happen in low-turnout primaries. Such was the case when followers of the authoritarian and perennial presidential candidate Lyndon LaRouche won the Democratic nomination for lieutenant governor and a few other statewide posts in Illinois in 1986. The results of that primary forced Democratic gubernatorial nominee Adlai Stevenson III to abandon the Democratic ticket so as to avoid running as a team with the LaRouche candidate. Party caucuses and conventions are certainly open to being captured by activists who represent certain extreme ideological divisions—as was the case when conservative religious activists took over the Republican parties in a number of states in the 1980s and 1990s. But these takeovers are usually by groups within a party's existing ideology. Additionally, takeovers cost the party votes in general elections, weakening the faction and returning the party to its more mainstream ideological position for the next round of elections.

Short of totally eliminating direct primaries, primaries could be rescheduled so as to eliminate at least one primary election every four years. This could be accomplished by scheduling presidential primaries on the same date as the primaries for congressional and state officeholders. This change would require a reordering of the presidential primary schedule, which at the moment is a haphazard, front-loaded schedule; each round, more states attempt to leapfrog in front of the rest in order to play an important role in presidential nominations. Reordering is necessary to create greater political equality in the nomination contests; this idea is discussed at greater length in what follows.

Summary: Reducing the Costs for Voters

Restructuring U.S. elections in order to make them less onerous for voters would greatly improve the overall health of America's elections. The worth of placing such a large number of decisions in the electoral arena is questionable. My suggestions will no doubt raise objections from some readers, who will decry them as undemocratic. But which is more democratic: an electoral system so weighted with demands that it effectively disenfranchises a large segment of the public and waters down the meaning of each decision voters make—or an electoral system in which more voters participate because the decisions are focused on a few key public offices in which more responsibility resides?

STRUCTURED ELECTORAL INEQUALITY

There are a number of causes of political inequality (that is, of the violation of the principle of one person, one vote) in the American electoral system. Some causes arise from weak laws governing the role of money in elections, some from the redistricting process, some from the unequal administration of voting laws, and some from the way elections are structured in the United States. This section addresses the structural causes of political inequality; later chapters deal with the other sources. The three structural causes of political inequality in America are the U.S. Senate, the Electoral College, and the presidential nomination process.

The U.S. Senate

As demonstrated in chapter 2, the U.S. Senate—in which every state, regardless of population size, has two senators—grants citizens of small states greater power than citizens of larger states in terms of the legislative process at the national level. Vermont's 624,000 people have the same number of votes in the U.S. Senate as do the 19.3 million people living just across Lake Champlain in New York. If the smaller states tend to have different policy preferences than the larger ones (which they often do), this imbalance can lead to policy outcomes that conflict with the preferences of the U.S. public as a whole.[388] Between 2000 and 2004 the Democrats "won two-and-a-half million *more* votes than the Republicans," yet by 2004 Democrats held "only 44 seats in that 100-person chamber because Republicans dominate the less populous states that are so heavily over-represented in the Senate."[389] When the Democrats finally won a majority (in both the electorate and in the chamber) in 2006, their ability to implement the policy changes they had campaigned on was thwarted by another aspect of the Senate that exacerbates the state-based representation inequality: the filibuster. A supermajority is needed in order to pass almost any major legislation in the Senate in the current era of highly polarized partisanship; this circumstance simply lends the minority greater influence than the majority when it comes to passing legislation—distorting political inequality even more.

The skewed state-based representation in the United States is a result of the great constitutional compromise that made the union of large and small states possible under the Constitution in 1787. One could easily question whether this form of state-based representation is justifiable today; a sound argument could be made that state boundaries do not necessarily enclose populations with common interests and that residents of certain types of communities have common interests regardless of their state of residence; urban residents, for example, have much more in common with city dwellers in other states than they do with the rural residents of their own states, and vice versa.[390]

I believe that it may be in the best interests of U.S. democracy to eliminate the body altogether because the U.S. Senate engenders unequal representation and because the need for equal representation of states qua states is questionable. But I hesitate to recommend such aggressive treatment as part of my prescription, primarily because it *is* an extremely aggressive approach—much more so than any other prescription offered in this book. The magnitude of constitutional and political change required to dissolve the Senate is substantial; it would mean not only changing constitutional provisions but also reallocating Senate respon-sibilities such as the senators' role in court appointments, treaties, and so forth. Such extensive changes would likely be accompanied by unin-tended consequences, carrying a risk that strikes me as far too large. It is, simply, a case in which the potential benefits are greatly outweighed by the potential risks. I should note, too, the value in the Senate's tendency to slow down the lawmaking process, an effect that the framers of the Constitution intended. While the Senate may be an undemocratic institu-tion from a majoritarian perspective, it does allow a larger set of inter-ests (including those in the minority) to be part of the decision-making process. Although the role of that minority has become dysfunctional of late the solution may be best sought in internal changes to the institution (particularly with regard to the filibuster) and in the way political debate is framed, as opposed to an elimination of the institution. And finally, though the state-based representation in the Senate does contribute to the political inequality and complexity of the system, the other sources of political inequality (both structural and legal) are more important. Ulti-mately, the elimination of the U.S. Senate is not part of my prescriptions to restore U.S. elections to health.

Adopt the Bonus Plan for the Electoral College

The Electoral College (EC) system for electing U.S. presidents, in which each state's presidential electors casts votes for the winner of the popular vote in that state, creates political inequality in at least four different ways. (1) It gives citizens of small states a disproportionate say in selecting the president because each state is granted two of its electors regardless of the size of the population (one for each senator). (2) It allows for the possibility that a candidate could win the most votes from the public and yet lose the election, as was the case in 2000 and could have been the case in 2004 had John Kerry won Ohio. (3) The Electoral College also leads to a campaign strategy whereby candidates make their appeals to and address the concerns of a small number of critical swing states, or battleground states, while essentially ignoring the rest of the country. (4) Finally, it leads people who live in a state where only one candidate has a chance of winning to question the value of their votes.

A number of different reforms have been promoted to deal with the inequities engendered by the Electoral College. Some have proposed abolishing the EC outright and replacing it with a direct popular vote, a move that would require a constitutional amendment. Others have proposed that EC votes be cast based on the votes of congressional districts (two states, Maine and Nebraska, already award some of their electoral votes this way) or in proportion to candidates' votes in the state—simply, a candidate who wins 50 percent of the vote from a state would get roughly 50 percent of the state's electoral votes.

One of the more interesting proposals is for the states to enact legislation declaring that they will award their electoral votes to the candidate who wins the nationwide popular vote, if other states representing a majority of the Electoral College commit to do the same. This solution, promoted by the reform group National Popular Vote, is both an innovative and a feasible solution to the problem of the EC.[391] Furthermore, it can be accomplished without amending the Constitution, which, after all, allows the states to appoint electors "in such Manner as the Legislature thereof may direct." All that is required is that states with a total of 270 electoral votes among them commit to choose their presidential electors who pledge to cast their vote for the winner of the popular vote nationwide. The legislation has already been adopted by Maryland and has been passed by a number of legislative chambers around the country.

There are problems with this proposal, however. It would, like any other plan for direct election of the president, reduce the likelihood that winning candidates would have the support of the majority of voters, and it would weaken the U.S. party system.

The EC system encourages people to back one of the top two choices for president, thereby increasing the probability that their choice will have the support of the majority vote of the EC. Indeed, the U.S. political party system developed in response to the EC. Direct election of the president would eliminate this incentive to build a majority around one candidate, weakening the political parties (a bad thing) and encouraging many contenders to enter the race. The EC's elimination would weaken political parties because it would obviate the need for them (and for their unique talent of building majorities) when it comes to winning the presidency. A candidate could become a serious contender with some celebrity status, a great deal of money, and perhaps an inflammatory single-issue cause. Without the EC, such candidates would not need the political parties' network of organizations across many states in order to win. They could run a successful campaign by buying the media access (TV ads, Internet, direct mail, etc.) needed to reach the voters. Party affiliation would become largely irrelevant in presidential contests held in this manner, making it more difficult for voters to choose (by taking away an important voting cue and adding complexity to the ballot), and consequently making it more difficult for voters to give direction to policy makers via elections.

Having many serious contenders for the presidency would also make winning a majority of the popular vote difficult, depriving the winner of majority support and increasing the possibility of an elected president who is opposed by the majority of voters. As historian Arthur Schlesinger, Jr., put it, direct election of the president

> would provide a potent incentive to single-issue zealots, freelance media adventurers and eccentric billionaires to jump into presidential contests. Accumulating votes from state to state—impossible under the electoral college system—splinter parties would have a new salience in the political process. We can expect an

outpouring of such parties—green parties, senior citizen parties, anti-immigration parties, right-to-life parties, pro-choice parties, anti-gun-control parties, homosexual rights parties, prohibition parties and so on down the single-issue line. The encouragement of multiple parties would be a further blow to a party structure already enfeebled by passage into the electronic age.[392]

As demonstrated in chapter 6, the last thing the U.S. electoral system needs is a weakening of the political party system. Parties in America's two-party model play a vital role in elections by structuring and simplifying the choices for voters and aggregating public preferences into governing majorities; without political parties, elections are meaningless. Tacking on an instant runoff system or holding runoff elections for president under a direct election system, as some have suggested, does not address this effect of a direct popular vote, and as already discussed, such voting systems introduce their own problems by complicating the task for voters.

As these critiques of reform proposals suggest, there are benefits to the EC. The question, then, is how to keep those benefits while eliminating the inequalities engendered by the EC. The Twentieth Century Fund[393] Task Force on Reform of the Presidential Election Process came up with a plan that would do just that, called the *bonus plan*.[394] This proposal suggests that the winner of the popular vote be awarded a bonus of 102 additional electoral votes (two for each state and the District of Columbia to counterbalance the two electoral votes awarded each state regardless of population). The plan practically guarantees that the winner of the popular vote will win the election, and the plan also maintains the benefits of the Electoral College system—namely, providing a role for the states in the process, particularly the smaller states. Under this system, candidates would still have to plan to win the requisite number of states, but they would also have an incentive to maximize their votes in every state—even those states they have no hope of winning (or losing, for that matter). The plan would "stimulate turnout, reinvigorate state parties, enhance voter equality and contribute to the vitality of federalism."[395]

Adopt the Patterson Proposal
for the Presidential Nomination Contest

The current process for nominating Democratic and Republican candidates for the presidency needs reordering not only to make it less complicated and fairer to all voters but also to make it more rational (for a general description of how each party selects its presidential nominees, see box 5.1). The process starts far too early, gives too much weight to a few early and unrepresentative states, and is chronologically too compressed. For the 2008 elections, the process started on January 3 with the Iowa caucuses; two days later Wyoming held its Republican caucuses, and three days after that New Hampshire held its primary.[396] A few other states held their primaries or caucuses in the ensuing weeks (Florida and Michigan did so against party rules). Then, less than a month after Iowa, twenty-five states and territories, constituting the bulk of delegates at stake, held their primaries or caucuses for one or both of the parties.

Box 5.1. Presidential Nomination Process

The best way to describe the manner in which the Democratic and Republican Parties choose their presidential nominees is to start at the end of the process and work backwards. Officially, the nominees are chosen by a majority vote of the delegates at each party's respective national convention, both of which meet once every four years. How does a candidate get the delegates at the convention to vote for him or her? Most delegates arrive at the convention pledged to support one of the candidates. Typically, one candidate has a majority of delegates pledged to his or her candidacy prior to the start of the convention. Candidates win the pledged delegates through the primaries and caucuses in the states and territories of the United States. Each primary election in each state determines the proportion of delegates from that state that will support each candidate in the race (though some states in the Republican contest, like California, do allocate their delegates on a winner-take-all basis). The state party conventions choose the specific people who are pledged to each candidate and will represent their state at the national convention. In caucus states, the whole process focuses on selecting delegates based on whom the delegates pledge to vote for at the national convention. Caucuses are local party meetings in which attendees discuss the candidates and select delegates to attend the next level of party meetings; delegates at those meetings, in turn, select pledged delegates to represent them at the next level, where pledged delegates are selected to represent voters at the state convention, where pledged delegates are finally selected for the national convention.

In each of the past several presidential election years, the nominating contests have been structured in such a way as to place them progressively earlier in the year and to compress the contests in the early days of the process. In 1984 the process started with Iowa caucuses on February 20, and it was not until May that three-fourths of the delegates were selected—a late date by recent standards. Usually by that point one candidate has enough delegates pledged that the nomination contest is effectively over. In 2004, for example, the process started on January 19, and three-fourths of the delegates had been selected by March 16.[397] And 2008 started even earlier and was even more heavily frontloaded. The Republican nomination in 2008 was settled by mid-February, the time when the 1984 process was just starting. In an unusual turn, the 2008 Democratic contest continued through the last primary in early June (though it was clear by early May that Hillary Clinton would not be able to overcome Barack Obama's lead in pledged delegates; nonetheless, Clinton remained in the contest until the end). The reason the contests have started earlier and have become more frontloaded is that in each successive presidential round, state after state decides it wants to be a critical part of the process and vies for attention from the presidential candidates and the press. In 2008 Michigan and Florida, for example, risked losing their seats at the party conventions in order to be among the early states.

The structure of the nominating process—the frontloading of contests, the importance of early contests, and the timing of it all—adds to the poor health of elections by increasing the demands on voters and by creating inequalities among voters and candidates, as well as between those who give large sums of money to candidates and those who do not. Additionally, it is not in the best interests of the political parties to schedule their nominations in this manner because it puts an emphasis on name recognition and fundraising acumen over other qualities that might enhance the parties' chances of winning in November. Moreover, the process, which is typically over shortly after it starts, does not provide a sufficient testing period for the potential nominee.[398]

The current nominating process is just one more aspect of the structure of U.S. elections that increases voters' burden by asking them to go to the polls on yet another occasion: most states move the date of only the presidential event and leave the congressional and state primaries at their original times later in the year, thus creating two primary dates in presidential election years. The current nomination process also adds to the costs of voting because it is so early in the year—research has shown that many voters actually have to relearn what they knew about the candidates when the general election rolls around in November.[399]

The presidential nominating process also creates inequality among voters. Candidates expend tremendous effort to win the hearts and minds of potential voters and caucus-goers in states with early contests—particularly Iowa, New Hampshire, and South Carolina. They make every effort to personally meet voters in these states and address their concerns. Those who live in states that hold their contests later in the process, after it is clear who will win the nomination, find that they and their concerns are, for all intents and purposes, ignored. Not only are they ignored, but in all except a few contests, their votes do not really count—that is, voters in those later states have no real influence on the choice of nominees. It is no surprise, then, that the citizens of states that come later in the process have less interest in the campaign and that very few of them turn out to vote in their primaries.[400] If there was some randomness to the process, if the states that went first were not always the same ones, then this lack of voice for voters in certain states would be less troubling. But the process as it stands grants the power to determine the nominees to the voters in the same states each time, unless and until some states choose to move their contests forward. Even then, they cannot legally vote before Iowa and New Hampshire, and the frontloading of all the other states makes such moves unlikely to benefit a state's voters, as Florida and Michigan found in 2008.[401]

Finally, the current manner of selecting nominees makes money a critical component to winning the nomination. Once they begin, the contests occur at a rate so fast and furious that candidates who have not raised large sums of money before the first contest have little to no chance of winning the nomination even if they do well in the early contests. Furthermore, the importance of having a large amount of money engenders political inequality by lending greater importance to those who can provide the needed funds. Despite the successes of recent campaigns in raising smaller contributions through the Internet, those who provide the most money for nominees are from the wealthier segments of society.[402] The amounts raised early for the 2008 campaign provide a sense of how much is needed, what it means, and where it comes from. Halfway through the year *before* the presidential nomination contests began, two Democratic candidates—Hillary Clinton and Barack Obama—had each raised over $50 million, twice the amount raised by their closest competitor.[403] On the Republican side, the top three candidates—Mitt Romney, Rudy Giuliani, and John McCain—had not at that point raised as much as the top two Democrats, but they had raised at least eight times as much as the next closest competitor. As of July 2007, the total of all candidates' fundraising was over $276 million, almost three times what had been raised at the same point in 2003. Seventy-three percent of the money raised at that early point in 2007 was in amounts of $1,000 or more.[404]

The problems associated with the structuring of the presidential nominating process have not escaped the attention of election scholars and observers, and many have suggested a variety of reforms to the process. Proposals include those that would create a national primary date, regional or other block primaries, or modifications to the existing system. A national primary represents the worst of the current system without any of its benefits. The role of one-on-one, retail-style, meet-the-voter politics—critical to winning small, single-state contests like Iowa and New Hampshire—would be eliminated and something good about the nomination contests would be lost. Money and name recognition would be of paramount importance. For example, given her name recognition and standing in national polls at the beginning of the nominating contest, Hillary Clinton would have won the Democratic nomination in 2008 if it had been determined by a national primary. Crowded fields of candidates would make the task of gathering information and making a decision more burdensome for more voters (the early contests usually winnow the field to a more manageable set of truly viable candidates). And the winners in the usual multicandidate contests would likely win the national primary without the support of a majority of primary voters—unless they were chosen through a runoff system, which, again, has problems of its own.

Some have proposed that the process be structured so that blocks of states vote together over several different primary dates. The National Association of Secretaries of State (NASS), for example, recommended that the country be divided up into four regions, which would hold primaries a month apart after the Iowa caucuses and the New Hampshire primary.[405] The order in which the regions would hold their primaries would be selected by lottery and then rotated. The Republican Brock Commission Plan would group the states by population and set up a series of dates on which each block of states would vote, starting with the group with the smallest populations and ending with the states with the largest populations. Both of these plans have advantages over a national primary and over the current system, though they would introduce a separate set of biases—the NASS plan would advantage a candidate from the region that went first and the Brock plan would give voters in small states a much greater role than voters in the largest states because the winner would undoubtedly emerge before the later contests took place. Media and money would still be of great importance during these block primaries.

As with the Electoral College, reform to the nominating system needs to maintain the positive aspects of the existing system while eliminating its inequities. The solution that does this the best is the one offered by political scientist Thomas E. Patterson in his book *The Vanishing Voter*. Patterson proposes that the parties hold five separate state primaries or caucuses over a period of eight weeks starting in mid-April, and that they then hold what he termed *ultimate Tuesday* a month later in the other forty-five states. The parties could allow Iowa and New Hampshire to take the first two contests (if the parties wished) and then randomly select and rotate states for the third through fifth contests, preferably in a way that would provide some regional balance. This would be fairer and less burdensome than the current system. The voters in the first five states (which would change from election to election) would narrow the field, while the voters in the forty-five remaining states would likely determine the nominee from the two or three remaining candidates. Voters in all states would play an important role. The small-scale, retail politics could be practiced in the first five states and would thus continue to be a part of the process. Candidates who cannot raise a great deal of money ahead of the contests or who do not have the benefit of national name recognition would have a chance to compete in the five opening states, and success in those contests would allow them to draw the needed attention and money to their campaign for the ultimate Tuesday contest. The contests would end about one month before the nominating conventions are held, allowing the process to build interest among voters that would culminate with the conventions and flow into the general election; voters would not be faced with the need to reacquaint themselves with the candidates in November.

CONCLUSION

The basic structure of elections, in terms of who is elected, when, and by what means plays an important role in the way elections operate. Poorly structured elections make it difficult for citizens to use elections as a means of popular control of government and give some citizens a more important role than others. Thus any attempt at restoring U.S. elections to health must address the problems generated by the way elections are structured.

Anthony Gierzynski, Ph.D.
Department of Political Science
The University of Vermont

Patient: U.S. Elections   D.O.B.: September 17, 1789

R$_X$

Stop complicating elections by asking voters to make more decisions with more choices.

Reduce the number of decisions asked of voters.

Hold elections less frequently.

Adopt the bonus plan for the Electoral College.

Restructure the presidential nomination process and start the process later.

Signature of the Prescriber: *Dr. Anthony Gierzynski*

CHAPTER 6

POLITICAL PARTIES
AND POLITICIANS

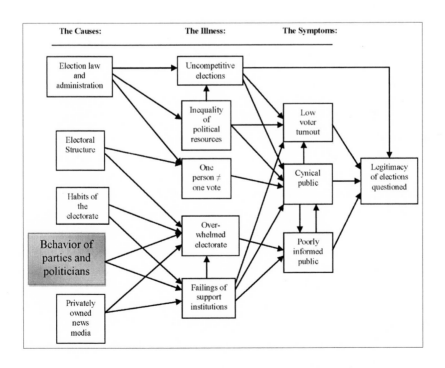

Political parties are a critical element of healthy elections; the failure of America's political system to make good use of political parties is a major contributing factor to the poor health of the country's elections. The Democratic and Republican Parties and their allies perform some tasks one would expect of political parties: they raise a lot of money; they recruit, train, and financially support their candidates; they provide a variety of services to their candidates; and they mobilize their voters on Election Day. But for a number of reasons—the nature of U.S. election campaigns, candidates' and party officials' rhetoric, the role of the mass media, and the low levels of knowledge and negative attitudes among the public with respect to the political parties—political parties are not effectively utilized to structure the choices in elections around ideological differences.[406] Were electoral decisions framed in terms of a choice between the competing ideologies of the parties the task of voting would be made simpler and elections would become a more effective means for citizens to control the policy direction of their governments.

The potential for the parties in the United States to be used in this manner exists; the policy and ideological differences between the Democrats and Republicans have rarely been more distinct than they are now, in the early twenty-first century. Citizens who are aware of the differences between the two parties are more likely to vote, follow politics, recall news stories about the campaigns, and talk about or give significant thought to the election (see figure 6.1).[407] But too many other citizens fail to recognize the differences and as a consequence see little reason for voting; if they do vote, they often base their votes on criteria (such as candidate likeability) that have little or nothing to do with the policies the candidates will promote once in office, or they vote based on wedge issues like stem cell research or same sex marriage that move them away from the party they agree with most.[408] This is not to say that these citizens are entirely to blame. The media certainly play a role, as do the politicians of both parties. In fact, there are a number of reasons why the U.S. system fails to take full advantage of political parties, leaving elections more candidate-centered than party-centered; American elections tend to be for, by, and about candidates rather than party programs or ideology. Making full use of political

FIGURE 6.1. Voting and interest levels by perception of party differences.

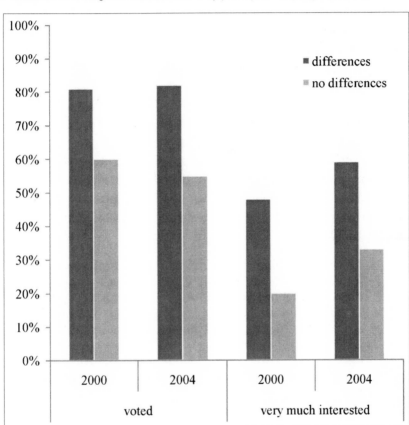

Source. American National Elections Studies, 2000 and 2004.
Questions: Do you think there are any important differences in what the Republicans and Democrats stand for? How interested are you in political campaigns?

parties by reversing this trend would do a lot to restore the health of U.S. elections. Doing so would require changes in the way the media cover elections (see chapter 4), changes in how the electorate perceives elections and political parties (see chapter 8), and changes in the way the Democrats and Republicans compete. This competition is the topic of this chapter.

The current state of competition between the Democrats and Republicans seems designed to distract voters from the real policy and ideological differences between the two parties. Candidates and elected officials of both parties (abetted by the media) tend to obfuscate the substantive differences by focusing on symbolic and wedge issues; by making politics a battle of labels, framing, and personal attacks; or by attempting to deceive the public as to the true effects of the policies the politicians pursue.[409] To cite an illustration from the world of sports, this behavior is akin to baseball teams fighting over who has the most attractive uniforms or the best fans or which team hits the ball with more authority—as opposed to actually competing on the field as the game was designed. American politics is currently focused on the wrong things. As *Daily Show* commentator Lewis Black put it in October of 2007,

> Anyone can talk about the issues, but it takes an experienced politician to know what really matters—the nonissues, and that's where our Congress really shines. Who else could turn a newspaper ad based on a stupid pun [the Moveon.org "General Petraeus ... or General Betray Us" ad] into a major patriotic crisis?

Black went on to cite Senate Democrats' focus on talk radio-show host Rush Limbaugh's reference to American troops as "phony soldiers," which focus was the Democratic response to Republican outrage at the "Betray Us?" advertisement. Continuing, Black said,

> Don't think of these nonissues as mere distractions from what is important. Sometimes they can *become* what's important. Look what happened to Barack Obama when he was spotted last week not wearing an American flag lapel pin [*followed by video clips of pundits on various news shows commenting on or expressing outrage about his decision not to wear the pin*] ... But it took *Fox News Live* to really place this in the pantheon of nonissues [*followed by a clip of a reporter stating that the way Obama said "that pin" was reminiscent of the way Bill Clinton said he had not had sex with "that woman," Monica Lewinsky."*].[410]

A political system cannot have healthy elections if its main adversaries (and the media) cannot refrain from focusing on such insignificant nonissues at the expense of what is truly important. If elections are to operate as a means of popular control of governmental decisions, then the competition between the Democrats and Republicans must be framed in terms of their policy and ideological differences. Changing the nature of the political discourse along these lines would do wonders for the health of U.S. elections and is therefore the first focus of the prescriptions discussed in this chapter. The second concerns voter mobilization and other campaign roles of the political parties. But proposals for change must be contextualized through an examination of the purpose of political parties, the reasons the United States has a two-party system, and the differences between the two major parties. In this context, I present prescriptions for encouraging a more meaningful political discourse and encouraging party organizational activities that enhance participation.

The Purpose of Political Parties

Most Americans are not convinced of the importance of political parties in a democracy and tend to see parties as an impediment to effective governing. For this reason, a few words about the vital role of political parties are appropriate here. To convey a sense of why political parties are critical to a well-functioning democracy, I often instruct my students to imagine that each of them, personally, wants to change what the government is doing about a number of different issues—for instance, global warming, reproductive rights, gun control, farm subsidies, the war in Iraq, welfare, taxes, and social security. What would an individual need to do in order to make the government do his or her bidding in these policy areas? As we discuss this question, students realize first that unless they have direct access to lawmakers and are capable of some version of the Jedi mind trick, they will not be able to accomplish their goals alone. Therefore they will need to find other like-minded people who want the same things from the government in these areas in order to effect the desired changes in government policy. Second, the conversation shows that a very *large* number of like-minded people is necessary—large enough to allow the group and its allies to take control of the executive branch and of a majority of legislative seats through the electoral process.

This thought may then lead students to a third realization: they will not be able to find enough people who want *exactly* the same things from government; then what are the options? In this situation, a person could either attempt to convince all the others to agree to what he or she wants (an unpromising approach) or a person could decide on an alliance with people who want *mostly* the same things with regard to these issues. Through this discussion, students see that they would need to ally themselves with people who want the same things with respect to (for example) global warming, reproductive rights, the war in Iraq, taxes, welfare, and social security, even though they might not agree on gun control or farm subsidies. Making such alliances increases the likelihood that a group could build a coalition of citizens constituting an electoral majority, which then allows that group to take control of the government via elections and make the government do *most* of the things they want it to do. In other words, in order to control the government through elections so that it will do what any one person wants, that person (or group) must build a majority coalition of people who share a similar set of preferences regarding what government should do; in other words, they must create a political party. This is the role that political parties play in democratic societies: they bring together citizens who share ideological and policy preferences to form governing majorities. There is simply no other way to do it, no other way to render elections institutions that allow the public to exercise influence over the decisions of their governments.

WHY TWO PARTIES? AND WHY THIRD PARTIES
AND INDEPENDENTS ARE NOT THE ANSWER

Political parties are critical to the health of elections because they are the only way to aggregate citizen preferences into ruling majorities. But why, many people ask, must U.S. voters' choices be limited to choosing between two parties? Wouldn't more choices make U.S. elections healthier and more democratic? Isn't that what the U.S. electoral system needs? The answer, in short, is no. Third parties are not the solution to the problems with U.S. elections.

Although third parties (and independent candidacies) can play an important role as minor players in the U.S. system by making sure the two major parties do not ignore popular issues, adding a third *major* party (or a fourth or fifth, or independent candidates) does nothing to address the reasons U.S. elections are in such dire condition. Adding more political parties would not address the inequality of political resources, restore political equality, make elections more competitive, boost the performance of key supporting institutions, or ease the burden on an overwhelmed electorate. Adding a third major party or independent candidate is at best ineffective medicine for the electoral system—like a placebo, it does nothing to alleviate the illness, it can only trick patients into temporarily thinking they feel better. Adding more choices to the ballot, in fact, has the potential to make the patient sicker; it would complicate the task of voting for the already overwhelmed electorate and make it more difficult for voters to see how their votes translate into action, as already discussed.

And finally, when it comes to getting the government to do what one wants it to, the number of parties is ultimately not very important. The bottom line is that governing requires majorities, which in turn requires some amount of compromise on ideological principles or issue positions. In a two-party system, election results usually make clear which party has the majority to govern, and that winning party is, ideally, the one that made its appeal ideologically broad enough to attract a majority of the voters. In multiparty systems, elections frequently conclude without any party's winning a majority. The basic math (more parties fighting for votes makes it less likely that any one party will emerge with a majority of the whole) and the fact that parties in such systems tend to tailor their ideological appeals more narrowly make winning control outright much more difficult. When no party wins a majority in a multiparty system, the party that wins the most votes must form a governing coalition with one or more of the other parties. In order to do so, the parties that form the coalition must compromise some of their party's policy positions in order to attract the support of other parties.

Thus *both systems end up at the same point in terms of representing the public*: governing coalitions that give their supporters most, but not all, of what they want from government. In two-party systems, parties are forced to build their majority coalitions before the election, making the necessary compromises on their policy positions in order to attract a majority of the vote. In multiparty systems the parties have more clearly defined ideological positions during an election but must compromise some of those positions in order to build a majority coalition after the election. Because of this last point, voters may actually exercise greater control in a two-party system because they are choosing from among the actual existing coalitions—that is, voters in a two-party system know when they vote what compromises have been made to attract a majority. In multiparty systems the governing coalitions are formed after the public votes so compromises are made after the election and are thus beyond the control of the voters. Finally, research has shown that the two-party system in the United States does as good a job offering choices and representing the public as do multiparty systems in Europe. Analyses show

> not only that the Democrats and Republicans are reasonably cohesive internally when compared with political parties in other systems, but also that their platforms are quite clearly differentiated from each other in an ideologically consistent fashion. They are thus as capable of giving a choice of policy alternatives to electors as are socialists and bourgeois parties in European democracies, and they are equally able to bring into effect their programs in government, despite institutional fragmentation.[411]

Given the growing ideological cohesiveness within the two American parties in recent years (evidence is cited in the next section), this is likely even more true today.

In the end, shifting to a multiparty system will not improve the health of U.S. elections or the representation they engender, so there seems to be no reason to undertake the major structural changes that would be required in order to make this change. To create multiparty competition, the United States would have to change the way voters elect legislators at the national, state, and local levels and would need to eliminate or effectively work around the Electoral College. Most legislative candidates in the country are selected in single-member districts, as opposed to the multimember districts necessary for multiparty systems.[412] Single-member districts create the electoral dynamic that leads to two-party systems. Any interest that wants to capture seats under a single-member district system must win a majority of the vote in order to preclude other interests from amassing a majority and winning the seat (whereas in proportional representation systems a party can win seats even if it does not win a majority of the vote). Thus the current form of representation prods those who have similar interests to work in advance of an election to secure seats by attempting to appeal to the majority of voters.

Consider, for example, what is needed to win seats in the U.S. House under the U.S. system as opposed to what would be needed in a multimember district with proportional representation. In single-member districts the incentive to parties is to make their appeal broad enough to win the most votes; this circumstance centers competition around two choices, both vying for the majority of votes in order to ensure victory. Candidates or parties that do not win the most votes in a district win nothing; parties whose support never comprises at least a plurality in any district do not win any representation. In a proportional representation system, however, parties win seats in proportion to their vote. Figure 6.2 illustrates the effects of the different election types. The figure shows a hypothetical rectangular state under two forms of representation: single-member districts and one multimember district, each electing ten members of U.S. House. Under the single-member district form of representation, the third party is unlikely to ever win any seats. So if they are interested in winning representation, third-party supporters have an incentive to join forces with one of the other parties behind a single candidate. Under the multimember, proportional representation system, the third party wins seats in proportion to the vote they receive

FIGURE 6.2. Effect of different representation schemes.

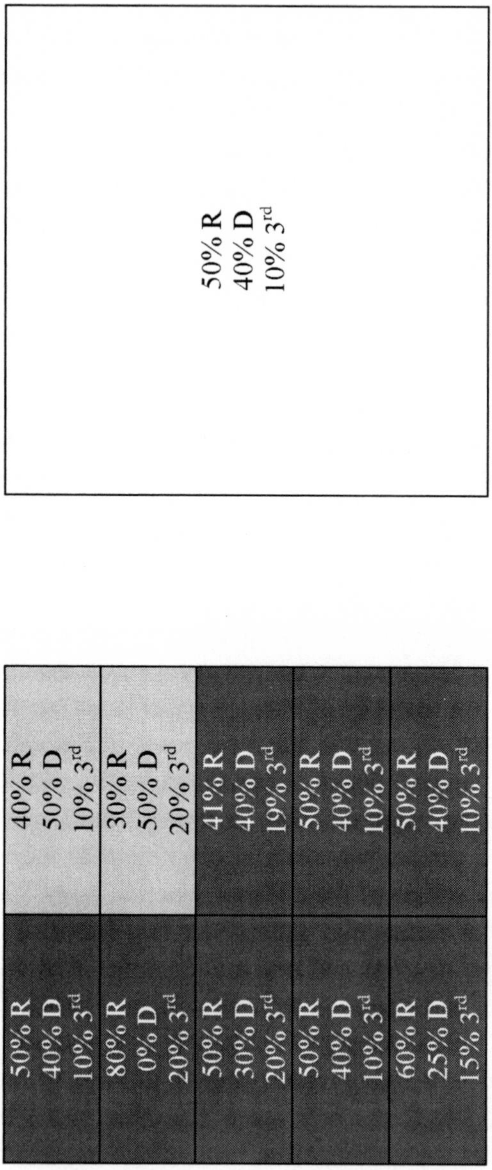

50% R 40% D 10% 3rd	40% R 50% D 10% 3rd
80% R 0% D 20% 3rd	30% R 50% D 20% 3rd
50% R 30% D 20% 3rd	41% R 40% D 19% 3rd
50% R 40% D 10% 3rd	50% R 40% D 10% 3rd
60% R 25% D 15% 3rd	50% R 40% D 10% 3rd

Single-member district, first-past-the post
Results: R = 8 seats, D = 2 seats, 3rd = 0 seats

50% R
40% D
10% 3rd

Multimember, proportional
Results: R = 5 seats, D = 4 seats, 3rd = 1 seat

D = percent of vote received by Democratic candidates
R = percent of vote received by Republican candidates
3rd = percent of vote received by 3rd party

on Election Day, and thus there is no incentive driving the group to work with another party before the election.

Thus, making U.S. elections into multiparty affairs would necessitate changing the form of representation to a proportional representation system with multimember districts for Congress. As argued earlier, there is no good reason to do so; such a change fails to address the ways in which U.S. elections are dysfunctional. Furthermore, shifting to proportional representation would be impossible in the seven states that elect only one member of the U.S. House and relatively meaningless for those other ten states that elect only two or three members of the U.S. House, and equally meaningless for the U.S. Senate seats as well. Supporters of expanding the number of parties might propose alternate voting systems, such as instant runoff voting (IRV), but as discussed in the previous chapter, this system has drawbacks of its own and would only aggravate the problem of overburdened voters while providing no gain; ultimately, legislators under such a system would still have to compromise in order to form a governing majority.

The people who tend to clamor for alternatives to the Democratic and Republican Parties are those on the ideological fringes (mainly the left) and those who are not yet aware of the actual differences between the Democrats and Republicans (primarily the young and the uninformed). Those on the far left or far right are unhappy with the more moderate positions the parties need to adopt in the U.S. system in order to win elections and govern. The uninformed simply lack an awareness of what the parties' positions actually are. And neither group seems to be aware that elections are about more than making choices; these citizens do not seem to understand that elections are also about building governing majorities.

PARTY DIFFERENCES IN THE UNITED STATES

In order for political parties to play their prescribed role in restoring the health of elections, they have to offer a choice to the electorate, a choice of different governing options. As I have asserted throughout this study, the Democrats and Republicans represent very different choices. These choices are rooted in different political value preferences that define the major ideological groups that comprise the political parties (and the public, as well).[413] Democrats believe governments should promote greater equality and greater personal freedoms. Republicans believe governments should be active in maintaining freedom in the marketplace and order in society, even at the cost of some personal freedom. These differences can be found in the party platforms, in the positions of the parties' candidates, in budget priorities, and in the distinctive ideological and partisan voting patterns of Democrats and Republicans who have been elected to government positions in national and state governments, as well as in party-line voting in Congress and state legislatures.[414] And despite what cynics may claim, the differences between the two parties matter in very real ways for voters, as perhaps best demonstrated by the research Larry Bartels published in his 2008 book, *Unequal Democracy*. In analyses of income changes since the 1940s, Bartels found that "under Republican administrations, real income growth for the lower- and middle-income classes has consistently lagged well behind income growth for the rich— and well behind the income growth rate for the lower and middle classes themselves under Democratic administrations."[415] These disparities "reflect consistent differences in policies and priorities between Democratic and Republican administrations." Furthermore, "the cumulative effect of these partisan differences has been enormous."[416]

Table 6.1 provides an illustration of the differences between the Democrats and Republicans on a more specific set of issues (those that were prevalent in late 2007). Where the two parties stand on these set of issues fits with their respective value preferences—Democrats supportive of a greater governmental role in the promotion of equality, Republicans supportive a greater governmental role in maintaining order—each in opposition to the role and scope of government promoted by the other. These differences are not as pronounced on all issues as some on the far left or right would like them to be (an end result of the parties' need to pitch their appeals broadly enough to win a majority); nonetheless, the bigger picture is that the differences are as great as many of the differences in European party systems,[417] as real as the system and public opinion

TABLE 6.1. Democratic v. Republican policy positions, 2007.

Issue	Democrats' General Position	Republicans' General Position	Evidence
Defense spending	Pre–Sept 11 support reduced spending; post–Sept 11 generally support increases (but have used allocations to attempt to set an end to Iraq war)	Support increases in spending and oppose use of funding bills to end Iraq war	Presidential budget proposals and congressional votes on budget
Interrogation methods	Most oppose torture and special interrogation methods (e.g., water boarding)	Most support use of torture or special interrogation methods	Candidates' positions, congressional votes, executive orders and directives
Legal rights of terrorism suspects	All citizens, noncitizens, enemy combatants have rights, including right to challenge detention in court	Limit the rights of terrorist suspects, detainees	Congressional votes, presidential actions, presidential candidates' positions
Government secrecy	Advocate minimal secrecy, more supportive of Freedom of Information Act	Support higher levels of secrecy for national security and executive privilege	Presidential administration actions, congressional actions
Anti-ballistic missile program	Oppose anti-ballistic program	Support anti-ballistic missile program	Presidential actions, congressional votes
Use of military force	More hesitant to use force, support its use for national security and protecting human rights	More inclined to use force but only to maintain national security; support preemptive action for national security purposes	Party platforms, congressional votes, administrative policies and actions

(continued on next page)

TABLE 6.1. (*continued*)

Issue	Democrats' General Position	Republicans' General Position	Evidence
NSA wiretapping	Infringes on citizens' right to privacy; require warrants through FISA court	Support NSA wiretapping without FISA court warrants	Congressional votes, presidential actions, presidential candidates' positions
Options for war in Iraq	Oppose increase in troops, favor setting timeline and benchmarks for withdrawal	Support troop increase ("surge"); oppose timelines and benchmarks for withdrawal	Congressional votes, party platforms, presidential candidates' positions
No Child Left Behind Act	Support act but express concern about money distribution, see funding as inadequate	Support act but express concern about increase of funding	Congressional votes, presidential budget proposals
Funds for primary and secondary education	Support increased funding for public education; oppose school-choice programs that divert money to religious and charter schools	Support less funding for public schools than Dems; support funds for religious and charter schools through school-choice programs	Congressional votes, presidential candidates' positions
Higher education	Support more funding: increase Pell Grants, cut interest rates on student loans, cut subsidies to lenders, create tax breaks for college costs	Support less funding: many (including G. W. Bush) opposed Democrats' initiatives on this issue	Congressional votes; presidential actions, positions
Income tax	Support progressive taxes (higher rates for wealthy); support rescinding Bush tax cuts on incomes over $250,000	Support lowering income taxes; oppose progressive tax. Support continuation of all Bush tax cuts, additional tax cuts.	Party platforms, presidential proposals, congressional votes

Issue	Democrat position	Republican position	Sources
Social security reform	Oppose taking funds from SS for private accounts; support increased taxes on higher incomes	Support private accounts, oppose raising taxes on higher incomes	Presidential candidate positions, presidential proposal
Immigration reform	Support border security, path to citizenship, protection of U.S. workers and wages	Support increased border security, penalties	Party platforms, congressional votes, presidential candidates' positions
Estate tax	Support maintaining estate tax	Support elimination of estate tax	Congressional votes, presidential candidates' positions
Free trade	Supportive, but conditioned on labor and environmental impact	Strongly in favor of free trade agreements	Congressional votes, candidates' positions, party platforms
Minimum wage	Favor significant increases in the minimum wage	Oppose increases or support small increases in minimum wage	Presidential candidates' positions, party platforms, congressional votes
Protecting wilderness areas	Clinton executive order halted all new road building, logging on 60 million acres of national forest land	G. W. Bush reversed Clinton administration's policy protecting roadless wilderness areas	Executive orders, administrative directives
Global warming	Support aggressive government action to combat global warming, offer detailed plans for capping emissions	Recognize issue (G. W. Bush not until late in second term); proposals less aggressive than Democrats'	Presidential candidates' positions; presidential actions, positions; congressional votes, party platforms
EPA budget	Advocate expansion of EPA budget	Seek to reduce EPA funding	Congressional votes, presidential budgets, presidential vetoes, party platform

(continued on next page)

TABLE 6.1. (continued)

Issue	Democrats' General Position	Republicans' General Position	Evidence
Endangered species	Support Endangered Species Act, oppose laws to weaken it (e.g., requiring compensation for property owners)	Support loosening restrictive laws, protection for property owners and developers	Congressional votes; presidential administration decisions, actions
Energy policy	Promote conservation, alternative energy sources	Promote domestic oil, gas, coal production (through, e.g., opening up ANWR, federal lands in West coastal areas)	Candidates' positions, presidential administration actions, congressional votes
Clean Air Act	Support aggressive government regulation of emissions, opposed Bush's attempt to loosen standards of act	Support less aggressive approach to regulating emissions, more voluntary	Congressional votes, actions in court, administrative decisions
Universal health care	Favor universal health care through expanding government health coverage, tax penalties for large businesses that do not insure employees	Favor expanding coverage through tax incentives, but without increasing role of federal government	Presidential candidates' positions, congressional leadership positions
Mental health parity	Support mental health coverage equivalent with coverage for other illnesses	Oppose mental health parity because it could drive up costs of coverage	Candidates' positions, congressional votes
Medicare Part D (Rx program)	Originally opposed bill as too confusing, too beneficial to insurance companies; support elimination of "donut hole"	Supported original bill with market-oriented approach; opposed government negotiation with drug companies	Congressional votes, presidential candidates' positions

Issue			
SCHIP	Created program; support expanding the program, increasing funding	Majority oppose expansion, claim it will lead to government-run health care	Presidential actions, statements; congressional votes; party platforms
Medicaid	Support fully funded program, expanding program as part of universal coverage proposals	Support reduced spending; advocate market-based Medicaid	Congressional votes, party platforms, presidential candidates' positions
Funding of public broadcasting	Support more spending on public broadcasting	Support reduced funding for public broadcasting	Congressional votes, news articles
Campaign finance reform	Support more regulations to restrict contributions, spending; support public funding	Oppose limits on contributions, spending; oppose public funding	Congressional votes, court challenges
Federal court appointments	Appoint liberal to moderate judges, justices	Appoint conservative judges, justices	Presidential nominations for Supreme Court, Senate votes
Consumer product safety	Support regulatory role of government; increased power, funding, staffing for Consumer Products Safety Commission	Support decreased funds and staff for inspections; support increased reliance on industry self-policing	G. W. Bush administration actions, budget priorities; congressional votes; party platforms
Gun control	Support greater restrictions on gun ownership (e.g., background checks, waiting periods); support ban on semiautomatic weapons; opposed ban on lawsuits against gun manufacturers	Oppose restrictions on gun owners; supported ban on lawsuits against gun manufacturers	Congressional votes, presidential candidates' positions, administrative decisions, party platforms

(continued on next page)

TABLE 6.1. (*continued*)

Issue	Democrats' General Position	Republicans' General Position	Evidence
Agricultural farm subsidies	Rural-state Dems support subsidies; Dems in general support ending subsidies for large farms, expanding food stamps, redirecting crop subsidies to pay for environmental conservation programs	Rural-state Republicans support subsidies; Republicans in general oppose crop subsidies, oppose expansion of food stamps and conservation programs	Congressional votes
Lobbying and ethics reform	Enacted stricter lobbying and ethics rules	Promoted weaker set of lobbying/ethics rules; did not enact reform while in control of Congress	Congressional votes
Same-sex marriage	Support same-sex marriage or civil unions; support allowing states to decide; oppose federal ban on same-sex marriage	Oppose same-sex marriage or civil unions; support federal-level definition of marriage as between man and woman only	Congressional votes, party platforms, positions of major candidates
Evolution	Support teaching of evolution	Oppose teaching evolution; support teaching of intelligent design	Senate vote, presidential candidates' statements
School prayer/ moment of silence	Most do not support prayer in school; many support daily moment of silence	Most support voluntary student-initiated prayer in public school, support moment of silence	Party platforms, House vote

Sex education, abstinence	Support promotion of increased awareness of STDs, of ways to avoid unwanted pregnancy; opposed to abstinence-only education	Promote abstinence till marriage, largely religious/moral perspective, oppose more exhaustive sex-education programs	Congressional votes; candidates' statements; presidential positions, actions
Abortion	Support women's right to choose abortion	Oppose abortion; support restrictions on abortions	Congressional votes, party platforms, presidential candidates' positions
Abortion pill (RU 486)	Support access to abortion pill	Oppose or restrict access to pill	Presidential executive orders, congressional votes
Plan-B contraception	Support over-the-counter access	Support access by prescription only	Congressional votes, candidates' positions, administrative actions
Laws governing labor unions	Generally support pro-labor union laws, advocate labor union rights	Support more restrictive labor union laws, including allowing workers to opt out of unions	Presidential candidates' positions, party platforms, congressional votes
TANF	Support increased TANF funding, child-care subsidies; oppose additional work requirements	Support reduced TANF funding; oppose child-care subsidies; added additional work requirements	Congressional votes, party platforms, presidential candidates' positions

allow them to be, and distinct enough to offer voters a clear choice. Were elections framed around these real differences, the work of the electorate would be simplified and elections would function in a much healthier manner.[418] The following section deals with how the parties' candidates could be encouraged to focus on these fundamental differences.

R$_x$: IMPROVE THE DISCOURSE

How does the United States get candidates, their campaigns, the political parties, and all of their supportive independent groups to contribute to an electoral debate that draws attention to the real choices the two sides represent? This question may provoke a cynical reaction among readers, and I admit that I myself am quite pessimistic about the feasibility of changing the behavior of candidates and of all the others involved in campaigns—especially because their approach comes from years of finding out what works, what wins elections. As with all prescriptions in this book, though, each must be understood in the context of all the others, for it is unlikely any one of the changes suggested will work on its own. Changing the nature of election discourse will require shifts in the media and in the public that will alter the incentives in ways that will help modify the behavior of politicians, parties, and their supporters.

My pessimism about changing how candidates, parties, and their surrogates behave was reinforced as I wrote this chapter by the early discourse of the 2008 general election (I wrote it in July 2008, just a few weeks after Barack Obama became the presumptive nominee). Serious issues confront the country, and the nominating contests ended in the selection of two candidates who promised a serious and civil electoral debate about how to deal with the issues confronting the nation. In the early stages of this general election campaign, however, the two camps quickly took up distractions and were far from civil. Frank Rich of the *New York Times* summed it up nicely:

> So much for a July Fourth week spent in idyllic celebration of our country's birthday. This year's festivities were marked instead

by a debate—childish, not constitutional—over who is and isn't patriotic. The fireworks were sparked by a verbally maladroit retired general, fueled by two increasingly fatuous presidential campaigns, and heated to a boil by a 24/7 news culture that inflates any passing tit for tat into a war of the worlds.

Let oil soar above $140 a barrel. Let layoffs and foreclosures proliferate like California's fires. Let someone else worry about the stock market's steepest June drop since the Great Depression. In our political culture, only one question mattered: What was Wesley Clark saying about John McCain and how loudly would every politician and bloviator in the land react?[419]

Before the extensive bloviating began over Wesley Clark's comment, the big distraction centered on a remark made by a McCain advisor about the impact a terrorist attack might have on McCain's chances of victory in the fall. And as the *Washington Post*'s Dan Balz pointed out, although candidates had been giving policy speeches, "whatever substance they may [have] contain[ed]" was "buried in negative counterattacks from the opposing camp, designed to turn ideas into stereotypes and candidates into caricatures."[420]

The state of electoral discourse, described in chapter 3 and illustrated by these cases, is *simply unacceptable*. It is a discourse that seems to try in every way possible to distract the public from the parties' fundamentally different positions on the issues. The tit-for-tat, "gotcha," and nit-picking mentality makes the public lose track of the big picture. Name-calling, simplifications, and distortions of comments taken out of context are used to make candidates, parties, and policy proposals into silly or threatening caricatures of themselves. It is nearly impossible to have healthy elections when this is the nature of political discourse, when debates between opposing ideological camps sound to the public like childish playground spats. This type of discourse not only distracts the public from the central meaning of their choice but also disheartens citizens and leads them to believe that politicians' only concern is defeating the other side, which perception in turn reduces the chance that they will vote.[421] Although electoral discourse has always had such aspects to

it, the modern media era has introduced incessant cable chatter, ubiquitous viral e-mails, and large-scale campaign microtargeting (the practice
of identifying interests of narrow segments of the public from consumer
data bases), forms of communication that overwhelm the voters in a del-
uge of trivialities in ways that can only obscure the true nature of the
electoral choice. Therefore an important step toward restoring the health
of U.S. elections is for politicians to change their behavior, change what
they and their organizations contribute to electoral discourse. Specifically, America needs its politicians to (1) stay focused on, or at least constantly return to the big picture, the fundamental nature represented by
the electoral choice, (2) maintain reasoned discourse over the merits of
their policies and those of opponents, (3) forgo exploiting wedge issues,
and (4) refrain from jumping on the other side's inconsequential gaffes.

The first principle can be seen as a generalized version of James
Carville's campaign directive embodied in the sign he penned for the
1992 Clinton campaign "War Room": *It's the economy, stupid ... and
don't forget health care.* That directive was posted to keep the candidate
and the organization focused on the core issues that would win them the
White House. Both issues were emblematic of the overall philosophy of
the campaign and of the Democratic Party, as well—namely, egalitarian
economic policies. If presidential (and other) candidates and their political parties followed this practice each election year—picking a few key
issues that are representative of their overall philosophies—and made
those issues the focus of their campaigns, then the nature of the choice
for voters might be made much clearer. Candidates and parties could
emphasize the issues that are their strongest (which they are likely to do
anyway[422]), as long as the issues they choose embody some aspect of the
party's basic philosophy. Campaigns already choose issues to emphasize,
but they are too quick to pounce on other nonissues that they believe will
help them win, or they are too willing to muddy the policy differences
on their opponents' driving issues.

None of this should be interpreted as an argument to limit electoral
discourse to a few issues. The debate should include discussion of many
other issues beyond the driving issues of the campaign, but if the key

issues appropriately reflect the fundamental values of the candidates' parties, then most all of the other issues will fit logically into the framework defined by those central issues—thus reinforcing the public's understanding of Republicans' and Democrats' differing philosophies.

Keeping the focus on core philosophical differences through emblematic, driving issues will not benefit elections if the discussion of those issues is muddied and distorted with faulty logic, questionable selection of the facts, and the inconsistent application of definitions and standards, all common today. Even when politicians focus on the issues (as opposed to nonissue distractions), the exchange between campaigns still falls far short of the type of reasoned discourse necessary in order to inform the public of the nature of the choice. Instead, the competition for votes is more analogous to baseball played with corked bats, spitballs, sign stealing, and performance-enhancing drugs—each team is trying to gain some sort of unfair advantage over the other. One need spend only a little time on FactCheck.org or Politifact.com or read Brooks Jackson and Kathleen Hall Jamieson's *unSpun* in order to be convinced of the prevalence of dishonest tactics, distortions, and spin.[423]

The second thing elections need from candidates, their campaigns and the political parties is a pledge to debate their fundamental policy differences or their driving issues as intelligent, logical adults who believe in fair play, support their arguments with consideration of all the relevant facts, and do not lose sight of the big picture. In other words, elections need the participants to make reasoned appeals to the voters and forgo deception. This does sound rather Pollyannaish; there are certainly no real incentives for candidates to behave in this way. The U.S. public in the television age seems to have lost its ability to differentiate between logical and illogical reasoning, to recognize real evidence as opposed to the anecdotal or selective fact, and to see the big picture; it is also possible that much of the public simply no longer cares about such standards of reasoned debate.[424] And the media, aside from a dwindling number of old-school journalists and the satire provided by outlets like *The Daily Show* and *The Colbert Report*, do little to challenge candidates' reasoning or evidence.[425] Moreover, campaigns spin and distort because these tactics work. Changes in the press and the public as suggested in this book, however, could create incentives for politicians to maintain more reasoned discourse. If voters and the media established a check on politicians' current practices through improved journalism and created an appetite for an honest, reasoned debate through better education (encouraging critical thinking and healthy skepticism), politicians would feel the pressure to reform the way they seek votes. To return to the sports analogy, professional baseball was cleaned up by the advent of press coverage and fans not inclined to tolerate unfair play. Politicians, after all (contrary to popular thought), believe in the policies that they promote; therefore they should be able to logically support those beliefs with reason and evidence.

Third, campaigns need to forgo the practice of microtargeting voters with wedge issues, the purpose of which is to encourage voting based on a single, emotion-laden issue, often against the voters' general preferences. This tactic, as D. Sunshine Hillygus and Todd G. Shields documented in their book *The Persuadable Voter*, is effective in persuading voters to vote against the party that more broadly represents their interests, and thus weakens the electorate's ability to influence the overall direction of government.[426]

Finally, the long political campaigns in the United States afford far too many opportunities for road-weary candidates or their staff or supporters to say something inappropriate or ill conceived. When this inevitably happens, the gaffe immediately becomes ammunition for the opposition and fodder for an always scandal-hungry media. Thus, the final way politicians must change the discourse is to resist the temptation to exploit such gaffes. Campaigns might defend this practice as a means to illustrate the issue positions of their opponents, but the result of such a practice is a caricature of the opposition. Most of the time, drawing attention to such gaffes is simply a distraction from the big picture, from the core differences between the candidates and their respective parties.

Motivating politicians to change the nature of electoral discourse along these lines would entail extracting a promise from the candidates and their political parties. Perhaps activists could cajole politicians into signing a pledge to campaign according to these principles, not unlike the pledges antitax groups obtained from many candidates not to raise taxes. A press that is more critical of politicians who distort, distract, and spin and a public that rewards reasoned, honest debate would certainly help. But the politicians need to be responsible, too, and change the way they talk about the choices they offer the voters.

Together, these changes in what politicians talk about and how they do so would lead to a significantly improved electoral discourse and healthier elections. It would be a discourse that reminds voters of the core differences between the major parties and candidates, of the fundamental nature of their choice. Such a reasoned and focused discourse would also reduce the level of political cynicism among members of the public.[427] When elections no longer resemble playground feuds over petty issues and look more like a reasonable debate between supporters of competing governing philosophies, the public might think more highly of the politicians and the system that produces them—and ultimately join in.

R_x: Maintain and Strengthen the Party Machinery

It is hard to overestimate how much properly functioning political parties contribute to healthy elections. In addition to structuring the choice in elections, political parties can contribute to the health of elections through a number of organizational activities, such as pooling resources, mobilizing voters, general electioneering, recruiting people to run for office, training candidates, and recruiting volunteers and paid staff. Such activities promote participation and enhance political equality and electoral competition. Consequently, any prescription for U.S. elections needs to include ways to encourage more of these activities. In this section I discuss the state of the parties with regard to these organizational activities and suggest prescriptions for maintaining, expanding and improving their performance. First, though, it is necessary to sketch the structure of those party organizations in the United States.

Much of the public probably perceives the parties as two unified, top-down organizations governed by the politicians in Washington, but this is a misperception. Both parties have national organizations, but the structure is looser than commonly thought. The Democratic National Committee (DNC) and the Republican National Committee (RNC) are each headed by a chairperson or two, and each party has a number of separate campaign committees, such as the Democratic Senatorial Campaign Committee and the Republican National Senatorial Committee, both dedicated to electing party members to the U.S. Senate; corresponding committees in both parties focus on the U.S. House. National governors associations and organizations to support the parties' candidates in state legislative contests also exist at the national level; each of these committees is governed separately. And while they are the supreme governing body of each party, the national party conventions concern themselves mainly with the presidential contest (selecting nominees for president and vice president and setting the rules for the next presidential nomination contest), the party platform, and selecting the national committees.

In addition to these national organizations, each party has state and local organizations. State party organizations include the state party conventions, state central committees (headed up by a state party chair and cochair), and legislative campaign committees (analogous to the congressional campaign committees at the national level). The national organizations do not control the state organizations. The national committees provide them with money and staff support (with some strings attached that are meant to direct the spending of the money in ways that strengthen the state party organizations) and they dictate how and when the state parties can select the delegates they send to the national party conventions. Local party organizations (depending on the state) include town, city, ward, precinct, county, and township committees (all lead by chairpersons) and the local party caucuses. Local party organizations, like the state party organizations, operate largely independently of the more centralized party organizations. A visual summary of the nature of party organizations in the United States is provided in figure 6.3. It is important to note that these organizations do not represent the full extent of party organizations in America; in addition to these formal committees of the political party organizations, a large number of organizations are

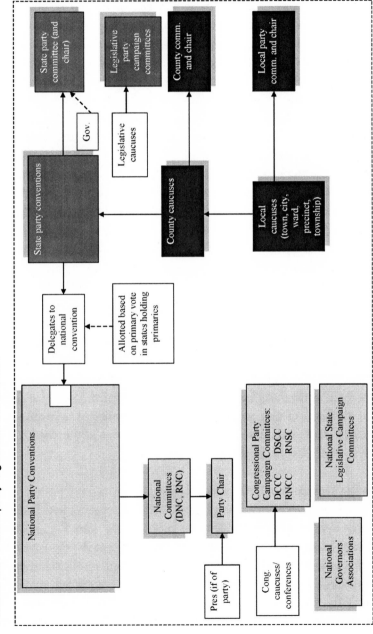

Figure 6.3. Formal party organization in the U.S.

affiliated with one of the two parties—party-connected committees (such as leadership PACs) and interest groups that primarily support one party and its candidates. These organizations are not depicted in figure 6.3.[428]

These party organizations exist for one purpose: to win elections. That purpose drives parties to engage in a number of activities that ultimately benefit democracy. The drive to win elections creates an incentive (1) to pool their resources, (2) to get the public registered and get them to vote on or by Election Day, (3) to campaign for all of their candidates, (4) to recruit quality candidates to run for office, (5) to train those candidates in the most effective campaign tactics, and (6) to recruit people to volunteer or work for the party and candidates. This aspect of U.S. elections—parties undertaking such activities—appears to be in good health. The past few decades have witnessed a rebirth of party organizations from the national level down.[429] Party committees, which in the wake of systemic, legal, and technological changes had been relegated to the electoral sidelines by the 1970s, are now reinvigorated. National, state, and local party committees are now involved and are often playing a major role in electoral contests, from the race for the presidency to contests for local offices. They are recruiting candidates, spending large amounts of money to support their candidates, providing training, services, personnel, and material support to candidates, and implementing massive grassroots voter mobilization programs. Most of this, I argue, benefits U.S. elections. There remain, however, a number of adjustments that could be made in order to enhance the contribution of party-organization activity to the health of elections.

Pooling Resources: Party Fundraising

There is no question that party organizations in the United States have greatly expanded their capacity to raise money (see Fig. 2.8 for the amounts raised over time). Party fundraising is probably associated in most people's minds with corruption, fat cats, and political bosses. Such associations may have been accurate in the age of corrupt party bosses (over fifty years ago), but the truth is that political party fundraising can be—and in a number of ways has been—beneficial to the healthy functioning of elections. This is because of the nature of fundraising and because the incentives that drive the modern party organization encourage party committees to spend the money in ways that enhance electoral competition and promote political equality.

Why Party Money is Healthy

There are several features of party fundraising that make it beneficial to an electoral system and that suggest that healthy elections should include substantial campaign fundraising by party organizations. One beneficial feature of party fundraising is its potential to weaken the connection between contributor and beneficiary (candidate) by imposing an intermediary between the two. Another is the way party fundraising can dilute the importance of any one contributor (or set of contributors) in a large pool of contributions.

First, when individuals or interests give money directly to candidates, there is a potential for such contributions to engender some sense of obligation on the part of the recipient to the contributor, opening the door to contribution-bought influence.[430] When money is instead contributed to a party organization, mingled with other contributions, and then used to support candidates, the direct connection between contributor and beneficiary—and consequently, the sense of obligation—is eliminated.[431] The fact that a significant source of party money in recent years has been the party's own elected officials (members of Congress, for example, transferred over $37 million from their own campaign committees to the House campaign committees in 2004)[432] adds yet another step between many contributors and the ultimate beneficiary (contributor → elected official → party committee → candidate), further weakening the direct impact of contributors. Thus encouraging money to flow through the political parties is healthy for the electoral system because it decreases the potential for corruption.

Though party fundraising weakens the direct connection between contributor and lawmaker, the question arises whether such fundraising gives contributors more power by centralizing their influence through the party organization, which might then be able to direct their elected members to support contributing interests. This should not be a problem as long as party organizations are not dependent on money from a narrow set of interests. Given that parties raise much more money than candidates do, it is likely that party money will originate from a more diverse set of contributors than candidate money, reducing the likelihood that the contributions from any one interest would constitute a significant share of party money. In this way parties should be less dependent on the money from any single interest than candidates are. Thus, party fundraising can function to dilute the influence of contributors, which reduces the political inequality that stems from private campaign contributions.

Whether party fundraising functions in this manner depends, in part, on how much any one interest can give to a party organization. If campaign finance rules allow very large or unlimited contributions to party organizations, then party organizations could come to be dependent on a set of interests that contribute very large amounts of money. While contributions to the national and to many state party organizations are limited in such a way as to prevent this sort of dependency, some states do allow unlimited contributions to party organizations. This point leads to the first prescription for party fundraising: state governments that currently do not do so should limit the contributions to state and local party organizations so as to prevent any party organization from becoming financially dependent on a narrow set of interests. These contribution limits do not have to be low; in fact, they should be much higher than the limits on contributions to candidates so as to channel a significant proportion of campaign money through the parties. Rather than being low, limits should be proportionate to the overall amounts of fundraising by the specific party committees so that any set of contributions from a particular interest may not comprise a critical percentage of the fundraising by the party. In other words, the size of the contribution allowed should be indexed to the typical amounts raised by the party committee in the state so that party committees in states that typically raise larger amounts of money should be allowed to accept larger contributions than party committees in states that tend to raise less.

The incentives that drive the modern party organization—primarily, winning control of the government through elections—also motivate party organizations to spend the money they raise in ways that enhance the health of elections. One way party spending is beneficial is related to how party spending distributes (or, more accurately, redistributes) political money. Party organizations, in order to maximize the effectiveness of their spending, put most of their financial effort into contests with uncertain outcomes and where they see a possibility of gaining a seat or, conversely, preventing the loss of a seat. In other words, parties concentrate their money on close contests, often ones involving nonincumbent candidates[433] who typically have difficulty attracting the campaign money they need.[434] This is in contrast to the tendency of most other contributors,[435] who tend to place their money on safe bets, contributing the bulk of their money to incumbent lawmakers in safe, uncompetitive districts and legislators whose extended tenure has usually resulted in powerful committee assignments. Such a pattern of giving is logical for nonparty contributors whose purpose is to have access to those in power following the election.[436] The money raised by the party organizations, then, goes to the competitive races, including the candidates in open seats and the candidates challenging incumbents—a set of candidates typically at a disadvantage in the campaign-finance system. When the party's incumbent officeholders transfer some of their funds to the party committees, money is effectively redistributed from incumbents in uncompetitive races to those in marginal races, making them more competitive. In these ways, party fundraising and party spending act to reduce campaign spending inequalities between incumbents and challengers and enhance electoral competition.

The benefits of such redistribution to date have been limited, however, because party committees too often get caught up in an ever-escalating spending contest with the other party over a few races and as a result concentrate massive sums of money on only a handful of races—especially for the U.S. Senate and House[437]—thus failing to effectively enhance competition and reduce campaign finance inequities. In 2006, for example, party committees focused on nine senate contests, with most money

going to five of those, and on forty to fifty house seats (though this number grew as the political climate put more seats into play and Election
Day drew near).[438] Overall in 2006, "the Democratic and Republican
Committees poured 81 percent of their candidate funding into nine Senate races and 27 House races."[439] The same intense focus on competitive
areas is evident in national party transfers to state parties and state party
fundraising for the presidential campaigns, which have also become
more concentrated on battleground states.[440]

Thus one might consider prescribing some changes that would result
in a greater scope of parties' redistribution of money in order to fuel
more competitive contests and offer voters a real choice in more contests; one obvious change (addressed in chapter 7) would be increasing the pool of competitive districts through changes in the redistricting
process. Continuing to craft campaign finance laws to encourage more
money to flow through the parties—as the Bipartisan Campaign Reform
Act (BCRA) did; see the following section—would mean the parties
would have more resources, hopefully, to support more of their candidates and thus to expand the number of competitive races. Limiting party
spending in districts or states is much more problematic.[441] While party
contributions to and coordinated spending on behalf of federal candidates are limited (direct contributions are limited to $5,000 per election
and, in 2008, coordinated spending limits were $42,100 and $84,100[442]
for House candidates and range from $84,100 to $2,284,900 for Senate
candidates, depending on each state's voting age population[443]), independent spending by party committees is not.[444] As a consequence, most
of the spending by parties takes the form of independent expenditures
(such expenditures composed 90 percent of the party money spent on
congressional elections in 2006),[445] allowing the parties to dedicate most
of their money to a handful of contests. Given that the courts will not
allow limits on independent expenditures and have rejected the logic
that parties by their nature cannot make "independent" expenditures, the
prospect of limiting this sort of party spending is rather dim, despite the
fact that independent spending is, as recognized by the Supreme Court,
less efficient and at times counterproductive, often carrying negative

consequences for the democratic process by muddling or confusing the message conveyed to voters about the contest.[446] Perhaps the best that can be done is, as campaign finance scholars Dwyre, Heberlig, Kolodny, and Larson recommended, eliminating the limits on coordinated party spending so that the parties can at least be more efficient with their spending; this would free up some money for other contests, making them more competitive.[447] Encouraging more coordinated party spending, however, might be accomplished by raising the limits on such spending to a much higher level (but still below the levels for independent spending). This change could curb the worst excesses of party arms-race spending in districts and, if done in tandem with contribution limits and public financing (as recommended in chapter 7), party resources might be used in a way to truly maximize competitiveness.

Furthermore, it should be noted that the resource sharing that is characteristic of party fundraising also creates a common sense of purpose for party members, strengthening party ties that can lead to a more unified and effective party in government, translating voters' party choices into policy.

> "There has been a sea change over the past decade in the way congressional election campaigns are conducted," said Michael J. Malbin, Executive Director of The Campaign Finance Institute. Noting that in 1994, the parties were responsible for a small fraction of the support for House and Senate candidates as in 2006, Malbin said that "Politics has shifted from being a one-on-one game, with the candidates all for themselves, to a team game. The parties have become crucial. You can see this in almost all of the close races in both chambers in 2006, but especially in the last minute spending that determined majority control in the Senate."[448]

Party spending has also benefited elections when funds are dedicated to building up the grassroots capacity of the party organization. Indeed, much of the money raised by the political parties in recent decades has fueled parties' return to their critical role of providing a choice (with each party recruiting and fielding candidates who offer opposing views on what government should do) and mobilizing the electorate.[449] The national party committees (chiefly the RNC) developed effective fundraising machinery in the 1980s and 1990s and poured money into the party system, building up national, state, and local organizations' capacity to play an important role in the electoral process (and to raise more money). The DNC, while lagging behind the RNC, had also developed more effective fundraising by the first elections of the new century. Both parties' fundraising allowed an infusion of money into state and local party organizations in order to build their capacity for organizing supporters, identifying potential candidates, and mobilizing voters. It also provided parties with a tool (substantial campaign support) to help recruit candidates. The Republicans built up their presence in the south in the 1980s this way. During his tenure as DNC Chair (2005–2008), Howard Dean committed the DNC to building party organizations in every state by funding a minimum number of party staffers for each state—a strategy that appears to have paid off for the Democrats in 2006 and 2008.

Party Fundraising and the BCRA

Party committees were able to raise the sums of money that helped them reestablish their role in elections thanks to party-friendly campaign finance law that allowed for the rise of *soft money*, money that could be contributed in amounts not regulated by federal campaign-finance law. During the soft money era, a 1979 amendment to the Federal Election Campaign Act and an accompanying rule interpretation by the Federal Election Commission allowed the national party committees to raise large sums of money outside of the FEC regulatory system,[450] money that came from corporations, wealthy individuals, unions, and other interest groups. As time passed, the parties and candidates learned how to tap this source, and massive sums of money flowed into the party coffers of both Democrats and Republicans, allowing each party to build up its organizational capacity and to funnel money to state party organizations (which also used some of this money to build up organizational capacity). This was, in part, a positive development for the electoral system because the enhanced organizational capacity of the party organizations served to enhance competition in elections and mobilize the electorate. But, as the sums and the size of the contributions increased, concern arose about the influence of those contributing soft money. In the absence of limits on the amounts that could be given, party committees could become dependent on a narrow set of interests, allowing those interests to exert disproportionate influence over the party and its elected officials.

Questions about high-value contributors to the DNC being hosted in the White House Lincoln bedroom in 1996 and the unfolding of the Enron scandal in 2002 highlighted the potential corrupting influence of such large and unregulated contributions. Ultimately, such concerns led to the adoption in 2003 of the Bipartisan Campaign Reform Act (BCRA), also called McCain-Feingold, which cut off the flow of soft money that had helped build up the party machinery. The long-term impact of the BCRA on party organizations remains to be seen. It eliminated a source of money that had been particularly beneficial to the Democratic Party (which had been tapping its wealthiest supporters to help catch up in the money race), but it also may have had a disproportionate influence on the Republican Party, which had long been more centrally organized and thus more dependent on money flowing to the RNC.[451] Though the BCRA outlawed soft money, it included a number of provisions that allowed the parties to make up for the loss of some of those funds in ways less harmful to the health of U.S. elections.

The BCRA increased the amount individuals may give to a national party committee from $20,000 per year to an inflation-adjusted $25,000. Individuals may also give up to $10,000 to each state and local party committee per year. The act also increased allowable total party giving up to $57,500 over a two-year election cycle (inflation adjusted; thus the 2009–2010 limits are $30,400 to any one party committee and $69,900 in total giving to parties). Increasing the overall limit on individual giving during an election also restricted how much of that total may go to candidates and nonparty committees to $37,500 per election cycle—in effect, encouraging contributors to give more to the national parties. The ban on soft money increased national party reliance on *hard money*, money that comes from contributions limited by law. Because of this—and because of the increasing effectiveness of Internet fundraising—parties turned to small contributions (under $200), which now make up a larger portion of fundraising (from 22 percent in 2002 to 34 percent in 2006), while the percentage of large contributions ($20,000 or more) decreased from 41 percent in 2002 to 7 percent in 2006.[452] The increase in contribution limits and the use of Internet fundraising allowed the parties to make up for the loss of soft money to some extent during the 2004 election. During 2008, however, as presidential candidates decided to reject public funding for their campaigns, more money flowed directly to the presidential campaigns (Obama's in particular) and left the national parties struggling to match their 2004 fundraising totals.[453]

The BCRA also allows former candidates and officeholders to transfer unlimited amounts of money from their own campaigns to a party committee. Driven by close competition for control of both chambers of Congress and a collective goal to win that competition, the total contributions from members of Congress to campaign committees increased substantially between 1996 and 2004, helping replace lost soft money with hard money.[454] As argued previously, this kind of fundraising is beneficial to the system because (1) it places an additional step between the contributors and the ultimate beneficiaries of the money—those candidates in close contests, (2) because the redistributive nature reduces inequality between incumbents and nonincumbents, and (3) because it strengthens the political parties' role.

State party committees were one of the main actors in the soft money era prior to the BCRA. In activities unregulated by most state governments, state party organizations raised vast sums of unlimited contributions and received similarly large sums of soft money in transfers from the national party organizations (often in exchange for hard money raised by the state parties).[455] State party committees used this soft money to mobilize voters and sponsor what are known as *issue ads*, electoral communications that avoid expressly advocating the election or defeat of a candidate.[456] The BCRA's ban of soft money put an end to these practices. In order to avoid sidelining state party organizations in federal elections, the Levin Amendment was tacked on to the BCRA, allowing state parties to collect up to $10,000 from a single contributor for use on voter mobilization if it was combined with hard money; however, because of the complexity of complying with the Levin Amendment, state parties made little use of this option.[457] Instead, state parties relied on hard money to conduct voter mobilization following the BCRA, and state party expenditures shifted away from issue ads toward mobilization and grassroots—a positive development stemming from the BCRA. The national parties made independent expenditures to run ads for their candidates in 2004 and 2008; 527 and 501(c) committees[458] took on the job of running issue ads and also worked independently to register voters and get them to the polls on Election Day—a not-so-positive consequence of the BCRA. [459] The shift to 527 and 501(c) committees weakened the state parties and made coordination of the electoral effort difficult, wasting money on overlapping administrative costs and allowing for inconsistent and sometimes competing messages. Additionally, because 527 and 501(c) committees act independently of candidates and political parties, there is no way to hold such groups accountable for the nature of their messages, which are among the worst in terms of lies, distortions, and overall nastiness—enough to put many voters off of the whole electoral process.

Curbing the excesses of 527 and 501(c) committees would undoubtedly be good medicine for U.S. elections. Given how the Supreme Court has consistently invalidated attempts to regulate the activities of such groups, the solution must come from rendering such committees unnecessary. The Court's unwillingness to allow governments to reign in the electoral activities of independent groups was reaffirmed in two rulings in 2006 and 2010. In 2006 the Court invalidated a provision of the BCRA that prevented the use of corporate or union money for electioneering communications (defined in the BCRA as communications that refer to a federal candidate, are aired within a certain period before an election, and target the federal candidate's constituency).[460] And in 2010 the Court not only eliminated the BCRA prohibitions on corporate and union spending but also completely erased a century-old ban on corporate and union spending in elections.[461] Requiring better disclosure of such committees' spending and revenues is possible, but placing limits on their financing or activities is apparently not. So the only remaining alternative is to render such committees unnecessary—a difficult though not altogether impossible task, as the lessons of the 2008 presidential election demonstrate.

In 2008 the use of 527 committees dropped dramatically, with spending declining from about $4.5 million in 2004 to about $2.6 million in 2008.[462] This decrease may be related in large part to Barack Obama's decision to forgo public funding for his presidential campaign.[463] By refusing public funding, Obama's campaign provided an opportunity for contributors to give directly to the campaign, an option unavailable if a candidate accepts public funding for the general election.[464] Though such contributions were limited (to $2,300 for the primary and another $2,300 for the general election), the option to give directly to the campaign (such donations are in addition to the sizeable amounts one could contribute to the party committees) must have siphoned off a significant amount of the funding that might have otherwise gone to independent committees. In other words, with more direct avenues for contributing kept open, the indirect routes through independent groups like the 527s become less attractive to contributors. Additionally, the money raised directly by the Obama campaign allowed it to do more of the things that previous presidential campaigns relied on 527s and 501(c)s to do, so such committees become less necessary from the perspective of the campaign and the party (with the added advantage that the campaign could coordinate activities to avoid redundancies in activities and inconsistencies in message).

The lesson of 2008, then, is that the activities of independent groups can be rendered less important if other options are available for contributors and campaigns. But is it possible to accomplish the same thing while maintaining the benefits of publicly funded campaigns? The BCRA did some good in this area by increasing the hard money limits for contributions to the political parties while shutting down the soft money option. Making it easier for state parties to use the Levin Amendment contributions would provide another useful channel to direct money to the parties. In chapter 7, I address how candidate campaign financing (and public funding) might also be reformed to channel political money in more productive ways.

Engaging in Activities that Support Elections

In addition to offering a choice in elections and pooling and redistributing money in the system, properly functioning political party organizations are also critical to the health of elections because of the work they do on the ground. Given that success or failure is measured by how well parties do at the polls, party organizations have a powerful incentive to register voters and motivate them to cast their votes on or before Election Day. Having competing organizations concerned with getting people to vote (even if they are concerned only with getting their own supporters to vote) is healthy for elections. The increase in voter turnout in the 2004 and 2008 presidential elections and the 2006 midterm election is likely the result, in part, of the refinement of massive voter-mobilization programs conducted by the two major political parties (other factors discussed in this book, particularly the abundantly clear nature of the partisan choice in these years, were more important, but that does not negate the significance of voter-mobilization efforts).[465]

Mobilizing voters involves three steps: (1) finding the voters, (2) registering the voters, and (3) getting them to cast their votes. Party organizations, usually in concert with their candidates' campaigns and with the aid of allied groups, have developed sophisticated and effective means to carry out all of these steps. They have built large computer-based voter files and enlisted the help of millions of volunteers to register voters and to motivate those people to vote.

In 2004 Republicans operated an incredibly effective grassroots organization in all fifty states connected to the national party (RNC) and Bush reelection campaign headquarters in Arlington, Virginia. Included in this party machine were paid top managers who coordinated the efforts of paid regional- and state-level coordinators, who in turn coordinated the work of more than one million county, city, and precinct volunteers—a network constructed by connections developed at the local level so that those who contacted prospective voters were, in effect, their neighbors.[466] This organization made use of an advanced voter database called the Voter Vault, created by the RNC from registration, voting history, magazine subscriptions, the types of cars owned, and other financial and consumer data.[467] RNC chair Ed Gillespie claimed that this machinery

> made over 15 million contacts, knocking on doors and making calls in the 72 hours before the polls closed. 7.2 million e-activists were contacting their family friends and coworkers. The RNC registered 3.4 million new voters, enlisted 1.4 million Team Leaders, and contacted—on a person to person basis—30 million Americans in the months leading up to and including Election Day.[468]

The RNC (and the McCain campaign) continued this effort in 2008, though at a slightly diminished level. The Democrats, however, proved more successful in 2008 through the efforts of the Obama campaign, the Democratic Party, and supportive independent groups.

In 2004 the Democrats relied largely upon state parties and outside groups—527 committees—to mobilize the electorate in the battleground states. The 527s—including America Coming Together (ACT), which spend $80 million in voter mobilization—operated largely in the suburban areas, while the state parties focused on urban areas.[469] In 2008, under the direction of the Obama campaign, Democratic Party efforts were more centralized and coordinated. The Obama campaign and the DNC copied the RNC in the development of a voter database, had volunteers contact voters (and record on a scale of one to five whether individuals were likely Obama supports or not), and then mounted a massive voter-mobilization effort that emphasized peer-to-peer contact—in other words, contact from friends, neighbors, or people from similar demographic groups.[470] The Obama campaign and the DNC also placed a special emphasis on younger voters. The 2008 mobilization efforts of both parties and campaigns again proved incredibly successful: voter registration increased by over 4 million in targeted states, with Democratic registration outstripping Republican;[471] 26 percent of voters told exit-poll workers that they had been contacted personally by the Obama campaign, and 18 percent reported contact from the McCain campaign.[472] Nationally, 25 percent of eighteen- to twenty-nine-year-old voters told exit-poll workers that they had been contacted by the Obama campaign, 13 percent by the McCain campaign. In targeted states, the number of young voters reporting contact from the Obama campaign was much higher: 54 percent in Pennsylvania and 61 percent in Nevada.[473] And research has demonstrated that such contact is effective in increasing voter turnout.[474]

By recruiting millions of volunteers (a disproportionate number of which are eighteen to twenty-nine years old), party organizations engage citizens more deeply in democratic politics. The typical activities of party volunteers—knocking on doors to register voters and distribute campaign literature, answering phones at party offices, phone banking in the days before the election, dropping off campaign signs, maintaining and updating voter lists—provide an avenue for participation in the system that goes beyond the relatively simple act of voting. These activities also enhance knowledge about the meaning of the election and the nature of the electoral system, engender excitement about elections, and build the personal connections that are at the foundation of social capital and, thus, of civic engagement.

Finally, party organizations support the health of elections by recruiting people to run for office and training those recruits to run effective, competitive campaigns. Without candidates, there are no elections and, as demonstrated in chapter 2, a large number of elections for Congress and state legislative contests feature only one serious contender. Such numbers would be worse if national, state, and local party organizations did not spend considerable effort to recruit candidates for office.[475] The Democratic and Republican Congressional campaign committees (for both the U.S. Senate and House) recruit and encourage large number of candidates for U.S. Senate and House seats, though they expend most of their effort recruiting candidates for competitive seats (and in some cases discouraging candidates whom they deem unlikely to win the general election).[476] State, state legislative, and local party committees also devote a great deal of effort to identifying and recruiting candidates for legislative seats,[477] in some cases attempting to ensure that they have a candidate in every legislative contest, in other cases concentrating their efforts on a select set of districts where they think they have the best chances of winning.[478] Party committees utilize their resources to induce candidates to run, offering money, help raising money, assistance with campaign communications, training, field workers, staff, facilities, and so forth.[479] Party recruitment has been critical to making elections contested and competitive and has ultimately contributed to the health of elections in the United States. Republican Party recruitment of candidates in southern states in the 1980s and 1990s, for example, played a key role in making that previously Democrat-dominated region competitive for the Republican Party.[480] In Vermont, Democrats helped turn a previously Republican-dominated legislature to one in which Democrats were at first simply competitive but are now the dominant majority party.[481] Similar examples abound.[482]

Box 6.1. The Dark Side? Campaign Consultants

In addition to recruiting candidates, running massive voter-mobilization efforts, maintaining voter information databases, helping candidates raise money, and making independent expenditures on behalf of their candidates, political party organizations (and their candidates) often contract out for polling services, media, and direct mail—that is, they hire campaign consultants. Campaign consultants have a notorious reputation; they are blamed for many of the evils of modern campaigns, including concern with image over substance, negative campaigns, and poll-driven politics. These "hired guns" have also been blamed for the weakening of political parties in the United States. Recent research, however, shows that campaign consultants are allies of the political parties rather than adversaries: most consultants work for only one party, most of them become consultants because of their political beliefs, and most consultants start their careers volunteering or working for party organizations.[483] Moreover, a sensible division of labor between party organizations and consultants has developed, leaving to each its respective strong suit—parties provide manpower, information, and money; campaign consultants deal with polling, media, direct mail, and the Internet.[484] The collaboration between party organizations and their corps of consultants extends the impact of party organizations on elections, providing critical services to candidates that promote competition. Where consultants (and their parties) may have a negative impact on the health of elections is in the ways they urge their candidates to compete and in the messages they craft for them.

The benefits of the activities of party organizations discussed in this section—mobilizing voters, recruiting candidates, pooling and redistributing campaign money—carry obvious benefits for U.S. elections, so it is clear that the health of the country's elections is closely tied to the health of political party organizations. Political parties should be encouraged to conduct more of these activities. In order to sustain and expand these activities, political party committees need money; therefore, the main prescription for encouraging these beneficial activities is to craft campaign-finance laws so that the easiest way for election money to flow is through the parties.

CONCLUSION

Although the American political parties have become involved in the practice of some activities that are detrimental to U.S. elections, healthy elections are unimaginable without strong, competitive political parties. In order to encourage the use of political parties as a means of structuring the choice in elections around philosophies of governance, one thing that needs to change is the rhetoric of the Democratic and Republican Parties and their candidates. If the rhetoric of partisans were more substantive, if it focused on the real nature of the choice that the parties offer voters (and not on irrelevant matters designed to distract voters or divert them from voting according to their overall interests), then members of the public could better understand what their electoral choices truly mean.

The typical activities of party organizations support the functioning of elections. Party organizations in the United States currently do quite a bit to support the health of elections, but they could do still more, and changes to the system could help. Campaign finance laws need to be altered to ensure that the bulk of the money in the campaign system flows through the political parties, and some adjustments are also needed in the way that parties use money on behalf of their candidates—adjustments to make elections more broadly competitive. Directing election money through the party organizations, after all, has a number of benefits: it dilutes the impact of individual contributing interests and it provides the resources parties need in order to encourage political participation in elections through voter mobilization, candidate recruitment, and more competitive elections.

Anthony Gierzynski, Ph.D.
Department of Political Science
The University of Vermont

Patient: U.S. Elections   D.O.B.: September 17, 1789

R_x

Parties must change what they talk about when they talk about politics by

- staying focused on (or at least constantly returning to) the big picture: the fundamental nature represented by the electoral choice
- maintaining reasoned discourse about the merits of policies
- forgoing the use of wedge issues
- refraining from jumping on the other side's inconsequential gaffes

State-set limits (albeit generous ones) on contributions to political parties

Increased national limits on party-coordinated spending

Campaign-finance laws that direct election money through party organizations

Signature of the Prescriber: *Dr. Anthony Gierzynski*

CHAPTER 7

ELECTION LAW
AND ADMINISTRATION

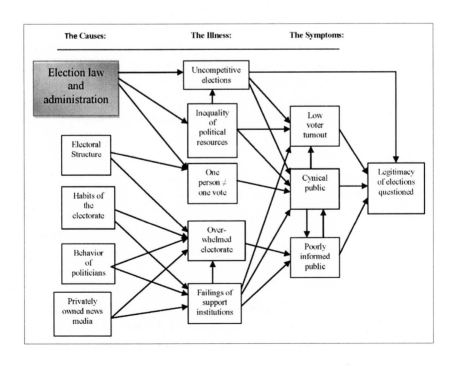

The Causes: The Illness: The Symptoms:

> Above everything, *the people are powerless if the political enterprise is not competitive.* It is the competition of political organizations that provides the people with the opportunity to make a choice. Without this opportunity popular sovereignty amounts to nothing.[485]

Competition is the very heart of elections; without it the people are stripped of their choices and thus of their power to influence the direction of governments. If the electoral system is open and fair, then elections, through the competition of contending philosophies of governance, can be a vehicle for transforming public preferences into governmental action. If the system is somehow biased, favoring one philosophy or segment of the society over another, then the overall health of the democracy is threatened. Governments establish laws that set the rules for elections so that elections will be fair, open, and competitive. Such policies are, naturally, highly controversial, for the rules of any game are rarely neutral. In setting the rules for the financing of elections, governments are confronted with a dilemma between measures that enhance equality and competition but that inevitably limit the freedom of some to bring their full resources to bear to influence the outcome of elections. If the laws that lay out the procedures for determining who votes with whom (that is, the laws for the delineation of legislative districts, for *redistricting*) allow one set of interests to arrange the distribution of voters in its own favor, then elections are likely to feature less competition between different governing philosophies, and control over legislative bodies is less likely to be responsive to changes in the preferences of the public. Laws that govern campaign financing and redistricting can have an effect on the health of elections by determining the levels of competitiveness. In the United States, poorly designed electoral laws are a leading cause of electoral dysfunction, and any prescription for healthier elections must therefore include improvements in such laws.

The way the actual act of casting votes is organized in U.S. elections (often labeled *election administration*) also has an effect on the health of elections. The current manner in which elections are administered often leads to the spoiling of voters' ballots, ambiguities in the vote count, difficulties registering to vote or staying registered, and a disproportionate burden on some voters (see chapter 3). This unevenness of electoral administration introduces inequities and can, in instances of close elections, leave the public questioning the legitimacy of elections.

This chapter examines some prescriptions for improving the health of elections through changes in the laws that govern campaign finance and redistricting and in election administration.

MONEY RULES: LAWS THAT GOVERN CAMPAIGN FINANCE

Campaign finance laws regulate money in elections; they may regulate who can contribute to whom, how much can be contributed, and how much can be spent. Campaign-finance laws may also provide public money to candidates and political party organizations. There is no question that money is an important political resource.[486] And there is no question that the distribution of money in the U.S. is highly unequal.[487] The overall purpose of campaign finance laws, then, is (or should be, if political equality is deemed an important democratic quality) to prevent the unequal distribution of an economic resource from becoming an unequal distribution of a political resource. To put it another way, campaign-finance laws are meant to prevent those with money from having undue influence over who gets elected and over the elected politicians' behavior. U.S. campaign-finance laws have not adequately done this.[488]

The purposes behind *laws that establish public financing* of campaigns vary depending on the law, but may include (1) enhancing competition by providing funds (or start-up funds) for candidates who, for reasons beyond their potential appeal (e.g., they are not incumbents or household names), might not otherwise be able to raise enough money; (2) promoting equality through the elimination of private money from elections and the leveling of the financial playing field; and (3) as an incentive for candidates to agree to spending limits.[489] Many public-funding laws, like campaign finance laws in general, have failed to achieve their purposes.

One reason most campaign-finance laws fail to achieve their designers' intent is that many of the laws were passed before the dynamics of campaign finance were fully understood; more recent laws have been designed in ignorance of it.[490] Prescribing effective campaign-finance laws requires an understanding of those dynamics. Extensive research on and experimentation with campaign-finance regulations demonstrates three critical things about the dynamics of money in elections: (1) money is a necessity in most elections, (2) it is impossible to keep private money out of elections, and (3) money flows to those who hold or are likely to hold political power within the political system—in the U.S. system, those are primarily incumbents (especially if they hold key committee assignments) and members of the majority party. The theory behind many campaign finance laws ignores these properties or sees the role of money in elections as purely dysfunctional, even evil. Policies that are driven by such theories seek to prevent, block, or dam up the flow of money, an unrealistic approach to campaign-finance reform and one that is bound to fail. Money is necessary to the proper functioning of elections, and the history of election financing in the United States has shown that money cannot be cut out of elections. Therefore a better approach is to conceive of the task not as cleaning the money out of the system but as *managing* the flow of money; instead of trying to cut funds off, laws should direct and redirect money in ways that eliminate or reduce the most harmful effects money has on elections.

The most harmful effects of money on elections can be summed up in one word: *inequality*. Because money is a political resource of great necessity to electoral campaigns—in particular, with respect to purchasing means to communicate with voters—the manner in which it is distributed among candidates, parties, and causes plays a critical role in determining the competitiveness of elections. If the distribution of money in elections is skewed so that one set or class of candidates has a significant advantage over another, elections are not competitive and fail to provide viable options for voters. As I wrote in a previous book on the matter:

> If you were holding a debate between two candidates or over a particular issue, would you think it fair if one side was allotted thirty minutes to make its case and the other side only one minute?

Would the audience of such a debate be able to make a rational and informed decision as to which side had more merit? Would it be fair if the sides had thirty and ten minutes, respectively? What about thirty and twenty minutes each? Since money in campaigns buys "time" with the voters, such questions are the issue facing us with the financing of political campaigns. If the contribution of different sides to the discourse in a political campaign is lopsided, and if other sources of information are limited, then the information voters have about the issue(s) will be dominated by that which comes from the side that has more money to spend.[491]

This is not to say that the amount of money has to be perfectly equal; after all, two different candidates could spend the same amount of money to very different effect. The problem arises when the imbalance is so great that the voice of one side is drowned out by the other and the outcome of the election turns not on the merit of the proposed policies but on which candidate, by means of financial advantage, had more chances to frame the debate and make more unanswered assertions. As demonstrated in chapter 2, such imbalances in campaign money are a very real feature of U.S. elections. Imbalances exist between incumbent candidates and their challengers, who typically have a fraction of what is available to the officeholders they run against, and between the Democratic and Republican Party committees (though some exceptions have appeared in recent years).

Because candidates and parties truly need money to communicate with voters in order to have a fighting chance at winning, the sources of electoral money also become important. When the money that candidates and parties rely on come disproportionately from one sector or interest in society, politicians become dependent on and indebted to those sources. This may then give the financial sources greater influence than everyone else. If such influence alters the outcome of the policy-making process, shifting it away from the direction supported by the voters, then elections are rendered less powerful and the system falls short of democracy because of the lack of political equality. Evidence exists to suggest that this is sometimes the case in America's political system, including obvious and blatant cases of corruption. For example, Democratic Illinois governor Rod Blagojevich was impeached and removed from office for selling state jobs, state contracts, and regulatory favors for campaign contributions, as well as for allegedly attempting to sell Barack Obama's U.S. Senate seat for campaign cash. (Illinois, incidentally, had no limits on campaign contributions as of 2008; four out of five recent governors have been charged with wrongdoing associated in some way with campaign contributions.) Another instance is the case of lobbyist Jack Abramoff, who was convicted of buying Congress members' votes with golf junkets and free dinners.

Beyond these headline cases, more subtle forms of such influence have also been uncovered by researchers—influence that affects the effort lawmakers put into promoting or opposing legislation, influence that affects votes on issues that are not very visible to the public or that are extremely important to the interests of the contributors.[492] Furthermore, polls suggest that the public believes that money does indeed buy influence. According to a 2008 poll conducted by Lake Research Partners and the Tarrance Group,

> over three-fourths of voters agree with the statement "I am worried that large political contributions will prevent Congress from tackling the important issues facing America today, like the economic crisis, rising energy costs, reforming health care, and global warming" (77% agree).[493]

In a 1997 Gallup poll, 53 percent of respondents thought that campaign contributions influence the policies supported by elected officials a great deal; another 33 percent, "a moderate amount." At the state level, a poll of Midwestern citizens found 37 percent "extremely concerned" about the role of money in state politics, ranging from 27 percent in Minnesota (which has publicly funded statewide and state legislative elections) to 46 percent in Illinois.[494]

These unhealthy aspects of the U.S. system—the evidence that corrupt influence takes place and that the financial playing field is uneven in many elections—demonstrate the need for improved campaign-finance laws at the national, state, and local levels in order to make U.S.

elections more democratic. The question, then, is how these laws should be modified.

The Campaign Finance System as It Is

Before any fixes to the campaign-finance system are proposed, it is critical to understand how the components of the system produce the outcomes that are detrimental to U.S. elections. To that end, figure 7.1 maps out the anatomy of the campaign-finance system for national elections in the United States. Perhaps the most striking characteristic is the system's incredible complexity (even without considering all the possible flows of money, some of which have been deliberately omitted from this figure to avoid making it utterly unreadable[495]). The anatomy of state and local elections is similar but varies with regard to the limits (some are stricter, some more lax, and some lack restrictions altogether) and with regard to the importance of the routes through which money flows—for instance, more money may flow through the political parties in some states, whereas in others, public funding of elections plays a critical role.

In the national system depicted in figure 7.1, money can flow from individuals directly to congressional or presidential candidates (unless presidential nominees accept public funding), to political party committees, to Political Action Committees (PACs), through individual fund-raisers called *bundlers* (because they bundle together checks from other contributors for the candidates), and to 527 committees or other independent groups. Campaign finance law has different rules for each of these ways to give—rules about how much can be given, including outright prohibitions (as for corporations and unions, not depicted in figure 7.1), set amounts (e.g., the $2,300 limit on individual contributions[496]), or no limits whatsoever. In the case of presidential contests, money can also flow from taxpayers who opt to dedicate $3 of their taxes to the Presidential Election Campaign Fund (PECF). This fund provides an option of public funding for candidates running for their parties' presidential nominations and for the parties' nominees during the general election (it also provides money for the parties' national conventions). The money that is contributed to these organizations can then be used for campaigning

FIGURE 7.1. Campaign finance system for 2008 national elections.

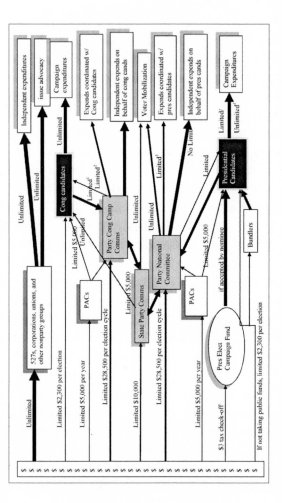

Note. Arrows represent options for individuals who wish to use their money to influence the process. Wider arrows indicate more money can flow through that route. Contributions from corporations, labor unions, and foreign nationals are prohibited.

[1] Limit = $5,000 to House candidates and $39,900 to Senate candidates per election.

[2] Limit varies for Senate and House districts based on population of the state, the number of congressional districts in the state and is adjusted for inflation, ranged from $42,100 to $2.28 million.

[3] Limit = $.02 x Voting Age Population in the United States; for 2008 it was $19,151,200.

[4] Limited if candidate accepts public funding, otherwise unlimited.

in its various forms—to communicate messages with voters via media or direct contact, to mobilize voters, or to purchase information and materials needed for an effective campaign. It may also be redistributed to other organizations—for example, from a candidate to a party committee or to other candidates, or from a PAC to a candidate.

As argued previously, some aspects of this system actually work in favor of equality and better competition, while others allow money to distort the system, favoring one set of candidates or interests and thus damaging the health of elections. As discussed in chapter 6, the role of the political party committees in the system is, for the most part, beneficial: they dilute the importance of any one contributor, redistribute money from incumbents in safe districts to more marginal elections (though they could disburse the money more widely), and utilize money in ways that encourage voter participation.

The public funding of presidential campaigns had worked from the mid 1970s until the 1990s to enhance political equality and competition by providing seed money for lesser known candidates to compete (some of whom later became president).[497] And for a time (until the actors in the system adjusted and the funding amounts and spending limits became too low), public funding worked to enhance political equality by diluting the influence of big contributors. As the decisions of recent candidates indicate, the public-funding system no longer seems to be working. The level of funding and the spending limits that accompany it have simply not kept up with the increasing costs of presidential campaigns. At first, candidates and their supporters used soft money to greatly increase what party organizations could do for their presidential candidates. When that was banned by the BCRA, supporters of the candidates shifted their financial support to 527 and 501(c) committees. Eventually it became clear to candidates that they could raise more through their own campaigns and thus avoid spending limits. Candidates George W. Bush, John Kerry, and Howard Dean rejected nomination funding in 2004; John McCain rejected such funds in 2008; and Barack Obama rejected both nomination and general-election funding in 2008. Obama's campaign ultimately raised almost four times the amount that he would have received in public funds for the general election.

Other independent (nonparty) groups, such as 527s and 501(c)s,[498] can raise money in unlimited amounts and spend that money campaigning for or against candidates (as long as they do so independently) or running what are known as *issue ads*—that is, campaign communications that do not expressly advocate the election or defeat of candidates.[499] This conduit gives individuals and groups with a lot of money the ability to influence elections disproportionately. Contributors can (and do) give large amounts of money to these organizations' campaigns, which campaigns then spend even larger amounts of money disseminating what are often the most negative, distracting, and dubious messages of the election.[500] These 527 and 501(c) committees can get away with saying almost anything because they are more or less anonymous and there is thus no practical way to hold them responsible for what they say. They operate under names like America Votes, American Solutions Winning the Future, the Fund for America, Patriot Majority Fund, Freedom's Watch, and Americans for Job Security, but their names give voters no clue as to who is actually paying for an ad or to which candidates or parties an ad might be connected.[501] Indeed, many of these groups—mainly 501(c)s—have no legal obligation to disclose the names of their financers. And these messages are simply too numerous—many that run well under the radar—for the already overwhelmed and increasingly understaffed mainstream press to check.

To cite a single illustrative example of how these groups operate, the top individual contributor to 527s in 2008 was Fred Eshelman of Pharmaceutical Product Development, Inc., who contributed nearly $5.5 million; the top group donor, Service Employees International Union, contributed over $34.5 million.[502] And although spending by such groups declined in 2008 relative to 2004 (527s, in particular, spent less; 501(c)s, however, spent more), they still spent approximately $400 million.[503] In addition to getting involved in presidential races, these groups tend to pour their money into the most competitive U.S. Senate and House contests, a circumstance that contributes to the spiraling financial escalation (or monetary "arms race") that is typical of such contests. At times, such independent expenditures and issue ads even make it difficult for the candidates themselves, whom these groups support, to get their own messages out through the deafening din of attacks and counterattacks. All this makes it quite evident that the operation of 527s, 501(c)s, and other independent groups is not good for the health of U.S. elections.

At this point, it is appropriate to note how the role of 527s and other independent groups in U.S. elections presents lessons on the difficulty of eliminating campaign finance practices that are harmful to democratic elections. Federal election campaign law has, through its various incarnations, sought to limit the corrupting influence of large contributors by banning corporate and union contributions and by limiting contributions to candidates, parties, and PACs.[504] Facing limits on contributions to candidates, PACs, and party committees, big money contributors have sought other ways to influence elections, and the U.S. Supreme Court provided the opening for this by first poking holes in the Federal Election Campaign Act and its amendments and then rejecting subsequent legislative attempts to patch those holes up.

In its landmark campaign-finance ruling *Buckley v. Valeo* (424 US 1, 1976) the Court equated campaign spending with speech, thus granting protection to campaign spending under the First Amendment's guarantee of freedom of speech. Based on that premise, the Court reasoned that any limits on what candidates, individuals, or groups may spend in elections are unconstitutional. From that point on, it has been impossible for governments to regulate campaign expenditures, including the expenditures of independent groups, individuals, and—as of 2010—corporations and unions.[505] In *Buckley* the Court also opened up a way to influence elections without having to follow federal election law by narrowly defining what would be considered *electioneering communications*. Communications that explicitly advocate the election or defeat of a candidate, using the words "*vote for, elect, support, cast your ballot for, Smith for Congress, vote against, defeat,* and *reject*"[506] were considered *express advocacy* or electioneering communications; all other forms of communication during elections (what became known as *issue advocacy*) lay outside election law. The effect of this definition was to allow groups to use unlimited amounts of money on issue ads, which are, for the most part, thinly veiled campaign ads that merely avoid the use of the specific words that would categorize them as electioneering ads. Indeed, research has shown that voters cannot distinguish between issue ads and electioneering ads; they see them all as attempts to persuade the electorate to vote one way or another.[507] Because such communications are not considered an attempt to affect the outcome of elections (despite all evidence to the contrary), groups that run issue advocacy campaigns are not regulated by the federal election law; instead, this activity is governed by federal tax laws (527 and 501(c) groups actually owe their names to the sections of the tax code that pertain to them). In 2002 Congress attempted to more realistically and broadly define electioneering communications as part of the Bipartisan Campaign Reform Act (BCRA), but the Supreme Court rejected the attempt.[508]

Political Action Committees (PACs; known as *multicandidate committees* under federal election law) can raise contributions from individuals in amounts up to $5,000 and can contribute up to $5,000 per candidate per election. Most PACs are part of an integrated lobbying effort on the part of interest groups; PACs give to members of Congress (especially to those on committees that deal with legislation of concern to the interest group) in order to ensure that their lobbyists have access to powerful lawmakers.[509] In a sense, much PAC money is geared not toward affecting election outcomes but toward making sure the group can have its say in the legislative process (indeed, incumbents and party leaders often make sure this is understood when they solicit PAC money; see for example, the case Republican Tom Delay made to Wal-Mart to persuade the company to begin contributing to Republicans[510]). Some PACs—those representing labor or ideological groups, for example—do focus on the outcome of elections, but such groups do not control the bulk of PAC money.

PACs were once the focus of much derision, the main culprit in many critiques of the campaign finance system. These days it is rare to hear reformers railing against PACs, but PACs do still pose some problems for the health of elections. One problem is that the PAC system is highly skewed in favor of one set of interests: business. Most PACs are business PACs, and business PACs are the source of most PAC money going to candidates (see chapter 2).[511] Consequently, the PAC system affords business interests greater access to lawmakers. The other problem is that most PACs shower those already in power with money while giving next to nothing to those who wish to challenge incumbent officeholders. This tendency on the part of PACs is a major contributor to the massive imbalances in campaign funds between incumbent candidates and challengers—imbalances that make competing incredibly difficult.

Contributions from individuals also play a key role in financing elections, especially presidential contests. Such contributions were limited to $2,300 per election in 2008 (an amount which is adjusted each election cycle for inflation and was $2,400 for the 2009–2010 election cycle). Individuals give for a variety of reasons—their ideology, their feelings about the candidate, their personal connections, and so forth[512]—and these contributions on their own (especially in smaller amounts) have no ill effect on elections. A ground swell of support in contributions, especially if they are in small amounts, can be seen as reflection of the popularity of a candidate or party (or of the opposing side's lack of popularity), and amassing support through small contributions does not violate most peoples' notion of democracy. Indeed, during the 2008 presidential election, much was made of Barack Obama's success in raising substantial amounts of money in small contributions—thanks, in part, to skillful use of the Internet—and rightly so. A study conducted by the Campaign Finance Institute found that 30 percent of the money the Obama campaign raised for the nomination contest came from contributors who gave $200 or less and that 34 percent of the money Obama raised for the general election came, again, from such small contributors. The percentage Obama raised from small contributors for the nomination exceeded that raised by John Kerry and by George W. Bush in 2004, as 20 percent of Kerry's nomination funds and 26 percent of Bush's came from contributors who gave $200 or less. Additionally, midrange contributors, those giving between $201 and $999 dollars, composed a substantial enough segment of Obama's financial support to keep him significantly less reliant on money from contributors who gave $1,000 or more (who were responsible for 43 percent of Obama's money nomination campaign funds and 42 percent of his general election funds) than was John McCain, who raised 60 percent of his funds for the nomination from contributors who gave $1,000 or more.[513] (McCain accepted public funding for the general election so there are no comparable numbers for that contest.)

Contributions from individuals are capped at a reasonable level and are thus unlikely to injure the health of elections on their own, but the rise of the bundlers of those individual contributions is less innocuous. Bundlers are wealthy individuals who tap their networks of friends, family, and associates in order to raise money for candidates. Those friends, family members, and associates write checks payable to the candidates (usually for the maximum allowable amount), and the bundlers give the bundle of checks to the grateful candidates.

> According to the Center for Responsive Politics (CRP), 561 "bundlers" had raised a minimum of $63 million for Obama by mid-August and 534 people had raised a minimum of $75 million for McCain. The bundlers undoubtedly were responsible for more than these amounts because the campaigns reported the bundlers in ranges and CRP's minimum totals were based conservatively on the low end of each range. A reasonable guess might estimate the real amount at the mid-point for each range. This would yield a total of about $90 million for Obama as of mid-August and more than $100 million for McCain. At the top of the bundlers were 47 of Obama's and 65 of McCain's who were listed by the campaigns in mid-August as being responsible for at least $500,000 each.[514]

The practice of bundling defeats the purpose of the individual contribution limits. Although each check comes from individuals who abide by the contribution limits, the ability of one individual to hand over a stack of checks totaling $100,000 or $500,000 to a campaign undoubtedly engenders a certain level of indebtedness to such individuals, almost all of whom are wealthy business executives, investors, realtors, lawyers, bankers, and lobbyists.[515] And bundlers *do* receive special treatment. Campaigns make them part of de facto clubs (the National Finance Committee for Obama bundlers and the Trailblazers and Innovators for McCain bundlers), grant them special privileges at party functions (e.g., the parties' national conventions), and give them personal access to the candidates.[516]

On the spending side of the system (the right-hand side of figure 7.1), there are no limits (except for party-coordinated expenditures). This produces one additional harmful dynamic in U.S. elections—namely, an upward spiraling escalation of spending in an arms-race mentality. Without spending limits, candidates become involved in a campaign-finance arms race because of the uncertainty posed by opponents' unlimited spending.[517] Not knowing how much the opponent is spending (or how much groups and party committees are spending on his or her behalf), the rational response is to raise and spend as much as possible (definitely more than was spent in the previous election) in order to avoid being outspent. Spending levels are thus determined not by what is necessary to publicize one's message but by previous levels of spending and by the need to counter the anticipated volume of messages coming from the opposing camp—and the volume levels in the highly contested races and battleground states have reached a deafening level. Furthermore, in such contests a great deal of money and time is spent raising more money as opposed to actually communicating with voters.[518]

The Campaign Finance System as It Should Be
The complexity of financing elections means that no simple fix will do. It also means that simple transparency (full-disclosure laws promoted by conservatives and libertarians) will not work as a check on the unhealthy practices that take place within the campaign finance systems; expecting the public to follow the money through the intricacies of these systems in a way that would allow them to hold candidates responsible is laughable, especially considering how little the public knows (or cares to know) and considering the questionable wisdom of further burdening the public.

At the other extreme, attempting to shut down or clean out this system, prohibiting people and groups from using their money for political purposes is not practical either. Nor is a system with strict contribution limits and expenditure limits; unrealistically restricting the flow of money through any of the routes in figure 7.1 merely results in the use of alternative routes, usually less regulated and more secretive than the original ones. Given the nature of money's role in elections and the complexity of the existing system, then, the best approach—and most likely the only workable one—is to enact a set of laws that see the system for what it is and modify it in ways that channel the money through the healthier routes. It is only through this sort of management that governments will be able to increase fairness and competition in the electoral system. Figure 7.2 maps out what the anatomy of such an improved campaign finance system might look like. (Though this figure and discussion focus on national elections, the same principles apply to elections at the state and local levels.)

Attaining the changes depicted in figure 7.2 would involve (1) an enhanced and expanded public financing program for both presidential and congressional candidates, (2) upward adjustments to the limits on money flowing through party organizations, (3) a more practical definition of *issue advocacy*, (4) limits on contributions to all groups involved in electioneering activities, and (5) limitations on bundling. Some of these alterations fly in the face of recent Supreme Court rulings, but the purpose of this study is to show what needs to be done, regardless of the current justices' opinions. Although the Court has the final word on the constitutionality of the law, its rulings should not limit the discussion of necessary changes. Supreme Court decisions often appear to be informed more by ideology than by an understanding of the empirical effects of campaign-finance practices on U.S. elections. Furthermore, recent Court reversals on the BCRA highlight the possibility that the Court may one day reverse its position as its members (and subsequently its ideology) change.[519]

R_x: Public Funding for Executive and Legislative Offices
Public funding is critical to achieving better levels of equality and competition in American elections. This is especially true now, following

FIGURE 7.2. Campaign finance system as it should be for national elections.

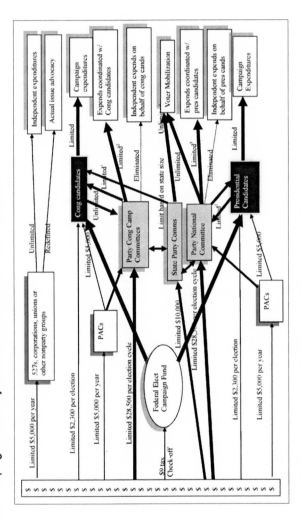

Note. Wider arrows indicate more money can flow through that route. Contributions from Corporations, Labor Unions and Foreign Nationals remain prohibited. All amounts subject to increases based on changes in inflation.

---

[1] Increase limits to equal coordinated expenditure limits.

[2] Triple limits using existing formula that varies for Senate and House districts based on population of the state and the number of congressional districts in the state range from $124,000 to $6.8 million.

[3] Increase limit = $.04 x Voting Age Population in the United States; for 2012 about $38 million.

the Supreme Court's 2010 *Citizens United* ruling, which removed the century-old ban on direct corporate spending in campaigns.[520] Public funding (1) can dilute the importance of big money contributors; (2) can provide the start-up money for lesser known but potentially appealing candidates, allowing them to compete; (3) if provided on a matching basis, can encourage small contributions while making those who can only give small amounts more important; and (4) if generous enough, can be used to induce candidates to accept reasonable spending limits and agree to debates, as discussed in chapter 4. Because public-funding programs are voluntary, they can be established without fear of violating current court rulings. Experience with public-funding systems has shown that they can work to meet these goals. The presidential system did so until it became outdated.[521] The state of Minnesota runs an effective public-funding program for its statewide and legislative candidates, a program that has reduced the financial disparities between incumbents and challengers and enhanced competition. Additionally, Minnesotans are less concerned about the influence of money in state politics than are citizens of neighboring states.[522] Studies of Arizona, Hawaii, Maine, Minnesota, and Wisconsin found increased competition and an increase in the number of candidates willing to challenge incumbents.[523] Finally, an analysis of gubernatorial elections found that candidate-based public funding, combined with reasonable spending limits, makes some elections (those involving a Democratic incumbent) more competitive.[524]

The public-funding system for presidential candidates is still on the books, but it is abundantly clear from the behavior of candidates, parties, and independent groups that the program, set up thirty years ago in the Watergate era, no longer works. There currently is no public-funding program for congressional candidates, but sixteen states and a number of local governments do have public funding programs. In seven states these programs cover statewide races; nine states fund both statewide and legislative contests. The types of public-funding programs include total public funding (what advocates call *clean money*) and partial or matching systems. Total public funding programs, in which candidate spending is effectively limited to government-provided money, are used in Maine, Connecticut, Arizona, New Jersey, North Carolina (for judicial candidates only), and New Mexico, as well as in local campaigns in Albuquerque, New Mexico. Partial public-funding systems that involve a mix of public money and money candidates raise from private citizens are used in nine states—Hawaii, Florida, Nebraska, Massachusetts, Michigan, Minnesota, New Jersey (gubernatorial campaigns), Rhode Island, and Wisconsin—and in New York City.[525]

A new public-funding program needs to be established for both presidential and congressional campaigns at the national level and for gubernatorial and state legislative campaigns in the states—without affecting existing effective programs. Because it is impossible to keep private money completely out of the system, a partial public-funding program is preferable to total public funding (whereby the only money candidates can spend comes from government grants). Partial public-funding programs, such as Minnesota's, seem to work better than total public-funding programs. The candidate participation rate (acceptance of public funding) in Minnesota's system, for example, is much higher than participation rates in full public-funding programs in Maine and Arizona, and it does not have the partisan slant to it evident in those states (in Arizona in 2006, only 47 percent of Republican legislative candidates participated in the public-funding system, compared with 76 percent of Democratic candidates and 89 percent of Republican legislative candidates in Minnesota).[526] Partial public-funding programs are less expensive to run—because taxpayers are providing only a portion of the money—and allow the implementation of higher spending limits than what might be possible if the public were paying the entire bill for campaigns. Finally, partial public funding still allows individuals the freedom to contribute money in legitimate ways, a freedom which, if limited, is by no means a bad thing for democracy. As history has shown, trying to prevent people from contributing at all within the regulated system of campaign finance laws simply provokes them to find ways to influence elections with their money outside of that system.

As part of a partial public-funding system, the government could also encourage small contributions (and thus enhance the importance of those small contributors) by providing the public funds through a matching system. A recent survey of campaign contributors has found that those who make small donations to campaigns are more representative of nondonors' policy views than are those who make large contributions. Perhaps even more importantly,

> large donors are more likely [than small donors] to indicate that their giving is motivated by a concern about narrowly targeted economic benefits for themselves. They are also more likely to contact lawmakers and their staff members about their own business, job, or industry.[527]

To encourage campaigns to focus on raising money from small contributors, the revamped public-funding system should offer a multiple match for the first so many dollars contributed by an individual. New York City, for instance, has a six-to-one match for the first $175, and a recent proposal by Fred Wertheimer of Democracy 21 and another by Common Cause both suggest a four-to-one match on the first $200 contributed to candidates.[528] This type of matching would, in effect, make those who contribute $200 as important to candidates as those who contribute $1,000. Some may ask, in light of recent successes in Internet use for campaign fundraising in small amounts (particularly by the Obama campaign), why small contributions need to be encouraged through public-funding matching. In fact, only about one-third of Obama's money came from donors who gave $200 or less, as already mentioned, and that portion is smaller for other candidates. Furthermore, using a matching system to encourage candidates to seek out small contributors could also provide a counterbalance to the bundlers.

Public funds for campaigns should have some strings attached for candidates who accept them. Candidates should first be required to demonstrate viability through a requirement of initial fundraising in small amounts, as is currently the case for presidential nominees; appropriate levels should be set for House, Senate, and state-level candidates. Public televised debates with the other major party candidate should be required (see chapter 4); bundling should be prohibited, and spending limits should be imposed. In crafting a workable public-funding pro-gram, the trick is to make sure that such requirements do not discourage participation in the program. The inducements offered by the program must outweigh the costs of participating. Debates are generally expected of candidates these days and hardly represent a cost. Although the law should prevent candidates who take public funds from accepting con-tributions in any way except directly from the contributors—in order to stop the practice of bundling—the money lost from bundlers would, in effect, be replaced with the program's public funds. Therefore that requirement should not prove to be much of a disincentive either.

Spending limits, however, must be set carefully—they cannot be too low, lest they discourage participation, nor too high, lest they have no practical effect. They are necessary, however, because without them campaigns, parties, and groups become drawn into a monetary arms race. Because candidates, parties, and groups do not want to be outspent by the other side in competitive contests and because they have no way of knowing how much the other candidate, party, and associate groups are spending until after the election is over, spending in elections spirals higher and higher—attaining levels beyond what is necessary to run a competitive campaign. This circumstance leads candidates, parties, and groups to spend as much as possible, as opposed to spending what is actually needed to communicate with voters. As a result, parties and groups narrowly focus their resources on a few hypercompetitive con-tests, effectively limiting competition to those few contests. The key in setting spending limits, then, is to find the point beyond which spending is unnecessary and simply starts to spiral into an escalating arms race. After all, the goal of spending money in elections is to inform voters of their choice, not to harass and confuse them with an endless barrage of over-the-top, simplistic, and distorted attacks and counterattacks that are characteristic of today's hypercompetitive contests. Additionally, if the prescriptions discussed in chapters 5, 6, and 8 are adopted, informing voters should not prove so extraordinarily expensive.

To find the appropriate spending limits, then, an examination of recent spending patterns is in order. Barack Obama's campaign spent

$424 million to win his party's 2008 nomination in what was an extremely competitive nominating contest and spent about $322 million on winning the general election against John McCain. Was this too much money? Obama's campaign received plaudits for its ability to reach deeply into and broadly across the country's citizenry in order to involve members of the public in the election. His campaign was able to take its message beyond the typical handful of battleground states where the energy and finances of most other presidential campaigns are concentrated. Obama was the first presidential candidate in many years to purchase network time in order to reach voters nationwide with his message, both in typical spot ads and in one thirty-minute spot that was broadcast simultaneously on a number of networks and cable channels. Because his campaign controlled most of the spending on his side (money which had in the past flowed to 527s or to the parties for independent expenditures), Obama was able to run a more unified campaign than those in the recent past (as well as McCain, his opponent in 2008), with a clear and focused message. And in concert with the DNC, he was able to build an impressive network of volunteers who contacted voters and encouraged them to cast a vote on or before Election Day. Despite these vast expenditures, I have not found any evidence or analysis to date suggesting that this campaign wasted money. Therefore it makes sense to set the spending limit for the *general election* for presidential candidates around the level of Obama's spending—say, $325 million for 2012—with adjustments for inflation for each subsequent presidential election cycle. The matching public funds should constitute about one-third to one-half of that. Such levels should make the program nearly irresistible to candidates. To sweeten the pot a bit more, an additional incentive that could encourage participation in the program is the free broadcast airtime discussed in chapter 4, the provision of which should be tied to the decision of the parties' presidential nominees to participate in the public-funding system.

For the *nomination contest*, the spending limit should be adjusted for the level of competition, and if the changes to the nominating contest suggested in chapter 5 are adopted, the spending level could probably be set substantially lower than what Obama spent. As I argued in chapter 5, the nominating contest should be reformed along the lines suggested by Thomas Patterson: it should start later in the year, involve five individual state contests over a period of eight weeks, followed by an ultimate Tuesday a month later for the rest of the states and territories. This would reduce the high costs associated with the long and haphazard nomination contest that takes place now. In this case, spending limits could be set for the first five state contests (so that there is more of an emphasis on retail, person-to-person campaigning; limits would be indexed to reflect the cost of some recent statewide campaigns in those states), and then another limit set for the ultimate Tuesday contest, the appropriate level for which may be more difficult to determine—though $200 to $250 million might be generous enough. Again, public funding would provide up to one-third of those limits. There would also have to be some system to govern the time between which a candidate secures the nomination on ultimate Tuesday and the candidate's national party convention, when he or she officially becomes the nominee, because this interim period is when the general election is likely to begin. Perhaps a portion of the general election spending could be allotted for use during this time.

For congressional contests, the spending limits for general election contests should also be set to reflect recent spending patterns. To find a suitable level, the spending of competitive campaigns can be examined as a gauge, and to avoid factoring in the financial arms race, the most expensive Senate and House contests should be excluded (with cost for Senate contests calculated on a per-voter basis in order to take into consideration the differing sizes of electorates—that is, state populations). The limit for House contests would be around $1 to $1.5 million, with between one-third and one-half coming from matching public funds.[529] The limit for Senate contests would vary by state population, again with between one-third and one-half coming from matching public funds. The spending limits would also vary depending on whether the candidate faced serious competition in the primary.

At this point, questions naturally arise about the cost of such a program and the way the government could pay for it. A number of reform groups promoting *full* public funding for congressional elections[530] estimate that the cost of full public funding for U.S. House and Senate contests would be about $1.75 billion per election year, or 0.04 percent of the federal budget (total spending for House and Senate candidates in 2006 was about $1.4 million).[531] The Congressional Budget Office estimated that the partial public-funding programs considered in the U.S. House and Senate in the early to mid-1990s would have cost between $95 and $190 million for the 1998 election.[532]

Table 7.1 presents calculations of the cost of a public-funding system based on the discussion up to this point. My estimates for a partial public-funding program that would cover about one-third of the costs of the 2008 presidential, House, and Senate elections come to just under $1.3 billion. If public funding was expected to cover half of what candidates spend, the cost would be closer to $1.9 billion. For House and

TABLE 7.1. Public funding estimate (in millions).

Presidential general election	Two candidates, at one-third the limit of $325	$216.7
Presidential nomination contests	Four candidates for entire campaign at one-third the limit ($325)	$433.3
	8 minor candidates who drop out after early contests (one-third of $60 million, about what the third-place Democratic and Republican candidates spent in 2008)	$160.0
Parties' national conventions	At approximately current funding levels	$35.0
U.S. Senate (primary and general elections)	One-third of 2008 total spending level	$136.7
U.S. House (primary and general elections)	One-third of 2008 total spending level*	$312.7
Total cost per presidential election cycle		$1,294.3
Total cost per nonpresidential election cycle		$449.3

Source. Data from http://www.opensecrets.org.

Senate elections when there is no presidential contest, the program would cost about $450 million ($674 million if public funding provided half of the money). These are only estimates; if other reforms suggested in this chapter produce more competitive House races, for example, those numbers could increase. Nonetheless, the costs of such a program are likely to remain close to these approximate numbers, which are rather small relative to the overall federal budget. Such costs might even be recouped if reform groups are correct in their argument that weakening influence of contributors through public funding would reduce the amount the federal government spends benefitting big-money interests—such as the $87 billion in subsidies to private businesses in 2001 or the $64 billion in earmarks in 2006.[533]

As for the source of the money, Congress could build on the already-existing Presidential Election Campaign Fund (PECF). The money for the PECF comes from taxpayers who opt to dedicate $3 of the taxes they already owe—although many tax payers mistakenly believe that this will add $3 to their taxes and do not check off the box on their 1040s. The percentage of taxpayers checking the box, once as high as 28.7 percent on 1980 returns, has dropped to 8.3 percent on 2007 returns, perhaps reflecting the decline in participation in the PECF by the major candidates in 2004 and 2008.[534] Like candidate participation in PECF, this aspect of the system had functioned effectively until recently (especially after the minor adjustment of increasing the amount from $1 to $3 in 1994), and with some small adjustments it could continue to be an important source of funding for a revamped federal election campaign fund. From 2004 to 2008, the tax-form option raised about $50 million per year—clearly not enough to fund the suggested program. In order to increase the revenues of the fund to provide the moneys for the suggested changes, the amount a taxpayer could dedicate to the fund should be increased to between $6 and $10. This, plus a campaign to inform the public as to the benefits and costs of the program (including the fact that it does not add to their taxes) could boost participation and funding levels. One alternative might be to change the form so that taxpayers would have to check the box to opt *out* of the public-funding system instead of checking it to opt in. This would likely greatly increase participation rates. If these changes worked and participation rates rebounded to the level in 1980 (just under four times the amount in 2007), the program could bring in close to $200 million a year; if the amount on the tax form were increased to $6, this would increase to $400 million a year; if increased to $9, revenues would hit $600 million a year, which is getting close to covering the costs estimated mentioned. In addition to tax check-off programs, there are other proposals for raising money for the public-funding program that could considered, including allocating general revenues to the program as Minnesota and Maine do, taxing campaign contributions, and assessing a fee or tax on lobbyists. Overall, it is evident that it would not be prohibitively difficult to fund a public-financing program for elections. For the U.S. elections, the health benefits of such programs—from more vigorously contested elections to greater political equality—would be well worth the costs.

Before moving on to other changes to campaign finance rules, it might be worth considering one additional aspect of Minnesota's law related to the public-funding program. Minnesota runs a Public Contribution Refund Program, which gives Minnesotans who make contributions to a Minnesota political party or a candidate for state office or legislature the ability to get a refund for the first $50 of the contribution amount—if the contribution goes to a candidate who agrees to spending limits.[535] According to research by the Campaign Finance Institute, this program made Minnesota unique in reliance on small contributors, with 45 percent of candidate funds (gubernatorial and legislative in 2006) coming from contributors who gave $100 or less.[536] Unfortunately, the program was suspended by Governor Tim Pawlenty in 2009 in order to trim spending to meet a budget shortfall. The program clearly worked to enhance the role of ordinary citizens and weaken the role of large contributors. It is worth considering such a program for other states and at the federal level in order to accomplish the same goals and provide another inducement for candidates to participate in the public-funding system.

R_x: A Bigger and More Honest Role for Political Parties

By adding public money and encouraging small contributions, a public-funding system similar to the one prescribed here should provide an effective counterbalance to the role of wealthy interests in the campaign-finance system. And the need for such a counterbalance is even more important following the 2010 *Citizens United* Supreme Court 558 U.S. ___ (2010) ruling allowing corporate electioneering spending. Adjusting the campaign-finance law to funnel the flow of most the remaining money in the system (whether from wealthy interests or those who give in small or moderate amounts) to the political parties would also benefit the health of elections. As pointed out in the previous chapter, the increase in the amount individuals can give to party committees under the BCRA was a positive step in this direction. State laws should follow this lead. But more needs to be done in this area to prompt party committees to spread their resources across more contests, in order to increase the number of competitive contests. What I suggest is a tradeoff for the parties: in exchange for increasing the limits on coordinated expenditures (perhaps tripling or even quadrupling the current limits), the parties would be required (preferably through legislation) to give up independent party expenditures. Again, with the parties allowed to coordinate more spending with candidates, spending would be more efficient, less wasteful, allowing them to support more candidates and expanding competition beyond the few hypercompetitive contests that receive the bulk of campaign funding today. Besides, the notion that parties and the candidates they nominate are separate actors in elections—the reasoning behind party-independent expenditures—is pure fiction. Candidates are part of the party and their purposes are the same. To further induce parties to agree to such a change in the law, governments should also condition the provision of free broadcast airtime on the agreement to eliminate independent spending.

R_x: Discourage Independent-Group Activity and Redefine Issue Ads

The partial public-funding system with practical spending limits and the changes to the rules governing political parties should encourage most of the money in the campaign-finance systems to flow either directly to the candidates or through the political parties as opposed to through 527s, 501(c)s, or other groups that use the funds for independent spending and issue ads. Nevertheless, it would also be good to have some laws in place that discourage money from flowing through these independent groups. In hopes that the Supreme Court will change its view in the not too distant future, legislative bodies should reassert their right to define what is and is not election activity. The definitions of electioneering activity in the BCRA seemed eminently reasonable and could provide the model. If groups run ads, send out mass mailings, or utilize other forms of mass communication during an election season that include the name or likeness of a candidate and are targeted to that candidate's constituents, such activity should be considered electioneering activity and consequently should be regulated under campaign-finance law. Such regulation simply recognizes the reality of such activity, the purpose of which, beyond any doubt, is to influence the outcome of elections. With a redefinition on the books, limits on such activities comparable to those that govern other election activity can be put into place; the $5,000 contribution limit applied to PACs seems fitting.

In sum, the prescription for campaign finance systems in America involves three main components: (1) a partial public-funding system for presidential and congressional races (gubernatorial and legislative races at the state level), (2) changes to the rules governing the role of party organizations so as to encourage the flow of money through the parties in a way that spreads competition, and (3) laws that curtail the electoral activities of independent groups. Such changes seem appropriate given the realities of the campaign-finance systems in the United States and offer the best chance to enhance electoral competition and promote political equality—both prerequisites for a democratic system.

DRAWING MORE COMPETITIVE ELECTORAL DISTRICTS

Another factor limiting electoral competition is the way that electoral districts are drawn in the United States.[537] Each member of the U.S.

House of Representatives, all state senators and state house members, as well as most city councilors or local government commissioners, represent populations located within defined geographical areas that are redrawn every ten years following the U.S. census. The characteristics of the populations of those geographic areas help determine the nature of electoral competition for those legislative seats. If the population of legislative districts comprises mostly partisans who favor one political party, only candidates from that party will have a reasonable chance of winning and electoral competition will be highly unlikely; furthermore, with few competitive districts, the number of legislative seats won or lost is less likely to reflect changes in the partisan preferences of the electorate, weakening the link between voting and control of the government. If the partisanship of the population of electoral districts is more evenly divided, candidates of either party will stand a reasonable chance of winning and elections will likely be contested vigorously. With more competitive districts, control of legislative bodies will be more sensitive to changes in the preferences of the electorate.

To illustrate this point, consider again the rectangular state (see figure 7.3), in which, for the sake of example, five districts must be drawn this time.[538] To attain an ideal level of competition, each district should include roughly equal numbers of Democrats and Republicans. Given the uneven distribution of partisans within and across states, this would be difficult to obtain; different states are disproportionately "red" or "blue," and different areas within states have higher concentrations of partisans—Democrats tend to dominate urban areas; Republicans, suburban and rural areas. Such complete balance, moreover, may not be entirely desirable, for at least two very good reasons. First, it would interfere with the creation of majority-minority districts that have promoted equality through the increase in minority representation. And second, if all districts were evenly divided, small swings in the party and independent votes could completely wipe out representation of the losing party in the legislature (if, for instance, because of partisan trends, either party gained 51 percent or more in all districts, that party would win every seat in Congress). Additionally, it is important to note that in

FIGURE 7.3. Various redistricting scenarios.

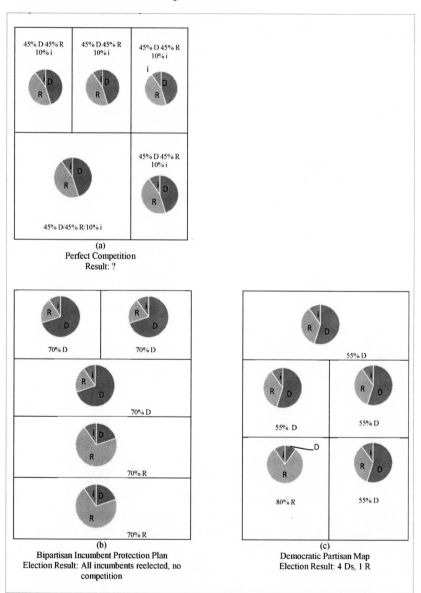

(a)
Perfect Competition
Result: ?

(b)
Bipartisan Incumbent Protection Plan
Election Result: All incumbents reelected, no
competition

(c)
Democratic Partisan Map
Election Result: 4 Ds, 1 R

terms of representation (as opposed to competition), lopsided districts ensure that the majority of the district receives representation in the legislative body. Clearly then, some mix of districts that are competitive and some that lean more toward one party is the desired goal. As documented earlier, U.S. electoral districts do not meet this standard; there are progressively fewer and fewer competitive electoral districts. The dearth of competitive districts needs to be addressed; more competitive districts are needed in order to increase the proportion of voters for whom electoral contests represent competitive choices. That, in turn, would increase the proportion of the electorate involved in determining who controls the legislative branches in the United States and increase the sensitivity of legislative representation to changes in the public's preferences.

Because the way district borders are drawn is critical for the nature of electoral competition, it is obvious that those who control the process of redrawing these political boundaries every ten years have the power to influence the level of competition in U.S. elections and to alter the partisan balance in the country's legislative bodies. Unfortunately, the dominant actors in the process—incumbent officeholders and political parties—have no interest in creating legislative districts that are competitive. Incumbents want to make their districts safe (or safer) for their own reelections, and the parties wish to maximize the number of districts that will safely elect their own members, which means packing their opponent's voters into as few uncompetitive districts as possible or spreading them around to reduce their influence. The district boundaries in figure 7.3*b* and *c* illustrate the effect of this gerrymandering. If incumbents of both parties compromise to protect their own interests, they secure reelection by rendering all of the districts uncompetitive. If one party draws the districts, some of the districts are more competitive than under incumbent compromise plans, but the districts are gerrymandered to favor the party that draws the map. Because incumbents and one party often control the process, redistricting as practiced in the United States tends to lead to electoral districts with partisan imbalances so extreme as to predetermine the outcome of elections, leading to minimal electoral competition and an unhealthy electoral system.

The effect can be seen in U.S. House and state legislative contests, progressively fewer of which have been competitive following recent redistricting cycles. In the elections immediately following the 1990 redistricting, eighty-four U.S. House contests were decided by a margin of 10 percent or less; in the elections immediately following the 2000 redistricting, only thirty-eight U.S. House seats were decided by a margin of 10 percent or less. Sixty-five percent of incumbents running for reelection in 1992 won with a margin of 20 percent or more; eighty-three percent won by similar large margins in 2002.[539] And there is evidence to show that the manner of redistricting has played a role in depressing the number of competitive elections for congressional elections.[540] In particular, fewer districts were competitive following the post-2000 census redistricting because more districts were drawn under bipartisan incumbent protection compromises (under which incumbents of opposing parties collaborate to draw electorally safe—that is, uncompetitive—districts for themselves). In 2000–2002, some 233 districts were drawn under such incumbent-protection compromises, compared to 147 drawn that way in 1990–1992.[541] Redistricting has also been found to discourage strong candidates from running for Congress by reducing their perceived chances of success.[542] The degree to which state legislators run unopposed has nearly doubled between 1968 (when 20 percent of seats were uncontested) and 2002 (when 39 percent of seats were uncontested).[543] Here, too, research has found that the redistricting practices have played an important role.[544]

How did this system develop—how is it that those who run in elections are permitted to choose their own voters? As with a great deal of electoral law in the U.S. federal system, the responsibility lies largely with state governments. States are responsible for drawing the boundaries of U.S. House districts (in those forty-three states that have more than one House district) and of their state-level house and senate districts (local governments draw their city council or commission districts in accordance with their state's constitution and laws). States, through their constitutions or statutes, determine who draws the districts and, for the most part, what rules must be followed in the process.[545] In most states the districts are mapped out through the legislative process, requiring approval of both chambers and the governor. A number of states, however, use other procedures for drawing electoral districts, procedures that may or may not involve the state legislature. For instance, twenty states use redistricting commissions of various forms at some stage of the process; the Iowa system utilizes the nonpartisan Legislative Service Agency to draw up maps that are voted on by the legislature; in Maryland's system the governor proposes redistricting plans that require approval of a majority of both chambers of the legislature, which, alternatively, can adopt its own plan with a two-thirds vote, and if they fail to do either, the governor's plan becomes law; and in Florida's and Kansas's processes, maps drawn by the legislature are submitted for approval to the state supreme court.[546]

In terms of the rules for the drawing of the district maps, some states set specific criteria to be used in the process, including the following: (1) requiring districts be contiguous and compact, (2) preventing or limiting the splitting up of political subdivisions (such as counties or towns), (3) requiring consideration of communities of interest, and (4) requiring maintenance of the core of previous districts. Some states have requirements about whether and how information on the residence of incumbent officeholders should be used in the process; some mandate the process be blind to the location of incumbents, others require the protection of incumbents so that their domicile is not carved out of the district or placed in a district with other incumbents. Two states, Arizona and Washington, call for the drawing of competitive districts.[547] Most states have at least one of the criteria for drawing state legislative districts in place (only three, Florida, Indiana, and Kentucky, have none of them), and most states have at least a requirement for compactness.[548] States typically have fewer requirements for the drawing of congressional districts than for their state legislative districts.[549]

Because of the perception that the redistricting process results increasingly in fewer competitive contests at both the national and state levels, reformers have taken up the cause of redistricting reform. Groups such as Common Cause (often joined by other organizations such as the League of Women Voters, the Brennan Center for Justice, and the Republican Main Street Partnership, individually or in an umbrella group called Americans for Redistricting Reform[550]) support

> redistricting reforms such as creating independent commissions to conduct redistricting, establishing criteria for how districts must be drawn, requiring a fair and transparent process for conducting redistricting, and creating "shadow" commissions to present their own recommendations.[551]

In Colorado, Florida, Indiana, Pennsylvania, and Minnesota, such groups have promoted state-level reforms that promote the creation of redistricting commissions. Advocates of reform were successful in California, where Proposition 11 (adopted by voters in 2008) created

> a qualified, diverse, and balanced independent commission to draw legislative districts and would require that both congressional and state districts be drawn according to criteria that prioritize the Voting Rights Act and preservation of communities of interest, neighborhoods, cities, and counties.[552]

These groups are also promoting legislation in Congress to require that states use independent commissions to draw congressional district lines. Within states, similar groups are campaigning; Fair Districts Florida, for instance, advocated amending the Florida state constitution in order to

> prohibit drawing districts to favor an incumbent or a party. While ensuring that racial and language minority voters have the equal opportunity to participate in the political process, the standards will require that districts be compact and community based.[553]

In 2010 the amendments they promoted to make such changes were endorsed by Florida voters.

Research on the effectiveness of reforming the process and the criteria used for redistricting has found that the most effective reforms are those that set the criteria for redistricting in the state's constitution. Jonathan Winburn's in-depth examination of the redistricting process in eight states led him to conclude that the most effective way to ensure greater electoral competition is to make criteria for redistricting part of the states' constitutions and that a key criterion for all maps is that the district boundaries do not split up political subdivisions.[554] A fifty-state comparative analysis by Richard Forgette and his colleagues supports Windburn's conclusions that such redistricting constraints are the most effective means to create more competitive and contested legislative districts from the redistricting process; these researchers also concluded that the more such criteria, the better.[555] Given the negative impact incumbents and parties have on competition through their redistricting plans, it makes sense to try to remove them from the process by establishing the independent redistricting commissions promoted by reform groups. Interestingly enough, however, none of the political science research has found any evidence to support the contention that redistricting commissions produce better maps.[556] It is simply too difficult to insulate the process from partisan and incumbent interests when the stakes are so high. And in this case, bipartisanship is not necessarily a good thing in that an agreement between the parties is most likely to lead to protection of each party's incumbents and thus minimize competition. Iowa's system is often cited as a successful way to carry out redistricting: Iowa's Legislative Service Agency (comprising nonpartisan staff of the state legislature) draws up maps for the legislature to approve or disapprove. Iowa has bucked the trend towards less competitive contests. As some have pointed out, though, it is not clear that this model would travel well to other states because most state legislative staff are not as nonpartisan as Iowa's and because Iowa's population is rather evenly distributed so that "no matter how one slices Iowa, you get back Iowa."[557]

R_x: Amend State Constitutions to Set Criteria for Redistricting

The most effective prescription in the case of redistricting, then, is for states to amend their constitutions with a set of criteria for drawing both state legislative and congressional districts, not unlike the reform being pursued by Fair Districts Florida. The criteria need to be outlined in the state's constitution as opposed to state statutes, which legislators could simply replace through the legislative process. The criteria should specify that any redistricting plan must do the following: (1) create the maximum number of competitive districts, (2) avoid splitting political subdivisions, (3) be blind to the location of incumbents, (4) be transparent and open to the public, and (5) take place only once every ten years (immediately following the release of census data).

Only two states currently call for districts to be drawn in such a way as to encourage competition; this low number does not serve democracy, given the importance of competition to the health of elections. Therefore one of the top criteria should be maximizing the competitiveness of the districts *to the degree possible in the context of the other criteria*, namely, the nature of the state's population, the distribution of its partisans within the state, and the desire to ensure minority representation through majority-minority districts. This competitiveness criterion would not create competition in every district—in many cases that is just not possible or even desirable—but there is no reason the process would not produce at least a significant increase in the proportion of competitive districts for both Congress and the state legislatures.

A criterion associated with greater competition and contestation in a number of studies is the requirement to keep political subdivisions (counties, towns, townships, and wards) together.[558] I would even suggest that states consider creating multimember districts in following such a rule (as Vermont does). The research unequivocally verifies the efficacy of avoiding such splits, but the mandate also makes sense in terms of making elections easier to understand. Understanding who one's representatives are is intuitive if the boundaries of legislative districts coincide with those of a ward or a town. Keeping these subdivisions together also makes sense in terms of the basis of representation, which without this requirement is based on an arbitrary chunk of land. Maintaining the integrity of these political units allows for representation of the interests of whole neighborhoods, towns, and even counties that might have a shared set of interests that should be represented in the state capital or U.S. House.

One of the toughest criteria to enact may be the requirement that the process ignore the location of incumbents. This might be hard on incumbents who find themselves in the same district as another incumbent or who find themselves in a radically different district from the one they had been used to representing. For this reason, the criterion might face the toughest political battle. The reason I include it is that incumbency is probably the biggest contributor to the uncompetitive nature of legislative elections in the United States today. Reelection success rates for members of the U.S. House and state legislative districts are consistently above 95 percent; in some elections all incumbents are reelected. Few quality candidates choose to challenge incumbents because of this record, leaving many races uncontested altogether. The reelection success of incumbents occurs because incumbents have tremendous electoral advantages, including (1) an ability to greatly outspend their opponent(s); (2) resources and benefits of the incumbent position that provide contact with potential voters (free mailing privileges, staff, and money for district projects); (3) regular coverage by the local media; and (4) district boundaries drawn to help them easily win reelection. The prescriptions in the first part of this chapter help address the monetary advantage. The other redistricting criteria listed should help weaken the ability of incumbents to draw safe districts for themselves on their own. Still, incumbent-blind redistricting may be valuable as one additional way to level the playing field and provide an added jolt to electoral competition.

Box 7.1. Why Not Term Limits?

Given that incumbency is the greatest deterrent to competition, why not simply limit the number of terms for legislators and members of Congress? I do not believe term limits are a good solution because the harmful aspects of incumbency can be mitigated without getting rid of the beneficial aspects. The prescriptions proposed in this book are aimed at reducing the advantages of incumbency, and the prescriptions are in the area of campaign finance and redistricting (though changes in the role political parties play as discussed in chapter 6 would also reduce the incumbency advantage). If such prescriptions are adopted, there is no need to prohibit incumbents from running for reelection. After all, some incumbents' success undoubtedly comes from their representing their districts well, and if the voters in that district support the incumbent, those outside the district (through a vote for term limits) should not prevent them from doing so. Long-serving legislators also enhance the functioning of the legislature—they provide needed leadership, develop policy expertise, and maintain an institutional memory that make legislatures more effective, independent, and better able to assert their role in the constitutional scheme of checks and balances. Research on the effects of term limits has found that term-limited legislatures experience a decline in committee seniority and expertise, weaker leadership in the lower chamber, a decline in legislative oversight, and an increase in executive control of the budget. In short, the result of term limits is weaker legislatures and stronger executives, not closer races or more party turnover.[559]

The process should be transparent and open to the public. Although members of the public have little familiarity with redistricting is or its importance, transparency in this case may have some positive effects. Opening meetings and deliberations to the public and the press may discourage the kind of deal making between interests that can lead to uncompetitive districts.

The final criterion limits the frequency of redistricting to once every ten years, immediately following the release of the decennial census data. Leaving open the possibility of more redistricting allows the interests with so much at stake more opportunity to alter the maps to their liking, thus depressing competition. The political debacle in Texas following the 2003 Republican takeover of the legislature provided a lesson in the dangers of leaving legislators free to redraw the maps whenever they are in power. Led by U.S. House majority leader Tom Delay, the Texas legislature redrew the congressional district map despite the objections of Democrats. The senate Democrats actually fled the state so as to deny senate Republicans the quorum needed to pass their new map; in response Delay instructed the Federal Aviation Administration to find them. The result of the new map, which eventually passed, was a Republican pickup of six congressional seats in the 2004 election—without the new map, Republicans would have lost seats in the U.S. House that year.

A rule that is not included in this list but that offers an interesting possibility for removing a degree of incumbent and party influence is Adam Cox's suggestion to delay the implementation of new electoral maps for several election cycles.[560] This would add some uncertainty to the process and thus reduce the influence of parties and incumbents. It is an idea that merits further study and perhaps experimentation in a few states.

Finally, there needs to be a way to seriously enforce these constitutional requirements, as the actors in redistricting in many states can and do ignore requirements that are not actively enforced.[561] One possibility is to set up independent commissions to review redistricting plans based on the criteria in the state constitutions, as suggested above, and to deter partisan and incumbent gerrymandering.[562] Adam Cox proposed a national administrative review of congressional district maps.[563] As Cox pointed out, such an administrative board or commission—with the proper configuration, empowerment, and resources—would be able to go beyond what the courts can do (currently only courts review redistricting). Each state might also consider setting up an administrative review of state senate and house maps (perhaps in lieu of creating commissions to do the redistricting) in order to determine whether they meet the states' constitutional requirements.

IMPROVING THE WAY WE VOTE

To avoid a crisis with respect to the legitimacy of electoral outcomes in the next close election and to ensure equality in the treatment of all voters, it is important to address the shortcomings of election administration in the United States as part of the prescription for a healthier democracy. As discussed earlier, the combination of localism and partisanship leads to "deferred maintenance" of the electoral infrastructure, leaving it in dire condition, much like the nation's physical infrastructure.[564] Although the Help America Vote Act of 2002 has improved the situation, it has not gone nearly far enough. The election infrastructure in the United States is still underfunded and unevenly funded. Poll workers are not well trained or well compensated. Ballot design and voting machines pose problems for many voters and administrators. The adoption of DRE voting machines has raised questions of vote security and accuracy. And those charged with running the elections are those who have a stake in the outcome.

What can be done to improve the operation of voting in the United States? First, the prescriptions that focus solely on technological fixes should be ruled out. Adding paper verification to DRE voting machines will do nothing to solve the greater problems with election administration, and as documented by Herrnson and his colleagues, such voter-verification fixes reduce the usability of voting machinery and actually make the voting experience worse for voters.[565] But problems with election administration will not be solved by rejecting electronic voting. Though there are legitimate concerns about hackers corrupting the machines, as Alvarez and Hall point out, concerns over the new technology echoes concerns voiced in the past about other voting technologies that are now trusted and accepted.[566] The solution to problems associated with DRE voting machinery is not to reject the system outright; the key is to develop the most usable and secure systems possible, whether that means DRE machines or some other type of voting equipment.

Likewise, the idea of centralizing responsibility for administering elections should be dismissed. Even though centralization seems logical given the ad hoc conglomeration of practices in the local administration of elections, most scholars who write about the problems associated with election administration do not advocate eliminating the local dimension of voting. Indeed, they point out the benefits of "experimentation, dispersed responsibility, voters' sense of efficacy and responsiveness" that accompany localism.[567] I see no reason to disagree with these scholars that local control of the administration of elections should continue. That said, there are a number of things that the national and state governments could do to improve election administration.

R$_x$: Increase Funding for the Administration of Elections

First and foremost, increased funding for election administration is needed to ensure that all localities have access to the best voting technology and enough money to train and compensate poll workers in a more professional manner. It would also be useful for the federal and state governments to invest money in studying which of the available options in voting machinery and ballot design are best in terms of usability for all voters.[568] I realize that this is yet another prescription calling for increased government expenditures at a time when the federal government is in debt and state and local governments struggle with their financing. But better funding for elections through any of the proposals involves minor costs relative to other budget items and reflects on how seriously the nation takes its democracy.

R$_x$: Transfer State Authority for the Administration of Elections to a Nonpartisan Election Official

Second, as recommended in chapter 5, states should remove the position of chief election officer (typically the secretary of state) from the ballot. Granting an elected partisan authority over elections in the states has been shown to be problematic, for it introduces an opportunity for that official to use the position to further the electoral interests of his or her party. States could simply appoint the secretary of state and require supermajorities for confirmation. Or as recommended by the Commission on Federal Election Reform, states could take the responsibility of conducting elections away from their secretaries of state and give it to chief elections officers, who would be a nonpartisan officials appointed with the approval of supermajorities in the state legislative chambers. Either approach would remove some of the partisan politics from decisions on the administration of elections—location of polling places, management of voter rolls, allocation of resources, and so forth.

R$_x$: Implement a "Democracy Index"

And finally, as many scholars who study the subject have pointed out, very few concrete data are available that would facilitate an assessment of election administration across the United States. Instead, anecdotal data bubbles to the surface when a close election leads to a crisis. Therefore the final prescription with regard to election administration is a recommendation that the United States adopt Heather Gerken's proposal to create a *democracy index* that ranks the administration of elections on measures of convenience, integrity, and accuracy.[569] The democracy-index ranking would not only create greater transparency in the process, aiding citizens, but as Gerken argued, it could also engender competition among administrators in ways that would improve the convenience, integrity, and accuracy of the way Americans vote.

CONCLUSION

Electoral competition is the lifeblood of elections; without it voters' chance to hold elected officials responsible or to effect desired changes in their government is limited. As I document in this chapter, laws that govern campaign finance and redistricting play a key role in determining the levels of competition in legislative contests. The laws as they exist today do more to diminish competition than to encourage it. So an important part of the plan to restore health to U.S. elections involves changing these laws in the manner prescribed in order to encourage greater interparty competition.

The way the United States manages the act of voting could also be improved in order to ensure equal treatment of voters and to avoid crises in the legitimacy of elections when contests are close. Greater funding of election administration is necessary so as to acquire the best voting equipment and so as to train and compensate poll workers. Taking the responsibility of running elections out of the hands of partisan secretaries of state and producing a democracy index to facilitate accountability would improve election administration and, as a result, contribute to elections' overall health.

Anthony Gierzynski, Ph.D.
Department of Political Science
The University of Vermont

Patient: U.S. Elections   D.O.B.: September 17, 1789

R_x

Provide partial public funding for candidates with four-to-one match for small contributions, spending limits that reflect the reality of campaign needs, a ban on bundling, and a requirement to debate.

Allow more money to flow through the parties for voter mobilization and coordinated spending while eliminating party-independent expenditures.

Discourage electoral activity of independent groups with a reasonable redefinition of electioneering activity.

Establish constitutional guidelines for redistricting that increase the number of competitive districts.

Increase funding for the administration of elections to test for and provide the most usable voting machinery and to train and compensate poll workers.

Transfer authority for elections from the partisan secretary of state's office to a nonpartisan election official appointed with approval of supermajorities in the state legislatures.

Implement a democracy-index ranking of local election administration.

Signature of the Prescriber: Dr. Anthony Gierzynski

CHAPTER 8

THE PUBLIC

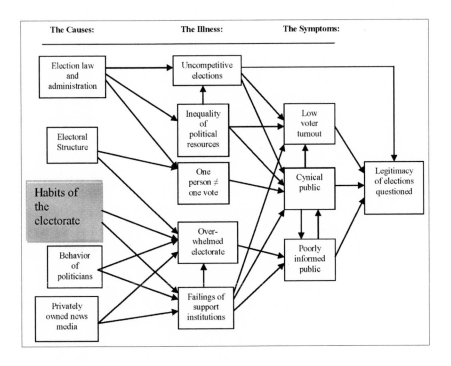

All of the prescriptions discussed thus far have dealt with the nature of elections (structure and laws) or the critical supportive institutions involved (the media and political parties). In other words, up to this point the focus has been on how to build a better electoral system, ignoring those for whom elections are designed, the citizens themselves. In this chapter the focus is turned on the citizenry because, unlike in *Field of Dreams*,[570] building a better system is no guarantee that voters will come. Just as a doctor may be able to prescribe medicines to fight disease and infection or perform surgery to clear arteries or replace or repair damaged organs, unless the patient discontinues the unhealthy habits that contribute to or worsen the illness, all the doctoring in the world is unlikely save that patient. Patients often need to change their behavior in order for treatment to be truly effective; the same is true for the health of the body electoral. Even if good journalism survives and is readily accessible to the public, if the electorate's choices are simplified and clarified, if the positive aspects of political parties are reinforced, and if campaign-finance reform, redistricting practices, and election administration are reformed to improve the competitiveness and fairness of elections—even if all these changes are realized, they can boost the levels and quality of political involvement only if the citizens themselves are part of the plan. They need to be part of the plan because citizens *are* part of the problem; certain cultural habits of the citizenry, developed and intensified over time, play a role in the poor health of elections.

Improving the health of elections is, therefore, dependent not only on changing elections and their supportive institutions but also on adjusting the public's harmful political "lifestyle" habits that impede the healthy functioning of elections. The damaging habits that do this are related to the way people think about elections, their use of one form of the mass media, and their fundamental approach to knowing about politics and government. More specifically, I argue in this chapter that the health of elections in the United States is impaired by (1) the very way people conceive of political action and elections; (2) the way the public thinks about and uses political parties; (3) the public's overuse of and reliance upon television; and (4) the propensity toward knee-jerk cynicism when thoughtful skepticism would serve people better.

When doctors counsel their patients to drop unhealthy habits, I imagine that it is difficult to avoid sounding like a scold; the very act of giving such counsel implies that the patient is doing something wrong. The same is true for the material in this chapter: the very act of suggesting that the public change some of its election-related habits may seem scolding and elitist, but such counsel cannot be avoided. As indicated throughout this book, the public cannot be left out of the prescription—indeed, the efficacy of the prescriptions offered up to this point depends in large part on the public, on the way ordinary people conceptualize elections and the manner in which they play their role as a citizens. The way elections work and what elections mean are shaped by the thinking, intentions, and behavior of the citizenry. Thus before I address the electorate's lifestyle choices that weaken elections, I want to clarify that the following discussion is not meant to scold or demean the public. I am not asserting that the problems with the electorate's habits are the result of flaws in the individuals that compose the citizenry; the public develops these habits not because they are lazy or stupid but largely, I believe, because this is what U.S. culture teaches American citizens about participation and political knowledge.

It is also worth pointing out here that the prescriptions in this book focus on making elections work for citizens in a way that takes into account the fact that people have many demands on their time. Elections should function as a means for the governed to control their government without requiring that people surrender their personal lives and other pursuits in order to spend endless hours on politics. Democracy does not—and indeed, *should not*—require that its people become political junkies. Unfortunately, as the diagnosis shows, elections in the United States have degenerated to this state, asking far more of U.S. citizens than most democracies worldwide ask of their citizens. For this reason, many of the prescriptions in this book are aimed at making elections *less* demanding and the choices clearer so that more of the public can easily see the meaning of the choice, feel empowered, and participate. For such changes to work in the manner prescribed, the public will need to make some changes, too—the changes discussed in the following pages. I thus make a request that the reader remain mindful of this intent and of the broader context of the entire book while reading this chapter.

R$_x$: New Civics Lesson I: Us, not Me

In American culture, the individual reigns supreme. An outsider analyzing the content of the country's cultural discourse as conveyed through its media might be struck by the way everything seems to revolve around the individual. Indeed, most of the discourse seems geared toward these questions: What are famous, attractive, familiar, or eccentric *individuals* up to? How does [the topic being covered] affect me individually? Who (as in which *individual*) is to blame for [the topic being covered]? And who (again, which *individual*) is going to do something about it? To confirm this point, simply tune in to the U.S. news media and watch as they feed the culture's obsession with celebrities, turn every societal problem or event into stories about individual people, and personalize government and politics. (By *personalizing government and politics*, I mean that the media portray the government as individual officeholders—the president, the governor, the mayor—and reduce ideological debates to personal conflicts between ambitious and petty politicians, all to the detriment of institutions, processes, and actual outcomes.) This cult of the individual is also apparent in U.S. entertainment—entertainment is so often a reflection and shaper of culture—in which the dominant problem-solving model focuses on a heroic individual who overcomes corrupt, evil, or diabolical institutions or organizations to win the day while others (those in the stories as well as viewers themselves) watch and maybe cheer, perhaps imagining themselves as that heroic individual.[571] Tocqueville's observation regarding the democratically healthy propensity of U.S. citizens to join civil associations and thus create collective identities no longer seems to characterize the U.S. political culture at the beginning of the twenty-first century;[572] we are now, as Robert Putnam demonstrated in his seminal work *Bowling Alone*, a much more atomized, solitary, and (I would add) all-about-me culture.[573]

If American culture writ large is focused on the individual, why should voting in the United States be any different? In fact, it is no exception. Voting (as well as most other forms of political participation) in the United States is individualized and personalized—it is all about *me* picking the right *person*. Americans are taught early in life to vote for the person rather than the party and are constantly told how important each individual vote is. The independent-minded voter who makes rational decisions without consideration of party or ideology is held in high esteem—when, in actuality, such people are often the least informed, the least interested, and the least likely to vote. Public officials who vote with their party or the president are put down as mindless ideologues who blindly follow party leaders; they are not thought of as people who share a set of political values with the party and have worked to collectively pursue those values. And groups, including those critical to the functioning of a democracy—political parties and interest groups—are demonized by the press, politicians themselves, and the entertainment media.[574] Because most of the public's exposure to elections comes through the greatest sales instrument ever created—the television—the U.S. public is primed to think of voting much as it thinks of the individual decision to purchase a product: if a political "product" isn't tailored exactly to consumers' specifications, or if they don't feel that what they "purchase" with their votes will improve their lifestyle, they won't buy it.

Thinking of elections this way—that is, framing elections in terms of *individual* citizens choosing *individual* leaders to run the government while ignoring or denigrating groups—is misleading, and it is disempowering. It is misleading because it paints a false picture of the U.S. political system, which is a system run not by individuals but by institutions—legislatures, courts, executive branches, and bureaucracies—whose decisions are influenced by other institutions—political parties and interest groups. In other words, the reality is that the power of the individual as such is limited in the U.S. political system. Thus the more U.S. culture celebrates the individual, the further it gets from political reality. In my opinion, the public intuitively knows this; citizens sense that the individual on his or her own is politically weak. They know that a single vote does not matter much in the grand scheme, and they probably also know that one elected person cannot change things on his or her own (even if this is often the expectation). But modern Americans live in a culture that constantly argues against this truth and that provides no alternative way of conceiving of elections—leading to disillusionment and feelings of powerlessness among the citizens.

The U.S. citizenry is schooled in stories (true and fictional) of close elections in which one vote or a handful of votes, it is said, would have made the difference—the 537 votes in Florida in 2000 and the movie *Swing Vote* are just two examples. Americans are subtly coaxed by television or YouTube videos to get to know the candidates as individuals and to choose them based on who they are rather than the philosophy of governance they represent—a process that inevitably leads to disillusionment when those politicians do things (personal or political) that the public did not expect or when they fail to do things because other powerbrokers in the system do not agree.[575] Although democratic elections comprise two basic components—the voters' choice and the building of a governing majority—nearly all discourse on elections focuses on the choice and emphasizes the individual aspect of it, either the individual candidates or the individual voters. Meanwhile, scant attention is paid to the fact that elections are about governing and that governing requires majorities to control the lawmaking branch of government and, in the United States, in order to elect any official.[576] For the health of U.S. elections and democracy, this individualistic way of thinking has to change because members of the public cannot fully understand their role in elections if they continue to see that role through this frame. Elections need to be reframed in the mind of U.S. citizens and in the discourse of the country's culture; a more accurate and encouraging way of thinking of elections must be substituted for the current individualistic frame. What is needed is a frame for elections that draws attention to the ways elections empower citizens through *collective* action and the *aggregation* of their interests, because the actions of majority coalitions shaped out of the aggregation of individual preferences can truly shape the decisions of governmental actors and institutions.

It is more realistic and empowering to think about elections as *vehicles for collective action*, as a way to combine the power of individuals with shared interests into governing majorities, than as instruments for acts of solitary individuals. This is true for a number of reasons. Despite the rhetoric about the power of the individual vote, most people know that politically, they cannot do anything on their own. If people can understand their involvement as part of a movement or collective action of millions of others who share their political goals, however, they will be more likely to feel that they can have a real effect. There *is* power in numbers, and elections are designed to be responsive to those numbers. Viewing elections as a way to simply voice one's individual opinion about the choices renders elections little more meaningful than giving an opinion to a pollster, but viewing elections as a way to be part of the group whose members become the governing majority is empowering. It is, in essence, the difference between asking *Where do my interests lie?* and *With whom do my interests ally me?*

If the public's thinking shifted to the second question, citizens' electoral habits of thought would change for the better; individuals would see that they are not alone, that they share political goals with millions of other citizens and groups (in and of itself an empowering thought), and that through voting (and other political activities) with their fellow partisans, aggregations of citizens with shared goals can exercise power, especially when that aggregation constitutes a majority. Framing elections in this way would not only empower the voter but should also lead to more empowering choices. In the U.S. system, the reality is that joining with others who have similar views (even if everyone does not necessarily agree on everything) increases the likelihood that the group will constitute a majority; joining with others thus improves the chance that a given group's preferences will be followed by the government and reduces the chances that the government will do things the group disagrees with (see chapter 6 for an extended discussion of this point). Had a fraction of the ninety thousand–plus Nader voters in Florida in 2000 seen the election from this aggregate perspective and voted accordingly, they could have overwhelmed the 537-vote margin by which George W. Bush won; and I strongly suspect that they—at least those who supported Nader because of his liberal positions on the issues—would have been much more satisfied with the presidential decision making in the four years that followed.

How, then, can the U.S. public be convinced to think about elections in terms of aggregates and not individuals? How can elections be reframed in the minds of the public? This is a difficult proposition given how deeply this perspective is ingrained in U.S. culture. Nevertheless, the changes in the focus of the media's election coverage suggested in chapter 4 and changes in the behavior of political parties and candidates as proposed in chapter 6 should help, to some degree, by drawing the public's attention to the central meaning of the electoral choice. Beyond that, the school systems and educators (grade school, high school and college level) should fundamentally rethink the way civics is taught in order to create a new curriculum that encourages students to think about elections in the more realistic and empowering manner suggested here.

Though there are excellent civics teachers, as I have learned from my university students over the years, and though there are some new, innovative civics programs (e.g., Kids Voting USA[577]), most high school civics courses offer bland history lessons about the Constitution and cast citizenship in the misleading individualistic manner critiqued earlier: the citizen's duty is to vote and to do so for the "best" candidate, without educating students on the fundamental nature of the choice found in the philosophical differences between the parties. The courses seem designed to avoid offending anyone and therefore usually fail to make clear the partisan nature of the electoral choice—even though notions about what makes someone the "best" candidate are impossible to separate from the candidate's party.

The new civics, while continuing to provide the necessary grounding in history and the Constitution, should highlight the power of aggregates of citizens over the minimal power of the individual and should show how major changes in government often come about as the result of pressure from collective efforts. This point can be illustrated by numerous historical examples, including the following: (1) the shared opposition to slavery that led to the creation of the Republican Party and eventual emancipation; (2) those most battered by the Great Depression pressured the government to act through the rise of the New Deal Democrats; (3) opposition to government involvement fueled group activity that led to the Reagan Revolution; and (4) the aggregation of interests opposed to the policies of the second Bush administration fueled major changes brought about by the Democrats and President Obama.[578] It should also be highlighted that conversely, when people do not take part in the work of those who share their interests, other—usually narrower—aggregations of interests determine the direction of the government, and this direction is frequently contrary to the broader public's interests.

The central idea for this type of civic education might be that political power is in numbers, and if any given voter does not lend his or her number to the effort, that voter's power and the power of those with shared interests will be marginalized. Such lessons should include instruction on the positive role of interest groups as vehicles for representation in the pluralistic democracy that is the American system. Supporting groups that share one's interests, it should be taught, is an effective way to exercise political power; the National Rifle Association (NRA) and the environmental movement could serve as case studies in such influence. In addition to the direct power exercised by an interest group, greater involvement of more people in those interest groups would result in a more representative balance of interests in the interest group system; today that system heavily favors businesses and the wealthier segments of society.

Finally, the new civics should also help change the other three habits that the public must shed if elections are to be restored to health: the counterproductive way most Americans think about the political parties, the way citizens get political information, and the knee-jerk cynicism that permeates U.S. culture. The new civics should teach people to vote for the party, not the person; the new civics should teach an awareness of the negatives effects of television and an awareness of the importance of *reading* good journalism about government and politics; and the new civics should teach citizens to be skeptics, not cynics.

R_x: New Civics Lesson II:
Vote for the Party, Not the Person

As argued in chapter 6, partisan voting strengthens elections because
the two major parties in the United States offer distinct choices in terms
of governing philosophies; were voters to choose candidates based on
the parties' platforms (as opposed to personality characteristics or some
wedge issue), elections would function better as means of popular control of governments. While political parties play this useful role for a
growing number of U.S. voters, too many others—voters and, more
importantly, nonvoters—do not recognize how the political parties can
empower them.[579] Many are unaware of what the parties offer in terms of
policy choices, and so all political arguments seem like pointless bickering to them. Other citizens express a preference for alternative party
choices that are "purer"—that is, parties that hold political views nearly
identical to their own—missing the point that the aggregation of somewhat diverse interests in elections is needed in order to build electoral
majorities. If any of these people are convinced to vote by friends, family, or get-out-the-vote drives, they usually base their votes on criteria
other than the policies the candidates will promote once in office. Instead
of considering policies, these voters may vote based on how likeable the
candidates are (or are not); how trustworthy, smart, or presidential they
deem the candidates to be (based on the media narrative and on what
they see in the personal demeanor of candidates on television); a wedge
issue that may provoke them to vote against the party with which they
agree the most overall; false information spread via the Internet, cable,
friends, family, or coworkers; or they may cast what could prove to be
a counterproductive vote for a third-party or independent candidate.[580]
It is certainly the prerogative of each voter to cast a vote as he or she
chooses, but if even a small portion of the electorate votes this way, the
message of the election gets muddled, making it unclear what the majority of the public actually wants and ultimately weakening elections as a
means of popular control (in elections as close as many recent contests
have been, a swing in only a few percentage points is enough to change

the outcome). Voting on these other criteria is, in short, self-defeating behavior for citizens in a democracy because elections that communicate nothing about the public's policy preferences fail to afford citizens the ability to control—through elections—what governments do.

What do elections say when a majority of voters preferred the issue stands of the losing candidates (Carter in 1980 and Gore in 2000, for example)?[581] And what do such elections communicate about candidates' claims of popular mandates to institute policy changes? Setting aside the fact that he did not win a majority of the vote, did Bill Clinton have a mandate for health-care reform following the 1992 election? Or was he elected because a large enough portion of the electorate sensed that he "felt their pain"? Did George W. Bush have a mandate for establishing personal accounts for social security following the 2004 election even though a significant proportion of the electorate was unaware of his proposal? Though both Clinton and Bush failed to enact these policies, both presidents claimed mandates and spent considerable time pushing for these policy changes. How many voters cast ballots for Barack Obama because of his rock-star personality? How many supported his health-care proposals, which ultimately became law? And what have the 2010 elections communicated about the public's views on policies that the Democrats have enacted under the leadership of the Obama administration? (Un)happiness with President Obama personally and stylistically? Discontent engendered by a poor economy? Frustration over how much time change takes? Or a real desire to have the government pursue different policies or continue on the same course? Or merely the typical surge and decline in participation that occurs between presidential elections and midterm elections?

As discussed earlier, the U.S. public might decide that it is acceptable for elections to serve the purposes reflected in those criteria identified previously (the personal qualities of the candidates, wedge issues, or misinformation); citizens might not care that elections do not, in fact, function as means of majority control of what the government does. But this is doubtful. An important component of the frustration with elections in the United States is, after all, that the public expects to exercise control over policy through elections but cannot, for a variety of reasons. And while various aspects of the electoral system are responsible for thwarting majority control, another reason citizens cannot exercise such control is the failure among large segments of the population to understand the value of policy preferences and to fully utilize political parties as a means of communicating those preferences.

If the United States is to strengthen elections as a means of popular control of government, then the country needs more of its people (especially nonvoters) to see the power that resides in communicating policy preferences through party-based voting. Changing the way people think about elections—shifting from understanding voting as an individual act to understanding it as a collective act—is the first step to increased party-based voting because parties are elections' principal groups. Based on policy preferences, parties aggregate people into majorities that then can control governments and convert those preferences into government policies. In this way elections empower the public. It would improve the health of elections if the U.S. public saw elections in this way.

How can the public come to see elections and parties this way? The new civics curriculum introduced previously is one way to accomplish this for the younger generations (some of the prescriptions in chapters 4 and 6 are also designed with this goal in mind). As part of its lessons in the power of the collective action, the new civics curriculum should explain the important role political parties play in elections. It could do so by making clear to students the philosophies and records of the two major parties, by showing how those philosophies and records predict what elected officials will do if they are elected, and by demonstrating that action based on this knowledge can empower the citizen.[582]

Policy-based partisan voting empowers citizens for a number of reasons. First, as mentioned earlier, it sends a clearer electoral message about the policy preferences of the public than elections currently do. When the public casts policy-based partisan votes, the message is, simply enough, that the majority wants the winning party to implement the policies that compose their platform. Second, increased policy-based voting would make the political parties more responsive to the public's policy preferences. Parties would need to tailor their appeal around their platforms and philosophy of governance more than they do today, a circumstance that would improve the electoral discourse and ensure that major concerns of the public are addressed. For if neither party addresses an issue of major concern to a large portion of the public, the opportunity arises for a third-party or independent candidate to draw voters away from the two major parties and cost them the election (indeed, this is the important role such parties play in the U.S. system).[583] And finally, policy-based partisan voting makes both the voter's choice and the connection between the vote and government action clearer and easier to understand. As a result, voter participation would increase, empowering more citizens.

This prescription to teach policy-based partisan voting may be a difficult proposition to enact in the public schools owing to the nature of the politics of primary and secondary education in the United States (though it should be less of an issue at the college level). Teachers would seem wise to avoid this aspect of civics education for fear of losing their jobs on the basis of claims about bias, especially in the current climate, where facts and evidence seem irrelevant to many people who support a cause (people who think the Bush administration was behind the attacks of September 11, proponents of intelligent design, those who claim Obama was not born in the United States, supporters of conspiracy theories of elite corporate control of government and media—more popularly known as "the man" theory—and opponents of the 2008 health-care reform who insisted that it included government "death panels" are just a few examples of what comes to mind). But civics lessons without a real discussion of the choices that the political parties present in elections are worthless; they will do little to improve the involvement of the citizenry. With proper care, the philosophies of the political parties and their records *can* be presented in a non-normative manner. The Kids Voting USA project attempts—successfully, it seems—to do this.[584] The textbook I have long used for my introductory American politics class, Kenneth Janda, Jeffrey Berry, and Jerry Goldman's *The Challenge of Democracy*, also does an excellent job framing political differences in terms of underlying value preferences for equality, freedom, or order.[585] Stressing to students the importance of determining which party is most closely aligned with their values is critical to engaging and involving anyone in politics; my own experience teaching for over eighteen years has convinced me that this is effective.

Such lessons can perhaps be more easily accepted if students are also taught some fundamentals about the nature of politics, starting with the ideas that politics is all about disagreements and that political disagreement is *okay*. Politics is, after all, the battle for control of the government so that the government will pursue the values certain groups deem important—and people simply do not agree about which values are more important. In that vein, the new civics curriculum should also teach the fundamental bases of political disagreements. Political disagreements arise when people disagree about the goals or values governments should pursue, the means of attaining those goals, or how the situation should be perceived.[586] Once acquired, such an understanding of political disputes can lead to acceptance of differences that are value based—for it is all but futile to try to convince someone that his or her values are inferior to someone else's—and can lead to rational, fact-based debate over the means and the nature of the situation, based on empirical claims. Lessons in sorting through facts would also be of great value and are discussed next in the section on skepticism.

Encouraging policy-based partisan voting through civics education would, if reinforced by the changes in political rhetoric prescribed in chapter 6 and by the improvements in the focus of the media's election coverage prescribed in chapter 4, clarify the messages communicated via voting and, as a result, empower citizens to control government policy through elections. The clearer and more simplified choices would ease the problem of an overwhelmed and confused electorate and consequently lead to higher levels of participation by a public that would, with these changes in place, have the requisite information to make an informed choice.

The higher voter turnout in 1992, 2004, and 2008 provides evidence that when the choice is clearer, more of the public will be engaged in the elections; no election reform took place that could explain the higher turnout in those years.[587] Likewise, the charismatic candidates Barack Obama, Bill Clinton, and Ross Perot can account for only a small portion of the higher turnout in 2008 and 1992. What accounts for most of the increase in voter turnout in these elections is that, despite all of the noise and distractions coming from the media and the candidates, the choice facing the voters was made clearer by events of the time and by candidacies that capitalized on those events; the choice was thus difficult to misinterpret. The economy in 1992 and 2008 and the war in Iraq in 2004 reflected the policies of the incumbent administrations in ways that made the differences clear. Such voting in these contests was certainly not all policy-based partisan voting; indeed, much of it was retrospective, "throw the bums out" voting (particularly 1992 and 2008) or voting based on the personal appeal of the candidates. Nevertheless, the policy choices were clear, and when more of the public saw those choices, more of the public knew what to do and acted. In 2004 and 2008 a greater partisan aspect came to the fore, in part because of the Bush administration's consistently conservative policies and the growing ideological polarization among the public.

That the clarity of the choice between the parties had become evident to the public can be seen in responses to the question asked by the American National Election Studies: "Do you think there are any important differences in what the Republicans and Democrats stand for?" The percentage of respondents answering yes to that question jumped from 64 percent in 2000 to 76 percent in 2004, where it stayed for 2008 (see figure 8.1). The effect of this increased clarity of choice can also be seen in research evidence, which indicates that the electorate has evinced greater ideologically consistent partisanship in recent years.[588] A continuation and expansion of that trend to more voters and to the large nonvoting segment of the population would improve the health of U.S. democracy.

An electorate thus focused on the parties as advocates of policies (in line with a particular philosophy of governance) also promises to alter the behavior of the political parties and politicians as prescribed

FIGURE **8.1.** Important differences between the Republicans and Democrats?

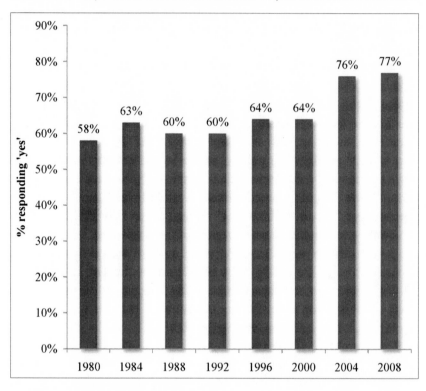

Source. American National Elections Study.
Note. Bars represent the percent of respondents answering yes to the question, "Do you think there are any important differences in what the Republicans and Democrats stand for?"

in chapter 6, making the parties more responsive to the general policy preferences of the public. It is likely that such an electorate would indirectly pressure the media, too, to alter the way they cover elections, demanding a greater focus on the essentials of the choice; and though the public might be amused and even incited to action by the silly little episodes that are bound to pepper election coverage, if citizens maintain an awareness of the central point of elections, they will be less distracted from the real nature of their choice by such trivia. To help ensure that members of the public stay focused and learn how to make policy-based judgments, the new civics curriculum should teach citizens where and how to get information.

R$_x$: NEW CIVICS LESSON III: CHANGING WATCHING HABITS

> I am gross and perverted,
> I'm obsessed and deranged,
> I have existed for years,
> but very little has changed...
> I may be vile and pernicious,
> But you can't turn away
> I make you think I'm delicious
> with the things that I say.
> I'm the best you can get.
> Have you guessed me yet?
> I'm the slime oozing out of your TV set.[589]

Perhaps Frank Zappa overstates the case a bit; there are certainly some benefits of television, including its entertainment value. Television is also beneficial to elections when it airs party convention speeches and candidate debates in their entirety, and it could benefit elections even more if free television time were given to the parties as prescribed earlier in this book. On balance, however, a review of the evidence—content analyses of what is available on television and research findings on the effects of television on the public—has led me to conclude that the way television is used in U.S. culture harms both elections and democracy more than it helps. Consequently, part of the prescription for a healthier democracy involves encouraging people to change the way they use television.

Television as it is currently used in the U.S. contributes to the poor health of democracy for three main reasons: (1) it adversely affects the public's understanding of politics and government, (2) it fails to support the type of journalism that a democracy needs, and (3) it erodes social capital.

The Adverse Effect of Television on the Public's Understanding of Politics and Government[590]

Television adversely affects the public's understanding of politics and government in a number of different ways, ranging from culture-wide changes in what it means to be informed to specific effects that derive from the television's tendency to make politics personal and cover it as if it were a sport. As several scholars have argued, these effects are compounded by the fact that on the whole, members of the American public are unaware of the deficiencies in their understanding of their political system—deficiencies that result from relying on television.

Television and the Discourse of a Culture

Twenty-five years ago, Neil Postman argued in his book *Amusing Ourselves to Death* that television had fundamentally altered the meaning of being informed in the United States.[591] Postman argued that television, as the dominant medium, had molded the culture's manner of discourse to conform to its own. Television's manner of discourse excels at *showing* what is happening, but it does a poor job *explaining* what happened or why. Additionally, television's mode of discourse means that America knows only what television can *show*; those aspects of the culture that cannot be videoed, such as institutions, abstract concepts, or chronic societal problems, are either ignored or personalized in ways that rob them of their meaning and importance.

Television's form of discourse does not provide an adequate understanding of the events of our world because the nature of the medium leads those who produce its programs to present events as a series of isolated happenings; these are rarely connected to larger causes or trends (a description that is true of election coverage, as well). Television provides snapshots of the world without the context, background, and analysis necessary for developing a coherent understanding of what is taking place and why. Put another way, television gives the public many pieces of the puzzle that represents the world out there, but television's way of knowing fails to show us how the pieces all fit together, fails even to suggest that they *should* fit together, leaving viewers with a confusing jumble of images and information—and incapable of holding public officials responsible.[592] In this way television fails to help build the complex cognitive structures needed for an understanding of the way government and politics work and for the processing of political information.[593] If citizens do not develop those cognitive structures through education or reading, for example, they will be at a loss to understand their political world as it is presented on television. Because television is the dominant mode of communication in U.S. culture, television's way of presenting the world has, according to Postman, become *the* way of knowing the world; as a result the public fails to develop the complex cognitive capacities for true understanding anywhere. The conversion of the culture to television's mode of discourse has thus meant that members of the public no longer *comprehend* their world; they simply know a number of unrelated things about it.

Finally, information that is presented without context, background, or analysis and that depends heavily on compelling video is good for only one purpose: entertainment. Such information is trivia with moving pictures. This is what television does best, what draws its largest audiences. Television is an entertainment medium, not a medium for serious, rational discourse. In its position as the dominant medium, it has thus shaped not only what we know and what we understand to be knowledge but in the process it has molded the culture's discourse to fit television's silly and nonsensical form of discourse.

The end result, Postman argued, is a culture incapable of reasoned discourse, incapable even of distinguishing reasoned discourse from the absurd, and a culture lacking in awareness about those things that do not fit the template of television discourse—in other words, that which does not amuse. Citizens in such a culture are highly susceptible to manipulation and spin. And such is the culture in the United States today. Postman's thesis about the cultural effects of television is, I would argue, even more true today than it was when he wrote his seminal book. As discussed earlier in this study, American political discourse is far too often absurd and nonsensical, and only a handful of citizens, journalists, politicians, and satirists seem to notice. There is a powerful anti-intellectual component to U.S. culture at the turn of the new millennium, as well as a "disdain for reason and evidence."[594] Large segments of the public believe theories or arguments that are founded on twisted logic and that blatantly ignore overwhelming evidence to the contrary—this is true of cultural issues such as evolution; global issues such climate change; and specific political issues, such as whether the attacks of September 11 were orchestrated by the Bush administration and whether the 2009 American Recovery and Reinvestment Act saved jobs.

The media produce—and the public cannot stop feeding on—stories that are high in entertainment value but of little or no significance—the building of a mosque two blocks from Ground Zero, the sensational declarations of Tea Party candidate Christine O'Donnell, a pastor's threat to burn the Koran are three examples from 2010.[595] Every year has its crop of stories that dominate coverage and monopolize the country's attention longer than they should. Although the media and the public do pay attention to serious news when it is high drama, this happens not necessarily because of its significance but because of its drama and novelty. For example, media coverage of the wars in Iraq and Afghanistan and of the BP oil spill in the Gulf of Mexico was initially quite significant, but as the novelty and drama of these events faded (though their significance did not), interest and concern also waned. The same can be said of elections: the media and public followed the 2008 election so closely largely for its drama—a battle between historic candidates. The activities and views of a small group of angry citizens—the Tea Party Movement—some of whom have said outrageous things, hijacked the focus of the 2010 midterm election. The culture in the United States is flooded with a sea of amusements and consists of a public and politicians who not only lack the ability to participate in reasoned discourse but who also disdain reason, evidence, and science. Television may not be the only cause of this state of affairs, but Postman's thesis makes a very strong case that television has played a dominant role. As long as the public remains unaware of how television has altered American culture's view of the world, and until people can recognize the shortcomings of television's way of knowing, they will have difficulty judging wrong from right, recognizing when they are being misled by politicians, and realizing when they are being distracted from the central meaning of elections.

Television Personalizes Politics

In addition to its broader cultural effect, television contributes to an unhealthy democracy because of a number of more specific habits it encourages in political news coverage. First among those is how it personalizes politics. Because people can be pictured, whereas abstractions like institutions, policies, and ideology cannot, television presents the political world in terms of people rather than abstract concepts. This approach engenders an impoverished understanding of a political system that is populated by institutions and abstractions. If ideas or ideologies or institutions come to be known solely by the people who support or compose them, then the success of such ideas or institutions will depend on the popularity of those people—not on the merit of the ideas themselves. Republicans' practice of calling the health-care legislation passed in 2010 "Obama Care" is an implicit recognition of this television-engendered cultural tendency to personalize policy. Public-opinion polls find this effect when they ask questions about issues that also mention the president's name; there was more public support for all the components of health-care reform proposed by Bill Clinton than there was for "Clinton's health-care reform," for example.

During elections television naturally focuses on the personalities and characters of the candidates, for candidates can be pictured—their ideas and governing philosophies cannot. This trend increases the salience of candidates' personal characteristics, which eventually influence the votes of television viewers more than issues, ideology, or party do.[596] This kind of coverage, according to Roderick Hart, also adds to people's false feeling that they are informed because they have come to "know" the candidates "personally" through television, and thus they feel that they know enough to vote.[597] By personalizing politics, television distracts the electorate and confounds its ability to use elections to control what the government does.

Television Engenders Impatience

Television's negative effect on citizens' ability to fully comprehend government and politics leaves them susceptible to another of the medium's effects in the twenty-first century. In the era of twenty-four-hour cable news coverage and the Internet, characterized by instantaneous, frenzied, and continuous coverage, television also creates the impatient citizen. The constancy of televised politics (whether delivered through cable, the Internet, hand-held devices, or broadcast) trains people to expect rapid and endless movement. People today want to see that "change we can believe in" and they want it now; they expect even complex and difficult problems to be solved and solved quickly. Cable television fills its news programs with an around-the-clock watch that inspires impatience, as around-the-clock watches tend to do. There is, after all, phenomenological truth in that old maxim that the watched pot never boils; and in politics, while the watched pot does not boil, the watchers might. The Internet helps feed this impatience by its sleepless watch and its speed. Modern media present politics instantaneously in a way that encourages instant gratification and endless consumption.

The process of converting electoral mandates into policy, in contrast, is slow, especially in a system which by design fractures political power—a feature carefully designed by the framers of the U.S. Constitution. Additionally, the problems that governments tackle are not as simple as they appear in television portrayals, whether in news programs or in entertainment programs. A government cannot simply remove all its troops from combat without catastrophic effects; ending combat operations in Iraq, for instance—as many people demanded during the Bush administration—is not a matter of merely giving the order. Likewise, no one person, group, or institution can effect instant economic recovery following a major recession. An understanding of the U.S. system includes an appreciation of the facts that it takes time to obtain agreement among all those institutions and actors that hold power in the system and that it takes time for policies to have an effect. But television, especially through its twenty-four-hour cable news with the sped up news cycle of the Internet age, allows for no such understanding;

television fosters, as Postman argued, a lack of a sense of history and ignorance of what is involved. Instead, the twenty-four-hour cable news' and Internet bloggers' constant watch inspires impatience, disillusionment, and an extremely short timeline, the opposite of what a democracy needs from its citizens. It would be helpful to democracy in the United States if citizens fought this tendency and took a longer perspective on the effects of their electoral choices. If citizens were to analyze all their gains and losses during the periods that different parties control government and remain cognizant of that broader context, they might maintain a better perspective on the nature and importance of their electoral choices. Television has made such a longer-term perspective difficult.

Television Portrays Politics as a Sport

Television news is more likely to be dominated by horse-race coverage of elections than print media are. The dominant mode of election coverage on television is the sporting-event mode, not unlike the coverage of, for example, a baseball game: after each inning the media judge the effort (candidates' motives, energy, etc.), add up the hits (fundraising successes, endorsements, appeals to the public) and runs (poll numbers), and speculate about how the game will end. Everything is framed in terms of what the candidates and their parties will do to win; little is framed in terms of what it will mean to the nation and its citizens if one side or the other wins. This tendency in television—and indeed, among the rest of the media these days, as they perhaps succumb to television's lead—is well documented through content analyses of television coverage (see chapter 4). This is not to say that horse-race coverage of elections has not always existed; the problem is that such coverage has so consumed the energies of the press that, as a former national political correspondent for the *Chicago Tribune* once told one of my classes, the media are forgetting to draw audiences' attention back to the central meaning of elections.[598]

While citizens cannot escape horse-race coverage by reading about elections (instead of relying on visual media), there is typically enough room in newspapers and on news websites for some serious policy coverage as well. An analysis by the Project for Excellence in Journalism, for example, found that 69 percent of television coverage in the 2004 election was framed around political internals (that is, "inside-baseball" coverage) and that 43 percent of newspaper coverage was framed that way. Even though 10 percent of television stories were framed around explaining policy issues versus 16 percent for newspaper stories—a difference of only six percentage points—given the space available to newspapers (either on paper or online), such a difference represents a substantial amount of additional information on policy issues.[599]

Television Uses Episodic Framing
The way television typically constructs its coverage also adds to the American public's impoverished understanding of the world. Television's predominant mode of framing issues is episodic, a strategy that presents issues such as poverty, crime, or terrorism in terms of single instances: a poor family, a violent murder, a terrorist attack.[600] The alternative—thematic framing—presents issues in broader terms, providing context, analysis, trends, and the bigger picture; thematic framing deals with the factors that explain poverty, crime, or terrorism, with the historical context and broad societal trends related to poverty, crime, and terrorism. Episodic framing, as Shanto Iyengar demonstrated, leads the public to conclude that the causes of events are located within flawed individuals, and so people fail to see the more complex reasons why things are the way they are—and so they do not think to hold public officials responsible for the societal conditions that also play a role in social circumstances.

Election stories on television, too, are framed in an episodic manner, covered as a string of events unrelated to and rarely compared with history or past patterns or the bigger electoral picture. Television news stories offer poll numbers and trends in the race but rarely provide a context for the typical ups and downs of campaigns that would aid the public in understanding what is and is not significant. When issues are covered, they are rarely tied to the overall governing philosophies of the candidates, and issues are never presented in the context of the fact, demonstrated by history, that candidates' issue stands and party platforms are excellent predictors of what they and fellow partisans will do if elected—issues are instead framed as another attempt to win the sporting contest. And the television media rarely focus on the big picture—that is, the meaning of the choice confronting voters. These circumstances feed the narrow, individual focus of elections as contests between people, not between philosophies of governance.

Television Propagates a False Sense of Being Informed

Through television members of the public acquire a sense of being informed when in fact they are not; chapter 1 of this study reviews the evidence for how poorly informed and even misinformed the public is. Simply put, television news broadcasts do not contain much politically relevant content and do not present the information needed to foster democratic citizenship (see chapter 4 for the evidence of this). The material television does provide is lacking in background and context. Not surprisingly, then, audiences of commercial television news are less informed than those who read newspapers; television audiences are more often misinformed than those who read the news.[601] While some of this difference in audience knowledge is due to a self-selection process—those who have the more advanced cognitive abilities needed to process print news are more likely to read the news—there is also a negative reinforcing effect: people with a poorer understanding of the world tend to rely on television, and thus receive poorer quality information.

Despite the differences evident in the knowledge of those who watch the news on television and those who read about it, many television viewers believe that they are informed. After all, they have instant access to twenty-four hours of news if they want it, with video available not just from television and cable but now also on the Internet and through a multitude of handheld media devices. Additionally, because television provides an opportunity to get to "know" the politicians, and because television audiences know all the ups and downs of the game of elections and the latest techniques for winning the vote, and because, as Neil Postman argued, television has fundamentally altered the culture's notions of what it means to be informed, the members of the public who rely on television are unaware of just how poor their understanding of elections has become.

The Adverse Effect of Television on Journalism

Television no longer supports a great deal of good journalism, that public watchdog so critical to maintaining an informed citizenry. Newspapers were always the largest employers of journalists, and after the staff cutbacks at the networks that started in the 1980s, this was even more so the case.[602] As newspapers fade and also cut back on the number of journalists they employ, the United States is in danger of finding itself without enough journalists to cover events thoroughly. Consuming television at the expense of reading articles about politics does little to support the good journalism critical for a democracy (see chapter 4 for an extended discussion of the importance of good journalism).

The Adverse Effect of Television on Social Capital

Finally, television seems to displace political participation and other social activities that tend to lead to political involvement. Television, according to Roderick Hart, makes viewers feel busy with politics and substitutes *watching* politics for *doing* politics.[603] Robert Putnam, in his book *Bowling Alone*, provides a wealth of evidence that shows television is damaging to cultural features critical to democratic societies— social capital and civic engagement.

> Americans at the end of the twentieth century were watching more TV, watching it more habitually, more pervasively, and more often alone, and watching more programs that were associated specifically with civic disengagement (entertainment, as distinct from news). The onset of these trends coincided exactly with the national decline in social connectedness, and the trends were most marked among the younger generations that are ... distinctively disengaged. Moreover, it is precisely those Americans most marked by this dependence on televised entertainment who were most likely to have dropped out of civic and social

life—who spent less time with friends, were less involved in community organizations and were less likely to participate in public
affairs.[604]

More specifically, Putnam documents, "each additional hour of television viewing per day means roughly a 10 percent reduction in most
forms of civic activism."[605] In contrast, readers of newspapers, regardless of age or education, were more engaged and more informed than
those who watched the news.

Changing the Way People See Television

The bottom line is that the more the U.S. public watches television (or
streams videos over the Internet[606]), the poorer the health of the country's elections will be and the weaker its democracy. Clearly, the health
of American democracy would improve if the public developed an
awareness of the negative effects of television on the comprehension of
politics and government and if citizens changed their habits with regard
to television, reducing the number of viewing hours and cultivating the
habit of reading high-quality journalistic accounts of government and
politics, either in newspapers or online. Only reading provides the context and background requisite for a meaningful understanding of the
issues and choices facing the nation (as well as state and local governments). Reading also helps create the complex and integrated cognitive
structures that the public needs to fully understand what is going on and
hold governmental officials accountable. And reading the news is associated with civic engagement.

I am not suggesting that people destroy their televisions and drop
watching entirely. What I propose is that U.S. citizens take the advice former television anchor and former NPR senior news analyst Daniel Schorr
offered to his granddaughter in a StoryCorps interview: "Would you read
now and then and turn off the television set?"[607] To be more specific, all
that is needed—especially in concert with the other changes suggested
throughout this book, changes that are designed to make elections less
burdensome and confusing—is to convince people who do not already

read their news to replace thirty minutes of television with reading four to five full-length news articles online or in print. The ubiquity of handheld devices that allow for reading wherever and whenever and the increased use of the Internet should facilitate such a change in habits. Additionally, it would be helpful for the state of democracy if those who do not already do so replaced one night a week of television watching and with some social activity. This does not necessarily have to be a political activity, as the title of Putman's book, *Bowling Alone*, indicates; any activity that allows for the development of personal connections with others in one's community builds social capital critical to political involvement.[608]

How can Americans be persuaded to follow this prescription and be made aware of the effects of television and television-watching habits? Incorporating lessons about television in the new civics curriculum would certainly help, as would exposure to and study of print news sources. Indeed, reading the news appears to be a habit that, when started at a young age, is maintained throughout life.[609] Awareness of the biases of the medium of television—or more broadly, videos, whether they are beamed from the old box or streamed online—needs to be a goal of the new civics curriculum.[610] The other changes to the civics curriculum prescribed earlier would also create incentives for citizens to change their news habits and help them focus their efforts on the essence of elections. With these changes in place, media monitoring of government and politics would serve a more simplified purpose of keeping tabs on whether the parties are following their philosophies of governance, whether the approach of the governing party is having an effect, and whether the times might call for an approach different from that followed by the current government. Changing the habits of the generations that have left school already will be a more difficult task, but introducing this knowledge about the damaging effects of television on citizenship into the cultural discourse might lead some to change. This knowledge is already presented in the form of satire on *The Daily Show*, *The Colbert Report*, and the *Onion News Network*, the "fake" news shows whose material is provided by the inane nature of television news as much as by the foibles of politicians; perhaps such satire about television is why the audiences of these shows tend to be more engaged and knowledgeable about politics.[611] But beyond the reach of that satire, these other changes in how the public sees elections and use the media may have to be something that spreads from the younger generations upward.

R$_x$: New Civics Lesson IV: Be Skeptics, Not Cynics

Finally, U.S. elections need the public to break the bad habit of reactionary cynicism, fed in part by television, and to learn instead to be skeptics. As demonstrated in chapter 1, much of the American public is highly cynical about government and politics. Indeed, U.S. culture seems to be in the midst of a relativistic period—the "truthiness era," if you will—in which reality and fact are deemed objectively unknowable. All claims, statements of fact, research findings, and so forth, are instead believed to be a product of personal and political biases. This idea feeds the cynics, who reject claims regardless of the evidence or facts. Large segments of the public are cynical about the motives of everyone involved in politics, especially the politicians and the mass media: politicians are self-serving and not to be trusted; the mainstream media is politically biased. Therefore the cynics believe no one who contradicts or challenges their own political beliefs. Many liberals believe to this day that there was a conspiracy around the assassination of President Kennedy and that the American government was behind the attacks of September 11. Many Republicans believe that Iraqi leader Saddam Hussein was involved in the attacks of September 11, even after a Republican-appointed government panel concluded that there was no connection and the Republican President Bush clearly reiterated that point. During the 2009 debate over changes to the health care system, opponents of the proposed changes disrupted congressional town meetings with claims that had absolutely no basis in fact (e.g., the claim that the Democrats were setting up "death panels"). A visit to FactCheck.org and a perusal of the "Ask FactCheck.org" questions and answers will provide readers with a multitude of different examples of the things people believe, often in the face of overwhelming contradictory information.

It is important to note here the negative aspects of partisanship that can feed this cynical reaction to information that contradicts a person's beliefs. When I propose in this book that people utilize political parties as a means of making elections more meaningful, I mean that people should support a party based on an informed awareness of the governing philosophies and policies advocated by the parties. Evidence indicates that more of the voting public is doing just that (though nonvoters are not).[612] Unfortunately, there is also evidence of a growing emotional component to partisanship—among the electorate and in the mass media—that can act as an impediment to political learning and result in a balkanization of knowledge about policy and politics. This affective component of partisanship (measured by the differences between how one feels about Democrats and Republicans, as opposed to reactions based on the policies and records of the parties) has increased in recent elections.[613] Fed by the news or entertainment media citizens choose to follow and the talk-show nature of political discourse in recent years, political party and ideology are now also used extensively for labeling partisan opponents as the "enemy" and demonizing them.[614] Moreover, too many people (including politicians and media personnel) have come to misuse partisanship and ideology, dismissing outright or shouting down disagreements and information contrary to their beliefs, ridiculing, caricaturing, and belittling opposing ideas and those who present them.[615] Emotions are certainly important to politics—they stimulate interest and motivate participation. But when the emotional side of partisanship becomes its overriding force such that people cannot come to a sensible agreement about the basic facts of the political debate—for instance, whether the economy is losing jobs, what is in proposed legislation, whether human activity is contributing to climate change, who benefits from various tax policies—then reasoned discourse is impossible and partisanship becomes a negative force in politics.

Political discourse in a culture is dysfunctional if it is dominated by affect, if neither side believes a word the other side says in dissent, or if no one believes anything critical journalists (the onetime arbiters of the facts) might have to say. Political debate is impossible without commonly accepted standards for what is and is not a fact. Thus if the public wants a healthy democracy, some reasonable standards must be in place as to what should and should not be accepted as fact or truth, and such standards must be applied to the claims made by *both* sides of the debate; citizens must hold their fellow partisans to these standards as rigorously as they do those with whom they disagree. Brooks Jackson and Kathleen Hall Jamieson attempt to encourage such standards in their book *unSpun: Finding Facts in a World of Disinformation*.[616] These authors present a set of guidelines for testing political claims, suggestions such as looking for general agreement among experts, checking primary sources, knowing what is being counted and how, knowing the reputation and biases of who is talking, and being skeptical but not cynical. Jackson and Jamieson have also developed a curriculum for teachers to help students incorporate these guidelines and develop their standards of evidence.[617] Greater dissemination of such skills through a new civics curriculum would certainly improve the nature of political discourse and would also create a demand for the fact-checking services traditionally provided by journalists. If journalists adopt the practices of assessing facts for their reporting as discussed in chapter 4, the new civics lessons would be nicely reinforced.

MANDATORY VOTING?

The final prescription discussed in this book is whether the government should, as some countries (most notably Australia) do, mandate by law that citizens vote. The idea may at first seem a nonstarter in U.S. culture: citizens in the United States do not like to be forced to do anything, and their first reaction would likely be to vote out of office any politician who legislated mandatory voting. From a practical standpoint, moreover, unless the changes in the structure of U.S. elections suggested in chapter 5 are adopted, the high frequency with which Americans are asked to vote might actually prove enough of a hardship on some citizens that the government would expend inordinate resources granting exceptions to the law. Additionally, given the information levels and reasoning powers of the U.S. public, one might wonder whether it be wise to force everyone to vote; but this question opens a much larger philosophical debate that I will leave to others.[618] Instead, I refer to the diagnosis outlined in the first three chapters of this book, a diagnosis that specifies low voter turnout as a *symptom* of other problems with the health of U.S. elections. To extend the medical metaphor, although it makes short-term sense to treat a sick patient's fever directly, in the long run the causes of the illness that generated the fever must be removed for the patient to fully recover. The prescriptions suggested in this book are aimed at the illness and the causes. If the proposals were fully implemented, I suspect that mandatory voting would simply reinforce the effects of those changes and that it would, perhaps, be unnecessary.

CONCLUSION

In the discussions I have had over the years with my students about reforming elections or the mass media, some students inevitably dismiss all of the institutional and legal reforms and lay the blame squarely on the public: "if the voters weren't so lazy..." and "if people would pay more attention...." In light of this book's content, my response to such comments should be obvious, but as the material in this chapter also indicates, those students have a valid point: the public must shoulder its share of the responsibility for the poor health of elections. Having people take responsibility for the state of elections and democracy, I might also point out, is the ideologically conservative solution for electoral problems. Over the years, thanks largely to the development of television and the perfection of its talent for endlessly amusing (which talent has now colonized the Internet), U.S. culture has inculcated in members of the public habits that diminish their ability to exercise the power of democratic citizenship. The habit of thinking about elections as an exercise in individual expression disempowers citizens and leads them to serial disillusionment. The cultural failure to recognize the power of policy-based partisan voting confuses the message of elections. The excessive reliance on television makes citizens spectators who lack a coherent understanding of events or of what election choices really mean. And the reactionary cynicism pervasive in the culture leads to intellectual laziness and an inability to properly sort through fact and fiction. Therefore part of nursing U.S. elections back to health requires that the American public break away from these bad habits. Democracy in the United States needs citizens (1) to see elections for what they are, namely, instruments of power for aggregations of like-minded people; (2) as a logical consequence of that more realistic view of elections, to vote based on the party, not the person; (3) to replace some of the time they spend watching television with reading about government and politics, and in the process support good journalism; (4) to become more involved their communities; and (5) to become thoughtful skeptics rather than reactionary cynics.

Anthony Gierzynski, Ph.D.
Department of Political Science
The University of Vermont

Patient: U.S. Elections   D.O.B.: September 17, 1789

R_x

Reconceptualize citizenship with a new civics curriculum that teaches the public to do the following:

- Think about elections not as acts of individual expression but in terms of how the actions of aggregations of like-minded people facilitate the exercise of power by choosing similarly like-minded governments
- Vote the party not the person
- Gain an awareness of the shortcomings of television's way of knowing about politics, replace thirty minutes of television time with reading good journalism about politics and government, and join a group
- Be skeptics, not cynics

Signature of the Prescriber: *Dr. Anthony Gierzynski*

CHAPTER 9

CONCLUSION

Anthony Gierzynski, Ph.D.
Department of Political Science
The University of Vermont

Patient: U.S. Elections   D.O.B.: September 17, 1789

R_x

Enhance public broadcasting through better (and dedicated) funding and greater insulation from political pressures.

Require broadcasters to fulfill public-service mandate through (1) compulsory (more thorough) coverage of conventions, (2) free airtime provided to the political parties, and (3) continued coverage of candidate debates.

Support journalists' drive to spread professional principles so that they can "provide people with the information they need to be free and self-governing." As part of this effort, establish a government-supported internship/fellowship program in order to increase the number of professionally trained journalists in news media organizations.

Stop complicating elections by asking voters to make more decisions with more choices and instead reduce the number of decisions asked of voters.

Hold elections less frequently.

Adopt the bonus plan for the Electoral College.

Restructure the presidential nomination process and begin the process later in the year.

Change political party discourse by (1) staying focused on or at least constantly returning to the big picture, the fundamental nature of the electoral choice; (2) maintaining reasoned discourse focused on the merits of policies; (3) forgoing the use of wedge issues; and (4) refraining from focusing on the other side's inconsequential gaffes.

At the state level, set limits (albeit generous ones) on contributions to political parties.

Establish partial public funding for federal and state candidates with four-to-one matching for small contributions with spending limits that reflect the reality of campaign needs, a ban on bundling, and a requirement to debate.

Allow more money to flow through the parties for voter mobilization and coordinated spending while eliminating party-independent expenditures.

Discourage electoral activity by independent groups through a reasonable redefinition of electioneering activity.

Establish constitutional guidelines for redistricting that increase the number of competitive districts.

Increase funding for the administration of elections, to test for and provide the most usable voting machinery and to train and compensate poll workers.

Transfer authority for elections from the partisan secretary of states' offices to a nonpartisan election official appointed with approval of supermajorities in the state legislatures.

Implement a democracy-index ranking of local election administration.

Reconceptualize citizenship with a new civics curriculum that teaches the public to do the following:

- Think about elections not as acts of individual expression but in terms of how the actions of aggregations of like-minded people facilitate the exercise of power by choosing similarly like-minded governments
- Vote the party not the person
- Gain an awareness of the shortcomings of television's way of knowing about politics, replace thirty minutes of television time with reading good journalism about politics and government, and join a group
- Be skeptics, not cynics.

Signature of the Prescriber: *Dr. Anthony Gierzynski*

THE PRESCRIPTIONS

The treatments I have prescribed in this book are what I believe are the most appropriate prescriptions given the diagnosis of the problems plaguing U.S. elections. These prescriptions utilize the diagnosis and the state of knowledge about elections in order to deal what is really making

U.S. elections sick—the condition of electoral law and election administration, the structure of elections, the damaging habits of the electorate
and politicians, and the misguided reliance on privately run, unregulated
media. These are the conditions that, in various combinations, are causing problems in the American electoral system. Treating or removing
these causes as I have prescribed would allow elections to get over the
high levels of uncompetitive contests, the political inequality, the overwhelmed electorate, and the failings of the key supportive institutions
(the mass media and political parties). And as elections recover from
these ailments, the symptoms of an uninvolved, uninformed, and cynical
electorate should fade. Elections thus mended would be capable of functioning more effectively as a means of popular control of government
policy, ultimately improving the well-being of the democracy that is so
dependent upon them for its health.

Getting from a diagnosis of the illness afflicting U.S. elections
to a healthier democracy is easily done in words; doing so in reality
is another matter. This is especially true given three factors: (1) elections are incredibly complex systems with highly interrelated problems;
(2) as in medical practice, prescribing the *right* treatment for the patient
is much more complicated than simply identifying the most effective
treatments; and (3) the effective prescriptions must compete with any
number of ineffective prescriptions to gain the attention of reformers
and policy makers. In considering the prescriptions presented throughout this book, I have attempted to deal with these difficulties in a number
of ways. First, in order to contend with the complex and interrelated
nature of the problems, I adopted a holistic approach to the treatment of
elections. A holistic approach not only deals with the interrelated nature
of the problems with elections, it also provides tactical support in the
political fight for reform by preempting opposing arguments that would
critically assess prescriptions in isolation. Second, in the process of finding the right treatment for elections, I went beyond considering what was
effective, taking into account the costs (or trade-offs) of treatments, their
possible side effects, and their political prices. And finally, by utilizing
a diagnosis based on the extant research concerning elections and by

plumbing that research for clues as to the effectiveness of various treatments for elections, I hoped to sort out the ineffective treatments—the "snake oil"—from the effective treatments. Although most reform proposals are motivated by good intent, the snake oil prescriptions have the unfortunate effect of diffusing the energy behind election reform, sending the effort in too many directions to be effective.

THE NECESSITY OF A HOLISTIC
APPROACH TO ELECTION REFORM

The diagnosis laid out in the first three chapters clarifies several points with respect to the problems besetting U.S. elections and the possible prescriptions to fix them. First, the problems with the health of U.S. elections are intricately intertwined. The reliance on privately owned, for-profit media, for example, means that the media fail to focus on important facts during elections and fail to act as watchdogs, keeping the politicians honest and on task. This means that the overwhelmed electorate (overwhelmed because of the structure of elections and because of the public's own failure to utilize partisanship in voting) receives little help deciphering information, which in turn leaves the public poorly informed, cynical, and unlikely to vote. To cite another example, the state of election law with respect to both the financing of elections and the drawing of legislative districts results in uncompetitive elections, unequal distribution of political resources, and a lack of equality in political influence—all of which in turn feed cynicism and suppress voter turnout. The diagram of the diagnosis in figure 2.1 shows how each problem is connected to the others.

Second, because the problems are so interconnected, the solutions must be, too. Tinkering with individual reforms here and there is unlikely to fully restore U.S. elections to health. What is needed is a holistic approach to reform that addresses the causes and attacks the election illness on multiple fronts; that was the approach I took in the process of considering electoral prescriptions for this book. As a consequence, the efficacy of the set of prescriptions I propose depends in large part on the patient's receiving the full treatment; most of the individual prescriptions will not do much good on their own. Providing better-funded public media and good electoral journalism, for example, will have little effect if the public does not recognize the value of these things and chooses endless entertainment instead. Changing redistricting practices will have a limited effect on competition if campaign-finance laws allow the politically lopsided distribution of electoral resources. Politicians are unlikely to change their habits of spin and distraction if the media and the public do not keep them focused on the bigger picture. For any of these prescriptions to work, all of them must be followed. If the demands on the voters are reduced by restructuring the electoral system in a more voter-friendly way; *and* if the electorate is encouraged to develop an understanding of the true nature of their electoral choices through a better understanding of the parties and a better functioning media; *and* partial public funding, adjustment to campaign-finance laws, and better criteria for redistricting are implemented in order to enhance competition and political equality—then and only then will the United States have healthier, more meaningful elections, elections that allow citizens to determine what their governments do.

A holistic approach to reform is not only essential for the prescriptions to work, but it is also critical to encouraging policy makers to write the prescriptions in the first place. There will be many interests vehemently opposed to the changes suggested here, mainly those interests that are advantaged by the poor health of elections in the United States today. We know from previous battles over electoral reform that one of the tactics opponents use against any proposed change is to charge that the reform, whatever it is, can easily be circumvented and that as a consequence the reform will not bring about healthier elections.[619] Opponents might argue, for instance, "If you require the major networks to cover the conventions, people will just change to some other channel," or "Starting the primaries and caucuses later will not prevent candidates from raising money and campaigning earlier," or "Supporting good journalism does not mean that people will actually read it." Such arguments can be effective because they have some merit when the proposed reforms are viewed in isolation—but only when they are viewed in isolation. A holistic approach, in prescribing a coherent *set* of treatments to address all the different aspects of the poor health of elections, counters such arguments and makes them irrelevant.

SNAKE OIL[620]

The diagnosis of the sickness afflicting U.S. elections, like any medical diagnosis, tells us not only which prescriptions are needed but also which prescriptions are useless or harmful. Throughout this book I have discussed a number of prescriptions for elections that either do not address any of the actual problems with U.S. elections or actually make them worse. Any prescription that increases the burden on voters—including national referenda, recall elections, nonpartisan elections, rank-order voting, and additional major political parties—will clearly make the situation worse. Prescriptions that address only the symptoms, such as "Rock the Vote"–style public-service campaigns to encourage people to vote and convenience voting (no-excuse absentee ballots, early voting, mail voting, and same-day registration) will do little to restore health to the system; according to some research, these approaches may even be harmful.[621] Prescriptions that impair the functioning of key institutions that support the health of elections should also be avoided, as they, too, would do more harm than good. Replacing the Electoral College with a national popular vote or establishing nonpartisan elections, for example, would damage the political parties, which are vital to the health of elections. Encouraging the development of a partisan press would only further weaken the media as an arbiter of electoral contests. And prescriptions that are not aimed at any of the actual problems in the electoral system—expanding the number of political parties; instituting rank-order (instant runoff) voting; introducing nonpartisan elections, proportional representation, full-disclosure with no-limits campaign finance laws, or bans on candidate advertisements—would do nothing to make elections healthier and, given the law of unintended consequences, would undoubtedly have some detrimental effects.

As in the medical field, prescriptions need to be informed by a diagnosis and by the results of the scientific research on the subject. Those fighting for healthier elections should avoid prescriptions made in ignorance of or in contradiction to a complete and research-based diagnosis like the one offered here. Such snake oil should be avoided not only because of its inefficacy and the possible harm it could cause but also because applying misguided (albeit often well-meaning) prescriptions is counterproductive to the overall political effort to improve the health of elections. The prevalence of so many snake-oil prescriptions distracts the reform effort from effective strategies and prevents those who recognize that there are problems with elections from supporting a coherent set of truly efficacious reforms.

OF PRAGMATISM, POLITICS, AND TRADE-OFFS

In medicine, doctors' prescriptions are informed not only by the diagnosis and the efficacy of various treatments but also by what can feasibly be done and in light of any trade-offs that the prescription may involve. Treatment options for health problems can range from conservative to aggressive options. On the conservative side, patients might be prescribed behavioral changes—specific diet or exercise programs, cessation of smoking, physical therapy—that carry long-term benefits if followed but have less dramatic immediate effects. On the aggressive side, the prescription might call for some invasive surgery that solves the immediate problem but may also be riskier and not as efficacious in the long run. I imagine that balancing these additional considerations is the most difficult thing for a medical doctor to do when deciding on treatment for patients. It is one thing to know what is wrong with a patient and that there are treatments available, but it is quite another to know which treatments to prescribe given the varying likelihood of success and the costs or trade-offs each treatment option poses for the patient. This is no less true when considering prescriptions for elections.

In choosing the prescriptions in this book, I considered practical and political issues as well as the trade-offs that each electoral prescription would entail and, as a result, ultimately settled on a mix of conservative and aggressive treatments. While I do prescribe more aggressive treatments in some areas, I do not call for any radical alteration of the U.S. electoral system that would require major surgery (e.g., major rewrites of the U.S. Constitution to establish a parliamentary system or to eliminate the U.S. Senate) because I believe that the uncertainties of such radical approaches are not worth the risks. Elections may be chronically ill in the United States, but they are not in need of a heart or liver transplant; health can be restored without such aggressive interventions.

In the end, consideration of the efficacy, costs, trade-offs, and possible side effects (as indicated by the social science research on elections) is what led to the mix of conservative and aggressive treatments prescribed here. Thus in campaign-finance reform, for example, I suggest surgery to redirect the flow of money in the existing system in beneficial ways and a dose of public funding. This is not as aggressive as an approach that would clear all private money out of the system (100 percent public financing), but it is, I believe, the better approach. It is better because research has shown it is likely to be more effective, with fewer side effects (full public funding leads private money to find other, less healthy means to fund elections), and fewer trade-offs (it still allows people freedom to contribute to candidates and parties). The conservative treatment for campaign-finance reform—attempting to modify behavior through simple disclosure of campaign finance activity—is the equivalent of merely monitoring the vital signs of the patient; it has been found to be entirely ineffective in treating the illness, political inequality.

With regard to redistricting, my prescription does not include the more aggressive treatment option of nonpartisan redistricting commissions because the research has failed to find any concrete benefit of such a reform. Instead, a more conservative set of incentives is proposed to change the behavior of actors involved in redistricting in order to attain the desired outcome of more competitive districts. With respect to the media, the most aggressive treatment—abolishing privately owned, for-profit media—is not feasible. So I prescribe more conservative treatments based on the findings of the research: strengthening the one countervailing force to the effect of the drive for profit within the media—journalism—and implementing mandatory debate coverage and free television time; the research shows that people actually learn policy positions from these options. I use the research findings to apply criteria meant to determine, for example, which decisions voters should be asked to make on the ballot and which ones are not worth the cost—the complexity they add to the ballot. The discussion of each prescription within the chapters of this book is steeped in such considerations.

The political considerations (what might be the parallel to affordability in medical practice) are undoubtedly, as I acknowledge throughout the book, the most difficult to deal with. After all, at issue here, to shift metaphors, are the rules of the election "game." And while those outside of the game (political scientists and reformers) may agree on what seems fair and efficacious, those playing the game (particularly the opposing teams on the field, the parties) are much less likely to. The special problem with reforming elections is that those playing are actually the ones who make the rules and would thus be the legislators of any reforms. Compounding the political problem of having competitors make the rules is the nature of the ideology of one of the teams—in this case, the Republicans. Because most prescriptions for improving the health of elections require government action, and because those actions increase the scope of government and the extent of government regulation, the proposals are likely to run afoul of conservative ideology, the dominant ideology within the Republican Party. It is entirely consistent for conservatives to apply their free-market, limited-government principles to elections and thus reject most election reform. Conservative opposition is also undoubtedly fueled in part by the fact that until the 2006 and 2008 elections, they and their party had become experts at winning under the current rules of the system. But as the 2006 and 2008 elections demonstrate, the current set of rules—or the elections' poor state of health—will not always benefit them.

In arriving at the prescriptions I suggest, I consider and propose solutions that require less government involvement. Indeed, many of the prescriptions are more conservative treatments (in both medical and ideological terms) than other proposals in the reform community. I accept, for example, that the media will continue to be controlled by for-profit businesses and therefore suggest more modest changes: additional requirements for those businesses (free airtime and coverage of party conventions and debates); indirect government subsidies for those media businesses in the form of a government-supported journalism fellowship program; and a relatively small boost in governmental support for nonprofit media in order to ensure that at least one set of media outlets can produce serious public-affairs coverage that the competitive market fails to provide. With regard to political parties and campaign finance, I reject the approaches that would deny the right of private interests to contribute money to election efforts (as many in the reform community propose with full-public-funding prescriptions) and instead suggest alterations to the current campaign finance system that would strengthen *competition* (a conservative value) and the ability of the political parties' to compete.

For conservatives to come to the "operating" table as "election doctors" and assist in treating the patient, they will need to be convinced that the health of elections is *not* ensured by free-market principles alone and that they—the conservatives—also suffer from the problems in the electoral system. Elections involve competition, certainly, but amassing profits or wealth is not the equivalent of amassing the most votes. Electoral success or health cannot be measured by mere vote totals but by whether the voting leads to representative government. In order for electoral competition to produce a government that does what the majority of the public wants it to do, elections must be a battle of ideas, not of tactics and personalities. The laissez-faire approach to elections, history shows, leads to elections focused on the latter and not the former. Additionally, viewing elections from a market perspective has the unfortunate corollary of seeing voters as consumers. This is problematic for a democracy. Voters clearly *can* be misled by fancy packaging and clever ad campaigns, and if that is what determines the outcome of elections, then the legitimacy of governments selected by those elections is cast into doubt. It should also be noted that a voter-as-consumer model of elections is a double-edged sword: while either side may win at times using such manipulative tactics, both sides will also lose at times, victim to the same tactics.

Additionally, there *are* flaws in the free-market approach and those flaws are more detrimental to elections than they are to the functioning of the market itself. In particular, the market faces problems of imperfect information and inequality. The ramifications of selecting a government based on imperfect information are typically much greater than the ramifications of purchasing a good without enough information (unless of course the good or service is hazardous to one's health). There is no returning a government, and the policies that governments pursue have a much greater impact on the world than a person's choice of consumer goods. And significant inequality is simply not acceptable to supporters of democracy. Indeed, *democracy* by definition requires political equality; without it a system no longer constitutes rule by the many and is instead rule by the few—it becomes *oligarchy*.

While any individual conservative might accept this reasoning, I am skeptical (as the reader may be) that in the current political environment in the United States—with the vitriol so extreme and the stakes perceived to be matters of life-and-death—that reason, evidence, and appeals to democratic principles will be effective. Therefore although I have asserted that all the prescriptions are necessary and dependent upon interactions with each other to create a successful treatment, I do not believe that they all have to be accomplished *simultaneously*, though that would be ideal. A pragmatic assessment of the current state of U.S. political culture would most likely lead to the conclusion that whereas the full prescription should certainly be followed, its elements may necessarily be implemented one step at a time. After all, doctors do not necessarily administer all of their prescribed treatments at once—they may operate on problems in stages or prescribe a course of drugs prior to an operation. Given the polarized and cynical climate of politics in the United States, perhaps the best starting point is those prescriptions that apply to the citizenry; these would prepare the way for other treatments.

As discussed in chapter 8, encouraging more of the public (1) to see elections as the avenue for aggregate action by citizens with similar preferences for government policy, (2) to vote according to which parties' governing philosophies reflect their broad preferences, and (3) to *read* about politics and government instead of only watching should start the process of refocusing the system on what elections and partisan competition are truly about. Changes in the media would then ensure that quality journalism is available to meet the increased demand for it. This, in turn, might provide the right incentives for politicians to reduce the level of incivility in their discourse and make an opening for a rational debate concerning the rest of the prescriptions. In some states or even at the national level, there may be opportunities at that point to start on other prescriptions as well—like reforming redistricting, campaign-finance laws, and developing a democracy index. With these changes in place, the proposals may have gained the momentum needed for complete implementation.

Finally, all prescriptions for reforming U.S. elections involve some trade-offs. When the discussion of any electoral reform is put into the broader context of American elections, the trade-offs that each reform entails become evident. Many prescriptions for improving elections might appear to be good ideas considered in isolation; reforms that give the public more choice, for example, often seem appealing on their own. But when one considers the effects of additional choices added to what is already a multitude of choices in U.S. elections, the trade-off becomes evident: should fewer people make more decisions, each of less importance than the last—or should more people make fewer decisions of greater importance? Consider, too, campaign finance reform. The nearly unconstrained freedom to contribute money to or spend on behalf of political campaigns at the national level and in many state and local contests comes with its price: an absence of political equality. Should people and interests have the freedom to throw all their weight (in dollars) behind candidates, parties, or groups—or should competitive elections be fostered and a closer approximation of political equality be pursued in the political system? And as for the nature of participation, exercising power through political participation means giving up some things one might want government to do in order to get government to do most of the things one wants. Is it all or nothing—or do voters want to exercise power so they can get the government to do *most* of what they want? Likewise, greater competition and more meaningful choice through political parties may sublimate the individuality of candidates to the goals of the party. Do voters want independence in candidates—or do voters want candidates to act as a team so the candidates when elected have the power to implement the majority's preferences? Finally, real democratic citizenship requires some civic responsibility, choosing to forgo the endless parade of cultural amusements from time to time for the sake of true political knowledge and involvement. Does the American public want a healthy democracy—or are people content with amusements?

In the end, doing nothing about the health of elections means accepting the trade-offs that have been made in the way elections run now, trade-offs that are implicit throughout this book, trade-offs that have put the health of U.S. elections in danger, trade-offs that have never actually been put before the public in order for them to choose. Does the public accept those trade-offs and the condition of elections today—or will Americans take action in order to render elections in the United States and the democracy that depends upon them healthier and more functional?

Notes

1. Jane Mayer, "Covert Operations: The Billionaire Brothers Who Are Waging A War Against Obama," *New Yorker*, August 30, 2010, accessed October 7, 2010, http://www.newyorker.com/reporting/2010/08/30/100830fa_fact_mayer.
2. Congressional Budget Office, "Estimated Impact of the American Recovery and Reinvestment Act on Employment and Economic Output from April 2010 through June 2010" (Washington, DC: Congressional Budget Office. August 2010).
3. T. W. Farnam and Dan Eggen, "Interest-Group Spending for Midterm Up Fivefold from 2006; Many Sources Secret," *Washington Post*, October 4, 2010, accessed October 7, 2010, http://www.washingtonpost.com/wp-dyn/content/article/2010/10/03/AR2010100303664.html?wpisrc=nl_headline&sid=ST2010100303814. [AG: please insert here "For the final numbers on group spending see The Campaign Finance Institute, "Table 1: Reportable Spending by Party and Non-Party Groups in Congressional Elections, 2006–2010," accessed February 20, 2011, http://www.cfinst.org/pdf/federal/PostElec2010_Table1_.pdf.
4. See Politifact.com and FactCheck.com for a depressing list and analyses of these incorrect claims. For the money pumped into airing these claims, see Farnam and Eggen, "Interest-group spending" and Michael Luo, "G.O.P Allies Drive Add Spending Disparity," *New York Times*, September 13, 2010.
5. The fourteenth-century barber, from a skit starring Steve Martin; the barber prescribed good bloodlettings and leaches for his patients; "Theodoric of York," *Saturday Night Live*, televised by NBC on November 4, 1978, http://www.nbc.com/saturday-night-live/video/clips/theodoric-of-york/2888/, accessed January 7, 2010. See NBC's website.
6. I was an expert witness in the cases that ultimately ended up in the U.S. Supreme Court under the title *Landell v. Sorrell* (548 U.S. __ [2006]) and in *Homans v. City of Albuquerque*, No. CIV 01-917 MV/RLP.
7. Jan-Erik Lane and Svante Ersson, *Democracy: A Comparative Approach* (New York: Routledge, 2003).
8. Gallup poll, October 3–5, 2008.
9. Democrats had done so in 1984, when Walter Mondale selected Geraldine Ferraro as his running mate.
10. Curtis Gans and Jon Hussey, "African-Americans, Anger, Fear and Youth Propel Turnout to Highest Level Since 1960: Possible Pro-Democratic

Realignment, GOP Disaster," a report produced by the Committee for the Study of the American Electorate, December 17, 2008, accessed June 26, 2009, http://www1.media.american.edu/electionexperts/2008%20Election%20Turnout_final_full.pdf.

11. Michael P. McDonald, "The Return of the Voter: Voter Turnout in the 2008 Presidential Election," *The Forum* Volume 6, Issue 4 (2008), accessed June 26, 2009, http://www.bepress.com/forum/vol6/iss4/.

12. Excluding southern states that had, until recently, suppressed their turnout levels with systematic attempts to disenfranchise black voters presents a truer picture of the general downward trend in turnout. See Thomas E. Patterson, *The Vanishing Voter: Public Involvement in an Age of Uncertainty* (New York: Knopf, 2002).

13. Committee for the Study of the American Electorate, "Turnout Exceeds Optimistic Predictions: More than 122 Million Vote," January 14, 2005, accessed June 26, 2009, http://election04.ssrc.org/research/csae_2004_final_report.pdf; Committee for the Study of the American Electorate, "African-Americans, Anger, Fear and Youth."

14. This is barely half the number of people who reported displaying the flag in August of 2002. Seventy-five percent reported displaying the flag in August 2002. See time trends in the Pew Research Center for the People and the Press, "Beyond Red and Blue: Republicans Divided about Role of Government—Democrats by Social and Personal Values," May 10, 2005, accessed September 1, 2005, http://people-press.org/reports/print.php3?PageID=953.

15. The United States Election Project, George Mason University, http://elections.gmu.edu/.

16. As a percentage of voting-age population; see Rafael Lopez Pintor and Maria Gratschew, *Voter Turnout Since 1945* (Stockholm, Sweden: International Institute for Democracy and Electoral Assistance, 2002), 84.

17. Patterson, *The Vanishing Voter*.

18. Ibid.

19. M. Margaret Conway, "The Scope of Participation in the 2008 Presidential Race," in *Winning the Presidency 2008*, ed. William J. Crotty (Boulder, CO: Paradigm, 2009), 111.

20. Curtis Gans, "2008 Primary Turnout Falls Just Short of Record Nationally, Breaks Record in Most States," News Release, Center for the Study of the American Electorate, American University, May 19, 2008, accessed August 26, 2009, http://www1.american.edu/ia/cdem/csae/pdfs/csae080519.pdf.

21. Curtis Gans, "The Primary Turnout Story: Presidential Races Miss Record High Senate and Governor Contests Hit Record Low," Report, Center for the Study of the American Electorate, American University, October 1, 2008, accessed August 26, 2009, http://www1.media.american.edu/election experts/2008%20Primary%20Turnout_Final.pdf.
22. Gans, "The Primary Turnout Story."
23. John F. Bibby and Thomas M. Holbrook, "Parties and Elections," in *Politics in the American States: A Comparative Analysis*, 8th ed., ed. Virginia Gray and Russell L. Hanson (Washington DC: Congressional Quarterly Press, 2004).
24. Bibby and Holbrook, "Parties and Elections."
25. Election statistics from the New Jersey Division of Elections, http://www.state.nj.us/lps/elections/results_2003_doe.html and the Virginia State Board of Elections, http://www.sbe.state.va.us/web_docs/election/results/2003/nov/. Eligible voting population from the United States Election Project, George Mason University.
26. Brian F. Schaffner, Matthew Streb, and Gerald Wright, "Teams Without Uniforms: The Nonpartisan Ballot in State and Local Elections," *Political Research Quarterly* 54 (March 2001): 7–30; Zoltan L. Hajnal, Paul Lewis, and Hugh Louch, *Municipal Elections in California: Turnout, Timing, and Competition* (San Francisco: Public Policy Institute of California, 2002).
27. Boston VOTES 2001, http://www.bostonvote.org/; Burlington City Clerk, "Annual City Election Statistics," Burlington, VT; Austin City Clerk's office, Austin, TX; and James A. Robinson, Clarence C. Elebash, and Andrea C. Hatcher, "Pensacola Votes by Mail: A Report on Pensacola's January 2001 Referendum," University of West Florida. March 30, 2001.
28. "Report: Some Sort of Primary Just Happened," *The Onion*, issue 41.39, September 28, 2005, accessed October 4, 2005, http://www.theonion.com/content/node/40979.
29. The definitive work on town meetings is Frank M. Bryan's *Real Democracy: The New England Town Meeting and How it Works* (Chicago: University of Chicago Press, 2004).
30. Arend Lijphart, "Unequal Participation: Democracy's Unresolved Dilemma," Presidential address, American Political Science Association, 1996, *American Political Science Review* 91, no. 1 (March 1997): 1–14; Patterson, *The Vanishing Voter*.
31. Between 1980 and 2008, an average of 26.5 percent of respondents in the American National Election Studies said they "follow what goes on in government and public affairs most of the time."

32. The Pew Research Center for the People and the Press, "Public Knowledge of Current Affairs Little Changed by News Information Revolutions," survey report, April 15, 2007, accessed August 26, 2009, http://people-press.org/report/319 .

33. Michael X. Delli Carpini and Scott Keeter, *What Americans Know About Politics and Why it Matters* (New Haven, CT: Yale University Press, 1996).

34. Delli Carpini and Keeter, *What Americans Know.*

35. Richard Morin, "Tuned Out, Turned Off: Millions of Americans know little about how their government works." *Washington Post National Weekly Edition*, Feb 5–11, 1996, p. 7.

36. Steven Kull, "Misperceptions, the Media and the Iraq War," Program on International Policy Attitudes, Center for International Security Studies at the University of Maryland, October 2, 2003, p. 5, accessed September 9, 2005, http://www.pipa.org/OnlineReports/Iraq/Media_10_02_03_Report.pdf.

37. Steven Kull, "Americans and Iraq" on the Eve of the Presidential Election," Program on International Policy Attitudes, Center for International Security Studies at the University of Maryland, October 28, 2004, accessed September 9, 2005, http://www.pipa.org/OnlineReports/Pres_Election_04/Report10_28_04.pdf.

38. Annenberg Public Policy Center, "Majority of 18 to 29 Year Olds Think Bush Favors Reinstating the Draft, Annenberg Data Shows," press release, October 8, 2004, accessed September 14, 2005, http://www.annenbergpublicpolicycenter.org/naes/2004_03_reinstate-the-draft_10-08_pr.pdf.

39. Steven Kull, "Americans on Climate Change: 2005," Program on International Policy Attitudes, July 5, 2005, accessed September 9, 2005, http://www.pipa.org/OnlineReports/ClimateChange/Report07_05_05.pdf.

40. American National Election Study, 2004.

41. Michael I. Norton and Daniel Ariely, "Building a Better America—One Wealth Quintile at a Time," *Perspectives on Psychological Science* (forthcoming), accessed October 12, 2010, http://www.people.hbs.edu/mnorton/norton%20ariely%20in%20press.pdf.

42. The term *truthiness* was coined by comedian Stephen Colbert. It means believing something from "the gut" without any consideration, and sometimes in direct contradiction to the actual facts.

43. Charles S. Taber and Milton Lodge, "Motivated Skepticism in the Evaluation of Political Beliefs," *American Journal of Political Science* 50, no. 3 (July 2006): 755–769; Charles S. Taber, Damon Cann, and Simona

Kucsova, "The Motivated Processing of Political Arguments," *Political Behavior* 31, no. 2 (June 2009): 137–155.

44. Delli Carpini and Keeter, *What Americans Know.*

45. Delli Carpini and Scott Keeter, *What Americans Know About Politics and Why it Matters*; Morin, "Tuned Out, Turned Off."

46. American National Election Study, 2004.

47. Delli Carpini and Keeter, *What Americans Know.*

48. Delli Carpini and Keeter, *What Americans Know*; Morin, "Tuned Out, Turned Off."

49. Pew Research Center for the People and the Press, "Public Knowledge of Current Affairs."

50. American National Elections Studies Cumulative Data File, 1948–2002; Pew Research Center for the People and the Press, "Public Knowledge of Current Affairs."

51. Delli Carpini and Keeter, *What Americans Know*, 133.

52. Pew Research Center for the People and the Press, "Public Knowledge of Current Affairs"; Markus Prior, *Post-Broadcast Democracy: How Media Choice Increases Inequality in Political Involvement and Polarizes Elections* (Cambridge: Cambridge University Press, 2007); Scott L. Althaus, *Collective Preferences in Democratic Politics* (Cambridge: Cambridge University Press, 2003); and Alan I. Abramowitz, *The Disappearing Center: Engaged Citizens, Polarization and American Democracy* (New Haven: Yale University Press, 2010).

53. Richard Morin, "Tuned Out, Turned Off."

54. Prior, *Post-Broadcast Democracy.*

55. Scott Keeter, as quoted in Richard Morin, "Tuned Out, Turned Off"; see also John D. Griffin and Brian Newman, "Are Voters Better Represented?" *Journal of Politics* 67, no. 4 (2005): 1206–1227.

56. For some it may be that support for the policies or the candidate lead to the misperceptions, as public opinion research suggests, but clearly for others, better information would lead to different attitudes toward the policy or the candidate—a dynamic also supported by public opinion research. See, for example, Richard R. Lau and David P. Redlawsk, "Advantages and Disadvantages of Cognitive Heuristics in Political Decision Making," *American Journal of Political Science* 45, no. 4 (2001): 952–971.

57. Kull, *Misperceptions, the Media and the Iraq War.*

58. Kull, *Misperceptions, the Media and the Iraq War.*

59. Patterson, *The Vanishing Voter*, 125.

60. William H. Flanigan and Nancy H. Zingale, *Political Behavior of the American Electorate*, 10th ed. (Washington, DC: CQ Press, 2001).

61. Registered voters are likely to be more knowledgeable than the public as a whole.

62. Annenberg Public Policy Center, "Majority of 18 to 29 Year Olds Think Bush Favors Reinstating the Draft, Annenberg Data Shows."

63. Pew Project for Excellence in Journalism, "2008 Trends," in *The State of the News Media 2009: An Annual Report on American Journalism*, 2009, accessed August 27, 2009, http://www.stateofthemedia.org/2009/narrative_yearinthenews_intro.php?cat=0&media=2.

64. Kathleen Hall Jamieson and Brooks Jackson, "Our Disinformed Electorate," special report, FactCheck.org, December 12, 2008, accessed August 26, 2009, http://www.factcheck.org/2008/12/our-disinformed-electorate/.

65. Delli Carpini and Keeter, *What Americans Know*,; Benjamin I. Page and Robert Y. Shapiro, *The Rational Public: Fifty Years of Trends in Americans' Policy Preferences* (Chicago: University of Chicago Press, 1992.

66. Samuel L. Popkin, *The Reasoning Voter: Communication and Persuasion in Presidential Campaigns*, 2nd ed. (Chicago: University of Chicago Press, 1994).

67. See Brooks Jackson and Kathleen Hall Jamieson, *unSpun: Finding Facts in a World of Disinformation* (New York: Random House Trade Paperbacks, 2007); Shanto Iyengar and Donald R. Kinder, *News that Matters: Television and American Opinion* (Chicago: University of Chicago Press, 1987); Shanto Iyengar, *Is Anyone Responsible? How Television Frames Political Issues* (Chicago: University of Chicago Press, 1991); Kathleen Hall Jamieson and Paul Waldman, *The Press Effect: Politicians, Journalists, and the Stories that Shape the Political World* (Oxford: Oxford University Press, 2003); David C. Barker, *Rushed to Judgment: Talk Radio, Persuasion, and American Political Behavior* (New York: Columbia University Press, 2002); and, Michael B. MacKuen, Robert S. Erikson, James A. Stimson, and Kathleen Knight, "Elections and the Dynamics of Ideological Representation," in *Electoral Democracy*, ed. Michael B. MacKuen and George Rabinowitz (Ann Arbor: University of Michigan Press, 2003).

68. Tom Ridge, the secretary of homeland security during the 2004 election, claims he was pressured by top advisors to President Bush to raise the alert levels just before the election; see Peter Baker, "Bush Official, in Book, Tells of Pressure on '04 Vote," *New York Times*, August 20, 2009.

69. Gerald M. Pomper, "The Presidential Election: The Ills of American Politics After 9/11," in *The Election of 2004*, ed. Michael Nelson (Washington, DC: CQ Press, 2005), 42–68.

70. National Annenberg Election Survey, 2004, http://www.annenbergpublicpolicycenter.org/naes/2004_03_%20Voters-and-the-issues_10-23_pr.pdf.

71. Annenberg Public Policy Center, "Bush Inauguration Comes with Nation Still Deeply Divided, Dubious on Iraq, Social Security, Annenberg Data Show," press release, January 17, 2005, accessed December 27, 2010, http://www.annenbergpublicpolicycenter.org/Downloads/Political_Communication/NAES/2005_03_inauguration_01-17_pr.pdf.

72. Annenberg Public Policy Center, "Bush Inauguration."

73. *New York Times*/CBS News Poll, September 9–13, 2005, accessed September 16, 2005, http://www.nytimes.com/packages/khtml/2005/09/14/politics/2050915_POLL.html.

74. This is the argument made by Kathleen Hall Jamieson and Joseph N. Cappella, *Echo Chamber: Rush Limbaugh and the Conservative Media Establishment* (Oxford: Oxford University Press, 2008). See chapter 4 in this book for a further discussion of the use of the bias claim against the media.

75. American National Election Study, 2004.

76. For a summary of the literature on unequal participation see Arend Lijphart, "Unequal Participation." Also see Sidney Verba, Kay Lehman Schlozman, and Henry E. Brady, *Voice and Equality: Civic Voluntarism in American Politics* (Cambridge, MA: Harvard University Press, 1995).

77. See Kathleen Hall Jamieson, *Everything You Think You Know about Politics and Why You're Wrong* (New York: Basic Books, 2000) for a summary of the literature on this point.

78. Some states use the votes of congressional districts to choose some of their electors.

79. State senate districts are different from state house districts, both of which constitute different electorates than those that choose governors or other statewide officials. Many local government positions are likewise selected by differing sets of voters.

80. Research conducted by Curtis Gans and the Center for the Study of the American Electorate over a series of elections has shown that convenience voting—mail voting, no-excuse absentee voting, early voting, and even election-day registration—does not help turnout and may even hurt it. Ten of the twelve states that saw a decline in voter turnout in 2008 as compared to 2004 offered convenience voting; seven of the thirteen states that saw

increases in voter turnout in 2008 did not offer any convenience voting. See Committee for the Study of the American Electorate, "African-Americans, Anger, Fear and Youth," December 17, 2008, accessed September 1, 2009, http://www.american.edu/spa/cdem/upload/2008pdfoffinaledited.pdf. See also Joseph D. Giammo and Brian J. Brox, "Reducing the Costs of Participation: Are States Getting a Return on Early Voting?" *Political Research Quarterly* 63, no. 2 (June 2010): 295–303.

81. I am not arguing here that there are *no* problems with openness; I am arguing that in the United States openness is not a debilitating problem. The country has come a long way in granting suffrage and access to the ballot, and given the weakness of campaign-finance laws, few impediments exist to contributing money. Concerns over disenfranchisement of classes of voters in the 2004 and 2000 election show that there is still a need for improvement. And as the U.S. Supreme Court's 2008 ruling shows (*Crawford et al. v. Marion County Election Board, et al.* on an Indiana voter identification law, rejecting "arguments that Indiana's law imposes unjustified burdens on people who are old, poor or members of minority groups and less likely to have driver's licenses or other acceptable forms of identification"), maintaining free and open elections is a continuing battle. David Stout, "Supreme Court Upholds Voter Identification Law in Indiana," *New York Times*, April 29, 2008. As argued in a later chapter of the present study, ballot access laws are not a problem.

82. E. E. Schattschneider, *The Semi-Sovereign People: A Realist's View of Democracy in America* (New York: Hold, Rinehart & Winston, 1960), 140.

83. Prior to this court-enforced redistricting, legislative districts in many states were grossly malapportioned so that legislators from urban areas represented many more people than those in rural areas, giving those in rural areas a disproportionate amount of power in the state legislatures.

84. Voting eligible population data from the United States Elections Project, George Mason University, accessed October 17, 2005, http://elections.gmu.edu/Voter_Turnout_2004.htm.

85. Thomas E. Patterson, *The Vanishing Voter: Public Involvement in an Age of Uncertainty* (New York: Knopf, 2002), 138.

86. Barak Obama's lead in delegates was basically insurmountable following the results of the May 6 primaries in North Carolina and Indiana.

87. Additionally, all candidates except Clinton removed their names from the Michigan ballot, and all candidates pledged not to campaign in Florida.

88. Thomas E. Patterson, *Out of Order* (New York: Alfred A. Knopf, 1993).

89. Patterson, *The Vanishing Voter*.

90. Based on 2004 U.S. Census data, http://quickfacts.census.gov/qfd/, accessed October 17, 2005.

91. Jacob S. Hacker and Paul Pierson, "The Center No Longer Holds: Why Bad Times for the Republicans do not Mean Good Times for the Democrats," *New York Times Magazine*, November 20, 2005, 32–36.

92. See also Sanford Levinson, *Our Undemocratic Constitution: Where the Constitution Goes Wrong (And How the People Can Correct It)* (Oxford: Oxford University Press, 2006).

93. See Frances E. Lee and Bruce Oppenheimer, *Sizing up the Senate: The Unequal Consequences of Equal Representation* (Chicago: University of Chicago Press, 1999); and Levinson, *Our Undemocratic Constitution*.

94. For an excellent analysis of this local dimension of elections, see Alec C. Ewald, *The Way We Vote: The Local Dimension of American Suffrage* (Nashville, TN: Vanderbilt University Press, 2009). For equally excellent analyses of the impact of various types of technology used for casting votes, see Paul S. Herrnson et al., *Voting Technology: The Not-So-Simple Act of Casting a Ballot* (Washington, DC: Brookings Institution Press, 2008); and R. Michael Alvarez and Thad E. Hall, *Electronic Elections: The Perils and Promises of Digital Democracy* (Princeton, NJ: Princeton University Press, 2008).

95. *Bush v. Gore*, 531 U.S. 98 (2000).

96. Kathleen Hall Jamieson and Paul Waldman, *The Press Effect: Politicians, Journalists, and the Stories that Shape the Political World* (New York: Oxford University Press, 2003). One can select the various standards for vote counting on a *New York Times* website, accessed October 18, 2005, http://www.nytimes.com/images/2001/11/12/politics/recount/. This conclusion comes from applying election rules and standards of the count equally to all ballots and absentee ballots, including the *over votes* (those ballots that registered more than one candidate for the presidency), apportioned to the candidates based on past voting patterns of counties' voters, and providing provisional ballots for those turned away from the polling places due to the states egregiously flawed purge of the voter registration rolls. Similar reversals in the handful of close states won by Gore, such as New Mexico, would not have given Bush enough electoral votes to win the presidency once the Florida electoral votes were awarded to Gore.

97. Based on the standard of one, person, one vote political equality, which would require that all voters be treated equally at the polling places and that all the votes be counted with consistent standards.

98. Jamieson and Waldman, *The Press Effect*; Jonathan N. Wand et al., "The Butterfly Did It: The Aberrant Vote for Buchanan in Palm Beach County, Florida," *The American Political Science Review* 95, no. 4. (December 2001): 793–810.

99. General Accounting Office Report on Elections, *The Scope of Congressional Authority in Elections Administration* (Washington, DC: General Accounting Office, 2001); R. Michael Alvarez, D. E. "Betsy" Sinclair, and Catherine H. Wilson, "Counting Ballots and the 2000 Election: What Went Wrong?" in *Rethinking the Vote: Politics and Prospects of American Election Reform*, ed. Ann N. Crigler, Mario R. Just, and Edward J. McCaffery (New York: Oxford University Press, 2004), 34–50.

100. Ford Fessenden, "Ballots Cast by Blacks and Older Voters Were Tossed in Far Greater Numbers," *New York Times*, November 12, 2001.

101. General Accounting Office Report on Elections, *The Scope of Congressional Authority in Elections Administration*; Alvarez, Sinclair, and Wilson, "Counting Ballots and the 2000 Election."

102. See Herrnson et al., *Voting Technology*; and Alvarez and Hall, *Electronic Elections*.

103. Tim Storey, "Helping America Vote," *State Legislatures*, April 2003, 13–15.

104. See Ewald, *The Way We Vote*.

105. See Herrnson et al., *Voting Technology*; and Alvarez and Hall, *Electronic Elections*.

106. Pew Research Center for the People and the Press, "Moral Values: How Important? Voters Liked Campaign 2004, But Too Much 'Mud-Slinging," November 11, 2004, accessed September 29, 2005, http://people-press.org/reports/display.php3?ReportID=233.

107. Eric A. Fischer and Kevin J. Coleman, "Election Reform and Local Election Officials: Results of Two National Surveys," CRS Report for Congress, February 7, 2008, accessed August 28, 2009, http://assets.opencrs.com/rpts/RL34363_20080207.pdf?emc=lm&m=212814&l=24&v=209825.

108. As reported in D. Sunshine Hillygus and Todd G. Shields, *The Persuadable Voter: Wedge Issues in Presidential Campaigns* (Princeton, NJ: Princeton University Press, 2008), 11. In 2008 Barack Obama's campaign advertised on national television networks.

109. These were the contests in states considered battlegrounds or in which one party was expected to win narrowly, according to "Election Results 2008," *New York Times*, December 9, 2008.

110. Ibid.
111. Gary C. Jacobson, "The Congress: The Structural Basis of Republican Success," in *The Election of 2004*, ed. Michael Nelson (Washington, DC: CQ Press, 2005), 163–186. Jacobson counted races as competitive based on *Congressional Quarterly* classifications: "tossups" and "leans Democrat/Republican" were counted as competitive.
112. Jacobson, "The Congress."
113. Federal Election Commission, "2003–2004 Financial Activity of Senate and House General Election Campaigns, January 1, 2003–December 31, 2004," accessed September 15, 2005, http://www.fec.gov/press/press2005/20050609candidate/gen2004.pdf.
114. Before the election the Senate had 51 Republicans, 48 Democrats and 1 independent; the House had 229 Republicans, 205 Democrats, and 1 independent.
115. Samuel Issacharoff and Jonathan Nagler, "Protected from Politics: Diminishing Margins of Electoral Competition in U.S. Congressional Elections," *Ohio State Law Journal* 68 (2007): 1121–1137.
116. The one independent senator, James Jeffords of Vermont, had been working with the Democrats since he defected from the Republican Party in 2001.
117. Jacobson, "The Congress." The single independent representative, Bernie Sanders (again of Vermont), tends to vote with the Democrats.
118. Christian R. Grose and Bruce I. Oppenheimer, "The Iraq War, Partisanship, and Candidate Attributes: Variation in Partisan Swing in the 2006 U.S. House Elections," *Legislative Studies Quarterly* 32 (2007).
119. Stephen Ansolabehere et al., "The Decline of Competition in U.S. Primary Elections, 1908–2004," in *The Marketplace of Democracy*, ed. Michael P. McDonald and John Samples (Washington, DC: Brookings Institution Press, 2006).
120. Ansolabehere et al., "Decline of Competition."
121. Calculated based on the *New York Times* classification of races as tossups or leaning toward one party; "Election Results 2008," *New York Times*, December 9, 2008, http://elections.nytimes.com/2008/results/house/votes.html, and "2006 Election Guide," *New York Times*, http://www.nytimes.com/ref/washington/2006ELECTIONGUIDE.html.
122. Ansolabehere et al., "Decline of Competition."
123. Keith E. Hamm and Gary F. Moncrief, "Legislative Politics in the States," in *Politics in the American States: A Comparative Analysis*, 8th ed., ed. Virginia Gray and Russell L. Hanson (Washington, DC: CQ Press, 2004), 157–193.

124. Schattschneider, *The Semi-Sovereign People: A Realist's View of Democracy in America.*

125. A tremendous amount of research has been published on this point. For a discussion of this literature see Anthony Gierzynski, *Money Rules: Financing Elections in America* (Boulder, CO: Westview Press, 2000), chapter 4.

126. Campaign Finance Institute, "A First Look at Money in the House and Senate Elections," press release, November 6, 2008, http://www.cfinst. org/pr/prRelease.aspx?ReleaseID=215, accessed August 28, 2009.

127. Gierzynski, *Money Rules.*

128. Gary C. Jacobson, "The First Congressional Elections after BCRA," in *The Election after Reform: Money, Politics, and the Bipartisan Campaign Reform Act*, ed. Michael Malbin (Lanham, MD: Rowman & Littlefield, 2005), 185–203.

129. Paul S. Herrnson, *Congressional Elections: Campaigning at Home and in Washington* (Washington, DC: Congressional Quarterly Press, 2008), 167.

130. Campaign Finance Institute, "Expenditures of Senate Incumbents and Challengers, by Election Outcome, 1974-2006" (Washington, DC: Brookings Institution, 2008), http://www.cfinst.org/data/pdf/VitalStats_t6.pdf.

131. Gierzynski, *Money Rules*; Gary Moncrief, "Candidate Spending in State Legislative Races," in *Campaign Finance in State Legislative Elections*, ed. Joel A. Thompson and Gary F. Moncrief (Washington, DC: Congressional Quarterly Press, 1998), 37–58; Robert E. Hogan and Keith E. Hamm, "Variations in District-Level Campaign Spending in State Legislatures," in *Campaign Finance in State Legislative Elections*, ed. Joel A. Thompson and Gary F. Moncrief (Washington, DC: Congressional Quarterly Press, 1998), 59–79.

132. Such factors include gross state product, candidate quality, competitiveness of the race, strictness of campaign finance laws, and party.

133. Anthony Gierzynski, "Gubernatorial and State Legislative Elections," in *Financing the 2000 Election*, ed. David Magleby (Washington, DC: Brookings Institution, 2002), 188–212.

134. Presidential candidates who accept federal public funds for the general election must adhere to spending limits.

135. Federal Election Commission, "2004 Presidential Campaign Financial Activity Summarized," February 3, 2005, accessed September 22, 2005, http://www.fec.gov/press/press2005/*20050203pressum*/20050203pressum.html.

136. See discussion later in this section about political party finances. In the past five presidential contests, the Republican nominee for president raised more than the Democratic nominee during the nomination phase; see Federal Election Commission, "2004 Presidential Campaign." And once incumbency, competitiveness, gross state product and other important factors are controlled for, Democratic gubernatorial candidates raise, on average, about $1.1 million less than Republican gubernatorial candidates; see Gierzynski, "Gubernatorial and State Legislative Elections." On presidential elections also see the analysis by Larry Bartels in *Unequal Democracy: The Political Economy of the New Gilded Age* (Princeton, NJ: Princeton University Press, 2008).

137. Federal Election Commission, "2004 Presidential Campaign."

138. Thomas B. Edsall and James V. Grimaldi, "On Nov. 2, GOP Got More Bang for Its Billion, Analysis Shows," *Washington Post*, December 30, 2004, A01.

139. The 2004 Democratic National Convention took place between July 26 and 29; the Republican National Convention between August 30 and September 2.

140. 527 committees are independent groups that spend money during elections. For a further explanation, please see chapter 7.

141. Edsall and Grimaldi, "On Nov. 2, GOP Got More Bang for Its Billion, Analysis Shows," *Washington Post*, December 30, 2004, A01.

142. Federal Election Commission, "2004 Presidential Campaign Summarized."

143. Center for Public Integrity "527s in 2004 Shatter Previous Records for Political Fundraising," December 16, 2004, accessed September 27, 2005, http://www.publicintegrity.org/527/report.aspx?aid=435&sid=300; Thomas B. Edsall and James V. Grimaldi, "On Nov. 2, GOP Got More Bang for Its Billion, Analysis Shows," *Washington Post*, December 30, 2004, A01.

144. Gerald M. Pomper, "The Presidential Election: The Ills of American Politics After 9/11," in *The Election of 2004*, ed. Michael Nelson (Washington, DC: CQ Press, 2005), 42–68.

145. Edsall and Grimaldi, "On Nov. 2, GOP Got More Bang for Its Billion, Analysis Shows," *Washington Post*, December 30, 2004, A01.

146. Campaign Finance Institute, "All CFI Funding Statistics Revised and Updated for the 2008 Presidential Primary and General Election Candidates," Press Release, January 8, 2010, accessed January 25, 2010, http://www.cfinst.org/pr/prRelease.aspx?ReleaseID=236.

147. Campaign Finance Institute, "All CFI Funding Statistics Revised."

148. Federal money can legally be spent on campaigns for federal offices, such as the presidency and U.S. Senate and House seats.

149. The DNC and the Democratic Senatorial Campaign Committee raised slightly more than their Republican counterparts, but the Republican National Congressional Committee and Republican state and local party committees raised substantially more federal money than their counterparts.

150. These organizations had previously been counted as part of the party's nonfederal (soft money) operation and were organized as 527 committees for 2003–2004.

151. Anthony Corrado, "Party Finance in the Wake of BCRA: An Overview," in *The Election after Reform: Money, Politics, and the Bipartisan Campaign Reform Act*, ed. Michael Malbin (Lanham, MD: Rowman & Littlefield, 2005).

152. Richard L. Hall and Frank W. Wayman, "Buying Time: Moneyed Interests and the Mobilization Bias in Congressional Elections," *American Political Science Review* 84 (1990).

153. Laura I. Langbein and Mark A. Lotwis, "The Political Efficacy of Lobbying and Money: Gun Control in the U.S. House, 1986," *Legislative Studies Quarterly* 15 (August 1990).

154. Stacy B. Gordon, *Campaign Contributions and Legislative Voting: A New Approach* (New York: Routledge, 2005).

155. Jacob S. Hacker and Paul Pierson, *Off Center: The Republican Revolution and the Erosion of American Democracy* (New Haven, CT: Yale University Press, 2005); Anthony Gierzynski, *Money Rules*; Sidney Verba, Kay Lehman Schlozman, and Henry E. Brady, *Voice and Equality: Civic Voluntarism in American Politics* (Cambridge, MA: Harvard University Press, 1995); Center for Responsive Politics, "The Big Picture: The Money Behind the Elections," http://www.crp.org/bigpicture/index.asp; Peter L. Francia et al., *The Financiers of Congressional Elections: Investors, Ideologues, and Intimates* (New York: Columbia University Press, 2003).

156. See Kathleen Hall Jamieson, *Everything You Think You Know About Politics and Why You're Wrong* (New York: Basic Books, 2000) for a review of the research on this point.

157. Paul S. Herrnson, *Congressional Elections: Campaigning at Home and in Washington* (Washington, DC: Congressional Quarterly Press, 2008); Gary F. Moncrief, Peverill Squire and Malcolm Jewell, *Who Runs for the Legislature* (Upper Saddle River, NJ: Prentice Hall, 2001); and Anthony

Gierzynski, *Legislative Party Campaign Committees in the American States* (Lexington: University Press of Kentucky, 1992).

158. Sarah A. Binder, "Elections, Parties, and Governance," in *The Legislative Branch*, ed. Paul J. Quirk and Sarah A. Binder (New York: Oxford University Press, 2005), 148–170; and Tim Storey, "The Real Race Is in the States," *State Legislatures*, September 2004, http://www.ncsl.org/programs/legman/statevote/real_race.htm, accessed October 11, 2005. Vol. 30, Issue 8, 22–24.

159. Kenneth Janda, Jeffrey M. Berry and Jerry Goldman, *The Challenge of Democracy: Government in America,* 8th ed. (Boston: Houghton Mifflin, 2005).

160. Patterson, *The Vanishing Voter.*

161. Jamieson and Waldman, *The Press Effect.*

162. An autopsy after Shiavo's death found extensive, irreversible brain damage.

163. FactCheck.org, "Foreign Money? Really?" October 11, 2010, accessed October 17, 2010, http://www.factcheck.org/2010/10/foreign-money-really/.

164. Terry Christensen and Peter J. Haas, *Projecting Politics: Political Messages in American Films* (Armonk, NY: M. E. Sharpe, 2005), 48–49.

165. Christensen and Haas, *Projecting Politics.*

166. FactCheck.org, "The Whoppers of 2008," September 25, 2008, accessed October 19, 2010, http://www.factcheck.org/elections-2008/the_whoppers_of_2008.html.

167. Patterson, *The Vanishing Voter*, 51.

168. Pew Research Center for the People and the Press, "Moral Values."

169. Pew Research Center for the People and the Press, "Most See Washington Dominated by Partisan Conflict," October 4, 2010, accessed October 17, 2010, http://pewresearch.org/pubs/1751/congressional-connection-partisan-bickering-hits-new-high.

170. Patterson, *The Vanishing Voter.*

171. Pew Research Center for the People and the Press, "Independents Oppose Party in Power ... Again," Washington, DC: Pew Research Center, September 23, 2010, accessed October 17, 2010, http://people-press.org/report/658/.

172. See Alison Dagnes, *Politics on Demand: The Effects of 24-Hour News on American Politics* (Santa Barbara, CA: ABC-CLIO, 2010).

173. Patterson, *Out of Order* .

174. The Pew Research Center for the People & the Press, "Internet Gains on Television as Public's Main News Source, January 4, 2011, accessed February 20, 2011, http://pewresearch.org/pubs/1844/poll-main-source-national-international-news-internet-television-newspapers.

175. See Patterson, *Out of* Order; Jamieson and Waldman, *The Press Effect*; and Brent Cunningham, "Re-Thinking Objectivity," *Columbia Journalism Review* (July/August 2003): 24–32.

176. Center for Media and Public Affairs, "Network News Flip-Flops on Candidates," press release, November 22, 2004, accessed October 3, 2005, http://www.cmpa.com/documents/04.11.19.Flip.Flop.Release.pdf.

177. Marion Just, Ann Crigler, and Tami Buhr, "Voice, Substance, and Cynicism in Presidential Campaign Media," *Political Communications* 16 (1999), 25–44.

178. Lear Center Local News Archive, a project of the USC Annenberg School and the University of Wisconsin, *Local TV News Coverage of the 2002 General Election*, accessed October 3, 2005, http://www.localnews-archive.org/pdf/LocalTV2002.pdf.

179. Jamieson and Waldman, *The Press Effect*.

180. *The Daily Show with Jon Stewart*, televised by Comedy Central on October 12, 2009. http://www.thedailyshow.com/watch/mon-october-12-2009/cnn-leaves-it-there, accessed 27 January 2010.

181. See Neil Postman, *Amusing Ourselves to Death: Public Discourse in the Age of Show Business* (New York: Penguin Books, 1985) and Roderick P. Hart, *Seducing America: How Television Charms the Modern Voter*, rev. ed. (Thousand Oaks, CA: Sage Publications, 1999).

182. For a framework to understand the relationship between political parties and allied groups see Paul S. Herrnson, "The Roles of Party Organizations, Party-Connected Committees, and Party Allies in Elections," *Journal of Politics* 71, no. 4 (October 2009): 1207–1224.

183. John F. Bibby and Thomas M. Holbrook, "Parties and Elections," in *Politics in the American States: A Comparative Analysis* 8th ed., ed. Virginia Gray and Russell L. Hanson (Washington, DC: Congressional Quarterly Press, 2004).

184. For the most recent work on the subject see Pippa Norris, *Count Every Voice: Democratic Participation Worldwide* (New York: Cambridge University Press, 2002); and Pippa Norris, "Do Institutions Matter? The Consequence of Electoral Reform for Political Participation," in *Rethinking the Vote: The Politics and Prospects of American Election Reform*, edited by Ann N. Crigler, Marion R. Just and Edward J. McCaffery (New York: Oxford University Press, 2004).

185. See Anthony Gierzynski, *Money Rules: Financing Elections in America* (Boulder, CO: Westview Press, 2000).

186. In the *Citizens United* ruling the Supreme Court reversed a century old ban on corporate and union campaign expenditures. For more on this case, see chapter 7.

187. Michael J. Malbin and Thomas L. Gais, *The Day After Reform: Sobering Campaign Finance Lessons from the American States* (Albany, NY: Rockefeller Institute Press, 1998); Donald A. Gross and Robert K. Goidel, *The States of Campaign Finance Reform* (Columbus: Ohio State University Press, 2003).

188. Edward D. Feigenbaum and James A. Palmer, *Campaign Finance Law 2002: A Summary of State Campaign Finance Laws* (Washington, DC: Federal Election Commission, 2003).

189. Anthony Gierzynski, "Gubernatorial and State Legislative Elections," in *Financing the 2000 Election*, ed. David Magleby (Washington, DC: Brookings Institution Press, 2002), 188–212. More recent cases include *Randall v. Sorrell* No. 04–1528, argued February 28, 2006, decided June 26, 2006; and *Citizens United v. Federal Election Commission*, No. 08–205, argued March 24, 2009, reargued September 9, 2009, decided January 21, 2010.

190. Campaign Finance Institute, "The $100 Million Dollar Exemption: Soft Money and the National Party Conventions," accessed October 7, 2005, http://www.cfinst.org/eguide/partyconventions/financing/cfistudy.html. Steve Weissman and Ruth Hassan, "527 Groups and BCRA," in *The Election after Reform: Money, Politics, and the Bipartisan Campaign Reform Act*, ed. Michael Malbin (Lanham, MD: Rowman & Littlefield, 2005).

191. As Micah Altman, Karin MacDonald, and Michael McDonald point out, advances in computer technology are not in of themselves the cause of less competitive districts; the problem lies in how such tools are used; see their "Pushbutton Gerrymanders? How Computing Has Changed Redistricting," in *Party Lines: Competition, Partisanship, and Congressional Redistricting*, ed. Thomas E. Mann and Bruce E. Cain (Washington, DC: Brookings Institution Press, 2005), 51–66.

192. The decision by Texas Republican lawmakers to redraw their congressional districts in 2003 (after they won unified control of the Texas government in the 2002 election) may set a precedent for more frequent redistricting.

193. Alan I. Abramowitz, *The Disappearing Center: Engaged Citizens, Polarization and American Democracy* (New Haven, CT: Yale University Press,

2010); Richard H. Pildes, "Why The Center Does Not Hold: The Causes of Hyperpolarized Democracy In America," *California Law Review* (forthcoming).

194. Gary C. Jacobson, "Modern Campaigns and Representation," in *The Legislative Branch*, ed. Paul J. Quirk and Sarah A. Binder (New York: Oxford University Press, 2005), 109–147.

195. Abramowitz, *The Disappearing Center*.

196. Keith E. Hamm and Gary F. Moncrief, "Legislative Politics in the States," in *Politics in the American States: A Comparative Analysis*, 8th ed., ed. Virginia Gray and Russell L. Hanson (Washington, DC: CQ Press, 2004).

197. Abramowitz, *The Disappearing Center*.

198. Heather K. Gerken, *The Democracy Index: Why Our Election System is Failing and How to Fix It* (Princeton, NJ: Princeton University Press, 2009), 13.

199. Alec C. Ewald, *The Way We Vote: The Local Dimension of American Suffrage* (Nashville, TN: Vanderbilt University Press, 2009).

200. Gerken, *The Democracy Index*.

201. Gerken, *The Democracy Index*, 19.

202. In addition to material cited in chapter 2 (note 181), see Richard W. Boyd, "The Effects of Primaries and Statewide Races on Voter Turnout," *Journal of Politics* 51 (August 1989): 730–739; Shaun Bowler, Todd Donovon, and Trudi Happ, "Ballot Propositions and Information Costs: Direct Democracy and the Fatigued Voter," *Western Political Quarterly* 45 (June 1992): 559–568; Arend Lijphart, "Unequal Participation: Democracy's Unresolved Dilemma: Presidential Address, American Political Science Association, 1996, *American Political Science Review* 91, no. 1 (March 1997): 1–14; and Robert W. Jackman, "Political Institutions and Voter Turnout in the Industrial Democracies," *American Political Science Review* 81 (June 1987): 405–423.

203. See Jan E. Leighley, *Mass Media and Politics: A Social Science Perspective* (New York: Houghton Mifflin, 2004) for a survey of the literature on this topic; see Leonard Downie, Jr., and Robert G Kaiser, *The News About the News* (New York: Alfred A. Knopf, 2002) for a perspective from those who work in the business; and see Darrell M. West, *The Rise and Fall of the Media Establishment* (Boston: Bedford/St. Martin's, 2001) for a historical perspective.

204. Pew Research Center's Project for Excellence in Journalism, *The State of the News Media 2009: An Annual Report on American Journalism* (Washington, DC: Pew Research Center, 2009).

205. Pew Research Center's Project for Excellence in Journalism, *The State of the News Media 2009.*

206. Downie and Kaiser, *The News About the News.*

207. Pew Center for the People and the Press, "Bottom-Line Pressures Now Hurting Coverage, Say Journalists Press Going Too Easy on Bush" (Washington, DC: Pew Research Center, May 23, 2004), accessed October 12, 2005, http://people-press.org/reports/display.php3?ReportID=214.

208. See Jamieson and Waldman, *The Press Effect: Politicians, Journalists, and the Stories that Shape the Political World* (Oxford: Oxford University Press, 2003); Thomas E. Patterson, *The Vanishing Voter: Public Involvement in an Age of Uncertainty* (New York: Knopf, 2002); and Thomas E. Patterson, *Out of Order* (New York: Knopf, 1993).

209. Roderick P. Hart, *Seducing America.*

210. *The Daily Show with Jon Stewart,* televised by Comedy Central on September 2, 2004.

211. Nirvana, "Smells Like Teen Spirit," *Nevermind,* Geffen Records, 1991.

212. John P. Robinson and Geoffrey Godbey, *Time for Life: The Surprising Ways Americans Use Their Time,* 2nd ed. (University Park: Pennsylvania State University Press, 1999).

213. Robert D. Putnam, *Bowling Alone: The Collapse and Revival of American Community* (New York: Simon & Schuster, 2000).

214. Project for Excellence in Journalism, an institute affiliated with Columbia University Graduate School of Journalism, "The State of the News Media: An Annual Report on American Journalism," (Washington, DC: Pew Research Center, 2005), accessed December 30, 2005, http://www.stateofthemedia.org/2005/narrative_networktv_contentanalysis.asp?cat=2&media=4.

215. Neil Postman, *Amusing Ourselves to Death: Public Discourse in the Age of Show Business* (New York: Penguin Books, 1985).

216. Julia R. Fox, Glory Koloen, and Volkan Sahin, "No Joke: A Comparison of Substance in *The Daily Show with Jon Stewart* and Broadcast Network Television Coverage of the 2004 Presidential Election Campaign," *Journal of Broadcast and Electronic Media* (forthcoming); and the Project for Excellence in Journalism, "Journalism, Satire, or Just Laughs? 'The Daily Show with Jon Stewart' Examined" (Washington, DC: Pew Research Center, May 8, 2008), accessed June 16, 2008, http://www.journalism.org/node/10953.

217. Pew Research Center for the People and the Press, "News Audiences Increasingly Politicized: Online News Audience Larger, More Diverse"

(Washington, DC: Pew Research Center, June 8, 2004), accessed October 13, 2005, http://people-press.org/reports/display.php3?PageID=833.

218. Pew Research Center for the People and the Press, "Popular Policies and Unpopular Press Lift Clinton Ratings: Scandal Reporting Faulted for Bias and Inaccuracy" (Washington, DC: Pew Research Center, February 6, 1998), accessed October 14, 2005, http://people-press.org/reports/display. php3?ReportID=96.

219. Bill Kovach and Tom Rosenstiel, *Warp Speed: America in the Age of Mixed Media* (New York: The Century Foundation Press, 1999); David T. Z. Mindich, *Tuned Out: Why Americans Under 40 Don't Follow the News* (New York: Oxford University Press, 2005).

220. See Postman, *Amusing Ourselves to Death*; Hart, *Seducing America*; and Putnam, *Bowling Alone*.

221. Sarah A. Binder, "Elections, Parties, and Governance," in *The Legislative Branch*, ed. Paul J. Quirk and Sarah A. Binder (New York: Oxford University Press, 2005), 153.

222. I personally ran in one such race, a contest for a Vermont state house seat.

223. *Crossfire*, Cable News Network, October 15, 2004.

224. CNN claims that Stewart's appearance had nothing to do with the cancellation of the show.

225. This idea is derived from Neil Postman's argument in *Amusing Ourselves to Death: Public Discourse in the Age of Show Business* (New York: Penguin Books, 1985).

226. Leonard Downie, Jr., and Robert G. Kaiser, *The News About the News* (New York: Alfred Knopf, 2002).

227. Pew Research Center's Project for Excellence in Journalism, "The Debate Effect: How the Press Covered the Pivotal Period" (Washington, DC: Pew Research Center), October 27, 2004, accessed March 15, 2006, http://www.journalism.org/node/163; Project for Excellence in Journalism, campaign data set, http://www.journalism.org/by_the_numbers/ datasets?sid=7213, accessed September 7, 2009.

228. Downie and Kaiser, *News About the News*, 220–221.

229. Bill Kovach and Tom Rosenstiel, *Warp Speed: America in the Age of Mixed Media* (New York: The Century Foundation Press, 1999), 7.

230. Downie and Kaiser, *News About the News*, 232.

231. Phyllis Kaniss, *Making Local News* (Chicago: University of Chicago Press, 1991).

232. Mark Fitzgerald, "Local TV News Lacks Substance," *Editor and Publisher* 24 (May 1997), 8–9.

233. Lear Center Local News Archive, a project of the USC Annenberg School and the University of Wisconsin, "Local TV News Coverage of the 2002 General Election," accessed October 3, 2005, http://www.localnewsarchive.org/pdf/LocalTV2002.pdf.

234. Martin Kaplan, Ken Goldstein, and Matthew Hale, "Local News Coverage of the 2004 Campaigns: An Analysis of Nightly Broadcasts in 11 Markets," Lear Center Local News Archive, February 15, 2005, accessed December 27, 2010, http://www.localnewsarchive.org/pdf/LCLNAFinal2004.pdf.

235. Kaplan Goldstein, and Hale, "Local News Coverage of the 2004 Campaigns."

236. David C. Barker, *Rushed to Judgment: Talk Radio, Persuasion, and American Political Behavior* (New York: Columbia University Press, 2002).

237. Kathleen Hall Jamieson and Joseph N. Cappella, *Echo Chamber: Rush Limbaugh and the Conservative Media Establishment* (New York: Oxford University Press, 2008), 191–192.

238. Pew Research Center's Project for Excellence in Journalism, *State of the News Media 2009*, "News Investment" (Washington, DC: Pew Research Center, 2009), accessed January 31, 2010, http://www.stateofthemedia.org/2009/narrative_audio_newsinvestment.php?cat=4&media=10.

239. Observations come from data collected by my "Politics & the Media" POLS137 class in the fall of 2009. Students coded forty-one *All Things Considered* (*ATC*) shows from 2009 and 1993 during the period between August and October in those years. Each student was given two dates, each the same day of the week. Years were chosen for similarity in terms of the stage in a new Democratic presidency (1993 and 2009 are the first years of the Clinton and Obama presidencies, respectively) and in terms of U.S. military involvement. Shows were coded for subject and relevance, and students were asked to make an open-ended assessment of the two shows. Thirty-two out of forty-one students thought that the 2009 *ATC* program provided less useful information and more entertainment and was "worse" than the show analyzed from sixteen years earlier; no student thought the 2009 show was better than the 1993 show. There were half as many stories on international events in 2009 as there were in 1993. More of the stories were coded as being for pure entertainment purposes as opposed to addressing a topic that was important to know or educational. Data and detailed methodology are available upon request. Also

see Peter Johnson, "Media Mix: NPR Staffers Grapple with Changes," *USA Today*, May 2, 2004.

240. Downie and Kaiser, *News About the News*.

241. Pew Research Center's Project for Excellence in Journalism, "The Debate Effect: How the Press Covered the Pivotal Period."

242. Pew Research Center's Project for Excellence in Journalism, *The State of the News Media 2005: An Annual Report on American Journalism* (Washington, DC: Pew Research Center, 2005).

243. Ibid.

244. Ibid.

245. See Postman, *Amusing Ourselves to Death*; Putnam, *Bowling Alone*; and Mindich, *Tuned Out*.

246. Darrell M. West, *The Rise and Fall of the Media Establishment* (Boston: Bedford/St. Martin's, 2001), Downie and Kaiser, *News About the News*; and Jan E. Leighley, *Mass Media and Politics: A Social Science Perspective* (New York: Houghton Mifflin, 2004).

247. This list may seem biased, as it list more journalistic revelations about Republican wrongdoings. However, this is because Republicans held power in the White House for eight of the last ten years. If journalists are to uncover similar abuses of power carried out by the Obama administration or failures in Obama policies, these will not become public until much nearer to the end of his term(s). I do not include the Monika Lewinsky reporting for several reasons: (1) because such reporting was not excellent journalism (see Bill Kovach and Tom Rosenstiel's documentation of this in *Warp Speed*), (2) because the scandal did not involve an abuse of power (Clinton's only crime in this case was lying under oath about this affair) and, (3) because the case's effects sans the media coverage would have been limited to those personally involved.

248. Lipton's investigations included (1) a story about members of Congress (Democrats and Republicans) setting up corporate-funded charities in the member of Congress' own name that allow them to, in effect, run permanent campaigns; (2) the lobbyists connections of John Boehner, the Republican who would likely become speaker of the House if Republicans win a majority of seats in November 2010; (3) the practice of corporate gifts establishing endowed chairs at universities in the names of members of Congress; (4) how corporations were finding a way around the earmark ban; and (5) reports on the House Ethics Committee investigations into the congressional Black Caucus.

249. Daniel C. Hallin and Paolo Mancini, *Comparing Media Systems: Three Models of Media and Politics* (Cambridge: Cambridge University Press, 2004).

250. Gail Russell Chaddock, "Bush Administration Blurs Media Boundary," *The Christian Science Monitor,* February 17, 2005, accessed December 28, 2005, http://www.csmonitor.com/2005/0217/p01s01-uspo.html.

251. Amy Goldstein, "GAO Says HHS Broke Laws with Medicare Videos," *Washington Post*, May 20, 2004, A01.

252. Chaddock, "Bush Administration Blurs Media Boundary."

253. The U.S. government does own media outlets—namely, the American Forces Radio and Television Service, which controls broadcasts to U.S. military posts; and the Voice of America Broadcast system, which airs U.S. government propaganda in other countries—but broadcasting such government-made programs within the United States itself is not allowed by law. Local governments in America do own local cable-access channels.

254. Jan E. Leighley, *Mass Media and Politics.*

255. Public Broadcasting PolicyBase, "Public broadcasting system revenues, 1982–2003," Current Publishing Committee and the National Public Broadcasting Archives, last updated June 10, 2005, accessed December 28, 2005, http://www.current.org/pbpb/statistics/totalrevs.html. Numbers cited are for FY 2003.

256. Ibid.

257. Pew Research Center's Project for Excellence in Journalism, *The State of the News Media 2005: An Annual Report on American Journalism,.*

258. Ibid.

259. Ibid.

260. Doris A. Graber, *Mass Media & American Politics*, 7th ed. (Washington, DC: Congressional Quarterly Press, 2006).

261. Paul Farhi, "Kenneth Tomlinson Quits Public Broadcasting Board," *Washington Post*, November 4, 2005.

262. Bill Carter, "Nightly News Feels the Pinch of 24-Hour News," *New York Times*, April 14, 2003, C1.

263. Pew Research Center for the People and the Press, "News Audiences Increasingly Politicized Online News Audience Larger, More Diverse" (Washington, DC: Pew Research Center; Pew Research Center's Project for Excellence in Journalism, *The State of the News Media 2004: An Annual Report on American Journalism*, "Executive Summary"

(Washington, DC: Pew Research Center, 2004), accessed December 30, 2005, http://www.stateofthenewsmedia.org/execsum.pdf.

264. Hallin and Mancini, *Comparing Media Systems*.

265. Pew Research Center's Project for Excellence in Journalism, *The State of the News Media 2005: An Annual Report on American Journalism*.

266. Ibid.

267. Hallin and Mancini, *Comparing Media Systems*.

268. Ibid.

269. Ibid.

270. Ibid.

271. Calculated for 2003 using Government Printing Office, "Budget of the United States Government: Historical Tables Fiscal Year FY2005," "Table 1.1 Summary of Receipts, Outlays, and Surpluses or Deficits (-): 1789–2009" (Washington, DC: GPO, accessed January 12, 2006, http://www.gpoaccess.gov/usbudget/fy05/hist.html; and Public Broadcasting Policy Base, "Public broadcasting system revenues, 1982–2003," accessed December 28, 2005, http://www.current.org/pbpb/statistics/totalrevs.html.

272. The general standard for acceptance of research findings by the scholarly community is whether the research has passed through a process of anonymous methodological scrutiny by other experts, or "peers" on the subject matter. My point here is that there is no such published research that supports the claim of bias.

273. Citizens for Independent Public Broadcasting, "The CIPB Proposal for A Public Broadcasting Trust," 2000, accessed January 12, 2006, http://www.cipbonline.org/trustMain.htm.

274. Bill McConnell, "Public Broadcasting's $20 Billion Pitch: Advocates push for new revenue source," *Broadcasting and Cable*, June 13, 2005, accessed January 12, 2006, http://www.broadcastingcable.com/index.asp?layout=articlePrint&articleID=CA607814.

275. Karen Everhart, "Advice from Chicago: 'Act like you don't have much time, because you don't': Trust Fund Possible Only with New Unity and Broad Support," *Current*, December 13, 2004, accessed January 12, 2006, http://www.current.org/funding/funding0423trustfund.shtml.

276. Hallin and Mancini, *Comparing Media Systems*.

277. Citizens for Independent Public Broadcasting, "The CIPB Proposal."

278. See Stephen T. Mockabee, "A Question of Authority: Religion and Cultural Conflict in the 2004 Election," *Political Behavior* 29, no. 3 (June 2007): 221–248.

279. Anne E. Kornblut, "Palin to Give Interview to ABC This Week," *Washington Post*, September 8, 2008, A02.

280. Hallin and Mancini, *Comparing Media Systems.*

281. See Jacob S. Hacker and Paul Pierson, *Off Center: The Republican Revolution and the Erosion of American Democracy* (New Haven, CT: Yale University Press, 2005).

282. Note to the reader: I ask that you withhold final judgment on each prescription until the end of the book because most of the prescriptions require the interactions created by the other "drugs" prescribed for the system. The impact of this first prescription, for example, is dependent upon whether the public would turn more often to a better public broadcasting system, a problem discussed in a later chapter.

283. 47 U.S.C.A §307(a), 1934.

284. Thomas E. Patterson, *The Vanishing Voter: Public Involvement in an Age of Uncertainty* (New York: Knopf, 2002).

285. University of Pennsylvania's National Annenberg Election Survey, "Despite Limited Convention Television Coverage, Public Learned about Campaign from Democrats, Annenberg Data Show," press release, August 29, 2004, accessed January 16, 2006, http://www.annenbergpublicpolicycenter.org/naes/2004_03_dnc-knowledge_08-30_pr.pdf.

286. Patterson, *The Vanishing Voter*, 120.

287. The Vanishing Voter Project, "Election Interest is Up Sharply but Convention Interest is Not," Harvard University, July 21, 2004, accessed January 18, 2006, http://www.vanishingvoter.org/Releases/release072104.shtml.

288. Pew Research Center's Project for Excellence in Journalism, *The State of the News Media 2005: An Annual Report on American Journalism.*

289. *The West Wing*, Season 3, "The Black Vera Wang," written by Aaron Sorkin, directed by Christopher Misiano. televised by CBS on September 22, 2002.

290. Barack Obama's campaign has been the only exception to this tendency in recent elections. See Project for Excellence in Journalism, *The State of the News Media 2005: An Annual Report on American Journalism.*

291. Center for Governmental Studies, "Chronology of Significant Efforts to Create Free TV Time for Candidates, 1928–2004," Center for Governmental Studies: Solutions for Democracy, accessed February 3, 2006, http://www.cgs.org/projects/media/Free_TV_Time_for_Candidates.pdf.

292. Advisory Committee on Public Interest Obligations of Digital Television Broadcasters (PIAC), "Charting the Digital Broadcast Future," 1998, February 3, 2006, http://www.ntia.doc.gov/pubintadvcom/piacreport.pdf.

293. Martin Kaplan and Matthew Hale, "Local TV Coverage of the 2000 General Election," Norman Lear Center Campaign Media Monitoring Project, 2000, accessed February 3, 2006, http://www.learcenter.org/pdf/campaignnews.PDF.

294. Newton Minow and Henry Geller, "Petition Of Newton Minow And Henry Geller For Expedited Rulemaking To Require Public Service Time For Political Broadcasts Of Significant Local Candidates Otherwise Not Covered," before the Federal Communications Commission, Washington, DC 20554, April 6, 2004, accessed February 3, 2006, http://www.campaignlegalcenter.org/attachments/1202.pdf.

295. Campaign Legal Center, Media Policy Program, "Our Democracy, Our Airwaves Act: Bill Summary," accessed February 3, 2006, http://www.campaignlegalcenter.org/attachments/1434.pdf.

296. Kaplan and Hale, "Local TV Coverage."

297. Presentation by Kathleen Hall Jamieson, "Free Air Time And Campaign Reform: A Report of the Conference held by the Annenberg Public Policy Center of the University of Pennsylvania and The Free TV for Straight Talk Coalition," funded by the Pew Charitable Trusts, Philadelphia, PA, March 11, 1997, accessed February 3, 2006, http://www.annenbergpublicpolicycenter.org/03_political_communication/freetime/REP15.PDF.

298. Presentation by Kenneth Rasinski (Senior Research Scientist, NORC) "Free Air Time And Campaign Reform: A Report of the Conference held by the Annenberg Public Policy Center of the University of Pennsylvania and the Free TV for Straight Talk Coalition," funded by the Pew Charitable Trusts, Philadelphia, PA, March 11, 1997, accessed, February 3, 2006, http://www.annenbergpublicpolicycenter.org/03_political_communication/freetime/REP15.PDF.

299. Paul Waldman, "Free Time and Advertising: The 1997 New Jersey Governor's Race," a report prepared for the Annenberg Public Policy Center and funded by the Pew Charitable Trusts, February 1998, accessed February 3, 2006, http://www.annenbergpublicpolicycenter.org/03_political_communication/freetime/REP18.PDF.

300. Hallin and Mancini, *Comparing Media Systems*.

301. Center for Responsive Politics, Commercial TV and Radio Stations, accessed September 3, 2009, http://www.opensecrets.org/industries/indus.php?cycle=2008&ind=C2100.

302. Graber, *Mass Media and American Politics*.

303. "Free Air Time," *NewsHour* online forum, PBS, accessed February 6, 2006, http://www.pbs.org/newshour/forum/march00/free_time2.html.

304. Polls may show that many voters claim to get what they need in order to make their electoral decisions, but such results are misleading. First, this does not mean that voters are getting information from television news programs. Second, many voters who are well informed enter the election with a large base of knowledge and thus know well in advance for whom they will vote; these voters swell the ranks of those who claim they learn enough. The least informed voters, who make their decisions late in the campaign and whose votes typically swing the election, should be a greater concern. Given these voters' lack of knowledge, it is unlikely that the information they need is available from television news programs.

305. Pew Research Center's Project for Excellence in Journalism, "2008 Trends," in *The State of the News Media 2009: An Annual Report on American Journalism* (Washington, DC: Pew Research Center, 2009), accessed August 27, 2009, http://www.stateofthemedia.org/2009/narrative_yearinthenews_intro.php?cat=0&media=2.

306. Pew Research Center's Project for Excellence in Journalism, *The State of the News Media 2005: An Annual Report on American Journalism*; University of Wisconsin Advertising Project, "Obama Outspending McCain 3 to 1 on TV; Nearly 75% of Presidential Ad Spending in Red States," press release, October 31, 2009, accessed September 3, 2009, http://wiscadproject.wisc.edu/wiscAds_release_103108.pdf.

307. For a study on the impact of media-choice environments, see Markus Prior, *Post-Broadcast Democracy: How Media Choice Increases Inequality in Political Involvement and Polarizes Elections* (New York: Cambridge University Press).

308. Patterson, *The Vanishing Voter*; University of Pennsylvania's National Annenberg Election Survey, "Voters Learned Positions on Issues Since Presidential Debates; Kerry Improves Slightly On Traits, Annenberg Data Show," Annenberg Public Policy Center, University of Pennsylvania, October 23, 2004, accessed February 14, 2006, http://www.annenbergpublicpolicycenter.org/naes/2004_03_%20Voters-and-the-issues_10-23_pr.pdf.

309. Patterson, *The Vanishing Voter*.

310. A 2005 nationwide survey by Lake Research Partners found that 84 percent of respondents rated "public debates/forums" as very or somewhat important a source of information on elections such as governor and state legislature (Lake Research Partners, "Public Opinion on Election Campaign Spending," December 5–9, 2005, accessed February 17, 2006, http://www.demos.org/pubs/VoterSurvey_010406.pdf). A 1998 survey of voters

in Albuquerque found that 91 percent of respondents cited "public debates and forum" as important in deciding how to vote during Albuquerque's mayoral election; Lake Snell Perry & Associates and John Deardourff/ The Media Company, "Public Perceptions of Campaign Spending Limits: Findings from a Survey of 400 Registered Voters in the City of Albuquerque, New Mexico."

311. Whether debates follow formal debating procedures is, I believe, a trivial issue (my apologies to debate coaches) that does not reduce the overall effectiveness of the debates as a means of providing the voters with useful, policy-based information.

312. Having minor candidates participate in debates will merely invite confusion and reduce the potential for voter learning from the debate.

313. See James B. Lemert et al., *News Verdicts, the Debates and Presidential Campaigns* (New York: Praeger, 1991); and Kathleen Kendall, "Presidential Debates Through Media Eyes," *American Behavioral Scientist* 40, no. 8 (1997).

314. NBC Nightly News, October 1, 2004; Dana Milbank, "Reaction Shots May Tell Tale of Debate; Bush's Scowls Compared to Gore's Sighs," *Washington Post*, October 2, 2004, Final Edition, A10.

315. Ross Perot was declared the winner of the first debate in 1992 because he was the most entertaining, whereas George H. W. Bush "lost" the town-meeting debate that year in part because the camera caught him looking at his watch. Michael Dukakis "lost" the debate with George H. W. Bush in 1988 when he failed to react with emotion to a hypothetical question of whether he would favor the death penalty if his wife had been raped and killed. Lloyd Bentsen bested Dan Quayle in the vice presidential debate that same year with his "you're no Jack Kennedy" line. Walter Mondale beat Gary Hart in a 1984 nomination debate with his "where's the beef?" line. And the list goes on.

316. Pew Research Center's Project for Excellence in Journalism, "The Debate Effect: How the Press Covered the Pivotal Period" (Washington, DC: Pew Research Center, 2004), 4.

317. Ibid., 5.

318. Pew Research Center's Project for Excellence in Journalism, "The Last Lap: How the Press Covered the Final Stages of the Presidential Campaign," (Washington, DC: Pew Research Center, 2000), accessed March 16, 2006, http://www.journalism.org/resources/research/reports/campaign2000/lastlap/default.asp.

319. Lemert et al., *News Verdicts, the Debates and Presidential Campaigns*.

320. Pew Research Center's Project for Excellence in Journalism, "The Debate Effect."

321. Pew Center for the People and the Press, "Bottom-Line Pressures Now Hurting Coverage, Say Journalists" (Washington, DC: Pew Research Center, May 23, 2004), accessed March 22, 2006, http://www.stateofthemedia. org/prc.pdf. This is a survey of journalists conducted by the Project for Excellence in Journalism and the Committee of Concerned Journalists.

322. Pew Research Center's Project for Excellence in Journalism, "About PEJ," http://www.journalism.org/who/pej/about.asp, accessed March 22, 2006.

323. Journalism.org, "About CCJ," accessed March 22, 2006, http://www. journalism.org/who/ccj/about.asp.

324. Bill Kovach and Tom Rosenstiel, *The Elements of Journalism: What Newspeople Should Know and the Public Should Expect* (New York: Crown Publishers, 2001), 17.

325. Kovach and Rosenstiel, *The Elements of Journalism*, 12–13.

326. Kathleen Hall Jamieson and Paul Waldman, *The Press Effect: Politicians, Journalists, and the Stories that Shape the Political World* (New York: Oxford University Press), 171–172.

327. *Citizen journalists* are private citizens who do their own web-based reporting on events; some suggest that this model could replace professional journalism. A study that compared citizen news sites and blogs found that citizens range of topics was narrower and their sourcing was thinner than those of professional journalists; see Pew Project for Excellence in Journalism, "2008 Trends," in *The State of the News Media 2009: An Annual Report on American Journalism* (Washington, DC: Pew Research Center, 2009), accessed September 16, 2009, http://www.stateofthemedia.org/2009/.

328. See Alexander Hamilton, James Madison, and John Jay, "Federalist No. 10," in *The Federalist Papers* (1787). Project Gutenberg Etext of *The Federalist Papers*, posted by The Library of Congress, accessed February 23, 2011, http://thomas.loc.gov/home/histdox/fedpapers.html"

329. See Robert A. Dahl, *How Democratic is the American Constitution?* (New Haven, CT: Yale University Press, 2001).

330. U.S. Census Bureau, *Census of Governments*, June 1995, accessed July 26, 2006, http://www.census.gov/Press-Release/cb95-18.txt.

331. The "costs" of voting include registering to vote, the time it takes to visit the polls on Election Day or obtain an absentee ballot, and—most importantly—the time it takes to gather enough information to make informed choices.

332. Decisions about the direction of government in our system require the cooperation of a large number of elected officials, each of whom has a claim of authority from constituents. The president needs the House and the Senate to pass legislation or acquiesce to executive use of power. Each member of Congress requires cooperation from a majority of other members in the House and Senate as well as from the president. Much of the nation's laws also require cooperation from each state government and its elected officials; state and local laws often require consent or cooperation from other elected officials within other levels of government, and so on. Although it is true that some elected officials have more influence over the direction of government than others, the nature of the U.S. system, with its multitude of elections, means that any one electoral choice is unlikely to determine what the government does.

333. For the most recent work on the subject, see Pippa Norris, *Count Every Voice: Democratic Participation Worldwide* (New York: Cambridge University Press, 2002); and Pippa Norris, "Do Institutions Matter? The Consequence of Electoral Reform for Political Participation," in *Rethinking the Vote: The Politics and Prospects of American Election Reform*, ed. Ann N. Crigler, Marion R. Just, and Edward J. McCaffery (New York: Oxford University Press, 2004), 133–148.

334. Steven E. Schier, *You Call This an Election? America's Peculiar Democracy* (Washington, DC: Georgetown University Press, 2003), 32.

335. The over votes included a much greater proportion of votes for Gore than for Bush, costing Gore tens of thousands of votes more than Bush (Bush's official margin of victory was 537 votes). See Jonathan N. Wand et al., "The Butterfly Did It: The Aberrant Vote for Buchanan in Palm Beach County, Florida," *The American Political Science Review* 95, no. 4. (December 2001): 793–810. Also see "Calculate the Results," an interactive feature of the *New York Times* website, http://www.nytimes.com/images/2001/11/12/politics/recount/.

336. See Anthony Gierzynski, "Testing Grounds: How Well Does Instant Runoff Voting Work?" *Campaigns and Elections: Special Case Study Edition* (May 2007): 52–56, accessed June 13, 2007, http://www.nxtbook.com/nxtbooks/intellisphere/ce0507-special/.

337. Democrat Andy Montroll was favored over Republican Kurt Wright majorities of 56 to 44 percent (930-vote margin), and over Progressive Bob Kiss 54 to 46 percent (590-vote margin). The following table provides the total number of voters choosing one candidate over another in one-on-one

match-ups (shaded cells represent winner of match-up between row and column).

No. of Voters who ranked	Kiss (Prog)	Montroll (D)	Wright (R)
Kiss (Prog) ahead of...		3,477	4,314
Montroll (D) ahead of...	4,067		4,597
Wright (R) ahead of...	4,064	3,668	

338. If you took away first round votes from the second place candidate and gave them to the winning candidate, that would bump up the candidate who came in third in the first round to second place. He then would have defeated the candidate who came in first when voters' other choice rankings were distributed to candidates. See Anthony Gierzynski, "Instant Runoff Voting," accessed February 5, 2010, http://www.uvm.edu/~vlrs/IRVassessment.pdf.

339. National Initiative for Democracy, accessed June 15, 2007, http://ni4d.us/index.htm; Initiative and Referendum Institute, accessed June 15, 2007, http://www.iandrinstitute.org/.

340. See Richard J. Ellis, *Democratic Delusions: The Initiative Process in America* (Lawrence: University Press of Kansas, 2002); Betty H. Zisk, *Money, Media and the Grass Roots: State Ballot Issues and the Electoral Process* (Newbury Park, CA: Sage, 1987); Shaun Bowler, Todd Donovan, and Trudi Happ, "Ballot Propositions and Information Costs: Direct Democracy and the Fatigued Voter," *Western Political Quarterly* 45 (1992) 559–568; Thomas E. Cronin, *Direct Democracy* (Cambridge, MA: Harvard University Press, 1989); David Magleby, *Direct Legislation: Voting on Ballot Propositions in the United States* (Baltimore: John Hopkins Press, 1984).

341. For an overview of the literature on this point see Anthony Gierzynski, *Money Rules: Financing Elections in America* (Boulder, CO: Westview Press, 2000). Also see material cited in the previous footnote.

342. National Conference of State Legislators, "Recall of State Officials," March 21, 2006, accessed June 15, 2007, http://www.ncsl.org/programs/legismgt/elect/recallprovision.htm.

343. See Brian F. Schaffner, Matthew Streb, and Gerald Wright, "Teams Without Uniforms: The Nonpartisan Ballot in State and Local Elections," *Political Research Quarterly* 54 (March 2001): 7–30; and Howard D. Hamilton, "The Municipal Voter: Voting and Nonvoting in City Elections," *American Political Science Review* 65 (December 1971).

344. Keith E. Hamm and Gary F. Moncrief, "Legislative Politics in the States," in *Politics in the American States: A Comparative Analysis*, 8th ed., ed. Virginia Gray and Russell L. Hanson (Washington, DC: CQ Press, 2004).

345. Clearly some parliamentary systems are entirely functional without separately elected chief executives.

346. Governor and lieutenant governor are chosen as a team in some states (just as president and vice president are) and are chosen in separate votes in other states.

347. Kendra A. Hovey and Harold A. Hovey, *CQ's State Fact Finder 2006* (Washington, DC: Congressional Quarterly Press, 2006).

348. The idea that follows was inspired by John McClaughry of the Ethan Allen Institute and his commentary on reducing the number of elected administrative officials in Vermont, "One Big Choice" which aired on Vermont Public Radio, April 22, 3003.

349. Commission on Federal Election Reform, *Final Commission Report: Building Confidence in U.S. Elections*, September 2005, accessed June 18, 2007, http://www.american.edu/ia/cfer/report/CFER_section6.pdf.

350. National Lieutenant Governors Association, "NLGA Fact Sheet: Team Election Data for the Office Of Lieutenant Governor," December 29, 2006, accessed August 23, 2007, http://www.nlga.us/web-content/About-NLGA/Fact_Sheets.htm.

351. Henry R. Glick, "Courts: Politics and the Judicial Process," in *Politics in the American States: A Comparative Analysis*, 8th ed., ed. Virginia Gray and Russell L. Hanson (Washington, DC: CQ Press, 2004), 232–260.

352. Gregory A. Huber and Sanford C. Gordon, "Accountability and Coercion: Is Justice Blind when It Runs for Office?" *American Journal of Political Science* 48, no. 2 (April 2004): 247–263.

353. Melinda Gann Hall, "Ballot Roll-off in Judicial Elections: Contextual and Institutional Influences on Voter Participation in the American States," Paper presented at the Annual Meeting of the American Political Science Association, Atlanta, GA, September 2–5, 1999.

354. Walsh Commission, *The People Shall Judge: Restoring Citizen Control to Judicial Selection* (Olympia, WA: Walsh Commission, 1996).

355. Brian F. Schaffner and Jennifer Segal Diascro, "Judicial Elections in the News," in *Running for Judge: The Rising Political, Financial and Legal Stakes of Judicial Elections*, ed. Matthew J. Streb (New York: New York University Press, 2007).

356. This is not necessarily true for state supreme court elections which are more likely to be contested in recent years; see Melinda Gann Hall,

"Competition as Accountability in State Supreme Court Elections," in *Running for Judge: The Rising Political, Financial and Legal Stakes of Judicial Elections*, ed. Matthew J. Streb (New York: New York University Press, 2007), 165–185.

357. Glick, "Courts: Politics and the Judicial Process."

358. Glick, "Courts: Politics and the Judicial Process"; Adam Liptak and Janet Roberts, "Campaign Cash Mirrors a High Court's Rulings," *New York Times*, October 1, 2006, 1.

359. "Not for Sale: The Caperton v. Massey Case," *Economist*, June 11, 2009, accessed 1 July 2009, http://www.economist.com/displayStory. cfm?story_id=13832427.

360. *Caperton v. Massey* (556 U.S. _____ 2009). Though the Court recognized this concern in the case, the Court also signaled that it will not be intervening in the future on this matter except in such extreme instances.

361. Melinda Gann Hall and Chris W. Bonneau, "Does Quality Matter? Challengers in State Supreme Court Elections," *American Journal of Political Science* 50, no. 1 (January 2006): 20–33.

362. These are part of the merit-selection process and work even less well than partisan or nonpartisan elections.

363. As quoted by Adam Liptak in "Rendering Justice, With One Eye on Re-election," *New York Times*, May 25, 2008, 13.

364. These are elected offices in at least one of the following states: Maine, Nebraska, North Carolina, Louisiana, Washington, Wisconsin, and Vermont.

365. To get a more complete sense of the scope of ballot measures, visit the National Conference of State Legislatures ballot measure database, accessed July 5, 2007, http://www.ncsl.org/programs/legismgt/elect/dbintro.htm.

366. National Conference of State Legislatures, "Initiative, Referendum and Recall," accessed July 5, 2007 http://www.ncsl.org/programs/legismgt/elect/initiat.htm.

367. Ellis, *Democratic Delusions*; the National Conference of State Legislatures, "Initiative and Referendum in the 21st Century: Final Report and Recommendations of the NCSL I&R Task Force," July 2002, accessed July 5, 2007, http://www.ncsl.org/programs/legismgt/irtaskfc/IandR_report.pdf.

368. Ellis, *Democratic Delusions*, 35.

369. See Alan Rosenthal, *The Decline of Representative Democracy: Process, Participation, and Power in State Legislatures* (Washington, DC: Congressional Quarterly Press, 1998).

370. See Robert S. Erikson, Gerald C. Wright, and John P. McIver, *Statehouse Democracy: Public Opinion and Policy in the American States* (Cambridge: Cambridge University Press, 1993).

371. James Monogan, Virginia Gray, and David Lowry, "Public Opinion, Organized Interests, and Policy Congruence in Initiative and Noninitiative U.S. States," *State Politics and Policy Quarterly* 9, no. 3 (Fall 2009): 304–324.

372. See Monogan, Gray, and Lowry, "Public Opinion"; Edward L. Lascher, Jr., Michael G. Hagen, and Steven A. Rochlin, "Gun Behind the Door? Ballot Initiatives, State Policies and Public Opinion," *Journal of Politics* 58 (1996): 760–775; and Michael G. Hagen, Edward L. Lascher, Jr., and John F. Camobreco, "Response to Matsusaka: Estimating the Effect of Ballot Initiatives on Policy Responsiveness," *Journal of Politics* 63 (2001).

373. Zisk, *Money, Media and the Grass Roots*.

374. Ellis, *Democratic Delusions*, 119.

375. David B. Magleby, *Direct Legislation*; and Shaun Bowler and Todd Donavan, *Demanding Choices: Opinion, Voting and Direct Democracy* (Ann Arbor: University of Michigan Press, 1998).

376. Monogan, Gray, and Lowry, "Public Opinion"; Lascher, Hagen, and Rochlin, "Gun Behind the Door?"; and Hagen, Lascher, and Camobreco, "Response to Matsusaka: Estimating the Effect of Ballot Initiatives on Policy Responsiveness."

377. Though perhaps less important than the issues of terrorism and the war in Iraq, the issue of gay marriage still had a measureable and significant effect on voters; see Herbert F. Weisberg and Dino P. Christenson, "Changing Horses in Wartime? The 2004 Presidential Election," *Political Behavior* 29, no. 2 (June 2007): 279–304.

378. Susan McManus, "The Resurgent City Councils," in *American State and Local Politics: Directions for the 21st Century*, ed. Ronald E. Weber and Paul Brace (New York: Chatham House Publishers, 1999), 166–193.

379. U.S. Conference of Mayors, "Mayoral Elections Scheduled for 2007," accessed July 10, 2007, http://www.usmayors.org/uscm/elections/election citiesfall2007.pdf; U.S. Conference of Mayors, "Mayoral Elections Scheduled for 2005," accessed July 10, 2007, http://www.usmayors.org/uscm/elections/electioncities11082005.pdf.

380. See McManus, "The Resurgent City Councils."

381. John E. Chubb, "Institutions, the Economy, and the Dynamics of State Elections," *American Political Science Review* 82 (1988): 133–154.

382. Tim Storey and Nicole Casal Moore, "Democrats Deliver a Power Punch: For the first time since 1994, the Democrats took control of the majority of the nation's state legislatures," *State Legislatures*, December 2006, accessed July 10, 2007, http://www.ncsl.org/programs/pubs/slmag/2006/06SLDec06_PowerPunch.htm.

383. Curtis Wood, "Voter Turnout in City Elections," *Urban Affairs* 38, no. 2 (November 2002): 209–231.

384. Richard W. Boyd, "The Effects of Primaries and Statewide Races on Voter Turnout," *Journal of Politics* 51 (August 1989): 730–739.

385. Center for the Study of the American Electorate, "Primary Turnout Narrowly Misses Record Lows: Interest in Late Primaries Higher than Early," September 26, 2002, accessed July 30, 2007, http://www.american.edu/ia/cdem/csae/pdfs/csae020926.pdf.

386. Competition in statewide and U.S. House races has declined. Only 12 percent of U.S. House races between 1960 and 2000 could be considered competitive. See Stephen Ansolabehere, John Mark Hansen, Shigeo Hirano, and James M. Snyder, Jr., "The Decline of Competition in U.S. Primary Elections, 1908–2004, in *The Marketplace of Democracy*, ed. Michael P. McDonald and John Samples (Washington, DC: Brookings Institution Press, 2006), 74–101.

387. Sarah M. Moorehouse, "Money versus Party Effort: Nominating for Governor," *American Journal of Political Science* 34 (1990): 706–724; David A. Breaux and Anthony Gierzynski, "'It's Money that Matters': Campaign Expenditures in State Legislative Primaries," *Legislative Studies Quarterly* 16 (1991): 429–443.

388. See Frances E. Lee and Bruce Oppenheimer, *Sizing up the Senate: The Unequal Consequences of Equal Representation* (Chicago: University of Chicago Press, 1999); and Sanford Levinson, *Our Undemocratic Constitution: Where the Constitution Goes Wrong (And How the People Can Correct It)* (Oxford: Oxford University Press, 2006).

389. Jacob S. Hacker and Paul Pierson, *Off Center: The Republican Revolution and the Erosion of American Democracy* (New Haven, CT: Yale University Press, 2005), 36.

390. For an extended discussion of why the Senate should be eliminated, see Levinson, *Our Undemocratic Constitution*.

391. See the groups website: http://www.nationalpopularvote.com/index.php, accessed July 19, 2007.

392. Arthur Schlesinger, Jr., "Fixing the Electoral College," *Washington Post*, December 19, 2000, A39.

393. The Twentieth Century Fund is now called the Century Fund.
394. Twentieth Century Fund, Task Force on Reform of the Presidential Election Process, *Winner Take All: Report Of the Twentieth Century Fund Task Force On Reform Of The Presidential Election Process* (New York: Holmes & Meier, 1978).
395. Arthur Schlesinger, Jr., "Fixing the Electoral College," *Washington Post*, December 19, 2000, A39.
396. See CNN.com/Politics , "Elections 101: Path to the Presidency," Cable News Network, 2008, accessed July 27, 2007, http://www.cnn.com/ELECTION/2008/path.presidency/.
397. Democratic National Committee, Commission on Presidential Nomination Timing and Scheduling, "Timing of Presidential Preference Primaries and Caucuses, 1976–2004," memorandum, March 10, 2005, accessed July 27, 2007, http://a9.g.akamai.net/7/9/8082/v001/democratic1.download.akamai.com/8082/pdfs/commission/20050325_calendars.pdf.
398. While the voting does not start until January, the contest actually begins much earlier, with candidates competing in the "money primary" and vying for media attention. Even so, most of the public does not pay serious attention to the contest until just before the voting starts.
399. Thomas E. Patterson, *The Vanishing Voter: Public Involvement in an Age of Uncertainty* (New York: Knopf, 2002).
400. See Patterson, *The Vanishing Voter*.
401. All the Democratic candidates except Clinton removed their names from the Michigan ballot and pledged not to campaign in Florida. Initially, both states were stripped of their delegates by the DNC; they were awarded half a vote for each delegate in a later DNC meeting just prior to the end of the nomination contest.
402. Michael J. Malbin, "Small Donors, Large Donors and the Internet: The Case for Public Financing after Obama," Campaign Finance Institute working paper, April 2009, accessed July 7, 2009, http://www.cfinst.org/president/pdf/PresidentialWorkingPaper_April09.pdf.
403. Campaign Finance Institute, "The Presidential Campaigns Are Setting Records," July 16, 2007, accessed July 27, 2007, http://www.cfinst.org/pr/prRelease.aspx?ReleaseID=155.
404. Ibid.
405. National Association of Secretaries of State, "NASS Rotating Regional Presidential Primaries Plan," accessed July 30, 2007, http://www.nass.org/index.php?option=com_content&task=view&id=74&Itemid=210.

406. Ideology can be defined as "a consistent set of values about the proper purpose and scope of government." Kenneth Janda, Jeffrey Berry, and Jerry Goldman, *The Challenge of Democracy*, 9th ed. (New York: Houghton Mifflin, 2007), 20.

407. See Alan I. Abramowitz, *The Disappearing Center: Engaged Citizens, Polarization and American Democracy* (New Haven, CT: Yale University Press, 2010); and Thomas E. Patterson, *The Vanishing Voter: Public Involvement in an Age of Uncertainty* (New York: Knopf, 2002).

408. See D. Sunshine Hillygus and Todd G. Shields, *The Persuadable Voter: Wedge Issues in Presidential Campaigns* (Princeton, NJ: Princeton University Press, 2008).

409. See Jacob S. Hacker and Paul Pierson, *Off Center: The Republican Revolution and the Erosion of American Democracy* (New Haven, CT: Yale University Press, 2005).

410. Lewis Black, "Back in Black," *The Daily Show*, October 3, 2007, accessed October 19, 2007, http://www.thedailyshow.com/video/index.jhtml?videoId=111130&title=back-in-black-%E2%80%93-limbaugh.

411. Hans-Dieter Klingemann, Richard I Hofferbert and Ian Budge, *Parties, Policies and Democracy* (Boulder, CO: Westview Press, 1994), 138.

412. Some state legislators and local government council members are elected in multimember districts.

413. William G. Jacoby, "Value Choices and American Public Opinion," *American Journal of Political Science* 50, no. 3 (July 2006): 706–723; Janda, Berry, and Goldman, *Challenge of Democracy*.

414. See Sarah A. Binder, "Elections, Parties, and Governance," in *The Legislative Branch*, ed. Paul J. Quirk and Sarah A. Binder (New York: Oxford University Press, 2005), 148–170 for evidence with regard to congressional voting. See Klingemann, Hofferbert, and Budge, *Parties, Policies and Democracy*; and John Gerrig, *Party Ideologies in America, 1828–1996* (New York: Cambridge University Press, 1998) for evidence drawn from platforms and speeches regarding the national parties. See Daniel J. Coffey, "State Party Activists and State Party Polarization," in *The State of the Parties: The Changing Role of Contemporary American Parties*, ed. John C. Green and Daniel J. Coffey (Lanham, MD: Rowman & Littlefield, 2007), 75–91; and Joel Paddock, "Explaining State Variation in Interparty Ideological Differences," *Political Research Quarterly* 51 (1998): 765–580 for evidence from state party platforms. For evidence that those state platforms predict parties' behavior in state legislatures, see Richard C. Elling, "State-Party Platforms and State Legislative Performance:

A Comparative Analysis," *American Journal of Political Science* 23 (1979): 383–405; and for evidence from state legislatures, see Tim Storey, "The Real Race Is in the States," *State Legislatures*, September 2004, http://www.ncsl.org/programs/legman/statevote/real_race.htm, accessed October 11, 2005. Vol. 30, Issue 8, 22–24.

415. Larry M. Bartels, *Unequal Democracy: The Political Economy of the New Gilded Age* (New York: Russell Sage Foundation, 2008), 30.

416. Bartels, *Unequal Democracy*, 30.

417. Klingemann, Hofferbert, and Budge, *Parties, Policies and Democracy*.

418. For a recent book-length argument about the benefits of partisanship along these lines see Nancy Rosenblum, *On the Side of the Angels: An Appreciation of Parties and Partisanship* (Princeton, NJ: Princeton University Press, 2008).

419. Frank Rich, "Wall-e for President," *New York Times*, July 6, 2008.

420. Dan Balz, "McCain-Obama So Far: Positively Negative," *Washington Post*, June 26, 2008.

421. Patterson, *The Vanishing Voter*.

422. See, for example, Thomas M. Carsey, *Campaign Dynamics: The Race for Governor* (Ann Arbor: University of Michigan Press, 2000).

423. Brooks Jackson and Kathleen Hall Jamieson, *unSpun: Finding Facts in a World of Disinformation* (New York: Random House, 2007). Also see Hacker and Pierson, *Off Center*.

424. See Neil Postman, *Amusing Ourselves to Death: Public Discourse in the Age of Show Business* (New York: Penguin Books, 1985); Jackson and Jamieson, *unSpun*; and Al Gore, *The Assault on Reason* (New York: Penguin Press, 2007).

425. See Kathleen Hall Jamieson and Paul Waldman, *The Press Effect: Politicians, Journalists, and the Stories that Shape the Political World* (Oxford: Oxford University Press, 2003).

426. Hillygus and Shields, *The Persuadable Voter*.

427. See, for example, Thomas A. Hollihan, *Uncivil Wars: Political Campaigns in the Media Age*, 2nd ed. (Boston: Bedford/St. Martin's, 2009).

428. See Paul S. Herrnson, "The Roles of Party Organizations, Party-Connected Committees, and Party Allies in Elections," *The Journal of Politics* 71, no. 4 (October 2009): 1207–1224.

429. Party organizations had, by the 1970s, witnessed a period of decline. They had been pushed to the sidelines of elections by the rise of candidate-centered campaigns, campaigns run by and for the candidates. Campaigns had become candidate centered thanks to a number of developments,

including the use of direct primaries and television, and the destruction of urban party machines brought about by the rise of the national welfare state and the reduction in political patronage.

430. For the most recent works on the subject, see Stacy B. Gordon, *Campaign Contributions and Legislative Voting: A New Approach* (New York: Routledge, 2005); and Lynda Powell, *The Influence of Campaign Contributions in State Legislatures* (Ann Arbor: University of Michigan Press, forthcoming).

431. By law, contributors to party organizations cannot direct the party organizations to spend the money on specific candidates.

432. Diane Dwyre, Eric Heberlig, Robin Kolodny, and Bruce Larson, "Committees and Candidates: National Party Finance after BCRA," in *The State of the Parties: The Changing Role of Contemporary American Parties*, ed. John C. Green and Daniel J. Coffey (Lanham, MD: Rowman & Littlefield, 2007).

433. *Nonincumbent candidates* refers to candidates who currently do not hold office and who are either running against an incumbent (and are thus called *challengers*) or running in a district in which no candidate is the current officeholder (often called *open-seat candidates*). Challengers find it harder to raise money than open-seat candidates in part because incumbents are hard to defeat. The ease with which open-seat candidates raise money depends on the candidates' chances of winning.

434. I first made this argument and provided evidence elsewhere: see Anthony Gierzynski, *Legislative Party Campaign Committees in The American States* (Lexington: University Press of Kentucky, 1992). Paul S. Herrnson demonstrated this at the national level in *Party Campaigning in the 1980s* (Cambridge, MA: Harvard University Press, 1988). For more recent evidence, see Anthony Corrado and Katie Varney, "Party Money in the 2006 Elections: The Role of National Party Committees in Financing Congressional Campaigns," A Campaign Finance Institute Report, 2007, accessed August 27, 2008, http://www.cfinst.org/books_reports/pdf/Corrado_Party-2006_Final.pdf.

435. Other contributors more likely to contribute to "safe" candidates are individuals, PACs, interest groups, unions, and corporations, where allowed.

436. This tendency is well documented in the literature. For an explanation of the pattern, see Anthony Gierzynski, *Money Rules: Financing Elections in America* (Boulder, CO: Westview Press, 2000).

437. Dwyre et al., "Committees and Candidates"; and Corrado and Varney, "Party Money."

438. Corrado and Varney, "Party Money."
439. Corrado and Varney, "Party Money," 18.
440. Raymond J. La Raja, Susan E. Orr, and Daniel A. Smith, "Surviving BCRA: State Party Finance in 2004," in *The State of the Parties: The Changing Role of Contemporary American Parties*, ed. John C. Green and Daniel J. Coffey (Lanham, MD: Rowman & Littlefield, 2007), 113–134.
441. Candidate and other group spending should also be limited (see chapter 7).
442. The higher amount is for House races in states that have only one House district.
443. Coordinated expenditures limits are adjusted each election; see FEC, "2008 Coordinated Party Expenditure Limits," http://www.fec.gov/info/charts_441ad.shtml, accessed January 28, 2009.
444. There are not limits because of Supreme Court rulings; see *Colorado Republican Federal Campaign Committee v. Federal Election Commission*, 518 U.S. 604 (1996).
445. Corrado and Varney, "Party Money."
446. Dwyre et al., "Committees and Candidates."
447. Ibid.
448. Campaign Finance Institute, "Candidates' Money was Up, but Party Spending was Way Up, and Crucial Flurry of Last-Minute Independent Spending by the Parties Caps an Election with Record Fundraising by the Senate and House Candidates," November 10, 2006, accessed August 27, 2008, http://www.cfinst.org/pr/prRelease.aspx?ReleaseID=82.
449. While the parties have spent a great deal of money building party infrastructure so as to better support candidates and mobilize the electorate (the extent to which they have done this is discussed in the section "Engaging in Activities that Support Election"), parties have also spent a tremendous amount of money on independent and coordinated expenditures on behalf of their candidates—spending so much, in fact, that they at times spend more than do the candidates' campaigns. See Dwyre et al., "Committees and Candidates."
450. *Soft money* is the term used to describe this unregulated money, the opposite of *hard money*, which was regulated by the Federal Election Campaign Act and by subsequent amendments.
451. Raymond J. La Raja, *Small Change: Money, Political Parties, and Campaign Finance Reform* (Ann Arbor: University of Michigan Press, 2008).
452. Corrado and Varney, "Party Money."

453. See Raymond J. La Raja, "Back to the Future? Campaign-Finance Reform and the Declining Importance of the National Party Organizations," in *The State of the Parties: The Changing Role of Contemporary American Parties*, Sixth Edition, ed. John C. Green and Daniel J. Coffey (New York: Rowman & Littlefield, 2010), 205–222.

454. Dwyre et al., "Committees and Candidates."

455. Diane Dwyre and Robin Kolodny, "Throwing Out the Rulebook: Party Financing of the 2000 Elections," in *Financing the 2000 Election*, ed. David Magleby (Washington, DC: Brookings, 2002).

456. Research has demonstrated, however, that voters are unable to distinguish between such issue ads and express advocacy advertisements; see David B. Magleby, "The Expanded Role of Interest Groups and Political Parties in Competitive U.S. Congressional Elections, in *Outside Money: Soft Money and Issue Advocacy in the 1998 Congressional Elections*, ed. David B. Magleby (Lanham, MD: Rowman & Littlefield, 2000), 1–16.

457. La Raja, Orr, and Smith, "Surviving BCRA."

458. These groups, 527 and 501(c) committees, are independent advocacy organizations governed by the federal tax code (as opposed to federal election law) and under that code they can raise and spend unlimited amounts of money advocating a cause as long as they do not coordinate with federal candidates or parties or become involved in expressly advocating the election or defeat of a candidate.

459. La Raja, Orr, and Smith, "Surviving BCRA."

460. *Wisconsin Right to Life, Inc. versus the Federal Election Commission*, 546 U. S. _____ (2006).

461. *Citizens United v. Federal Election Commission* (No. 08-205), January 2010.

462. Center for Responsive Politics, OpenSecrets.org, "527s: Advocacy Group Spending in the 2008 Election," May 14, 2009, accessed June 22, 2009, http://www.opensecrets.org/527s/index.php.

463. Candidate Obama did not opt to take public financing for either the nomination contest or for the general election contest; here I am discussing his decision to opt out of the public financing for the general election. He was the first candidate to do so since the fund was established in 1974.

464. Candidates who accept public funding for the general election campaign receive a block of money ($84.1 million in 2008) and must limit their campaign spending to that amount; they are not allowed to raise any money from any other source for their campaign.

465. M. Margaret Conway, "The Scope of Participation in the 2008 Presidential Race," in *Winning the Presidency 2008*, ed. William J. Crotty (Boulder, CO: Paradigm, 2009).

466. Peter Ubertaccio, "Machine Politics for the Twenty-First Century," in *The State of the Parties: The Changing Role of Contemporary American Parties*, ed. John C. Green and Daniel J. Coffey (Lanham, MD: Rowman & Littlefield, 2007), 173–186.

467. Conway, "Scope of Participation."

468. Pauline East, "Notes from the Campaign Chair," *RWLC Blog*, accessed October 4, 2004, www.rwlc.net.

469. La Raja, Orr, and Smith, "Surviving BCRA."

470. Conway, "Scope of Participation."

471. Alec MacGillis and Alice Crites, "Registration Gains Favor Democrats: Voter Rolls Swelling in Key States," *Washington Post*, October 6, 2008.

472. Edison Media Research/Mitofsky International 2008 Exit Poll, November 4, 2008, accessed June 26, 2009, http://www.cnn.com/ELECTION/2008/results/polls/#val=USP00p2.

473. Scott Keeter, Juliana Horowitz and Alec Tyson, "Young Voters in the 2008 Election," Pew Research Center for the People and the Press Report, November 12, 2008, accessed June 26, 2009, http://pewresearch.org/pubs/1031/young-voters-in-the-2008-election.

474. But some forms of contact are more effective than others; see Donald P. Green and Alan S. Gerber, *Get Out the Vote: How to Increase Voter Turnout*, 2nd ed. (Washington, DC: Brookings Institution Press, 2008).

475. Paul S. Herrnson and Colton C. Campbell, "Modern Political Campaigns in the United States," in *Routledge Handbook of Political Management*, ed. Dennis W. Johnson (New York: Routledge, 2009), 11–23.

476. Herrnson and Campbell, "Modern Political Campaigns."

477. One survey of candidates in eight states found that between one-third and one-half of candidates running against incumbents or in open seats had been approached by local, state, and legislative party committees. Gary F. Moncrief, Peverill Squire, and Malcolm E. Jewell, *Who Runs for the Legislature?* (Upper Saddle River, NJ: Prentice Hall, 2001).

478. Moncrief, Squire, and Jewell, *Who Runs for the Legislature?*; Malcolm E. Jewell and Sarah M. Morehouse, *Political Parties and Elections in American* States (Washington, DC: Congressional Quarterly Press, 2001); and Gierzynski, *Legislative Party Campaign Committees*.

479. Herrnson and Campbell, "Modern Political Campaigns"; Moncrief, Squire, and Jewell, *Who Runs for the Legislature?*; Gierzynski, *Legislative Party Campaign Committees*; Jewell and Morehouse, *Political Parties*.

480. Jewell and Morehouse, *Political Parties*.

481. Ralph G. Wright, *Inside the Statehouse: Lessons from the Speaker* (Washington, DC: Congressional Quarterly Press, 2005).

482. Jewell and Morehouse, *Political Parties*.

483. Maik Bohne, Alicia Kolar Prevost, and James Thurber, "Campaign Consultants and Political Parties Today," in *Routledge Handbook of Political Management*, ed. Dennis W. Johnson (New York: Routledge, 2009), 497–508; Robin Kolodny and Andrea Logan, "Political Consultants and the Extension of Party Goals," *PS: Political Science and Politics* 31, no. 2 (June 1998).

484. Bohne, Prevost, and Thurber, "Campaign Consultants and Political Parties Today."

485. E. E. Schattschneider, *The Semi-Sovereign People: A Realist's View of Democracy in America* (New York: Hold, Rinehart and Winston, 1960), 140 (emphasis added).

486. Again, a tremendous amount of research has been published on this point. For a discussion of this literature see Anthony Gierzynski, *Money Rules: Financing Elections in America* (Boulder, CO: Westview Press, 2000), chapter 4.

487. For a recent book with a wealth of evidence on this point, see Larry M. Bartels, *Unequal Democracy: The Political Economy of the New Gilded Age* (New York: Russell Sage Foundation, 2008).

488. See Gierzynski, *Money Rules*.

489. The Supreme Court has invalidated all laws that set spending limits; see *Buckley v. Valeo* (424 U.S. 1, 1976).

490. Other reasons campaign-finance reform fails include (1) court rulings that provide major loop holes in the laws and (2) the adaptive behavior of campaigns, political parties, groups, and contributors.

491. Gierzynski, *Money Rules*.

492. For the most recent research on this subject see Stacy B. Gordon, *Campaign Contributions and Legislative Voting: A New Approach* (New York: Routledge, 2005); and Lynda Powell, *The Influence of Campaign Contributions in State Legislatures* (Ann Arbor: University of Michigan Press, forthcoming).

493. Lake Research Partners and the Tarrance Group, 2008, accessed August 7, 2009, http://www.campaignmoney.org/polling#_edn1.

494. Belden Russonello and Stewart Research and Communications, Midwest Democracy Network, "Midwestern Attitudes on Political Reform: Highlights From a Five-State Survey," June 2008, accessed September 10, 2009, http://midwestdemocracynetwork.org/files/pdf/Five_State_2008_PollReport.pdf.

495. Examples include the funding for the parties' national conventions, which comes from the Presidential Election Campaign Fund and from other private contributors who can give to the host city's committee; PACs' independent expenditures or issue ads; a candidate's giving to other candidates; a candidate's forming leadership PACs (separate from those of their campaigns), which they then use to contribute to other candidates; and PACs' giving to state party committees.

496. The limit on individual contributions is adjusted for inflation each election cycle.

497. Michael J. Malbin, "Small Donors, Large Donors and the Internet: The Case for Public Financing after Obama," Campaign Finance Institute Working Paper, April 2009, accessed June 29, 2009, http://www.cfinst.org/president/pdf/PresidentialWorkingPaper_April09.pdf.

498. The best description of these organizations comes from the Campaign Finance Institute: Certain organizations, 501(c)s (as identified by the tax code) can use unlimited contributions for three main kinds of campaign spending. Some, "ideological" corporations 501(c) (4) groups—which do not take corporate or union money, have no shareholders, and do not receive business income—may make "express advocacy" appeals to the general public to vote for or against candidates, so long as this does not constitute "their major purpose." Others, 501(c) (4), (5), and (6) organizations, may make certain television and radio, "electioneering communications" that name candidates and are distributed in the relevant constituency 60 days before a general election or 30 days before a primary one as long as they are not the "functional equivalent of express advocacy." Such groups are free to make an even broader class of similar communications to television and radio voters outside of the above "window" periods, distribute other non–express advocacy messages concerning candidates via newspaper and Internet ads, direct mail, e-mail, telephone and canvassing, and pay for related polling and market research. The Campaign Finance Institute, "Soft Money Political Spending by 501(c) Nonprofits Tripled in 2008 Election," accessed July 6, 2009, CFI working paper, http://www.cfinst.org/pr/prRelease.aspx?ReleaseID=221. Press release, March 25, 2009.

499. Express advocacy is determined by use of a set of words, e.g., *vote for*, *vote against, elect, support*, and so forth, listed in a footnote of the 1976 *Buckley v. Valeo* (424 U.S. 1, 1976) U.S. Supreme Court decision.

500. Mary Deason and Caitlin Sause, "The Impact of Organized Interests on the Campaign Environment," paper prepared for presentation at the Midwest Political Science Association Meeting, Chicago, April 20–23, 2006; the Campaign Finance Institute Task Force on Disclosure, "Issue Ad Disclosure: Recommendations for a New Approach," Campaign Finance Institute, February 2001, accessed July 7, 2009, http://www.cfinst.org/disclosure/pdf/issueads_rpt.pdf.

501. These first four—America Votes, American Solutions Winning the Future, the Fund for America, Patriot Majority Fund—are the names of four of the top six 527s (in terms of spending) in the 2008 election; Service Employees International Union and EMILY's List are the other two in the top six (see OpenSecrets.org). Very little information is available about 501(c)s, of which Freedom's Watch and Americans for Job Security are two.

502. OpenSecrets.org, the Center for Responsive Politics, "527s: Advocacy Groups Spending in the 2008 Election,", accessed July 7, 2009, http://www.opensecrets.org/527s/index.php.

503. Compared to $426 million in 2004. Campaign Finance Institute, "Soft Money Political Spending by 501(c) Nonprofits Tripled in 2008 Election," CFI working paper, accessed July 6, 2009, http://www.cfinst.org/pr/prRelease.aspx?ReleaseID=221).

504. For a history of campaign-finance law, see Gierzynski, *Money Rules*, chapter 3; or Raymond J. La Raja, *Small Change: Money, Political Parties and Campaign Finance Reform* (Ann Arbor: University of Michigan Press, 2008).

505. Ruling this way most recently in *Citizens United v. Federal Election Commission* (No. 08-205), January 2010; also see *Randall v Sorrell* (548 U.S. __ [2006]).

506. *Buckley v. Valeo*, 424 U.S. 1, 1976, n52.

507. David B. Magleby, "Getting Inside the Outside Campaign: Issue Advocacy in the 2000 Presidential Primaries," Report of a Grant Funded by the Pew Charitable Trusts, 2000; David B. Magleby, *The Other Campaign: Soft Money And Issue Advocacy In The 2000 Congressional Elections* (Lanham, MD: Rowman & Littlefield, 2002).

508. See *Wisconsin Right to Life, Inc. v. Federal Election Commission* (551 U.S.___ [2007] and *Citizens United v. Federal Election Commission* (No. 08-205), 2010.

509. For a study of PAC strategies see, Robert Biersack, Paul S. Herrnson, and Clyde Wilcox, eds., *Risky Business? PAC Decisionmaking in Congressional Elections* (New York: M. E. Sharpe, 1994).

510. Jacob S. Hacker and Paul Pierson, *Off Center: The Republican Revolution and the Erosion of American Democracy* (New Haven, CT: Yale University Press, 2005); also see Frank J. Sorauf, *Inside Campaign Finance: Myths and Realities* (New Haven, CT: Yale University Press, 1992).

511. Although the top-spending PACs tend to include union PACs, most PAC money overall is from business PACs (see chapter 2).

512. Wesley Y. Joe, Michael J. Malbin, Clyde Wilcox, Peter W. Brusoe, and Jamie P. Pimlott, "Do Small Donors Improve Representation?: Some Answers from Recent Gubernatorial and State Legislative Elections," the Campaign Finance Small Donor Project, paper presented at the Annual Meeting of the American Political Science Association, August 28–31, 2008, Boston, MA, accessed July 9, 2009, http://www.cfinst.org/books_reports/SmallDonors/APSA_2008_SmallDonors.pdf.

513. Campaign Finance Institute, "All CFI Funding Statistics Revised and Updated For the 2008 Presidential Primary and General Election Candidates," press release, January 8, 2010, accessed February 7, 2010, http://www.cfinst.org/pr/prRelease.aspx?ReleaseID=236. Also see Michael J. Malbin, "Small Donors."

514. Malbin, "Small Donors."

515. OpenSecrets.org, the Center for Responsive Politics, "Capital Eye Blog: Bundlers for McCain, Obama Are among Wall Street's Tumblers," September 18, 2008, accessed July 7, 2009, http://www.opensecrets.org/news/2008/09/bundlers-for-mccain-obama-are.html.

516. Michael Luo and Christopher Drew, "Big Donors, Too, Have Seats at Obama Fund-Raising Table," *New York Times*, August 5, 2008.

517. California Commission on Campaign Financing, *Money and Politics in the Golden State: Financing California's Local Elections* (Los Angeles: Center for Responsive Government, 1989); Michael J. Malbin and Thomas L. Gais, *The Day After Reform: Sobering Campaign Finance Lessons from the American States* (Albany, NY: Rockefeller Institute Press, 1998).

518. California Commission on Campaign Financing, *Money and Politics*.

519. For example, had a President Al Gore—instead of President George W. Bush—nominated the replacements for Justices Rehnquist and O'Connor, the Court's recent decisions on the BCRA, *Citizens United v. Federal Election Commission* (No. 08-205, 2010), *Wisconsin Right to Life, Inc. v. Federal Election Commission* (551 U.S.___, 2007), and on Vermont's

campaign finance law, *Landell v Sorrell* (548 U.S. __ , 2006), would have been very different.

520. *Citizens United v. Federal Election Commission* (No. 08-205), January 2010.

521. Malbin, "Small Donors."

522. R. Sam Garrett, "Public Financing of Congressional Elections: Background and Analysis," CRS Report of Congress, July 2, 2007, accessed July 21, 2009., http://fpc.state.gov/documents/organization/94355.pdf; Joel A. Thompson, and Gary F. Moncrief, eds., *Campaign Finance in State Legislative Elections*, 112; Anthony Gierzynski, Kevin Channel, and Surbhi Godsay, "Minnesota's Public Campaign Finance Program," The Vermont Legislative Research Shop, March 30, 2009, accessed July 8, 2009, http://www.uvm.edu/~vlrs/PoliticalProcess/MinnesotaPublic Financing.pdf.

523. Kenneth R. Mayer, Timothy Werner, and Amanda Williams, "Public Funding Programs and Competition," in *The Marketplace of Democracy: Electoral Competition and American Politics*, ed. Michael P. McDonald and John Samples (Washington, DC: Brookings Institution Press, 2006), 245–267; Neil Malhorta, "The Impact of Public Financing on Electoral Competition: Evidence from Arizona and Maine," *State Politics and Policy Quarterly* 8, no. 3 (Fall 2008): 263–281.

524. Donald A. Gross and Robert K. Goidel, *The States of Campaign Finance Reform* (Columbus: Ohio State University Press, 2003).

525. Garrett, "Public Financing."

526. Minnesota's system is plagued by independent spending, which cannot be regulated. As evident in the discussion of national elections above, this problem is not limited to Minnesota; it is also a problem for other public-funding states. Additionally, most of the independent spending is done by political party committees, which is not necessarily all bad and can be fixed by changing the law to redefine party-independent spending as coordinated spending (see chapter 6).

527. Joe et al., "Do Small Donors Improve Representation?," 2–3.

528. Malbin, "Small Donors."

529. A higher limit would be set for House contests in states with only one congressional district, reflecting the formula currently used to set the limits on party-coordinated expenditures.

530. Groups that advocate full public funding include the Brennan Center for Justice, Common Cause, Democracy Matters, Public Campaign, Public Citizen, and US Public Interest Research Group.

531. Brennan Center for Justice, Common Cause, Democracy Matters, Public Campaign, Public Citizen and US PIRG, "Breaking Free with Fair Elections: A New Declaration of Independence for Congress," March 2007, accessed July 21, 2009, http://www.cleanupwashington.org/documents/breaking_free.pdf.

532. Garrett, "Public Financing."

533. Brennan Center et al., "Breaking Free with Fair Elections."

534. Federal Election Commission, "Presidential Election Campaign Fund (PECF)," accessed July 21, 2009, http://www.fec.gov/press/bkgnd/fund.shtml.

535. Campaign Finance and Public Disclosure Board, "Agency Profile," February 15, 2011, accessed 23 February 2011, http://www.mmb.state.mn.us/doc/budget/profiles/campaign.pdf.

536. Campaign Finance Institute, "Minnesota's $50 Political Contribution Refunds Ended on July 1: The Refund Helped Stimulate Unparalleled Participation by Small Donors," A CFI Press Release, July 8, 2009, accessed July 22, 2009, http://www.cfinst.org/states/pdf/20090708_MN_refund_w-Charts.pdf.

537. As pointed out in chapter 3, redistricting is not the only or even the main cause of the decline in competition, but it does play a role; changes in the way redistricting is done can increase competition in the future.

538. For purposes of this hypothetical example, the state lost five seats in reapportionment (the process through which Congress allots the number of House seats per state based on population changes as measured by the decennial census).

539. Richard Forgette, Andrew Garner, and John Winkle, "Do Redistricting Principles and Practices Affect U.S. State Legislative Electoral Competition?" *State Politics and Policy Quarterly* 9, no. 2 (Summer 2009): 151–175.

540. Michael P. McDonald, "Redistricting and Competitive Districts," in *The Marketplace of Democracy*, ed. Michael P. McDonald and John Samples (Washington, DC: Brookings Institution Press, 2006), 222–244; Gary W. Cox and Jonathan N. Katz, *Elbridge Gerry's Salamander: The Electoral Consequences of the Reapportionment Revolution* (Cambridge: Cambridge University Press, 2002).

541. McDonald, "Redistricting"; and Bruce E. Cain, Karin MacDonald, and Michael McDonald, "From Equality to Fairness: The Path of Political Reform since *Baker v. Carr*," in *Party Lines: Competition, Partisanship,*

and Congressional Redistricting, ed. Thomas E. Mann and Bruce E. Cain (Washington, DC: Brookings Institution Press, 2005), 6–30.

542. L. Sandy Maisel, Cherie D. Maestas, and Walter J. Stone, "The Impact of Redistricting on Candidate Emergence," in *Party Lines: Competition, Partisanship, and Congressional Redistricting*, ed. Thomas E. Mann and Bruce E. Cain (Washington, DC: Brookings Institution Press, 2005), 31–50.

543. Forgette, Garner, and Winkle, "Redistricting Principles."

544. Jonathan Winburn, *The Realities of Redistricting: Following the Rules and Limiting Gerrymandering in State Legislative Redistricting* (New York: Lexington Books, 2008); Forgette, Garner, and Winkle, "Redistricting Principles."

545. The U.S. Supreme Court has mandated that districts be of equal population under the one person, one vote rule—see *Baker v. Carr* (368 U.S. 186, 1962)—and that race be considered but not the predominant criterion in the process; see *Shaw v. Reno* (509 U.S. 630, 1993). The Voting Rights Act requires certain states (those which had used the redistricting process in the past to discriminate against minorities) to get clearance for the district plans from the Department of Justice or the Washington, DC, District Court.

546. McDonald, "Redistricting."

547. Ibid.

548. Forgette, Garner, and Winkle, "Redistricting Principles."

549. Ibid.

550. See the group's website: http://www.americansforredistrictingreform.org/html/about_us.html, accessed August 4, 2009.

551. Common Cause, "Redistricting," accessed August 4, 2009, http://www.commoncause.org/site/pp.asp?c=dkLNK1MQIwG&b=4773689.

552. Ibid.

553. Fair Districts Florida, "About Redistricting," accessed August 4, 2009, http://www.fairdistrictsflorida.org/whatis.php.

554. Winburn, *Realities*.

555. Forgette, Garner, and Winkle, "Redistricting Principles"; McDonald, "Redistricting and Competitive Districts."

556. Winburn, *Realities*; Forgette, Garner, and Winkle, "Redistricting Principles"; McDonald, "Redistricting."

557. McDonald, "Redistricting," 238.

558. Bruce Cain, John Hanley, and Thad Kousser, "Term Limits: A Recipe for More Competition?" in *The Marketplace of Democracy*, eds. Michael P.

McDonald and John Samples (Washington, DC: Brookings Institution Press, 2006), 199–221.

559. Winburn, *Realities*; Forgette, Garner, and Winkle, "Redistricting Principles."

560. Adam B. Cox, "Designing Redistricting Institutions," *Election Law Journal* 5, no. 4 (2006): 412–424.

561. Winburn, *Realities*.

562. A number of regions must submit their district maps to the Justice Department for review to prevent racial gerrymandering; the sort of review Cox proposes would be in addition to this Voting Rights Act mandated review.

563. Cox, "Designing Redistricting Institutions."

564. Heather K. Gerken, *The Democracy Index: Why Our Election System is Failing and How to Fix It* (Princeton, NJ: Princeton University Press, 2009).

565. Paul S. Herrnson et al., *Voting Technology: The Not-So-Simple Act of Casting a Ballot* (Washington, DC: Brookings Institution Press, 2008).

566. R. Michael Alvarez and Thad E. Hall, *Electronic Elections: The Perils and Promises of Digital Democracy* (Princeton, NJ: Princeton University Press, 2008).

567. Alec C. Ewald, *The Way We Vote: The Local Dimension of American Suffrage* (Nashville, TN: Vanderbilt University Press, 2009), 155.

568. Herrnson et al., *Voting Technology*; and Alvarez and Hall, *Electronic Elections*.

569. Gerken, *Democracy Index*.

570. The film *Field of Dreams* is based on the book *Shoeless Joe* by W. P. Kinsella (New York: Mariner Books, 1999).

571. Terry Christensen and Peter Haas, *Projecting Politics: Political Messages in American Films* (New York: M. E. Sharpe, 2005).

572. Alexis de Tocqueville, *Democracy in America, 1835–1839*, ed. Richard D. Heffner (New York: Mentor Books, 1956).

573. There is some debate about several of Putnam's conclusions regarding the decline social capital, but I find his analysis, which is based on a number of different sets of data on cultural trends, most convincing. While interest groups abound, peoples' willingness to actively participate in associations has declined. My argument, though, goes beyond what Putnam was arguing: I contend that the U.S. cultural discourse, which takes place almost exclusively via the mass media and is clearly reflected in the media, shows this obsession with the individual. It is a perspective that owes its origins to writings and research on the media by Neil Postman, Roderick Hart,

Shanto Iyengar, W. Lance Bennett, Terry Christensen and Peter Haas, and others.

574. Christensen and Haas, *Projecting Politics*.

575. See Roderick P. Hart, *Seducing America: How Television Charms the Modern Voter*, rev. ed. (Thousand Oaks, CA: Sage, 1999).

576. While some candidates are elected with a plurality—that is, having one the most votes, but not a majority—any candidate that receives a majority of the popular vote (except presidential candidates, who need a majority of the Electoral Vote) will win.

577. Kids Voting USA, https://netforum.avectra.com/eWeb/StartPage. aspx?Site=KVUSA.

578. I am not arguing here that all these causes were supported by the majority; my point is that they show how the aggregation of interests propelled them to successful changes in government policy.

579. See Larry Bartels, "Partisanship and Voting Behavior, 1952–1996," *Public Opinion Quarterly* 66, no. 1 (Spring 2002): 67–79; Markus Prior's analysis of partisan polarization in *Post-Broadcast Democracy* (Cambridge: Cambridge University Press, 2007); and Alan I. Abramowitz, *The Disappearing Center: Engaged Citizens, Polarization and American Democracy* (New Haven, CT: Yale University Press, 2010).

580. See chapter 1 for a discussion of the political science research and debate on this topic. Also see D. Sunshine Hillygus and Todd G. Shields, *The Persuadable Voter: Wedge Issues in Presidential Campaigns* (Princeton, NJ: Princeton University Press, 2008); Thomas E. Patterson, *The Vanishing Voter: Public Involvement in an Age of Uncertainty* (New York: Knopf, 2002); Brooks Jackson and Kathleen Hall Jamieson, *unSpun: Finding Facts in a World of Disinformation* (New York: Random House Trade Paperbacks, 2007); Kathleen Hall Jamieson and Paul Waldman, *The Press Effect: Politicians, Journalists, and the Stories that Shape the Political World* (Oxford: Oxford University Press, 2003).

581. Patterson, *The Vanishing Voter*.

582. There have been some developments in civics education along the lines I discuss here, such as the work of Kids Voting USA, which engages students by having them gather the information needed to vote in mock elections with a ballot that parallels the actual ballot used during the election. Research has shown that this program has been effective. See Michael McDevitt and Spiro Kiousis, "Experiments in Political Socialization: Kids Voting USA as a Model for Civic Education Reform," working paper 49, August 2006; the Center for Information and Research on Civic Learn-

ing and Engagement, accessed, February 23, 2011, http://civicyouth.org/
PopUps/WorkingPapers/WP49McDevitt.pdf; and Kids Voting USA's
classroom activities page: http://netforum.avectra.com/eWeb/StartPage.as
px?Site=KVUSA&WebCode=HomePage, accessed September 26, 2010.
Unfortunately, the value of such learning is not reflected in the aspects
of civics knowledge tested for in the U.S. Department of Education's
National Assessment of Education Progress; see "Civics: What Do 12th-
Graders Know and What Can They Do?," accessed September 26, 2010,
http://nces.ed.gov/pubs2001/2001461.pdf.

583. There is a difference, however, between failing to address a pressing issue
of concern to a large portion of the public and not being pure enough
on an issue. By 1992, both parties had basically ignored the continuing
budget deficits and growing national debt, providing the main fuel for
Ross Perot's candidacy (though George H. W. Bush and the congressional
Democrats did make a budget deal to reduce the ballooning deficit, a deal
in which Bush broke his "no new taxes" promise). In 2000, Ralph Nader
claimed that Al Gore was weak on, among other things, the environment
(this claim is ironic considering that Gore ultimately won a Nobel prize
for his environmental activism). The 1992 Perot vote made sense because
neither party offered a real choice given their histories. But with apologies to the man who sold my previous book on his website, the 2000 vote
for Nader made little sense because there was a clear choice between the
two major parties on the environment (as the alignment of environmental groups behind Gore reflected), even if it wasn't a perfect choice in
the eyes of some. The same could be said about the other issues Nader
campaigned on; the problem was not a lack of choice but that the choice
between the two major-party candidates was not pure enough. The resulting eight years of Bush administration policies is clear enough proof of
the Nader supporters' error. Following Perot's 1992 independent candidacy, the Democrats adopted a more fiscally responsible approach under
the Clinton administration, which administration, with added pressure
from the Republicans (who gained the majority in 1995), helped turn budget deficits to surpluses.

584. McDevitt and Kiousis, "Experiments in Political Socialization."

585. Kenneth Janda, Jeffrey Berry, and Jerry Goldman, *The Challenge of
Democracy*, 10th ed. (Boston: Wadsworth, 2009).

586. This point, too, can be found in Janda, Berry and Goldman's *The Challenge of Democracy*.

587. The National Voter Registration Act of 1993 (also known as the motor-voter bill) had been in effect for the 1996 and 2000 elections with no noticeable effect on voter turnout. And given the rise of 527s following the Bipartisan Campaign Reform Act of 2003 (BCRA, or the McCain-Feingold bill), it is unlikely that BCRA had much effect on the public's faith in elections.

588. Abramowitz, *The Disappearing Center*; and Bartels, "Partisanship and Voting Behavior, 1952–1996."

589. Frank Zappa and the Mothers of Invention, "I'm the Slime," *Over-Nite Sensation*, Rykodisk, 1995.

590. There is a debate and conflicting research regarding how much people actually learn from television news. My focus is on whether people can develop an understanding of government, politics, and the choice in elections from television as opposed to simply gaining an awareness of issues or events. While some research, such as that reported on by W. Russell Neuman, Marion R. Just, and Ann N. Crigler in *Common Knowledge: News and the Construction of Political Meaning* (Chicago: University of Chicago Press, 1992), shows how people pick up awareness of issues and events through television, the medium does not, I argue here, help people comprehend the political world in the specific ways that are necessary for democratic citizenship.

591. Neil Postman, *Amusing Ourselves to Death: Public Discourse in the Age of Show Business* (New York: Penguin Books, 1985).

592. Shanto Iyengar, *Is Anyone Responsible? How Television Frames Political Issues* (Chicago: University of Chicago Press, 1991).

593. On the role of cognitive structures, or schema, in the processing of the news, see Doris A. Graber, *Processing the News: How People Tame the Information Tide* (New York: Longman, 1988). Also see W. Russell Neuman, *The Paradox of Mass Politics: Knowledge and Opinion in the American Electorate* (Cambridge, MA: Harvard University Press, 1986).

594. For more material on this point, see Susan Jacoby, *The Age of American Unreason* (New York: Pantheon Books, 2008), xvii.

595. These news stories dominated media coverage across sectors when they occurred (see the Weekly News Index produced by the Project for Excellence in Journalism, www.journalism.org).

596. Matthew A. Baum, "Talking the Vote: Why Presidential Candidates Hit the Talk Show Circuit," *American Journal of Political Science* 49, no. 2 (April 2005): 213–234; Scott Keeter, "The Illusion of Intimacy: Television

and the Role of Candidate Personal Qualities in Voter Choice," *Public Opinion Quarterly* 51, no. 3 (1987): 344–358.

597. Hart, *Seducing America*.

598. Jon Margolis, in a discussion with University of Vermont students of POLS137, "Politics & the Media," April 7, 2008.

599. Pew Research Center Project for Excellence in Journalism, "The Debate Effect: How the Press Covered the Pivotal Period of the 2004 Presidential Campaign" (Washington, DC: Pew Research Center, 2004), accessed March 15, 2006, http://www.journalism.org/resources/research/reports/debateeffect/thedebates.asp.

600. Iyengar, *Is Anyone Responsible?*

601. Pew Research Center for the People and the Press, "Public Knowledge of Current Affairs Little Changed by News and Information Revolutions" (Washington, DC: Pew Research Center, April 15, 2007), accessed May 30, 2007, http://people-press.org/reports/display.php3?ReportID=319; Steven Kull, *Misperceptions, the Media and the Iraq War*, Program on International Policy Attitudes, Center for International Security Studies at the University of Maryland, October 2, 2003, accessed September 9, 2005, http://www.pipa.org/OnlineReports/Iraq/Media_10_02_03_Report.pdf; John P. Robinson and Mark R. Levy, *The Main Source: Learning from Television News* (Beverly Hills, CA: Sage, 1986); John P. Robinson and Mark R. Levy, "News Media Use and the Informed Public: A 1990s Update," *Journal of Communication* 6, no. 2 (2006): 129–135.

602. Leonard Downie, Jr., and Robert G Kaiser, *The News About the News* (New York: Alfred A. Knopf, 2002); David T. Z. Mindich, *Tuned Out: Why Americans Under 40 Don't Follow the News* (New York: Oxford University Press, 2005); Pew Research Center Project for Excellence in Journalism, *The State of the News Media 2010: An Annual Report on American Journalism* (Washington, DC: Pew Research Center, 2010), accessed September 27, 2010, http://www.stateofthemedia.org/2010/.

603. Hart, *Seducing America*.

604. Robert D. Putnam, *Bowling Alone: The Collapse and Revival of American Community* (New York: Simon & Schuster, 2000), 246.

605. Putnam, *Bowling Alone*, 228.

606. One positive aspect of the video available on the Internet is that people can view longer clips, such as a speech in its entirety, as opposed to the sound bites presented on news broadcasts. Millions of people, for example, watched candidate Barack Obama's speech about race on YouTube. Because often the only way to accurately and fully understand a person's

complex argument is to listen to it all, the availability of such full-length videos of speeches has the potential to enhance the public's understanding of political issues. Whether and to what extent it does will be determined by future research.

607. Dan Schorr with his son, Jonathan, for StoryCorps National Day of Listing Project, as quoted in "A Last Conversation with Daniel Schorr," NPR Staff, November 20, 2010, accessed December 31, 2010, http://www.npr.org/templates/story/story.php?storyId=131465619.

608. My own outlet is playing baseball with the Montpelier Monties in the Vermont Senior Baseball League. Please don't look up my batting average.

609. Mindich, *Tuned Out*.

610. This is what Neil Postman prescribes in *Amusing Ourselves to Death*.

611. Anthony Gierzynski and Kensington Moore, "The New Guard: Entertainment Talk Shows and the Not-so-fake News," in *Voting in America*, ed. Morgan E. Felchner (Westport, CT: Praeger, 2008), 165–173; National Annenberg Election Survey, "Daily Show Viewers Knowledgeable About Presidential Campaign, National Annenberg Survey Shows," September 21, 2004, accessed May 30, 2007, http://www.annenbergpublicpolicycenter.org/Downloads/Political_Communication/naes/2004_03_late-night-knowledge-2_9-21_pr.pdf; Pew Research Center for the People and the Press, "Public Knowledge of Current Affairs Little Changed by News and Information Revolutions," April 15, 2007, accessed May 30, 2007, http://people-press.org/reports/display.php3?ReportID=319; Jody Baumgartner and Jonathan S. Morris, "*The Daily Show* Effect: Candidate Evaluations, Efficacy, and American Youth," *American Politics Research* 34, no. 3 (May 2006): 341–367.

612. Abramowitz, *The Disappearing Center*; Larry Bartels, "Partisanship and Voting Behavior, 1952–1996"; and Markus Prior's analysis of partisan polarization in *Post-Broadcast Democracy: How Media Choice Increases Inequality in Political Involvement and Polarizes Elections* (Cambridge: Cambridge University Press, 2007).

613. See Prior's analysis of partisan polarization in *Post-Broadcast Democracy*; and see Kathleen Hall Jamieson and Joseph N. Cappella's discussion of polarization and balkanization in, *Echo Chamber: Rush Limbaugh and the Conservative Media Establishment* (Oxford: Oxford University Press, 2008).

614. On the effect of media choices, see Prior, *Post-Broadcast Democracy*. For an analysis of the content of opinion media and a discussion of its effects, see Jamieson and Cappella, *Echo Chamber*.

615. See Jamieson and Cappella, *Echo Chamber*.

616. Brooks Jackson and Kathleen Hall Jamieson, *unSpun: Finding Facts in a World of Disinformation* (New York: Random House, 2007).

617. The curriculum is available at http://www.factchecked.org/, accessed August 20, 2009.

618. For one of the best, in my opinion, see Alan Wertheimer, "In Defense of Compulsory Voting" in *Participation in Politics*, ed. J. Roland Pennock and John V. Chapman (New York: Lieber-Atherton, 1975), 276–296.

619. Other typical tactics are to deny that there is a problem in the first place (an argument which collapses under the weight of the research evidence used to generate the diagnosis in the first three chapters), and to argue that the prescriptions violate some other cherished value, especially freedom of speech—which I have addressed in the context of the prescriptions that are perceived to be in conflict with that value.

620. I use the term *snake oil* loosely here; I am not suggesting an attempt to deceive on the part of reformers with whom I disagree.

621. See Committee for the Study of the American Electorate, "African-Americans, Anger, Fear and Youth Propel Turnout to Highest Level Since 1960: Possible Pro-Democratic Realignment, GOP Disaster," December 17, 2008, accessed June 26, 2009, http://www1.media.american.edu/electionexperts/2008%20Election%20Turnout_final_full.pdf.

BIBLIOGRAPHY

Abramowitz, Alan I. *The Disappearing Center: Engaged Citizens, Polarization and American Democracy*. New Haven, CT: Yale University Press, 2010.

———. "Explaining Senate Election Outcomes." *American Political Science Review* 82 (June 1988): 385–403.

Advisory Committee on Public Interest Obligations of Digital Television Broadcasters (PIAC). "Charting the Digital Broadcast Future Final Report of Advisory Committee on Public Interest Obligations of Digital Television Broadcasters." 1998. Accessed February 3, 2006. http://www.ntia.doc.gov/pubintadvcom/piacreport.pdf.

Althaus, Scott L. *Collective Preferences in Democratic Politics*. Cambridge: Cambridge University Press, 2003.

Altman, Micah, Karin MacDonald, and Michael McDonald. "Push-button Gerrymanders? How Computing Has Changed Redistricting." In *Party Lines: Competition, Partisanship, and Congressional Redistricting*, edited by Thomas E. Mann and Bruce E. Cain, 51–66. Washington, DC: Brookings Institution Press, 2005.

Alvarez, R. Michael, D. E. "Betsy" Sinclair, and Catherine H. Wilson. "Counting Ballots and the 2000 Election: What Went Wrong?" In *Rethinking the Vote: Politics and Prospects of American Election Reform*, edited by Ann N. Crigler, Marion R. Just and Edward J. McCaffery, 34–50. New York: Oxford University Press, 2004.

Alvarez, R. Michael, and Thad E. Hall. *Electronic Elections: The Perils and Promises of Digital Democracy*. Princeton, NJ: Princeton University Press, 2008.

Annenberg Public Policy Center. "Bush Inauguration Comes with Nation Still Deeply Divided, Dubious on Iraq, Social Security, Annenberg Data

Show." Press release, January 17, 2005. Accessd December 27, 2010. http://www.annenbergpublicpolicycenter.org/Downloads/Political_ Communication/NAES/2005_03_inauguration_01-17_pr.pdf.

————. "Majority of 18 to 29 Year Olds Think Bush Favors Reinstating the Draft, Annenberg Data Shows." Press release, October 8, 2004. Accessed September 14, 2005. http://www.annenbergpublicpolicycenter.org/ naes/2004_03_reinstate-the-draft_10-08_pr.pdf.

Ansolabehere, Stephen, John Mark Hansen, Shigeo Hirano, and James M. Snyder, Jr. "The Decline of Competition in U.S. Primary Elections, 1908–2004." In *The Marketplace of Democracy*, edited by Michael P. McDonald and John Samples, 74–101. Washington, DC: Brookings Institution Press, 2006.

Baker, Peter. "Bush Official, in Book, Tells of Pressure on '04 Vote." *New York Times*, August 20, 2009. Accessed August 27, 2009. http://www. nytimes.com/2009/08/21/us/21ridge.html?scp=2&sq=homeland%20 security%20department&st=cse.

Barker, David C. *Rushed to Judgment: Talk Radio, Persuasion, and American Political Behavior*. New York: Columbia University Press, 2002.

Bartels, Larry M. "Partisanship and Voting Behavior, 1952–1996." *Public Opinion Quarterly* 66, no. 1 (Spring 2002): 67–79

————. *Unequal Democracy: The Political Economy of the New Gilded Age*. Princeton, NJ: Princeton University Press, 2008.

Baum, Matthew A. "Talking the Vote: Why Presidential Candidates Hit the Talk Show Circuit." *American Journal of Political Science* 49, no. 2 (April 2005): 213–234.

Baumgartner, Jody, and Jonathan S. Morris. "*The Daily Show* Effect: Candidate Evaluations, Efficacy, and American Youth." *American Politics Research* 34, no. 3 (May 2006): 341–367.

Bibby, John F., and Thomas M. Holbrook. "Parties and Elections." In *Politics in the American States: A Comparative Analysis*, 8th edition, edited by Virginia Gray and Russell L. Hanson, 62–99. Washington, DC: Congressional Quarterly Press, 2004.

Biersack, Robert, Paul S. Herrnson, and Clyde Wilcox, eds. *Risky Business? PAC Decisionmaking in Congressional Elections*. New York: M. E. Sharpe, 1994.

Binder, Sarah A. "Elections, Parties, and Governance." In *The Legislative Branch*, edited by Paul J. Quirk and Sarah A. Binder, 148–170. New York: Oxford University Press, 2005.

Bohne, Maik, Alicia Kolar Prevost, and James Thurber. "Campaign Consultants and Political Parties Today." In *Routledge Handbook of Political Management*, edited by Dennis W. Johnson, 497–508. New York: Routledge, 2009.

Boyd, Richard W. "The Effects of Primaries and Statewide Races on Voter Turnout." *Journal of Politics* 51 (August 1989): 730–739.

———. "Election Calendars and Voter Turnout." *American Politics Quarterly* 14 (January–April 1986): 89–104.

Bowler, Shaun, and Todd Donavan. *Demanding Choices: Opinion, Voting and Direct Democracy*. Ann Arbor: University of Michigan Press, 1998.

Bowler, Shaun, Todd Donovon, and Trudi Happ. "Ballot Propositions and Information Costs: Direct Democracy and the Fatigued Voter." *Western Political Quarterly* 45 (June 1992): 559–568.

Breaux, David A., and Anthony Gierzynski. "'It's Money that Matters': Campaign Expenditures in State Legislative Primaries." *Legislative Studies Quarterly* 16 (1991): 429–443.

Brennan Center for Justice, Common Cause, Democracy Matters, Public Campaign, Public Citizen, and US PIRG. "Breaking Free with Fair Elections: A New Declaration of Independence for Congress." March 2007. Accessed July 21, 2009. http://www.cleanupwashington.org/documents/breaking_free.pdf.

Bryan, Frank M. *Real Democracy: The New England Town Meeting and How it Works*. Chicago: University of Chicago Press, 2004.

Cain, Bruce E., John Hanley, and Thad Kousser. "Term Limits: A Recipe for More Competition?" In *The Marketplace of Democracy*, ed. Michael P. McDonald and John Samples, 199–221. Washington, DC: Brookings Institution Press, 2006.

Cain, Bruce E., Karin MacDonald, and Michael McDonald. "From Equality to Fairness: The Path of Political Reform since *Baker v. Carr*." In *Party Lines: Competition, Partisanship, and Congressional Redistricting*, edited by Thomas E. Mann and Bruce E. Cain, 6–30. Washington, DC: Brookings Institution Press, 2005.

California Commission on Campaign Financing. *Money and Politics in the Golden State: Financing California's Local Elections*. Los Angeles: Center for Responsive Government, 1989.

Campaign Finance and Public Disclosure Board. "Agency Profile." n.d. Accessed 23 February 2009. http://www.mmb.state.mn.us/doc/budget/profiles/campaign.pdf.

Campaign Finance Institute. "The $100 Million Dollar Exemption: Soft Money and the National Party Conventions." July 2007. Washington, DC. Accessed October 7, 2005. http://www.cfinst.org/eguide/party conventions/financing/cfistudy.html

————. "All CFI Funding Statistics Revised and Updated for the 2008 Presidential Primary and General Election Candidates." Press release, January 8, 2010. Accessed January 25, 2010. http://www.cfinst.org/pr/prRelease.aspx?ReleaseID=236.

————. "Candidates' Money was Up, but Party Spending was Way Up, and Crucial Flurry of Last-Minute Independent Spending by the Parties Caps an Election with Record Fundraising by the Senate and House Candidates." November 10, 2006. Accessed August 27, 2008. http://www.cfinst.org/pr/prRelease.aspx?ReleaseID=82.

———. "Expenditures of Senate Incumbents and Challengers, by Election Outcome, 1974–2006." Washington, DC: Brookings Institution, 2008. http://www.cfinst.org/data/pdf/VitalStats_t6.pdf.

———. "A First Look at Money in the House and Senate Elections." Press release, November 6, 2008. Accessed August 28, 2009. http://www.cfinst.org/pr/prRelease.aspx?ReleaseID=215.

———. "Minnesota's $50 Political Contribution Refunds Ended on July 1: The Refund Helped Stimulate Unparalleled Participation by Small Donors." A CFI Press Release, July 8, 2009. Accessed July 22, 2009. http://www.cfinst.org/states/pdf/20090708_MN_refund_w-Charts.pdf.

———. "The Presidential Campaigns Are Setting Records." July 16, 2007. Accessed July 27, 2007. http://www.cfinst.org/pr/prRelease.aspx?ReleaseID=155.

———. "Soft Money Political Spending by 501(c) Nonprofits Tripled in 2008 Election." CFI working paper, 2009. Accessed July 6, 2009. http://www.cfinst.org/pr/prRelease.aspx?ReleaseID=221.

Campaign Finance Institute Task Force on Disclosure. "Issue Ad Disclosure: Recommendations for a New Approach." Washington, DC: Campaign Finance Institute, February 2001. Accessed July 7, 2009. http://www.cfinst.org/disclosure/pdf/issueads_rpt.pdf.

Campaign Legal Center, Media Policy Program. "Our Democracy, Our Airwaves Act: Bill Summary." Accessed February 3, 2006. http://www.campaignlegalcenter.org/attachments/1434.pdf.

Carsey, Thomas M. *Campaign Dynamics: The Race for Governor*. Ann Arbor: University of Michigan Press, 2000.

Center for Governmental Studies. "Chronology of Significant Efforts to Create Free TV Time for Candidates, 1928–2004." Accessed February 3, 2006. http://www.cgs.org/projects/media/Free_TV_Time_for_Candidates.pdf.

Center for Responsive Politics. "527s: Advocacy Groups Spending in the 2008 Election." Accessed July 7, 2009. http://www.opensecrets.org/527s/index.php.

————. "The Big Picture: The Money Behind the Elections." Accessed September 26, 2005. http://www.crp.org/bigpicture/index.asp.

————. "Capital Eye Blog: Bundlers for McCain, Obama Are among Wall Street's Tumblers." Accessed July 7, 2009. http://www.opensecrets.org/news/2008/09/bundlers-for-mccain-obama-are.html.

Center for the Study of the American Electorate. "Primary Turnout Narrowly Misses Record Lows: Interest in Late Primaries Higher than Early." September 26, 2002. Accessed July 30, 2007. http://www.american.edu/ia/cdem/csae/pdfs/csae020926.pdf.

Chaddock, Gail Russell. "Bush Administration Blurs Media Boundary." *Christian Science Monitor,* February 17, 2005. Accessed December 28, 2005. http://www.csmonitor.com/2005/0217/p01s01-uspo.html.

Christensen, Terry, and Peter J. Haas. *Projecting Politics: Political Messages in American Films.* Armonk, NY: M. E. Sharpe, 2005.

Chubb, John E. "Institutions, the Economy, and the Dynamics of State Elections." *American Political Science Review* 82 (1988): 133–154.

Coffey, Daniel J. "State Party Activists and State Party Polarization." In *The State of the Parties: The Changing Role of Contemporary American Parties,* edited by John C. Green and Daniel J. Coffey, 75–79. Lanham, MD: Rowman & Littlefield, 2007.

Commission on Federal Election Reform. *Final Commission Report: Building Confidence in U.S. Elections.* September 19, 2005. Accessed June 18, 2007. http://www.american.edu/ia/cfer/.

Committee for the Study of the American Electorate. "African-Americans, Anger, Fear and Youth Propel Turnout to Highest Level Since 1960: Possible Pro-Democratic Realignment, GOP Disaster." December 17,

2008. Accessed June 26, 2009. http://www1.media.american.edu/electionexperts/2008%20Election%20Turnout_final_full.pdf.

———. "Turnout Exceeds Optimistic Predictions: More than 122 Million Vote." January 14, 2005. Accessed June 26, 2009. http://election04.ssrc.org/research/csae_2004_final_report.pdf.

Common Cause. "Redistricting." Accessed August 4, 2009. http://www.commoncause.org/site/pp.asp?c=dkLNK1MQIwG&b=4773689.

Congressional Budget Office. "Estimated Impact of the American Recovery and Reinvestment Act on Employment and Economic Output from April 2010 through June 2010." Washington, DC: Congressional Budget Office, August 2010.

Conway, M. Margaret. "The Scope of Participation in the 2008 Presidential Race." In *Winning the Presidency 2008*, edited by William J. Crotty, 110–122. Boulder, CO: Paradigm, 2009.

Corrado, Anthony. "Party Finance in the Wake of BCRA: An Overview." In *The Election after Reform: Money, Politics, and the Bipartisan Campaign Reform Act*, edited by Michael Malbin. Lanham, MD: Rowman & Littlefield, 2005.

Corrado, Anthony, and Katie Varney. "Party Money in the 2006 Elections: The Role of National Party Committees in Financing Congressional Campaigns." Campaign Finance Institute Report, 2007. Accessed August 27, 2008.http://www.cfinst.org/books_reports/pdf/Corrado_Party-2006_Final.pdf.

Cox, Adam B. "Designing Redistricting Institutions." *Election Law Journal* 5, no. 4 (2006): 412–424.

Cox, Gary W., and Jonathan N. Katz. *Elbridge Gerry's Salamander: The Electoral Consequences of the Reapportionment Revolution*. Cambridge: Cambridge University Press, 2002.

Cronin, Thomas E. *Direct Democracy*. Cambridge, MA: Harvard University Press, 1989.

Cunningham, Brent. "Re-Thinking Objectivity." *Columbia Journalism Review* (July/August 2003): 24–32.

Dagnes, Alison. *Politics on Demand: The Effects of 24-Hour News on American Politics*. Santa Barbara, CA: ABC-CLIO, 2010.

Dahl, Robert A. *How Democratic is the American Constitution?* New Haven, CT: Yale University Press, 2001.

Deason, Mary, and Caitlin Sause. "The Impact of Organized Interests on the Campaign Environment." Paper presented at the Midwest Political Science Association Meeting, Chicago, April 20–23, 2006.

Delli Carpini, Michael X., and Scott Keeter. *What Americans Know About Politics and Why it Matters*. New Haven, CT: Yale University Press, 1996.

Democratic National Committee, Commission on Presidential Nomination Timing and Scheduling. "Timing of Presidential Preference Primaries and Caucuses, 1976–2004." Memorandum, March 10, 2005. Accessed July 27, 2007. http://a9.g.akamai.net/7/9/8082/v001/democratic1.down load.akamai.com/8082/pdfs/commission/20050325_calendars.pdf.

de Tocqueville, Alexis. *Democracy in America, 1835–1839*. Edited by Richard D. Heffner. New York: Mentor Books, 1956.

Downie, Leonard, Jr., and Robert G. Kaiser. *The News About the News*. New York: Alfred A. Knopf, 2002.

Dwyre, Diane, Eric Heberlig, Robin Kolodny, and Bruce Larson. "Committees and Candidates: National Party Finance after BCRA." In *The State of the Parties: The Changing Role of Contemporary American Parties*, edited by John C. Green and Daniel J. Coffey, 95–112. Lanham, MD: Rowman & Littlefield, 2007.

Dwyre, Diane, and Robin Kolodny. "Throwing Out the Rulebook: Party Financing of the 2000 Elections." In *Financing the 2000 Election*, edited by David Magleby, 133–162. Washington, DC: Brookings Institution Press, 2002.

East, Pauline. "Notes from the Campaign Chair." *RWLC Blog*. Accessed October 4, 2004. www.rwlc.net.

Elling, Richard C. "State-Party Platforms and State Legislative Performance: A Comparative Analysis." *American Journal of Political Science* 23 (1979): 383–405.

Ellis, Richard J. *Democratic Delusions: The Initiative Process in America*. Lawrence: University Press of Kansas, 2002.

Erikson, Robert S., Gerald C. Wright, and John P. McIver. *Statehouse Democracy: Public Opinion and Policy in the American States*. Cambridge: Cambridge University Press, 1993.

Everhart, Karen. "Advice from Chicago: 'Act Like You Don't Have Much Time, Because You Don't': Trust Fund Possible Only with New Unity and Broad Support." *Current*, December 13, 2004. Accessed January 12, 2006, http://www.current.org/funding/funding0423trustfund.shtml.

Ewald, Alec C. *The Way We Vote: The Local Dimension of American Suffrage*. Nashville, TN: Vanderbilt University Press, 2009.

Federal Election Commission. "2003–2004 Financial Activity of Senate and House General Election Campaigns, January 1, 2003–December 31, 2004." Accessed September 15, 2005. http://www.fec.gov/press/press2005/20050609candidate/gen2004.pdf.

———. "2004 Presidential Campaign Financial Activity Summarized." Washington, DC: Federal Election Commission, February 3, 2005. Accessed September 22, 2005. http://www.fec.gov/press/press2005/2 *0050203pressum*/20050203pressum.html.

———. "Presidential Election Campaign Fund (PECF)." Accessed July 21, 2009. http://www.fec.gov/press/bkgnd/fund.shtml.

Feigenbaum, Edward D., and James A. Palmer. *Campaign Finance Law 2002: A Summary of State Campaign Finance Laws*. Washington, DC: Federal Election Commission, 2003.

Fischer, Eric A., and Kevin J. Coleman. "Election Reform and Local Election Officials: Results of Two National Surveys." CRS Report for Congress, February 7, 2008. Accessed August 28, 2009. http://assets. opencrs.com/rpts/RL34363_20080207.pdf?emc=lm&m=212814&l= 24&v=209825.

Fitzgerald, Mark. "Local TV News Lacks Substance." *Editor and Publisher* 24 (May 1997): 8–9.

Flanigan, William H., and Nancy H. Zingale. *Political Behavior of the American Electorate*. 10th ed. Washington, DC: CQ Press, 2001.

Forgette, Richard, Andrew Garner, and John Winkle. "Do Redistricting Principles and Practices Affect U.S. State Legislative Electoral Competition?" *State Politics and Policy Quarterly* 9, no. 2 (Summer 2009): 151–175.

Fox, Julia R., Glory Koloen, and Volkan Sahin. "No Joke: A Comparison of Substance in *The Daily Show with Jon Stewart* and Broadcast Network Television Coverage of the 2004 Presidential Election Campaign." *Journal of Broadcast and Electronic Media* (forthcoming).

Francia, Peter L., Paul S. Herrnson, John C. Green, Lynda W. Powell, and Clyde Wilcox. *The Financiers of Congressional Elections: Investors, Ideologues, and Intimates*. New York: Columbia University Press, 2003.

Gans, Curtis. "2008 Primary Turnout Falls Just Short of Record Nationally, Breaks Record in Most States." News Release, Center for the Study of the American Electorate, American University, May 19, 2008. Accessed August 26, 2009. http://www1.american.edu/ia/cdem/csae/pdfs/csae080519.pdf.

———. "The Primary Turnout Story: Presidential Races Miss Record High Senate and Governor Contests Hit Record Low." Report, Center for the Study of the American Electorate, American University, October 1, 2008. Accessed August 26, 2009, http://www1.media.american.edu/electionexperts/2008%20Primary%20Turnout_Final.pdf.

Garrett, R. Sam. "Public Financing of Congressional Elections: Background and Analysis." CRS Report of Congress, July 2, 2007. Accessed July 21, 2009. http://fpc.state.gov/documents/organization/94355.pdf.

General Accounting Office Report on Elections. *The Scope of Congressional Authority in Elections Administration*. Washington, DC: General Accounting Office, 2001.

Gerken, Heather K. *The Democracy Index: Why Our Election System is Failing and How to Fix It*. Princeton, NJ: Princeton University Press, 2009.

Gerrig, John. *Party Ideologies in America, 1828–1996*. New York: Cambridge University Press, 1998.

Giammo, Joseph D., and Brian J. Brox. "Reducing the Costs of Participation: Are States Getting a Return on Early Voting?" *Political Research Quarterly* 63, no. 2 (June 2010): 295–303.

Gierzynski, Anthony. "Gubernatorial and State Legislative Elections." In *Financing the 2000 Election*, edited by David Magleby, 188–212. Washington, DC: Brookings Institution Press, 2002.

———. *Legislative Party Campaign Committees in the American States*. Lexington: University Press of Kentucky, 1992.

———. *Money Rules: Financing Elections in America*. Boulder, CO: Westview Press, 2000.

———. "Testing Grounds: How Well Does Instant Runoff Voting Work?" *Campaigns and Elections: Special Case Study Edition* (May 2007): 52–56. Accessed June 13, 2007. http://www.nxtbook.com/nxtbooks/intellisphere/ce0507-special/.

Gierzynski, Anthony, and David A. Breaux. "Legislative Elections and the Importance of Money." *Legislative Studies Quarterly* 21 (1996): 337–357.

———. "Money and Votes in State Legislative Elections." *Legislative Studies Quarterly* 16 (1991): 203–217.

Gierzynski, Anthony, Kevin Channel, and Surbhi Godsay. "Minnesota's Public Campaign Finance Program." The Vermont Legislative Research Shop, March 30, 2009. Accessed July 8, 2009. http://www.uvm.edu/~vlrs/PoliticalProcess/MinnesotaPublicFinancing.pdf.

Gierzynski, Anthony, Paul Kleppner, and James Lewis. "Money or the Machine: Money and Votes in Chicago Aldermanic Elections." *American Politics Quarterly* 26 (1998): 160–173.

Gierzynski, Anthony, and Kensington Moore. "The New Guard: Entertainment Talk Shows and the Not-so-fake News." In *Voting in America*, edited by Morgan E. Felchner, 165–173. Westport, CT: Praeger, 2008.

Glick, Henry R. "Courts: Politics and the Judicial Process." In *Politics in the American States: A Comparative Analysis*, 8th ed., edited by Virginia Gray and Russell L. Hanson, 232–260. Washington, DC: Congressional Quarterly Press, 2004.

Gordon, Stacy B. *Campaign Contributions and Legislative Voting: A New Approach*. New York: Routledge, 2005.

Gore, Al. *The Assault on Reason*. New York: Penguin Press, 2007.

Graber, Doris A. *Mass Media and American Politics*. 7th ed. Washington, DC: Congressional Quarterly Press, 2006.

———. *Processing the News: How People Tame the Information Tide*. New York: Longman, 1988.

Green, Donald P., and Alan S. Gerber. *Get Out the Vote: How to Increase Voter Turnout*. 2nd ed. Washington, DC: Brookings Institution Press, 2008.

Green, Donald Philip, and Jonathan S. Krasno. "Salvation for the Spendthrift Incumbent: Reestimating the Effects of Campaign Spending in House Elections." *American Journal of Political Science* 32 (1988): 884–907.

Griffin, John D., and Brian Newman. "Are Voters Better Represented?" *Journal of Politics* 67, no. 4 (2005): 1206–1227.

Grose, Christian R., and Bruce I. Oppenheimer. "The Iraq War, Partisanship, and Candidate Attributes: Variation in Partisan Swing in the 2006 U.S. House Elections." *Legislative Studies Quarterly* 32 (2007): 531–558.

Gross, Donald A., and Robert K. Goidel. *The States of Campaign Finance Reform.* Columbus: Ohio State University Press, 2003.

Hacker, Jacob S., and Paul Pierson. "The Center No Longer Holds: Why Bad Times for the Republicans do not Mean Good Times for the Democrats." *New York Times Magazine,* November 20, 2005, 32–36.

———. *Off Center: The Republican Revolution and the Erosion of American Democracy.* New Haven, CT: Yale University Press, 2005.

Hagen, Michael G., Edward L. Lascher, Jr., and John F. Camobreco. "Response to Matsusaka: Estimating the Effect of Ballot Initiatives on Policy Responsiveness." *Journal of Politics* 63 (2001): 1257–1263.

Hajnal, Zoltan L., Paul Lewis, and Hugh Louch. *Municipal Elections in California: Turnout, Timing, and Competition.* San Francisco: Public Policy Institute of California, 2002.

Hall, Melinda Gann. "Ballot Roll-off in Judicial Elections: Contextual and Institutional Influences on Voter Participation in the American States." Paper presented at the Annual Meeting of the American Political Science Association, Atlanta, GA, September 2–5, 1999.

———. "Competition as Accountability in State Supreme Court Elections." In *Running for Judge: The Rising Political, Financial and Legal Stakes of Judicial Elections,* edited by Matthew J. Streb, 165–185. New York: New York University Press, 2007.

Hall, Melinda Gann, and Chris W. Bonneau. "Does Quality Matter? Challengers in State Supreme Court Elections." *American Journal of Political Science* 50, no. 1 (January 2006): 20–33.

Hall, Richard L., and Frank W. Wayman. "Buying Time: Moneyed Interests and the Mobilization Bias in Congressional Elections." *American Political Science Review* 84 (1990): 797–820.

Hallin, Daniel C., and Paolo Mancini. *Comparing Media Systems: Three Models of Media and Politics.* Cambridge: Cambridge University Press, 2004.

Hamilton, Howard D. "The Municipal Voter: Voting and Nonvoting in City Elections." *American Political Science Review* 65 (December 1971): 1135–1104.

Hamm, Keith E., and Gary F. Moncrief. "Legislative Politics in the States." In *Politics in the American States: A Comparative Analysis,* 8th ed., edited by Virginia Gray and Russell L. Hanson, 157–193. Washington, DC: CQ Press, 2004.

Hart, Roderick P. *Seducing America: How Television Charms the Modern Voter.* Rev. ed. Thousand Oaks, CA: Sage, 1999.

———. *Congressional Elections: Campaigning at Home and in Washington.* Washington, DC: Congressional Quarterly Press, 2008.

Herrnson, Paul S. *Party Campaigning in the 1980s.* Cambridge, MA: Harvard University Press, 1988.

———. "The Roles of Party Organizations, Party-Connected Committees, and Party Allies in Elections." *Journal of Politics* 71, no. 4 (October 2009): 1207–1224.

Herrnson, Paul S., and Colton C. Campbell. "Modern Political Campaigns in the United States." In *Routledge Handbook of Political Management,* edited by Dennis W. Johnson, 11–23. New York: Routledge, 2009.

Herrnson, Paul S., Richard G. Niemi, Michael J. Hammer, Benjamin B. Bederson, Frederick C. Conrad, and Michael W. Traugott. *Voting Technology: The Not-So-Simple Act of Casting a Ballot.* Washington, DC: Brookings Institution Press, 2008.

Hillygus, D. Sunshine, and Todd G. Shields. *The Persuadable Voter: Wedge Issues in Presidential Campaigns.* Princeton, NJ: Princeton University Press, 2008.

Hogan Robert E., and Keith E. Hamm. "Variations in District-Level Campaign Spending in State Legislatures." In *Campaign Finance in State Legislative Elections*, edited by Joel A. Thompson and Gary F. Moncrief, 59–79. Washington, DC: Congressional Quarterly Press, 1998.

Hollihan, Thomas A. *Uncivil Wars: Political Campaigns in the Media Age*. 2nd ed. Boston: Bedford/St. Martin's, 2009.

Hovey, Kendra A., and Harold A. Hovey. *CQ's State Fact Finder 2006*. Washington, DC: Congressional Quarterly Press, 2006.

Huber, Gregory A., and Sanford C. Gordon. "Accountability and Coercion: Is Justice Blind when It Runs for Office?" *American Journal of Political Science* 48, no. 2 (April 2004): 247–263.

Issacharoff, Samuel, and Jonathan Nagler. "Protected from Politics: Diminishing Margins of Electoral Competition in U.S. Congressional Elections." *Ohio State Law Journal* 68 (2007): 1121–1137.

Iyengar, Shanto. *Is Anyone Responsible? How Television Frames Political Issues*. Chicago: University of Chicago Press, 1991.

Iyengar, Shanto, and Donald R. Kinder. *News that Matters: Television and American Opinion*. Chicago: University of Chicago Press, 1987.

Jackman, Robert W. "Political Institutions and Voter Turnout in the Industrial Democracies." *American Political Science Review* 81 (June 1987): 405–423.

Jackson, Brooks, and Kathleen Hall Jamieson. *unSpun: Finding Facts in a World of Disinformation*. New York: Random House Trade Paperbacks, 2007.

Jacobson, Gary C. "The Congress: The Structural Basis of Republican Success." In *The Election of 2004*, edited by Michael Nelson, 163–186. Washington, DC: CQ Press, 2005.

———. "The First Congressional Elections after BCRA." In *The Election after Reform: Money, Politics, and the Bipartisan Campaign*

Reform Act, ed. Michael Malbin, 185–203. Lanham, MD: Rowman & Littlefield, 2005.

———. "Modern Campaigns and Representation." In *The Legislative Branch*, edited by Paul J. Quirk and Sarah A. Binder, 109–147. New York: Oxford University Press, 2005.

———. *Money in Congressional Elections*. New Haven, CT: Yale University Press, 1980.

Jacoby, Susan. *The Age of American Unreason*. New York: Pantheon Books, 2008.

Jacoby, William G. "Value Choices and American Public Opinion." *American Journal of Political Science* 50, no. 3 (July 2006): 706–723.

Jamieson, Kathleen Hall. *Everything You Think You Know About Politics and Why You're Wrong*. New York: Basic Books, 2000.

———. "Free Air Time And Campaign Reform: A Report of the Conference held by the Annenberg Public Policy Center of the University of Pennsylvania and The Free TV for Straight Talk Coalition." Funded by the Pew Charitable Trusts, Philadelphia, PA, March 11, 1997. Accessed February 3, 2006, http://www.annenbergpublicpolicycenter. org/03_political_communication/freetime/REP15.PDF.

Jamieson, Kathleen Hall, and Joseph N. Cappella. *Echo Chamber: Rush Limbaugh and the Conservative Media Establishment*. Oxford University Press, 2008.

Jamieson, Kathleen Hall, and Brooks Jackson. "Our Disinformed Electorate." Special report, FactCheck.org, December 12, 2008. Accessed August 26, 2009. http://www.factcheck.org/2008/12/our-disinformed-electorate/.

Jamieson, Kathleen Hall, and Paul Waldman. *The Press Effect: Politicians, Journalists, and the Stories that Shape the Political World*. Oxford: Oxford University Press, 2003.

Janda, Kenneth, Jeffrey M. Berry, and Jerry Goldman. *The Challenge of Democracy: Government in America*. 9th ed. Boston: Houghton Mifflin, 2007.

Jewell, Malcolm E., and Sarah M. Morehouse. *Political Parties and Elections in American States*. Washington, DC: Congressional Quarterly Press, 2001.

Joe, Wesley Y., Michael J. Malbin, Clyde Wilcox, Peter W. Brusoe, and Jamie P. Pimlott. "Do Small Donors Improve Representation? Some Answers from Recent Gubernatorial and State Legislative Elections." The Campaign Finance Small Donor Project. Paper presented at the Annual Meeting of the American Political Science Association, Boston, August 28–31, 2008. Accessed July 9, 2009. http://www.cfinst.org/books_reports/SmallDonors/APSA_2008_SmallDonors.pdf.

Just, Marion, Ann Crigler, and Tami Buhr. "Voice, Substance, and Cynicism in Presidential Campaign Media." *Political Communications* 16 (1999): 25–44.

Kaniss, Phyllis. *Making Local News*. Chicago: University of Chicago Press, 1991.

Kaplan, Martin, Ken Goldstein, and Matthew Hale. "Local News Coverage of the 2004 Campaigns: An Analysis of Nightly Broadcasts in 11 Markets." Lear Center Local News Archive, February 15, 2005.

Kaplan, Martin, and Matthew Hale. "Local TV Coverage of the 2000 General Election." Norman Lear Center Campaign Media Monitoring Project, 2000. Accessed February 3, 2006. http://www.learcenter.org/pdf/campaignnews.PDF.

Keeter, Scott. "The Illusion of Intimacy: Television and the Role of Candidate Personal Qualities in Voter Choice." *Public Opinion Quarterly* 51, no. 3 (1987): 344–358.

Keeter, Scott, Juliana Horowitz, and Alec Tyson. "Young Voters in the 2008 Election." Pew Research Center for the People and the Press Report, November 12, 2008. Accessed June 26, 2009. http://pewresearch.org/pubs/1031/young-voters-in-the-2008-election.

Kendall, Kathleen. "Presidential Debates Through Media Eyes." *American Behavioral Scientist* 40, no. 8 (1997): 1193–1207.

Klingemann, Hans-Dieter, Richard I. Hofferbert, and Ian Budge. *Parties, Policies and Democracy*. Boulder, CO: Westview Press, 1994.

Kolodny, Robin, and Andrea Logan. "Political Consultants and the Extension of Party Goals." *PS: Political Science and Politics* 31, no. 2 (June 1998): 155–159.

Kovach, Bill, and Tom Rosenstiel. *The Elements of Journalism: What Newspeople Should Know and the Public Should Expect*. New York: Crown Publishers, 2001.

———. *Warp Speed: America in the Age of Mixed Media*. New York: The Century Foundation Press, 1999.

Kull, Steven. "Americans and Iraq on the Eve of the Presidential Election." Program on International Policy Attitudes, Center for International Security Studies at the University of Maryland. October 28, 2004. Accessed September 9, 2005. http://www.pipa.org/OnlineReports/Pres_Election_04/Report10_28_04.pdf.

———. "Americans on Climate Change: 2005." Program on International Policy Attitudes. July 5, 2005. Accessed September 9, 2005. http://www.pipa.org/OnlineReports/ClimateChange/Report07_05_05.pdf.

———. "Misperceptions, the Media and the Iraq War." Program on International Policy Attitudes, Center for International Security Studies at the University of Maryland. October 2, 2003. Accessed September 9, 2005. http://www.pipa.org/OnlineReports/Iraq/Media_10_02_03_Report.pdf.

Lane, Jan-Erik, and Svante Ersson. *Democracy: A Comparative Approach*. New York: Routledge, 2003.

Langbein, Laura I., and Mark A. Lotwis. "The Political Efficacy of Lobbying and Money: Gun Control in the U.S. House, 1986." *Legislative Studies Quarterly* 15 (August 1990): 413–440.

La Raja, Raymond J. "Back to the Future? Campaign Finance Reform and the Declining Importance of the National Party Organizations." In *The State of the Parties: The Changing Role of Contemporary American*

Parties, 6th ed., edited by John C. Green and Daniel J. Coffey, 205–222. Lanham, MD: Rowman & Littlefield, 2010.

———. *Small Change: Money, Political Parties, and Campaign Finance Reform*. Ann Arbor: University of Michigan Press, 2008.

La Raja, Raymond J., Susan E. Orr, and Daniel A. Smith. "Surviving BCRA: State Party Finance in 2004." In *The State of the Parties: The Changing Role of Contemporary American Parties*, edited by John C. Green and Daniel J. Coffey, 113–134. Lanham, MD: Rowman & Littlefield, 2007.

Lascher, Edward L., Jr., Michael G. Hagen, and Steven A. Rochlin. "Gun Behind the Door? Ballot Initiatives, State Policies, and Public Opinion." *The Journal of Politics* 58 (1996): 760–775.

Lau, Richard R., and David P. Redlawsk. "Advantages and Disadvantages of Cognitive Heuristics in Political Decision Making." *American Journal of Political Science* 45, no. 4 (2001): 951–971.

Lear Center Local News Archive, a project of the USC Annenberg School and the University of Wisconsin. *Local TV News Coverage of the 2002 General Election*. 2002. Accessed October 3, 2005. http://www.localnewsarchive.org/pdf/LocalTV2002.pdf.

Lee, Frances E., and Bruce Oppenheimer. *Sizing up the Senate: The Unequal Consequences of Equal Representation*. Chicago: University of Chicago Press, 1999.

Leighley, Jan E. *Mass Media and Politics: A Social Science Perspective*. New York: Houghton Mifflin, 2004.

Lemert, James B., William R. Elliott, James M. Bernstein, William L. Rosenberg, and Karl J. Nestwold. *News Verdicts, the Debates and Presidential Campaigns*. New York: Praeger, 1991.

Levinson, Sanford. *Our Undemocratic Constitution: Where the Constitution Goes Wrong (And How the People Can Correct It)*. Oxford: Oxford University Press, 2006.

Lijphart, Arend. "Unequal Participation: Democracy's Unresolved Dilemma." Presidential address, American Political Science Association, 1996. *American Political Science Review* 91, no. 1 (March 1997): 1–14.

Lopez Pintor, Rafael, and Maria Gratschew. *Voter Turnout Since 1945.* Stockholm, Sweden: International Institute for Democracy and Electoral Assistance, 2002.

MacKuen, Michael B., Robert S. Erikson, James A. Stimson, and Kathleen Knight. "Elections and the Dynamics of Ideological Representation." In *Electoral Democracy*, edited by Michael B. MacKuen and George Rabinowitz, 200–237. Ann Arbor: University of Michigan Press, 2003.

Magelby, David B. *Direct Legislation*. Baltimore: John Hopkins Press, 1984.

———. "The Expanded Role of Interest Groups and Political Parties in Competitive U.S. Congressional Elections." In *Outside Money: Soft Money and Issue Advocacy in the 1998 Congressional Elections*, edited by David B. Magleby, 1–16. Lanham, MD: Rowman & Littlefield, 2000.

———. "Getting Inside the Outside Campaign: Issue Advocacy in the 2000 Presidential Primaries." Report of a grant funded by the Pew Charitable Trusts, 2000.

———. *The Other Campaign: Soft Money and Issue Advocacy In The 2000 Congressional Elections*. Lanham, MD: Rowman & Littlefield, 2002.

Maisel, L. Sandy, Cherie D. Maestas, and Walter J. Stone. "The Impact of Redistricting on Candidate Emergence." In *Party Lines: Competition, Partisanship, and Congressional Redistricting*, edited by Thomas E. Mann and Bruce E. Cain, 31–50. Washington, DC: Brookings Institution Press, 2005.

Malbin, Michael J. "Small Donors, Large Donors and the Internet: The Case for Public Financing after Obama." Campaign Finance Institute working paper, April 2009. Accessed July 7, 2009. http://www.cfinst. org/president/pdf/PresidentialWorkingPaper_April09.pdf.

Malbin, Michael J., and Thomas L. Gais. *The Day After Reform: Sobering Campaign Finance Lessons from the American States*. Albany, NY: Rockefeller Institute Press, 1998.

Malhorta, Neil. "The Impact of Public Financing on Electoral Competition: Evidence from Arizona and Maine." *State Politics & Policy Quarterly* 8, no. 3 (Fall 2008): 263–281.

Mayer, Jane. "Covert Operations: The Billionaire Brothers Who Are Waging A War Against Obama." *New Yorker*. August 30, 2010. Accessed October 7, 2010. http://www.newyorker.com/reporting/2010/08/30/100830fa_fact_mayer.

Mayer, Kenneth R., Timothy Werner, and Amanda Williams. "Public Funding Programs and Competition." In *The Marketplace of Democracy: Electoral Competition and American Politics*, edited by Michael P. McDonald and John Samples, 245–267. Washington, DC: Cato Institute, Brookings Institution Press, 2006.

McChesney, Robert W., and John Nichols. *The Death and Life of American Journalism: The Media Revolution That Will Begin the World Again*. New York: Nation Books, 2010.

McConnell, Bill. "Public Broadcasting's $20 Billion Pitch: Advocates Push for New Revenue Source." *Broadcasting and Cable*, June 13, 2005. Accessed January 12, 2006. http://www.broadcastingcable.com/index.asp?layout=articlePrint&articleID=CA607814.

McDevitt, Michael, and Spiro Kiousis. "Experiments in Political Socialization: Kids Voting USA as a Model for Civic Education Reform." Working paper 49, August 2006. The Center for Information and Research on Civic Learning and Engagement. Accessed

September 27, 2010. http://www.civicyouth.org/PopUps/Working-Papers/WP49McDevitt.pdf

McDonald, Michael P. "Redistricting and Competitive Districts." In *The Marketplace of Democracy*, edited by Michael P. McDonald and John Samples, 222–244. Washington, DC: Brookings Institution Press, 2006.

————."The Return of the Voter: Voter Turnout in the 2008 Presidential Election." *The Forum* 6, no. 4 (2008). Accessed June 26, 2009. http://www.bepress.com/cgi/viewcontent.cgi?context=forum&article=1278&date=&mt=MTI0NjA0MDUwNA==&access_ok_form=Continue.

McManus, Susan. "The Resurgent City Councils." In *American State and Local Politics: Directions for the 21st Century*, edited by Ronald E. Weber and Paul Brace, 166–193. New York: Chatham House Publishers, 1999.

Mindich, David T. Z. *Tuned Out: Why Americans Under 40 Don't Follow the News*. New York: Oxford University Press, 2005.

Minow, Newton, and Henry Geller. "Petition Of Newton Minow And Henry Geller For Expedited Rulemaking To Require Public Service Time For Political Broadcasts Of Significant Local Candidates Otherwise Not Covered." Federal Communications Commission, Washington, DC 20554. April 6, 2004. Accessed February 3, 2006. http://www.campaignlegalcenter.org/attachments/1202.pdf.

Mockabee, Stephen T. "A Question of Authority: Religion and Cultural Conflict in the 2004 Election." *Political Behavior* 29, no. 3 (June 2007): 221–248.

Moncrief, Gary F. "Candidate Spending in State Legislative Races." In *Campaign Finance in State Legislative Elections*, edited by Joel A. Thompson and Gary F. Moncrief, 37–58. Washington, DC: Congressional Quarterly Press, 1998.

Moncrief, Gary F., Peverill Squire, and Malcolm Jewell. *Who Runs for the Legislature*. Upper Saddle River, NJ: Prentice Hall, 2001.

Monogan, James, Virginia Gray, and David Lowry. "Public Opinion, Organized Interests, and Policy Congruence in Initiative and Noninitiative U.S. States." *State Politics & Policy Quarterly* 9, no. 3 (Fall 2009): 304–324.

Moorehouse, Sarah M. "Money versus Party Effort: Nominating for Governor." *American Journal of Political Science* 34 (1990): 706–724.

Morin, Richard. "Tuned Out, Turned Off: Millions of Americans Know Little About How Their Government Works." *Washington Post National Weekly Edition*, Feb 5–11, 1996, p. 7.

National Annenberg Election Survey. "*Daily Show* Viewers Knowledgeable About Presidential Campaign, National Annenberg Survey Shows." September 21, 2004. Accessed May 30, 2007. http://www.annenberg publicpolicycenter.org/Downloads/Political_Communication/naes/ 2004_03_late-night-knowledge-2_9-21_pr.pdf.

———. "Voters Learned Positions on Issues Since Presidential Debates; Kerry Improves Slightly On Traits, Annenberg Data Show." October 23, 2004. Accessed February 14, 2006, http://www.annenbergpublicpolicy center.org/naes/2004_03_%20Voters-and-the-issues_10-23_pr.pdf.

National Association of Secretaries of State. "NASS Rotating Regional Presidential Primaries Plan." Accessed July 30, 2007. http://www.nass. org/index.php?option=com_content&task=view&id=74&Itemid=210.

National Center for Education Statistics. "Civics: What Do 12th-Graders Know and What Can They Do?" October 2001. Accessed September 26, 2010. http://nces.ed.gov/pubs2001/2001461.pdf

National Conference of State Legislatures. "Initiative and Referendum in the 21st Century: Final Report and Recommendations of the NCSL I&R Task Force." July 2002. Accessed July 5, 2007. http://www.ncsl. org/programs/legismgt/irtaskfc/IandR_report.pdf.

National Conference of State Legislators. "Recall of State Officials." March 21, 2006. Accessed June 15, 2007. http://www.ncsl.org/programs/ legismgt/elect/recallprovision.htm.

National Lieutenant Governors Association. "NLGA Fact Sheet: Team Election Data for the Office Of Lieutenant Governor." December 29, 2006. Accessed August 23, 2007. http://www.nlga.us/web-content/AboutNLGA/Fact_Sheets.htm.

Neuman, W. Russell. *The Paradox of Mass Politics: Knowledge and Opinion in the American Electorate*. Cambridge, MA: Harvard University Press, 1986.

Neuman, W. Russell, Marion R. Just, and Ann N. Crigler. *Common Knowledge: News and the Construction of Political Meaning*. Chicago: University of Chicago Press, 1992.

Norris, Pippa. *Count Every Voice: Democratic Participation Worldwide*. New York: Cambridge University Press, 2002.

———. "Do Institutions Matter? The Consequences of Electoral Reform for Political Participation." In *Rethinking the Vote: The Politics and Prospects of American Election Reform*, edited by Ann N. Crigler, Marion R. Just and Edward J. McCaffery, 133–148. New York: Oxford University Press, 2004.

Norton, Michael I., and Daniel Ariely. "Building a Better America—One Wealth Quintile at a Time." *Perspectives on Psychological Science* (forthcoming). Accessed October 12, 2010. http://www.people.hbs.edu/mnorton/norton%20ariely%20in%20press.pdf.

Paddock, Joel. "Explaining State Variation in Interparty Ideological Differences." *Political Research Quarterly* 51 (1998): 765–780.

Page, Benjamin I., and Robert Y. Shapiro. *The Rational Public: Fifty Years of Trends in Americans' Policy Preferences*. Chicago: University of Chicago Press, 1992.

Patterson, Thomas E. *Out of Order*. New York: Alfred A. Knopf, 1993.

———. *The Vanishing Voter: Public Involvement in an Age of Uncertainty*. New York: Knopf, 2002.

Pew Research Center Project for Excellence in Journalism. "The Debate Effect: How the Press Covered the Pivotal Period of the 2004 Presidential Campaign." Washington, DC: Pew Research Center, 2004. Accessed March 15, 2006. http://www.journalism.org/resources/research/reports/debateeffect/thedebates.asp.

———. "Journalism, Satire, or Just Laughs? 'The Daily Show with Jon Stewart' Examined." Washington, DC: Pew Research Center, 2008. Accessed June 16, 2008. http://www.journalism.org/node/10953.

———. "The Last Lap: How the Press Covered the Final Stages of the Presidential Campaign." Washington, DC: Pew Research Center, 2000. Accessed March 16, 2006. http://www.journalism.org/resources/research/reports/campaign2000/lastlap/default.asp.

———. *State of the News Media 2004: An Annual Report on American Journalism.* Washington, DC: Project for Excellence in Journalism, 2004.

———. *The State of the News Media 2005: An Annual Report on American Journalism.* Washington, DC: Project for Excellence in Journalism, 2005.

———. *The State of the News Media 2009: An Annual Report on American Journalism.* Washington, DC: Project for Excellence in Journalism, 2009. Accessed September 3, 2009. http://www.stateofthemedia.org/2009/index.htm.

———. *The State of the News Media 2010: An Annual Report on American Journalism.*" Washington, DC: Project for Excellence in Journalism, 2010. Accessed September 27, 2010. http://www.stateofthemedia.org/2010/.

Pew Research Center for the People and the Press. "Beyond Red and Blue: Republicans Divided about Role of Government—Democrats by Social and Personal Values." Washington, DC: Pew Research Center, May 10, 2005. Accessed September 1, 2005. http://people-press.org/reports/print.php3?PageID=953.

————. "Bottom-Line Pressures Now Hurting Coverage, Say Journalists: Press Going Too Easy on Bush." Washington, DC: Pew Research Center, May 23, 2004. Accessed October 12, 2005. http://people-press.org/reports/display.php3?ReportID=214.

————. "Independents Oppose Party in Power ... Again." Washington, DC: Pew Research Center, September 23, 2010. Accessed October 17, 2010. http://people-press.org/report/658/.

————. "Moral Values: How Important? Voters Liked Campaign 2004, But Too Much 'Mud-Slinging." Washington, DC: Pew Research Center, November 11, 2004. Accessed September 29, 2005. http://people press.org/reports/display.php3?ReportID=233.

————. "Most See Washington Dominated by Partisan Conflict." Washington, DC: Pew Research Center, October 4, 2010. Accessed October 17, 2010. http://pewresearch.org/pubs/1751/congressional-connection-partisan-bickering-hits-new-high.

————. "News Audiences Increasingly Politicized; Online News Audience Larger, More Diverse." Washington, DC: Pew Research Center, June 8, 2004.

————. "Popular Policies and Unpopular Press Lift Clinton Ratings: Scandal Reporting Faulted for Bias and Inaccuracy." Washington, DC: Pew Research Center, February 6, 1998. Accessed October 14, 2005. http://people-press.org/reports/display.php3?ReportID=96.

————. "Public Knowledge of Current Affairs Little Changed by News and Information Revolutions." Survey report. Washington, DC: Pew Research Center, April 15, 2007. Accessed May 30, 2007. http://people-press.org/reports/display.php3?ReportID=319.

Pildes, Richard H. "Why The Center Does Not Hold: The Causes of Hyperpolarized Democracy In America." *California Law Review* (forthcoming).

Pomper, Gerald M. "The Presidential Election: The Ills of American Politics After 9/11." In *The Election of 2004*, edited by Michael Nelson, 42–68. Washington, DC: CQ Press, 2005.

Popkin, Samuel L. *The Reasoning Voter: Communication and Persuasion in Presidential Campaigns*. 2nd ed. Chicago: University of Chicago Press, 1994.

Postman, Neil. *Amusing Ourselves to Death: Public Discourse in the Age of Show Business*. New York: Penguin Books, 1985.

Powell, Lynda. *The Influence of Campaign Contributions in State Legislatures*. Ann Arbor: University of Michigan Press, forthcoming.

Prior, Markus. *Post-Broadcast Democracy: How Media Choice Increases Inequality in Political Involvement and Polarizes Elections*. Cambridge: Cambridge University Press, 2007.

Project for Excellence in Journalism, an institute affiliated with Columbia University Graduate School of Journalism. "The State of the News Media: An Annual Report on American Journalism," 2005 edition. Accessed December 30, 2005. http://www.stateofthemedia.org/2005/narrative_networktv_contentanalysis.asp?cat=2&media=4.

Putnam, Robert D. *Bowling Alone: The Collapse and Revival of American Community*. New York: Simon & Schuster, 2000.

Rasinski, Kenneth. "Free Air Time And Campaign Reform: A Report of the Conference held by the Annenberg Public Policy Center of the University of Pennsylvania and the Free TV for Straight Talk Coalition." Funded by the Pew Charitable Trusts, Philadelphia, PA. March 11, 1997. Accessed February 3, 2006. http://www.annenbergpublicpolicycenter.org/03_political_communication/freetime/REP15.PDF.

"Report: Some Sort of Primary Just Happened." *The Onion*, issue 41.39, September 28, 2005. Accessed October 4, 2005, http://www.theonion.com/content/node/40979.

Robinson, John P., and Geoffrey Godbey. *Time for Life: The Surprising Ways Americans Use Their Time*.

Robinson, James A., Clarence C. Elebash, and Andrea C. Hatcher. "Pensacola Votes by Mail: A Report on Pensacola's January 2001 Referendum." Pensacola: University of West Florida, March 30, 2001.

————. "News Media Use and the Informed Public: A 1990s Update." *Journal of Communication* 6, no. 2 (2006): 129–135.

Rosenblum, Nancy. *On the Side of the Angels: An Appreciation of Parties and Partisanship*. Princeton, NJ: Princeton University Press, 2008.

Rosenthal, Alan. *The Decline of Representative Democracy: Process, Participation, and Power in State Legislatures*. Washington, DC: Congressional Quarterly Press, 1998.

Schaffner, Brian F., and Jennifer Segal Diascro. "Judicial Elections in the News." In *Running for Judge: The Rising Political, Financial and Legal Stakes of Judicial Elections*, edited by Matthew J. Streb, 115–139. New York: New York University Press, 2007.

Schaffner, Brian F., Matthew Streb, and Gerald Wright. "Teams without Uniforms: The Nonpartisan Ballot in State and Local Elections." *Political Research Quarterly* 54 (March 2001): 7–30.

Schattschneider, E. E. *The Semi-Sovereign People: A Realist's View of Democracy in America*. New York: Hold, Rinehart & Winston, 1960.

Schier, Steven E. *You Call This an Election? America's Peculiar Democracy*. Washington, DC: Georgetown University Press, 2003.

Sorauf, Frank J. *Inside Campaign Finance: Myths and Realities*. New Haven, CT: Yale University Press, 1992.

Storey, Tim. "Helping America Vote." *State Legislatures*, April 2003, Vol. 29, Issue 4, 13–15."

————. "The Real Race Is in the States." *State Legislatures*, September 2004. Vol. 30, Issue 8, 22–24 Accessed October 11, 2005. http://www. ncsl.org/programs/legman/statevote/real_race.htm.

Story, Tim, and Nicole Casal Moore. "Democrats Deliver a Power Punch: For the First Time Since 1994, the Democrats Took Control of the Majority of the Nation's State Legislatures." *State Legislatures*, December 2006. Accessed July 10, 2007. http://www.ncsl.org/programs/pubs/slmag/2006/06SLDec06_PowerPunch.htm.

Squire, Peverill. "Challenger Profile and Gubernatorial Elections." *Western Political Quarterly* 45 (1992): 125–142.

Taber, Charles S., Damon Cann, and Simona Kucsova. "The Motivated Processing of Political Arguments." *Political Behavior* 31, no. 2 (June 2009): 137–155.

Taber, Charles S., and Milton Lodge. "Motivated Skepticism in the Evaluation of Political Beliefs." *American Journal of Political Science* 50, no. 3 (July 2006): 755–769.

Thomas, Scott J. "Do Incumbent Expenditures Matter?" *Journal of Politics* 51 (1989): 965–976.

Thompson, Joel A., and Gary F. Moncrief, eds. *Campaign Finance in State Legislative Elections*. Washington, DC: Congressional Quarterly Press, 1997.

Twentieth Century Fund, Task Force on Reform of the Presidential Election Process. *Winner Take All: Report Of The Twentieth Century Fund Task Force On Reform Of The Presidential Election Process*. New York: Holmes & Meier, 1978.

Ubertaccio, Peter. "Machine Politics for the Twenty-First Century." In *The State of the Parties: The Changing Role of Contemporary American Parties*, edited by John C. Green and Daniel J. Coffey, 173–186. Lanham, MD: Rowman & Littlefield, 2007.

United States Elections Project. George Mason University. http://elections. gmu.edu/.

Verba, Sidney, Kay Lehman Schlozman, and Henry E. Brady. *Voice and Equality: Civic Voluntarism in American Politics*. Cambridge, MA: Harvard University Press, 1995.

Waldman, Paul. "Free Time and Advertising: The 1997 New Jersey Governor's Race." A report for the Annenberg Public Policy Center and funded by the Pew Charitable Trusts, February 1998. Accessed February 3, 2006. http://www.annenbergpublicpolicycenter.org/03_political_communication/freetime/REP18.PDF.

Walsh Commission. *The People Shall Judge: Restoring Citizen Control to Judicial Selection.* Olympia, WA: Walsh Commission, 1996.

Wand, Jonathan N., Kenneth W. Shotts, Jasjeet S. Sekhon, Walter R. Mebane, Jr., Michael C. Herron, and Henry E. Brady. "The Butterfly Did It: The Aberrant Vote for Buchanan in Palm Beach County, Florida." *American Political Science Review* 95, no. 4. (December 2001): 793–810.

Weisberg, Herbert F., and Dino P. Christenson. "Changing Horses in Wartime? The 2004 Presidential Election." *Political Behavior* 29, no. 2 (June 2007): 279–304.

Weissman, Steve, and Ruth Hassan. "527 Groups and BCRA." In *The Election after Reform: Money, Politics, and the Bipartisan Campaign Reform Act*, edited by Michael Malbin, 79–101. Lanham, MD: Rowman & Littlefield, 2005.

Wertheimer, Alan. "In Defense of Compulsory Voting." In *Participation in Politics*, edited by J. Roland Pennock and John V. Chapman, 276–296. New York: Lieber-Atherton, 1975.

West, Darrell M. *The Rise and Fall of the Media Establishment.* Boston: Bedford/St. Martin's, 2001.

Winburn, Jonathan. *The Realities of Redistricting: Following the Rules and Limiting Gerrymandering in State Legislative Redistricting.* New York: Lexington Books, 2008.

Wood, Curtis. "Voter Turnout in City Elections." *Urban Affairs* 38, no. 2 (November 2002): 209–231.

Wright, Ralph G. *Inside the Statehouse: Lessons from the Speaker.* Washington, DC: Congressional Quarterly Press, 2005.

Zisk, Betty H. *Money, Media and the Grass Roots: State Ballot Issues and the Electoral Process.* Newbury Park, CA: Sage Publications, 1987.

INDEX

ABOUT THE AUTHOR

Anthony Gierzynski is an associate professor of political science at University of Vermont and the director of the Vermont Legislative Research Service of the James M. Jeffords Center. He holds a PhD from the University of Kentucky. Dr. Gierzynski's previous publications include *Money Rules: Financing Elections in America* and *Legislative Party Campaign Committees in the American States*. He has published in several journals, such as *Legislative Politics Quarterly* and *American Politics Quarterly*, and is also the author of several book chapters. Dr. Gierzynski was a member of a number of research teams that have been awarded grants from the National Science Foundation and the Joyce Foundation to study campaign finance. He was also an expert witness in court cases involving campaign finance laws for the State of Vermont (Landell v Sorrell (548 U.S.— [2006])) and the City of Albuquerque, New Mexico.

9 781604 977523